Gardening For Canadians For Dummies®

Drought is a relatively common experience on the prair... ...ion in other parts of Canada. And as gardeners become more ... ...y plants, drought-tolerant shrubs, trees, perennials, and ... ...of choice. So here we provide you with several quick lists ... ...trees, and perennials. For annuals, please turn over the page.

D1622839

Drought-Tolerant Trees, Shrubs and Groundcovers

Amur maple. *(Acer ginnala)* Zone 2

Bearberry. *(Arctostaphylos uva-ursi)* Zone 3

Bearberry conteaster. *(Cotoneaster dammeri)* Zone 4

Beautybush. *(Kolkwitzia ababilis)* Zone 5b

Buffalo berry. *(Shepherdia canadensis)* Zone 1

Butterfly bush. *(Buddleia davidii)* Zone 5b

Common juniper. *(Juniperus communis)* Zone 2b

Creeping juniper. *(Juniperus horizontalis)* Zone 2

Easter red cedar. *(Junperus virginiana)* Zone 3

Euonymus. *(Euonymus fortunei)* Zones 4 and 5

Honey locust. *(Gledititsia species)* Zone 5

Japanese flowering quince. *(Chaenomeles speciosa)* Zone 5b

Locust. *(Rabina species)* Zone 4

Mock Orange. *(Philadelphus coronarius)* Zone 5

Ninebark. *(Physocarpus opulifolius)* Zone 2b

Prairie rose. *(Rosa setigera)* Zone 3

Rockspray cotoneaster. *(Cotoneaster horizontalis)* Zone 5

Rose daphne. *(Daphne cneorum)* Zone 5

Rugosa rose. *(Rosa rugosa)* Zone 2b

Russian olive. *(Elaeagnus angustifolia)* Zone 3

Sea buckthorn. *(Hippophae rhamnoides)* Zone 2b

Shrub bush clover. *(Lespedeza bicolor)* Zone 4

Small leaf cotoneaster. *(Cotoneaster microphylla)* Zone 7

Smooth sumac. *(Rhus glabra)* Zone 2b

Trailing arbutus or mayflower. *(Epigaea repens)* Zone 5b

White birch or paper birch. *(Betula papyrifera)* Zone 2

Drought-Tolerant Perennials

Artemisia. *(Artemisia species)* Zone 5

Aster. *(Aster species)* Zone 4 or 5

Bellflower. *(Campanula carpatica)* Zone 4

Chamomile. *(Chamaemelum nobile)* Zone 5

Coreopsis. *(Coreopsis species)* Zone 3

Dianthus. *(Dianthus species)* Zone 4

Daylily. *(Hemerocallis species).* Zone 3

Heather. *(Calluna vulgaris)* Zone 6

Purple coneflower. *(Echinacea purpurea)* Zone 3

Rudbeckia. *(Rudbeckia fulgida)* Zone 4

Sedum. *(Sedum species)* Zone 4

Yarrow. *(Achillea species)* Zone 3

...For Dummies®: Bestselling Book Series for Beginners

Gardening For Canadians For Dummies®

Cheat Sheet

Measurement Conversions

1 centimeter ≈ 0.4 inch	1 inch ≈ 2.5 centimeters
1 meter ≈ 39 inches ≈ 1.1 yards	1 yard ≈ 0.9 meter
1 kilometer ≈ 0.6 mile	1 mile ≈ 1.6 kilometers
1 liter ≈ 1.1 quarts	1 quart ≈ 0.9 liter
1 kilogram ≈ 2.2 pounds	1 pound ≈ 0.4 kilogram
1 gram ≈ 0.04 ounce	1 ounce ≈ 31 grams

Drought-Tolerant Annuals

Bachelor buttons. (*Centaurea cyanus*)

Black-eyed Susan. (*Rudbeckia hirta*)

California poppy. (*Eschscholzia californica*)

Chinese forget-me-not. (*Cynoglossum amabile*)

Cosmos. (*Cosmos* species)

Flowering tobacco. (*Nicotiana alata*)

Marigold. (*Tagetes* species)

Morning glories. (*Ipomoea purpurea*)

Petunia. (*Petunia hybrida*)

Pot marigold. (*Calendula officinalis*)

Verbena. (*Verbena hybrida*)

Zinnia. (*Zinnia elegans*)

Quick Pronunciation Guide to Common Plant Names

Abies	aa-bees
Acer	aa-sir
Betula	bet-you-la
Cercis	kerr-kiss (or sir-sis)
Chamaecyparis	ka-mee-qu-pa-ris
Cotoneaster	ko-tone-ee-aster
Dianthus	dee-anth-us
Echinacea	ee-kee-nah-kee-a
Eleagnus	e-lee-egg-nus
Floribunda	flor-a-bun-da
Hemerocallis	hay-mee-row-kay-lis
Heuchera	hew-kee-ra
Lagerstroemia	law-ger-strom-ee-a
Lathyrus odoratus	lay-thi-rus
Lilium	lee-lee-um
Liriope	lee-ree-o-pay (or lear-ee-ope)
Muscari	mus-kah-ree
Parthenocissus	par-then-o-kiss-us
Quercus	kwer-kus
Rudbeckia	rude-beck-ee-a
Trachelospermum	tra-kay-low-sperm-um
Trillium	tril-lee-um

...For Dummies®: Bestselling Book Series for Beginners

™

References for the Rest of Us!™

BESTSELLING BOOK SERIES

Do you find that traditional reference books are overloaded with technical details and advice you'll never use? Do you postpone important life decisions because you just don't want to deal with them? Then our *...For Dummies*® business and general reference book series is for you.

...For Dummies business and general reference books are written for those frustrated and hard-working souls who know they aren't dumb, but find that the myriad of personal and business issues and the accompanying horror stories make them feel helpless. *...For Dummies* books use a lighthearted approach, a down-to-earth style, and even cartoons and humorous icons to dispel fears and build confidence. Lighthearted but not lightweight, these books are perfect survival guides to solve your everyday personal and business problems.

> *"...Dummies books consistently live up to their brand-name promise to transform 'can't into can.' "*
> — Ottawa Citizen

> *"...set up in bits and bites that are easy to digest, full of no-nonsense advice."*
> — The Calgary Herald

> *"...clear, straightforward information laced with a touch of humour."*
> — The Toronto Star

Already, millions of satisfied readers agree. They have made *...For Dummies* the #1 introductory level computer book series and a best-selling business book series. They have written asking for more. So, if you're looking for the best and easiest way to learn about business and other general reference topics, look to *...For Dummies* to give you a helping hand.

IDG BOOKS WORLDWIDE

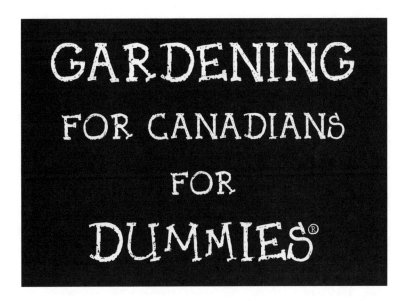

GARDENING FOR CANADIANS FOR DUMMIES®

by **Liz Primeau**
The Editors of *Canadian Gardening*
Michael MacCaskey
Bill Marken
The Editors of The National Gardening Association

CDG Books Canada, Inc.

IDG Books Worldwide, Inc.
An International Data Group
Company

Toronto, ON ◆ Foster City, CA ◆ Chicago, IL ◆ Indianapolis, IN ◆ New York, NY

Gardening For Canadians For Dummies ®

Published by
CDG Books Canada, Inc.
99 Yorkville Avenue
Suite 400
Toronto, ON   M5R 3K5
www.cdgbooks.com (CDG Books Canada Web Site)

www.idgbooks.com (IDG Books Worldwide Web Site)
www.dummies.com (Dummies Press Web Site)

Canadian Cataloguing in Publication Data

Primeau, Liz

Gardening for Canadians for dummies

Includes index.
ISBN: 1-894413-03-2

1. Gardening — Canada. I. MacCaskey, Michael. II. Marken, Bill. III. National Gardening Association (U.S.). IV. Title.

SB453.3.C2P753 1999   635'.0971   C99-931303-2

Printed in the United States of America

1 2 3 4 5 IDGB 03 02 01 00 99

We acknowledge the financial support of the Government of Canada through the Book Publishing Industry Development Program for our publishing activities.

1O/RV/QZ/ZZ/IN

Distributed in Canada by CDG Books Canada, Inc.

For general information on CDG Books, including all IDG Books Worldwide publications, please call our distribution center: HarperCollins Canada at 1-800-387-0117. For reseller information, including discounts and premium sales, please call our Sales department at 1-877-963-8830.

This book is available at special discounts for bulk purchases by your group or organization for resale, premiums, fundraising and seminars. For details, contact CDG Books Canada, Special Sales Department, 99 Yorkville Avenue, Suite 400, Toronto, ON, M5K 3K5; Tel: 416-963-8830; Email: spmarkets@cdgbooks.com.

For press review copies, author interviews, or other publicity information, please contact our Marketing department at 416-963-8830, fax 416-923-4821, or e-mail publicity@cdgbooks.com.

For authorization to photocopy items for corporate, personal, or educational use, please contact Cancopy, The Canadian Copyright Licensing Agency, One Yonge Street, Suite 1900, Toronto, ON, M5E 1E5; Tel: 416-868-1620; Fax: 416-868-1621; www.cancopy.com

is a trademark under exclusive license to CDG Books Canada, Inc. from International Data Group, Inc.

is a registered trademark under exclusive license to IDG Books Worldwide, Inc. from International Data Group, Inc.

About the Authors

For close to a decade, **Liz Primeau** was the editor-in-chief of *Canadian Gardening* magazine, the foremost periodical about gardening in Canada. An avid and experienced gardener, she has been a featured speaker at gardening conferences, trade shows, and garden clubs. The author of several successful gardening titles, for the past three seasons she has been the host of *Canadian Gardening Television* on the Life Network.

Canadian Gardening is one of Canada's most popular gardening magazines. Published since 1990, *Canadian Gardening* is the industry leader and has become the definitive source for novice and expert gardening enthusiasts. For more information about this great magazine, check out their Web site at www.canadiangardening.com.

Michael MacCaskey began his college career as a creative arts student at San Francisco State University in 1969, but in the process became instead a passionate gardener. By 1976, he received a Bachelor of Science degree in ornamental horticulture from California State Polytechnic University, San Luis Obispo. He was appointed Editor-in-Chief of Vermont-based *National Gardening* magazine in 1994. Since then, he's been learning about gardening in a short-season, cold-winter region. His magazine writing has been honored by both the Western Magazine Publishers Association and the Garden Writers of America.

Bill Marken is the editor-in-chief of eHow.com and the founding editor of *Rebecca's Garden* magazine, a publication based on the popular television show. A lifelong resident of California, Bill served as editor-in-chief of *Sunset*, the magazine of Western Living, from 1981 to 1996. Earlier in his career, he wrote for the magazine's garden section, pitched in on several editions of the best-selling *Western Garden Book*, and generally nurtured his interests in subjects related to gardening, landscaping, travel, and other aspects of the good life in the West. A vacation garden at 6,200-feet elevation gives him insight into cold-winter climates with 100-day growing seasons.

The National Gardening Association is the largest member-based, nonprofit organization of home gardeners in the U.S. Founded in 1972 (as 'Gardens for All') to spearhead the community garden movement, today's National Gardening Association is best known for its bimonthly publication, *National Gardening* magazine. Reporting on all aspects of home gardening, each issue is read by some half-million gardeners worldwide. For more information about the National Gardening Association, write to 180 Flynn Ave., Burlington, VT 05401 USA; or see its Web site at www.garden.org on the Internet.

ABOUT IDG BOOKS WORLDWIDE, INC.
AND CDG BOOKS CANADA, INC.

Welcome to the world of IDG Books Worldwide and CDG Books Canada.

IDG Books Worldwide, Inc., is a subsidiary of International Data Group, Inc., the world's largest publisher of computer-related information and the leading global provider of information services on information technology. IDG was founded more than 30 years ago and now employs more than 9,000 people worldwide. IDG publishes more than 295 computer publications in over 75 countries (see listing below). More than 90 million people read one or more IDG publications each month.

Launched in 1990, IDG Books Worldwide is today the #1 publisher of best-selling computer books in North America. IDG Books Worldwide is proud to be the recipient of eight awards from the Computer Press Association in recognition of editorial excellence and three from *Computer Currents'* First Annual Readers' Choice Awards. Our best-selling *...For Dummies®* series has more than 55 million copies in print with translations in 31 languages. In record time, IDG Books Worldwide has become the first choice for millions of readers around the world who want to learn how to better manage their businesses.

In 1998, IDG Books Worldwide formally partnered with Macmillan Canada, a subsidiary of Canada Publishing Corporation, to create CDG Books Canada, a dynamic new Canadian publishing company. CDG Books Canada is now Canada's fastest growing publisher, bringing valuable information to Canadians from coast to coast through the introduction of Canadian *...For Dummies®* and *CliffsNotes™* titles.

Every one of our books is designed to bring extra value and skill-building instructions to the reader. Our books are written by experts who understand and care about our readers. The knowledge base of our editorial staff comes from years of experience in publishing, education, and journalism — experience we use to produce books to carry us into the new millennium. In short, we care about books, so we attract the best people. We devote special attention to details such as audience, interior design, use of icons, and illustrations. And because we use an efficient process of authoring, editing, and desktop publishing our books electronically, we can spend more time ensuring superior content and spend less time on the technicalities of making books.

You can count on our commitment to deliver high-quality books at competitive prices on topics you want to read about. At IDG Books Worldwide and CDG Books Canada, we continue in the IDG tradition of delivering quality for more than 30 years. You can learn more about IDG Books Worldwide and CDG Books Canada by visiting www.idgbooks.com, www.dummies.com, and www.cdgbooks.com.

IDG BOOKS WORLDWIDE

John Kilcullen
President and Publisher
IDG Books Worldwide, Inc.

Steven Berkowitz
Chairman and CEO
IDG Books Worldwide, Inc.

Hart Hillman
President
CDG Books Canada, Inc.

CDG BOOKS CANADA

Eighth Annual
Computer Press
Awards ≥1992

Ninth Annual
Computer Press
Awards ≥1993

Tenth Annual
Computer Press
Awards ≥1994

Eleventh Annual
Computer Press
Awards ≥1995

Dedication

We dedicate this book to new gardeners, individuals who sow a packet of seeds, plant a tree, or otherwise nurture a plant for the first time.

Acknowledgments

You wouldn't be reading this book if it weren't for Tina Forrester, researcher and proofreader extraordinaire, who was an invaluable help in getting this Canadian edition to the printer. She provided inspiration and just plain facts. Tina is a pro, and we couldn't have done without her.

Joan Whitman, Acquisitions Editor, and Kim Herter, Assistant Editor, were both joys to work with. Their patience, humour, and professionalism saw us through many tight deadlines. Thanks, too, to Janet Davis, who let us mess up her workplace with hundreds of slides as we chose the right ones for the book, provided us with the perfect cover shot, and for being able to identify the cultivars of the plants she'd photographed.

For their patience and assistance in checking facts and plants: Eric Hambly at Siloam Orchards in Uxbridge, Ont.; The Canadian Rose Society; Ken Carey at the Guelph Turfgrass Institute; and Shirley Froelich at Prairie Originals.

Michael McCaskey, Bill Marken, and the NGA thank the Chicago staff of IDG Books Worldwide: Kathy Welton, publisher, and Holly McGuire, acquisitions editor. We especially thank Sarah Kennedy, former executive editor, for her support and enthusiastic promotion of ...*For Dummies* gardening books. Of the IDG team in Indianapolis, we thank senior project editor Kyle Looper who not only demonstrated excellent organizational and editorial skills, but great trust and patience as well. (A book this size and this complex is an act of faith as much as writing and editing!) We also thank Patricia Yuu Pan for her close reading and knowledgeable editing of the text. Thanks to artists Ron Hildebrand (most of the illustrations in the book) and Shane Kelly (USDA Zone maps) for their excellent work, and to IDG's Alison Walthall, Shelley Lea, and Brent Savage for their help with the color inserts. At NGA, thanks to President David Els; Vice-President, Publishing, Larry Sommers; and the excellent magazine staff of Linda Provost, Shila Patel, Charlie Nardozzi, and Kim Mitchell. Special thanks to Second Edition contributors Karen E. Fletcher and Kathy Bond Borie, and to First Edition contributors Lynn Ocone, Vicky Congdon, Lance Walheim, Barbara Pleasant, Susan McClure, Robert Kourik, and Sally Williams. Thanks, finally, to technical editors and good friends Deb Brown, Denny Schrock, and Dick Dunmire for their consistently good advice.

Publisher's Acknowledgments

We're proud of this book; please register your comments through our IDG Books Worldwide Online Registration Form located at http://my2cents.dummies.com.

Some of the people who helped bring this book to market include the following:

Acquisitions, Editorial, and Media Development

Editor: Colleen Totz

Acquisitions Editor: Joan Whitman

Assistant Editor: Kim Herter

Cover and Interior Photography: Janet Davis

Special Help
Tina Forrester, Michael Kelly, Michelle Vukas, Diane Graves Steele, Tom Hopkins

Production

Project Coordinator: E. Shawn Aylsworth

Layout and Graphics: Amy M. Adrian, Brian Drumm, Angela F. Hunckler, Kate Jenkins, Barry Offringa, Jill Piscitelli, Douglas L. Rollison, Brent Savage, Janet Seib, Michael A. Sullivan, Maggie Ubertini, Mary Jo Weis, Dan Whetstine

Proofreaders: Vickie Broyles, Melissa Martin, Marianne Santy, Ethel Winslow

Indexer: Sharon Hilgenberg

General and Administrative

IDG Books Worldwide, Inc.: John Kilcullen, CEO; Steven Berkowitz, President and Publisher

CDG Books Canada, Inc.: Ron Besse, Chairman; Hart Hillman, President; Robert Harris, Vice President and Publisher

IDG Books Technology Publishing Group: Richard Swadley, Senior Vice President and Publisher; Walter Bruce III, Vice President and Associate Publisher; Steven Sayre, Associate Publisher; Joseph Wikert, Associate Publisher; Mary Bednarek, Branded Product Development Director; Mary Corder, Editorial Director

IDG Books Consumer Publishing Group: Roland Elgey, Senior Vice President and Publisher; Kathleen A. Welton, Vice President and Publisher; Kevin Thornton, Acquisitions Manager; Kristin A. Cocks, Editorial Director

IDG Books Internet Publishing Group: Brenda McLaughlin, Senior Vice President and Publisher; Diane Graves Steele, Vice President and Associate Publisher; Sofia Marchant, Online Marketing Manager

IDG Books Production for Dummies Press: Michael R. Britton, Vice President of Production; Debbie Stailey, Associate Director of Production; Cindy L. Phipps, Manager of Project Coordination, Production Proofreading, and Indexing; Tony Augsburger, Manager of Prepress, Reprints, and Systems; Laura Carpenter, Production Control Manager; Shelley Lea, Supervisor of Graphics and Design; Debbie J. Gates, Production Systems Specialist; Robert Springer, Supervisor of Proofreading; Kathie Schutte, Production Supervisor

Dummies Packaging and Book Design: Patty Page, Manager, Promotions Marketing

◆

The publisher would like to give special thanks to Patrick J. McGovern, without whom this book would not have been possible.

◆

Contents at a Glance

Introduction *1*

Part I: Getting Going with Gardening *7*

Chapter 1: Just a Few Ground-Level Questions and Answers 9

Chapter 2: Zoning Out: What You Can and Can't Grow 17

Chapter 3: Planning Your Landscape 29

Part II: Colour Your World *45*

Chapter 4: Annuals 47

Chapter 5: Perennials 61

Chapter 6: Bulbs 75

Chapter 7: Roses 89

Part III: Sculpting with Plants *109*

Chapter 8: Trees and Shrubs 111

Chapter 9: Lawns and Ground Covers 133

Chapter 10: Vines 155

Part IV: At Ground Level *168*

Chapter 11: Understanding and Improving Soil 169

Chapter 12: Raising Plants from Seeds 187

Chapter 13: Choosing and Planting Seedlings, Trees, and Shrubs 201

Part V: Caring for Your Plants *213*

Chapter 14: Feed Me, Seymour! Watering, Feeding, and Composting 215

Chapter 15: A Snip Here, a Snip There: Pruning and Propagating 235

Chapter 16: Fighting Pests, Diseases, and Weeds 245

Chapter 17: Tools of the Trade 275

Part VI: Special Gardens *287*

Chapter 18: Food Gardens 289

Chapter 19: Container Gardens 307

Part VII: The Part of Tens *324*

Chapter 20: Ten Provinces, Three Territories, Twelve Official Flowers 325

Chapter 21: Perfumed Garden Flowers 333

Appendix A: Gardening Resources *341*

Appendix B: Mail-Order Resources *361*

Index *385*

Book Registration Information ....*Back of Book*

Cartoons at a Glance

By Rich Tennant

page 7

"Something's about to die in your cactus container."

page 109

page 45

"That should do it."

page 287

page 167

page 323

page 213

Fax: 978-546-7747 • E-mail: the5wave@tiac.net

Table of Contents

Introduction 1

    How to Use This Book 2
        Part I: Getting Going with Gardening 2
        Part II: Colour Your World 3
        Part III: Sculpting with Plants 3
        Part IV: At Ground Level 3
        Part V: Caring for Your Plants 3
        Part VI: Special Gardens 4
        Part VII: The Part of Tens 4
        Appendixes 4
    Icons Used in This Book 5

Part I: Getting Going with Gardening 7

    Chapter 1: Just a Few Ground-Level Questions and Answers 9
    How Do I Make My Plants Grow Rather Than Die? 10
        Your climate and microclimates 10
        Sun or shade 11
        Soil and water 12
        Plants that are most at home in your garden 12
    What Can I Use My Garden For? 13
    Do I Have to Learn a Foreign Language? 14
        The fancy name 15
        Common names 16

    Chapter 2: Zoning Out: What You Can and Can't Grow 17
    Plant Hardiness 18
        Cold hardiness 18
        Winter injury 18
    Plant Hardiness Zones of Canada 19
        U.S. and Canadian zones: How they compare 20
    Working with microclimates 20
    Length Counts: How Long Is Your Season? 21
    Stretching Your Garden Season 23
        Planting earlier in the year 23
        Gardening into autumn 25
    Maximizing Winter Hardiness 26

Chapter 3: Planning Your Landscape 29

Taking Stock of What You Have .30
Dreaming Up the Perfect Landscape 33
Who will use your yard? 34
When will you use your yard? 34
What's your neighbourhood like? 34
How much maintenance are you ready for? 35
What Goes Where: Designing the Plan 36
Using your space effectively .37
Defining areas and ways to move through them 37
The hardscape 39
The plants 40
Creating a Final Plan 42
Using your computer 43
Field testing 44

Part II: Colour Your World 45

Chapter 4: Annuals 47

What's an Annual? 47
Getting Cozy with Annuals 49
Some annuals are cool and some like it hot 49
Sun and shade 50
How to Buy Annuals 50
What You Can Do with Annuals 51
Playing with colour 52
Using shape, height, and structure 53
Designing for fragrance 53
Getting annuals together 55
Containing annuals 55
Taking Care of Your Annuals 56
Our Favourite Annuals 57
Cool-season annuals 57
Warm-season annuals 59

Chapter 5: Perennials 61

What's a Perennial? 61
Beds and Borders 62
Designing a Perennial Border .63
Beyond borders 64
Planting Perennials . . . and Afterwards 65
Watering and feeding 65
Pinching and pruning perennials 66
Our Favourite Perennials 68

Chapter 6: Bulbs **75**

What Are Bulbs? 75

What You Can Do with Bulbs 77

When and How to Buy Bulbs 77

Spring-blooming bulbs 77

Summer-blooming bulbs 78

Shopping tips 79

Ode to the Lily 79

Planting Bulbs 81

What's your style? 82

Beware the creatures 82

Caring for Bulbs 83

Dividing and Propagating Bulbs 83

Bulbs in Containers 84

Favourite Bulbs 86

Chapter 7: Roses **89**

Kinds of Roses 90

Trying out hybrid teas 91

Fun with floribundas 92

The experts' choice 92

Hail to the queen 93

Climbing high with roses 93

"Honey, I shrunk the roses!" 93

When a rose is a tree 94

Shrub roses 94

Landscaping with Roses 100

Buying Roses 101

Planting Roses 103

Fertilizing and Watering 104

The Mystery of Pruning 106

Other Rose Quirks 107

Helping Roses Survive Winter 108

Part III: Sculpting with Plants *109*

Chapter 8: Trees and Shrubs **111**

What Trees Can Do for You 111

Lower heating and cooling expenses 112

Make you look marvelous 112

Choosing the Right Tree 113

Don't Try This at Home 115

Our Favourite Trees 116

Rub-a-Dub-Dub, What's a Shrub? 122

What Shrubs Can Do for You 122
   Design considerations 123
   Organizing shrubs by height 124
Our Favourite Shrubs 124

Chapter 9: Lawns and Ground Covers 133

Lawn Decisions 134
   How big? 134
   Which grass is for you? 134
   Turfgrass short list 135
Putting in a New Lawn 137
Planting Lawn from Seed 138
   Shopping for seed 138
   How much seed to buy 138
   Planting day 139
Planting Lawn from Sod 142
   Buying sod 143
   Laying sod 143
Care and Feeding of Lawns 146
   Weeding 147
   Mowing 147
   Fertilizing 148
   Tune-ups and face-lifts 148
Ground Covers instead of Lawns 149
Planting Ground Covers 149
Top Ground Cover Choices 151
Over in the Meadow 154

Chapter 10: Vines 155

Let's Do the Twist 155
Using Vines Effectively 156
   Don't let vines grow where they shouldn't 156
   Provide sturdy support 156
   Prune for healthy vines 157
Lean on Me 157
Choosing a Vine Support 158
   Bamboo teepees 159
   Chain-link fences 159
   Metal trellises 160
   Latticework trellises 160
   Fan trellises 160
   Plastic netting 161
   Pillars 161
   Wall-mounted supports 161
   Arbours 162
Vines We Love 162
Annual Vines 164

Part IV: At Ground Level *167*

Chapter 11: Understanding and Improving Soil 169

Clearing the Site 169
    Stripping sod 170
    Other soil-clearing methods 171
Meeting Your Soil 172
    Soil texture 172
    Soil structure 174
    One more big thing: Soil pH 176
    Your soil, in detail 177
Improving Your Soil 177
    Exactly what do you add? 178
    Changing pH 180
    Adding nutrients 180
    Green manure crops and cover crops 181
Loosening the Soil 181
    Time for a tiller 182
    Double digging 183
    Simple raised beds 184

Chapter 12: Raising Plants from Seeds 187

    What Those Needy Seeds Need 188
Smart Shopping 188
Sowing Seeds Right in the Ground 189
    A Dozen Easy Annuals to Direct-Sow 191
Starting Seeds Indoors 194
A Dozen Easy Annuals to Start Indoors 198

Chapter 13: Choosing and Planting Seedlings, Trees, and Shrubs 201

Buying and Planting Seedlings 202
Figuring Out Spacing for Transplants 202
Planting Seedlings, Step by Step 203
Container-Grown Trees and Shrubs 206
    Choosing container-grown trees and shrubs 206
    Transplanting trees and shrubs from containers 207
Bare-Root Planting 209
    Choosing bare-root plants 210
    Planting bare-root plants 210
Burlap-Wrapped Root Balls 211
    Choosing balled-and-burlapped plants 211
    Planting balled-and-burlapped plants 211

Part V: Caring for Your Plants 213

Chapter 14: Feed Me, Seymour! Watering, Feeding, and Composting 215

Watering Basics 215
    Getting water to your garden 216
    Determining the amount and frequency of watering 220
    Conserving water 221
Providing a Balanced Diet for Your Plants 221
Don't Compromise, Fertilize! 223
    Common fertilizer terms 223
    Kinds of fertilizers for various plants 225
    Organic fertilizers 226
Piling onto the Compost Bandwagon 227
    From refuse to riches 227
    Bin there, done that! 228
    To build or to buy? 228
    Composting aids . . . who needs them? 231
    Heapin' it on 232
A-Mulching We Will Go 232
    Inorganic mulches 233
    Fertile mulches 233

Chapter 15: A Snip Here, a Snip There: Pruning and Propagating 235

Practical Pruning 235
    How pruning affects plant growth 236
    The kindest cuts 237
    Pruning trees 238
    Pruning in winter 240
    Pruning in summer 240
    Pruning tools 241
Down-to-Earth Propagating 242
Getting Plants for Free 243

Chapter 16: Fighting Pests, Diseases, and Weeds 245

Preventing Bad Things from Happening 246
Identifying Damage 248
Insect Pests You're Most Likely to Encounter 249
Managing Pests 257
    Encouraging "good" insects 258
    Safe and effective pest chemicals 259
Preventing Plant Diseases 263
    Solarization 265
    Fourteen dirty diseases: What to do 265
    Least-toxic disease remedies 269

Controlling Weeds 269
  Weed-control basics 269
  Thirteen common weeds 271

Chapter 17: Tools of the Trade **275**
  Hand Tools 275
    The magnificent seven tools 275
    Hand-tool maintenance 276
    Five more tools to buy 278
  Powering Up Your Tools 278
    Lawn mowers 279
    Trimmers 282
    Tillers and chipper-shredders 282
  Where to Shop for Garden Tools 285
    Nurseries 285
    Other sources for tools and garden supplies 285

Part VI: Special Gardens **287**

Chapter 18: Food Gardens **289**
  Planning a Vegetable Garden 289
    Seasonal preferences 290
    Choose the right location 291
    Make the garden the right size 292
    Designing the garden 292
    Improving the soil 293
    What to start with 294
    It's all in the timing 294
    Have a happy harvest 296
  You Can't Go Wrong with These 296
  What about Hybrids and Heirlooms? 298
  Squeezing in Herbs 299
  Is There Fruit in Your Future? 300
    Six steps to a fruit tree harvest 301
    Planning a fruit garden 303
    Fruits for the home garden 303

Chapter 19: Container Gardens **307**
  Choosing the Right Pots 307
  Designing with Container Plants 310
    Style points 310
    One special plant 312
    Combining plants in containers 312
    How to arrange containers 312
  Putting It All Together 314

Favourite Container Combos 315
    Perennial accents 315
    Delectable edibles 316
A Container for Four Seasons 317
A Primer on Soil for Pots 317
How to Plant Containers 320
Is Everybody Happy? 321
    A fertilizing plan 321

Part VII: The Part of Tens *323*

Chapter 20: Ten Provinces, Three Territories, Twelve Official Flowers .... .325

British Columbia 326
Alberta 326
Saskatchewan 327
Manitoba 327
Ontario 328
Quebec 328
New Brunswick 329
Nova Scotia 329
Prince Edward Island 330
Newfoundland/Labrador 330
Northwest Territories 331
Yukon Territory 331

Chapter 21: Perfumed Garden Flowers 333

Getting the Most for Your Whiff 333
Flowers Most Possessed with Scent 334
Fragrance after Dark 335
The Most Aromatic Herbs 336
Heavenly Scented Trees, Shrubs, and Vines 336
Best Bulbs for Fragrance 337
Redolent Roses 338

Appendix A: Gardening Resources 341

Books and Magazines 342
Gardening Online 346
Weather and Climate Online 351
Gardening Software 358

Appendix B: Mail-Order Resources 362

Index *385*

Book Registration Information ....*Back of Book*

Introduction

When it comes to gardening books, Canadians used to feel left out in the cold. And no wonder — virtually all the books on the shelves tell you how to raise roses where Jack Frost drops in maybe a couple of times a year, or show to-die-for perennial beds impossible in our climate but prospering in places like Sticky Wicket, Dorset, England. (We're not kidding — such a place exists.) We slavered, and we yearned, and we've ended up feeling like less-than-adequate gardeners, if not downright sorry for ourselves that we lived in such an unkind country.

Well, things have changed. The gardening boom of the last few years has proved that gardening in Canada is not an oxymoron — in fact, gardens here have their own distinctive style and beauty, just like the gardens of other countries. We just had to find ourselves — to grow up, if you will — and to realize that while we can't winter over mandevilla or raise artichokes, we can grow plants gardeners in many countries find difficult, such as lilacs, tulips, and apple trees. We have gorgeous native grasses and blooming plants, such as ironweed, trilliums, and blazing star. We have impressive conifers, the showy but dainty spring-blooming redbud tree, and we have autumn colour that's envied by gardeners and tourists from other countries. Adjectives can't do this season justice, but we who live here know how incredibly beautiful it can be.

Canadian garden writers have surfaced, too, and each spring and fall now brings a new crop of books about gardening in Canada. We wrote this book for you, the Canadian gardener. We made sure that the advice given and plants suggested are appropriate for Canadian gardeners. You'll find a wide range of information, from rose varieties hardy in Canada's climates to scab-resistant apple trees available in Canada. We made sure the products mentioned are available here, too. Be sure to check out the appendixes on gardening resources and mail-order resources — they are invaluable. They tell you where to buy daylilies or wildflower seed, and how to find your local agricultural office for specific advice pertaining to your area. We've also picked out photos that represent beautiful, lush, and most important, *possible* Canadian gardens.

Our job was made easier because the American edition of this book was our style of gardening: down-to-earth, basic, common-sense stuff. The advice on garden design, composting, and mulching was what we'd have said if we'd written it first, and it remains essentially the same. We liked the book's style, too: It doesn't take gardening too seriously, and we hope we've maintained that slightly irreverent tone — we can guarantee a few laughs along the way!

Gardening For Canadians For Dummies is for beginning gardeners who like to have fun and need straight-from-the-shoulder advice. We trust we've provided it here, for Canadian gardeners.

How to Use This Book

You have in your hands a gardening encyclopedia in miniature — all you need to know to get off to a good start. No matter what area of gardening interests you — growing roses or perennials or just cutting the grass — you'll find good advice here. And when you outgrow the level of information that we provide here, you can turn to the appendixes at the back of this book for pointers on where to look next, and to other *...For Dummies* books on other related topics.

In every chapter, our goal is to give you the information you need to plant or prune what you want. Novices aren't the only ones who will find this useful. Gardening is such a huge topic that no one ever comes close to knowing everything about it. (That's one reason why gardening has become one of the most popular hobbies of all time.) If, for example, you are a seasoned rose grower but know almost nothing about starting a salad garden or pruning trees, you can find excellent advice in Chapters 18 or 15, respectively.

This book offers lists of plants that you can choose from to create a beautiful garden. We list the plants by the common name first, followed by the botanical name. The lists are alphabetized according to the botanical name.

For international gardeners, we've added approximate metric equivalents for plant heights, planting depths, and other pertinent measurements.

Part I: Getting Going with Gardening

Before you buy your first six-pack of flower seedlings in spring, you need to decide just where and when to start digging.

Chapter 1 begins at root level, guiding you through what your plants need to what you want from a garden.

Chapter 2 helps you determine which plants will grow in your climate.

Chapter 3 gets into the details of designing or planning a garden, with emphasis on making a rudimentary plan that you can refer to and refine later.

Part II: Colour Your World

Here's where the real fun starts! This part is the heart of the book because, for most people, the essence of gardening is putting in colourful plants and watching them grow.

Chapter 4 tells you about those comets of the garden, flowering annuals.

Chapter 5 is about the colourful stalwarts, the perennials.

Chapter 6 deals with bulbs for all seasons — not just spring.

Chapter 7 covers the world's most famous flower, the rose.

Part III: Sculpting with Plants

Chapter 8 goes over the garden's skeleton — the trees, shrubs, and ornamental grasses that form your yard's foundation.

Chapter 9 discusses the plants of the horizontal plane (lawns and ground covers), while the vertical plane (vines) gets similar treatment in Chapter 10.

Part IV: At Ground Level

This section is the nitty-gritty of gardening — literally. The three chapters in this part are about working with soil and getting your plants started.

Chapter 11 helps you understand and improve your soil.

You find the basics of starting seeds in Chapter 12, and other plant-starting methods (seedlings, bulbs, and transplants) in Chapter 13.

Part V: Caring for Your Plants

In a nutshell, this section covers long-term garden maintenance.

Chapter 14 covers everything you need to know about the basics of plant care: watering, feeding, and composting.

Chapter 15 covers pruning, Chapter 16 common sense pest control, and Chapter 17 all those tools you need to accomplish as much as you'd like.

Part VI: Special Gardens

It's back to the fun stuff — plants and planting — in this section!

If you want to grow at least some of your own food, check out Chapter 18. In Chapter 19, discover what it takes to grow a garden in a container.

Part VII: The Part of Tens

No ...*For Dummies* book is complete without the Part of Tens, so we offer a compendium of expert tips for achieving interesting, low-care gardens and a rundown of our country's official flowers.

Appendixes

One exciting feature about gardening is the endless amount of information available on whatever aspect you find most compelling. The appendixes that we've compiled here are intended to help you in that effort.

Appendix A: Gardening Resources

Just as this book can't possibly include all the plants that might grow in your garden, no book, even the biggest, fattest, most expensive ones, include more than a fraction of what you may want to know someday. That's why we believe so strongly in this section of resources. This appendix is the place to go if or when you want to know more about the following:

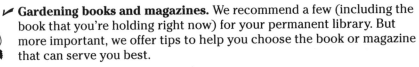

- ✔ **Gardening books and magazines.** We recommend a few (including the book that you're holding right now) for your permanent library. But more important, we offer tips to help you choose the book or magazine that can serve you best.

- ✔ **Gardening online.** Going online is often the quickest way to get your questions answered. We should know. The National Gardening Association has answered more gardening questions for longer than any other organization. In this appendix, you find some of our favorite gardening Web sites and automatic mailing lists. If you have any questions or comments after reading this book, you can contact us at `nga@garden.org`.

Appendix B: Mail-Order Resources

The variety of plants, seeds, and tools that you can buy through the mail and have delivered the next day is astounding. Mail-order is the way to go, especially if you're looking for anything the least bit unusual. You can outfit your entire garden through the mail, from plants, to tools, to fertilizers, to ornaments.

Icons Used in This Book

Points Suggests ways to save money.

Points out ecological tips and ways to be earth-friendly.

Flags information that even some experienced gardeners may not know.

Marks tips that experienced gardeners live by.

Offers international gardening advice and data.

Demystifies gardening lingo. Although we've made this book as jargon-free as possible, you need to know some terms.

Gives addresses and/or phone numbers for ordering special gardening equipment. (You can also find sources in the appendixes.)

Watch out! Alerts you to avoid bad gardening experiences, including some that may cause injury.

Part I
Getting Going with Gardening

The 5th Wave   By Rich Tennant

"Well, Roger wanted to design the garden, and, of course, I <u>knew</u> he was a paleontologist, but I had no idea..."

In this part . . .

You've probably heard about the green thumbs and the brown thumbs. Some people seem to have an almost magical ability to raise beautiful, healthy plants, whereas others seem to turn out only withering brown husks.

No matter which group you identify with, take note: Anyone can become a gardener. Like any other interest that's worth pursuing, gardening requires knowledge, experience, attention, and enthusiasm. If you're willing to dedicate some time and attention to gardening, you can move from the brown thumb camp into the green thumb camp. If you already consider yourself to have a green thumb, you undoubtedly know that gardening never ceases to surprise you, and you never finish learning.

Part I gives you a basic understanding of some of the key issues that gardeners face: what plants require in order to thrive, what you can do with your garden, how climate affects what you can grow, and how to take the space you have and maximize it.

Well, what are you waiting for? Get going!

Chapter 1

Just a Few Ground-Level Questions and Answers

• •

In This Chapter

▶ Understanding what plants need from you

▶ Knowing what your garden can do for you

▶ Speaking the garden language

• •

*I*f you want to learn more about gardening — and you must if you are read-ing this — just where do you start? We could start with some heavy-duty science, tossing around terms like *cotyledon, cambium,* and the ever-popular *tilth.* Or we could start talking about beautiful gardens as if we were critics of fine paintings, employing words like *composition, energy, focal point,* and such.

We don't mean to suggest anything but respect for scientists and artists. In fact, the chance to combine science and art is what draws many of us to gar-dening in the first place — especially if you throw in a little farming and a few old wives' tales (of course, you should — or shouldn't — plant sweet peas at the full moon).

All we really want to do here is to get you through a few basic principles of plant growth and garden planning so you can rush out into the yard when the weather's right for planting and the soil is ripe for digging.

First, any questions?

How Do I Make My Plants Grow Rather Than Die?

Like other living things, plants have certain requirements for good health. For example, they require the right amounts of sunlight, moisture, and nutrients. Plants also need an equitable range of temperatures — neither too hot nor too cold.

When selecting plants, you can meet their requirements in one of two ways. The first involves selecting your favourites and then doing your best to alter the growing conditions at the planting site to meet their needs. You can change the growing conditions by adding sprinkler irrigation, incorporating fertilizer, hauling in fresh topsoil, pruning some trees, or covering plants with blankets in winter. But this is the backward approach.

A better way to make sure plants grow well — and need less care in the process — is to learn about the conditions in your garden first, and then choose plants that grow under those conditions. Of course, you're going to choose some plants that are accustomed to conditions different from those you have, and those plants are going to need some attention to stay happy. But the better you match plants to the planting site, the longer they'll live, the better they'll look, and the less work (watering, pruning, fertilizing, and controlling pests) you'll have to do to care for them.

Your climate and microclimates

Matching a plant to a site needs to be done on both a large and a small scale. On the large scale, the biggest consideration is Old Man Winter. Is the plant you want to grow winter hardy in your climatic zone? (You can find more information in Chapter 2, which is devoted to Canada's zone system.) For example, you wouldn't try to grow a palm tree in Regina, although you might be successful in certain parts of British Columbia. But there are so many beautiful, hardy herbaceous perennials, shrubs, and trees to choose from you won't miss the palm tree, or even a bougainvillea, unless you're willing to treat it as an annual and let it succumb to frost when winter comes. By the way, don't worry about annuals for the larger picture — they grow for one summer season only, and in fact thrive in the long, sunny days of the northern parts of Canada.

Rainfall is another big-picture consideration. If you live where the annual rainfall is low, choose drought-resistant plants unless you're prepared to give them supplemental irrigation.

On a smaller scale, consider the localized climates of your garden, called *microclimates*. They can vary from cold, windy and shady on the northeast side of your house to dry and baking hot on the west. The warmth radiated by a light-coloured brick wall can heat up a bed so it's several degrees warmer than a more exposed part of your garden. It may even qualify as a zone higher. An area like this might allow you to push the limits and grow plants that aren't considered hardy in your zone. On the other hand, plants otherwise hardy in your zone might succumb to winter chill on that exposed, windswept hill in the back forty. (For more about microclimates, see Chapter 2.) If you have the luxury of the time, observe the conditions in your garden for a year before you decide what plants will grow best in it.

Sun or shade

All plants need light to grow properly. However, different plants need different amounts of light.

Many plants require full sun for at least six to eight hours per day. Plants that don't get enough sunlight become *leggy* (long, spindly stems), because they're stretching out for more light. Plants that don't get enough sunlight also tend to flower poorly.

Some plants prefer shade for the entire day, or at least part of it. Many different types of shade exist, and each type creates a different microclimate. For example, consider the area on the east side of your house. For at least half a day — in the morning — this area is sunny and warm. In the afternoon, it's shady and a little cooler.

The west side of the house is usually the opposite — shady in the morning but hot and sunny in the afternoon. Heavy, all-day shade appears on the north side of the house, and filtered shade is found under trees. To further confuse the matter, shade can change with the seasons as trees lose their leaves and as the sun moves on the horizon. If the weather is very hot, some normally sun-loving plants prefer at least partial afternoon shade.

Here's an obvious rule for gardening in the shade: Grow *shade-loving* plants in the shade. Sun-worshipping plants just won't make it. Don't fret. Hundreds of incredible shade-lovers (some with showy flowers and others with attractive foliage and form) are available to choose from.

To complicate matters a little, a plant's shade tolerance varies both by region and by specific garden conditions. For example, many plants that need full sun in cool, northern parts of Canada (or in coastal areas) tolerate or require some afternoon shade when grown in the banana belt areas of southern Ontario and British Columbia.

Soil and water

The kind of soil in your garden — heavy clay or porous sand, for example — and soil moisture are closely related. Chapters 11 and 14 detail the importance of these two factors and the ways in which they affect plant growth. Those chapters also cover cultural practices such as tilling, watering, and fertilizing. Whether you see prairies, mountains, or rolling hills when you look out your window, you can find plants that are well adapted to almost every situation. Wet, soggy clay soil is very difficult to correct, but certain plants grow, and even thrive, under those conditions. Choosing plants to fit existing soil conditions is usually a great deal easier than altering the soil conditions themselves.

Plants that are most at home in your garden

Nothing epitomizes the principle of choosing plants appropriate to the site more than growing *native plants*. Natives are plants that grow naturally in a specific region or locality. Over hundreds (probably thousands) of years, these plants have become superbly adapted to their conditions and in those areas — or in similar areas — they grow with health and vigour without the help of gardeners. These abilities also make them very valuable as landscape plants.

Native plants have become very popular with gardeners, and for good reason. They get by on what nature provides, especially when it comes to water. Many have adapted to wet or boggy areas, and others to more arid areas, especially on the prairies. They don't need extra irrigation, and conserving natural resources always makes sense.

Native plants grown in conditions they've adapted to also bloom dependably, according to their habit, without extra help from fertilizers or coddling by the gardener. Many, like Solomon's seal, small-flowered alum root and Dutchman's breeches, are subtle in their flower habit. Others, such as purple coneflower, camassia, and butterfly weed, are the showgirls of the native plant garden.

Natives plants are also terrific for attracting birds, butterflies, bees, and other fauna that depend on them for food and shelter.

Many retail nurseries can help you select native plants. Some mail-order catalogues also specialize in native plants, especially wildflowers. (See Appendix B for a full listing of gardening suppliers.)

So what is a native plant, anyway?

A true native plant is one that grew here before Columbus discovered America. It evolved over millennia with everything else in a particular area as part of the ecology — including animals — and adapted to all the habitat's conditions.

Naturalized plants are another flora entirely, and it's easy not to know the difference between them and native plants. Naturalized plants arrived here as immigrants with European settlers, as seeds they brought to plant in the New World, or on their own, as stowaways in cargo or a ship's ballast. They may have been planted in settlers' gardens, but soon they escaped to thrive in the wild. Like native plants, naturalized ones are survivors that grow easily in nature's own conditions. Many, like the dandelion, are considered weeds, but others like the oxeye daisy and Queen Anne's lace, are admired as wildflowers.

The native plant police would not like to see you grow naturalized plants if you aspire to a natural garden. Less rigid gardeners are happy to welcome them into their garden, as long as they don't want to be the boss. That's something to be careful of: These plants were able to escape over the garden fence and naturalize in fields because they're tough and hardy, and sometimes they're invasive.

What Can I Use My Garden For?

True, you can buy plants, stick them in the ground and let it go at that. But many of us want a "garden," which, by our definition, contains enough organization and space to allow room for growing plants plus other purposes — playing, relaxing, outdoor dining, entertaining, and more.

A garden can make your life more comfortable, healthier, more colourful, and more convenient. A garden lets you expand your living area to the outdoors, harvest fresh food, and pick your own flowers. Take a look at the different ways that a garden can enhance your life.

- ✔ **A private getaway.** Imagine taking a vacation in your own backyard or relaxing in a shady spot, secluded from the hustle and bustle of daily living. This dream can be yours, if you begin by creating a private area for your own pleasure.

- ✔ **A place for entertaining.** Whether you like large get-togethers with the extended family or business associates, or a quiet dinner with a few friends, your garden can provide an ideal atmosphere. You need a few key ingredients to make your garden perfect for entertaining.

- ✔ **Don't forget Junior . . . or Spot.** Who will use your garden? Take into account children and pets — they have different garden interests than grownups.

- **Harvesting the fruits of your labour.** One of the most delicious aspects of your garden is that it can produce wonderful vegetables, fruits, and herbs. You can grow gourmet produce, rare and special crops, and grow them organically.

- **A practical work area.** Being outdoors means more than fun and games. You may need a place in your yard to keep your garden tools, fuel tank, firewood, clothesline, or garbage cans. Organize all of these less-than-attractive outdoor necessities in the same out-of-the way location — a workstation separate from your entertaining and play areas. Ideally, the location should be handy, near the garage or driveway, but far enough away from handsome views or gardens so that the workstation is not a distraction.

- **Take time to relax.** Anywhere that seems cozy and pleasant is a great place to put a sitting nook. The area doesn't have to be fancy, just a place for you to relax and, perhaps, watch the kids play. Start with a comfortable bench or chair and position it in shade beneath a magnificent oak, at the end of your vegetable garden, or at the back of your yard near the swing set. If you put in all-weather footing — gravel or mulch, for example — you can sit outside regardless of the soil conditions.

The possibilities for your garden are almost endless. Take some time to jot down everything you may possibly want in your yard. Chapter 3 shows you how to pull together all your needs and wishes in a garden plan.

Do I Have to Learn a Foreign Language?

The language spoken in gardening circles can be quirky. For example, dirt isn't just *dirt,* it's *soil.* Dirt is what you make mud pies with; it's the stain on your shirt. Soil, on the other hand, is full of promise and good nutrients. And some gardenholics tend to go on and on about plant names. You may catch them at the nursery asking, "Which Latin name is *most* correct, the old one or the new one?" or "What is the proper pronunciation for that plant?" Real garden snobs don't even recognize the common names, and tend to look down on you if you do. Don't be too hard on these people. Not only can they not help themselves, but you may find yourself behaving the same way someday.

In other words, learning something about plant names helps you appreciate gardening more — and helps you get through this book.

The fancy name

The proper (scientific) *botanical name* of a plant consists of two parts, much in the same way that people have a first and a last name. However, in plant language, the last name comes first.

The most important name is the *genus* — the "Smith" of Joe Smith, if you will. (The genus name always begins with a capital letter when used as part of a multipart name.) A genus is a group of closely related plants. Just as in your own family, some of the plant cousins look a lot alike, while others don't bear much resemblance at all. Also like your family, some closely related individuals have very different comfort levels. One uncle lives in Winnipeg, Manitoba, and loves its hot, dry summers. His sister thinks that Oxford, England, is quite warm and dry enough, thank you very much. It's the same for plants.

The second name, the "Joe" part of Joe Smith, is the species name. The species name usually describes some feature of the plant or its preferred habitat, or serves as a tribute to whoever discovered the plant. But the species name is disguised in pseudo-Latin, of course, just to keep things interesting. Consider, for example, *Hosta undulata.* Hosta is the genus name. The species name, *undulata,* describes the undulating shape of the leaf.

The plain old-fashioned, natural species of some plants acquire new status in face of prodigiously hybridized plants — tulips, for example. In those cases, the norm for the plant is some kind of hybrid of indeterminate botanical origin. That's why when gardeners finally have in their gardens an actual natural, non-hybridized type of tulip they say something like, "And this is my species tulip." Gardeners are funny, aren't they? (In this book, we use the abbreviation spp. for species.)

Occasionally, a third name follows the *species* name — the variety. Varieties are members of the same species but are different enough to deserve their own name. Just as you may have one redhead in a family of brunettes, some plants are quite dissimilar to their siblings. For example, *Lychnis coronaria* bears magenta flowers. Her sister *Lychnis coronaria alba,* however, wears a white *(alba)* flower.

Another part of a botanical name is the "cultivated variety," or *cultivar.* Whoever discovered or created the plant decided that it was special enough to have its own name. And the cultivar is also special enough to be maintained by cuttings, grafting, line-bred seed propagation, or tissue culture. The cultivar name appears after the species or variety name. The cultivar name is the only part of the botanical name that isn't in italics but is always enclosed with single quotation marks. For example, a very nice form of *Lychnis coronaria* with a pink blush is called *Lychnis coronaria* 'Angel Blush.'

Common names

Of course, ordinary people don't go around using long Latin botanical names in everyday conversation. Instead, they use a sort of botanical nickname, called a *common name*. Common names are less formal and easier to pronounce than botanical names. They're also less precise. Just as your Aunt Norma calls you "Pumpkin" and Uncle Bob calls you "Big Guy," many plants have several nicknames.

Often, the common name describes some distinguishing characteristic of the plant. For example, the plant called blue star has starry blue flowers. Sometimes, the origin of the name is lost in the mythology of a former time. Does anyone have a clue just who was the Susan of black-eyed Susan fame?

Finding that several unrelated flowers share the same common name isn't unusual at all. Unfortunately, regular English flower names are often just as silly as their highfalutin Latin cousins, if for different reasons. For example, two distinct plants share the name "mock orange," and at least five different plants go by "dusty miller." At least three unrelated perennials are called coneflowers: *Echinacea purpurea,* the *Rudbeckia genus,* and the *Ratibida genus.* On the other hand, many plants have no common name! Go figure.

The long and short of it is that the Latin or botanical name is the most precise. You need to pay attention when reading the plant tags at the nursery plant names — if only to avoid buying the wrong plant.

Chapter 2

Zoning Out: What You Can and Can't Grow

In This Chapter

▶ Understanding which permanent plants can grow in your garden

▶ Looking at Agriculture Canada's Hardiness Zones for plants' winter hardiness

▶ Creating frost-free days for annuals and vegetables

▶ Extending the growing season

▶ Maximizing winter hardiness

*W*e hate to admit it, but gardeners with a superior streak sometimes like to lord it over beginning gardeners. They ask questions like "And what zone are *you* in?" expecting a blank look. If you have no idea how you'd respond, this chapter is for you. Read it and consult Agriculture Canada's Hardiness Zones Map in the colour section of this book, and you'll be able to answer with authority in a trice, and maybe even tell your garden snob something he or she didn't know.

But this chapter will do more than that. It will also help you understand why knowing your zone is important and how it helps you choose permanent plants — trees, shrubs, ground covers, vines and herbaceous perennials — that will grow well in your garden. It will also help you understand when to abide by your zone and when to ignore it.

First of all, what is a *hardiness zone*? Simply put, it defines an area's climate. Knowing what zone you live in is important because it helps you predict what permanent plants will survive winter in your area. You don't need to worry about hardiness with most vegetables and annual flowers because they don't start growing still spring, and then they die in fall. What's important for annuals and vegetables is the *length* of that growing season, the number of days between frosts. (You read more about frost-free days later in this chapter.)

Plant Hardiness

Gardeners are keenly aware of the seasonal effects of temperature, particularly freezing temperatures, on the growth of landscape plants. Terms such as *cold hardy, frost hardy,* and *winter hardy* describe plants that can survive varying degrees of freezing temperatures without injury during winter dormancy.

Some very large and substantial plants curl their toes and turn mushy if exposed long enough to low temperatures. Imagine a palm tree thriving all summer in Brandon, Manitoba, and then imagine what happens to it in September. On the other hand, some plants can survive freezing, and even frigid, temperatures. Bulbs and many perennials escape the cold by hiding underground or under snow until spring. Others, such as hardy trees and shrubs, undergo metabolic changes between summer and winter.

Cold hardiness

The genetic capacity of a plant to acclimatize determines its cold hardiness. When plants acclimatize, they transform themselves from a nonhardy to hardy condition that allows them to withstand freezing temperatures. But absolute temperature, as devastating as its effects can be, is not the only criterion of hardiness. Many plants are not injured in winter by low temperatures, but they suffer damage during the changing weather of spring or fall. At those times, while they're not growing at full tilt, plants are not fully hardy either. Winter temperatures that move up and down from freeze to thaw can be damaging too. In places like Toronto, where a winter can be pleasantly mild with little snow cover and suddenly the temperature plunges to below zero, plants can suffer badly. This is also true of the area around Calgary, where warming winter chinooks can turn winter into spring for a day, melting snow and fooling plants (and people) into yawning and stretching and thinking about a young bud's fancy. Then Jack Frost returns, and there goes your favourite plant. . . . So you can see that determining where and when a plant is hardy can be complicated. Temperatures are crucial, but so are a region's climate patterns and how the plant responds. So, too, are microclimates, but more about them later.

Winter injury

Winter injury is easy to diagnose when you see lots of brown leaves or dried needles on an evergreen plant, injured or dead flower buds, or splitting bark. But sometimes damage from winter temperatures is difficult to see, manifested only in delayed bud development or slightly reduced growth. Trees and shrubs may limp along for several years and suddenly succumb during a harsh winter — especially if they were only borderline hardy in your region to begin with. Perhaps the safest course to ensure plant adaptability is to grow plants native to your particular region. Such plants are the best bets to have the constitution to survive in your garden. And for the most part, local nurseries stock only plants that are known to survive in their region. However, plants don't stay in their regions of origin any more than gardeners do. Plants native to China, Siberia, or even Mexico thrive alongside each other in many Canadian gardens. Furthermore, mail order allows a gardener in Halifax to easily obtain that native prairie plant he's always wanted, and soon he's passing out cuttings to his neighbours. New plants that no one knows a lot about constantly debut on the retail market, and gardeners always want to experiment. In these cases, gardeners need some way to compare their gardens' climates with the climate where the plant grows well. Canada's zones map plays a critical role here.

Plant Hardiness Zones of Canada

Canada's zones map was compiled for Agriculture Canada in 1967, which seems like a long time without an update. But it's the only one we have, and experts say it still works because it's the only zones map in North America with any Canadian detail. And overall our weather patterns haven't changed significantly — despite fears about global warming, there's still not enough change to warrant a new map. The main factor in delineating the zones is mean minimum winter temperature (because that's what governs whether a tree or shrub will survive in an area), and the next most important is the length of the frost-free period. Rainfall, maximum winter temperature, snow cover and wind strength entered the equation to a lesser degree. Geographical areas that share a common climate and sustain similar plant material, especially woody perennials like shrubs and trees, are considered to be in the same zone. If you look at the Plant Hardiness Zones Map in the colour section of this book, you see that these zones extend horizontally across Canada in sweeping wavy lines like the pattern of oil on water. Canada's zones number from 0 (the coldest) to 9 (the mildest) and each zone is divided into a colder section (a) and a milder one (b). Plant species and cultivars hardy to those zones — and warmer zones — have been identified and the zone number is sometimes noted on the plant tag. Catalogues also list zone hardiness. If you live in Zone 4, generally speaking it makes sense to purchase woody perennials tagged for your zone.

Something to remember: Growers often don't put zone information for herbaceous perennials on plant tags because the factors that affect their hardiness can differ from those of woody perennials. The amount of insulating snow cover, for example, or where it's planted — on a windy hill or beside a warm brick wall. Factors like these are often more important to an herbaceous perennial than how cold the weather gets.

The message is that gardening was never meant to be followed with a set of rules. Be daring: Try plants you like that are hardy within a zone and a half either way of your own zone. As a wise gardener of our acquaintance says: "If you kill something off, so what? Where else could you learn so much for such a modest investment?"

U.S. and Canadian zones: How they compare

Canadian gardeners are easily seduced by the plants appearing in U.S. and British magazines and books, which often list hardiness zones. Odds are the U.S. zone rating is from the U.S. Department of Agriculture (USDA) map, which can differ from ours to the tune of a half zone to two full zones. And no easy formula is available for figuring out the difference because the two systems use different criteria to arrive at their zone boundaries. For example: Toronto is listed as Zone 5b on the USDA map, and Zone 6b on the Canadian map. A ha! you might say, I'll just count down one zone to figure out my hardiness rating according to U.S. standards. Well, not exactly: Calgary, on the other hand, is considered 3b on the USDA map, 3a on the Canadian one. And the USDA map conveys little information for Canadians: Vancouver Island, from the mild coastline to the harsher interior, shows up as a single hardiness zone, something island gardeners know is not true.

You seldom see a British map, but if you do, ignore it. Absolutely no relation exists between British and Canadian zone designations.

Working with microclimates

Gardeners love to fling about references to their "microclimate" as if they have a corner on the market. Well, don't let them fool you — everybody has at least one microclimate in their garden, just as the larger zones have areas of different climates. A microclimate is simply an area that's more protected than others, or more windy and harsh. In your garden you can have beneficial microclimates as well as harsh ones.

- **Frost pockets** collect in low-lying areas when cold, denser air flows down a slope and settles. They also occur on the north side of a solid wall or dense hedge. Thin the hedge to allow circulation of air, or build up the soil in the hollow. Stick to hardy, deep-rooted plants and mulch heavily.

- **Wind tunnels** occur between buildings or lines of trees, and can damage plants severely. Plan carefully when putting in trees or adding structures to your garden. To deal with an existing wind tunnel, put in low, wind-resistant plants, or build an open, slatted fence at one end as a windbreak.

✔ **Heat traps** are areas in sunny, sheltered parts of the garden, and they're ideal sites for heat-loving vegetables and tender flowering plants. To be sure they don't become too dry, amend the soil with lots of compost or moisture retaining peat moss, and use mulches. Create a protected spot for sitting or for more exotic plants you want to grow by creating an enclosure using a fence, wall, or hedge. Remember to leave some open spaces in the wall or fence for wind to flow through, so it doesn't create a downdraft as it blows over the top.

✔ **Air pollution** from passing traffic or city smog can damage plants as well as people. A low wall near the road may help, or plant tolerant trees and shrubs such as aralia, caragana, Russian olive, euonymus, honeysuckle, and alpine currant.

Length Counts: How Long Is Your Season?

You can grow most vegetables and annual flowers anywhere. Some of the largest, most beautiful vegetables we've ever seen were from avid gardeners in the Yukon. If you can grow vegetables where the sun doesn't shine for six months of the year, you know they are easy to grow.

Which zone you live in isn't as critical for vegetables or other annuals as it is for fruits, perennial flowers, trees, and shrubs. The length of your growing season is much more important.

A *growing season* is the average number of days between frosts. Sometimes it's referred to as "frost-free days." Some vegetables are very quick to grow and mature, so they require relatively little time. Others need a long season. Usually, seed packets or garden catalogues show this as the "number of days to harvest," or a similar phrase, and it's meant as a guide. Using Table 2-1, which lists the approximate dates of the last spring frost and the first fall frost for several cities in Canada, you can figure out roughly how many growing days to expect in your region. If you live outside an area listed, call your regional Environment Canada office (the number is listed in the blue pages of the phone book) or visit Environment Canada's Web site at `www.cmc.ec.gc.ca/climate/normals/eprovwmo.htm`.

Of course, we're all smart enough to know it would make no sense for a gardener in Mississauga, Ontario, to grow a semi-tropical vegetable like jicama, which requires 200 frost-free days to mature. It would freeze to death before it ever had a chance to produce. Where these dates do come in handy is in choosing particular varieties of, say, tomatoes, that have a shorter maturing time than others and should result in a more successful harvest. For instance, the beefsteak tomato 'Siberia' starts ripening in 54 days from the time of transplanting to the garden, compared to Tomato Beef King's 75 days. By looking at the "days to harvest" number, you'll quickly realize that there are some vegetables, like tomatoes, peppers and eggplant, that require a head start. That's why we start some vegetable and flowers seeds indoors under lights six to eight weeks before the last spring frost. The early start means sturdy little plants are ready for the garden as soon as the danger of frost passes. Naturally, things are not as simple as they seem: You should use the "days to harvest" number only as a guide, because so many variables affect a plant's growth, such as temperature and rainfall.

You can read a lot more about the needs of specific vegetables and growing seasons in *Vegetable Gardening For Dummies* by Charlie Nardozzi and the Editors of The National Gardening Association (IDG Books Worldwide, Inc.).

Table 2-1	Typical Number of Frost-Free Days		
City or Town	*Last Frost Date*	*First Frost Date*	*Typical Number of Frost-Free Days*
St. John's	June 2	Oct. 12	132
Halifax	May 6	Oct. 20	167
Montreal	May 3	Oct 7	157
Toronto	May 9	Oct 6	150
Winnipeg	May 25	Sept. 22	120
Regina	May 21	Sept. 10	112
Calgary	May 23	Sept 15	115
Yellowknife	May 27	Sept 15	111
Whitehorse	June 11	Aug. 25	75
Vancouver	Mar. 28	Nov. 5	222
Victoria	Mar 1	Dec. 1	275

As a general rule, move seedlings of tomatoes, cucumbers, peppers, eggplant, and melons that you've either purchased or started indoors into their final planting place in the garden in May or June, depending on your region, and sow seed of veggies that like cooler weather, like lettuce, peas, and spinach, right in the garden a month or so before that.

Stretching Your Garden Season

When you live above the 49th parallel, you deal with a shorter growing season than if you live in the more southern regions of Canada. On the other hand, the more north you get the more hours of daylight you have in the summer, and this encourages quick plant growth. Nevertheless, in all parts of Canada you need to squeeze in a few extra weeks of plant growth at the beginning and the end of the season if you want to increase your garden bounty. By using some of the techniques described here, you can enjoy the advantages that gardeners have in one or two zones milder.

Planting earlier in the year

Gardeners are master manipulators and have devised all sorts of ways to get a jump on spring. The first simply is to plant early. Here's how to get away with fooling Mother Nature:

- **Start plants indoors.** Some plants, such as snapdragons or lettuce, prefer cooler weather and even tolerate light frosts. Start them indoors, timed so they're ready for transplanting in the garden three to four weeks before the average last frost date.

  You can also take a chance and put frost-tender plants — such as marigolds, tomatoes, sweet peppers and eggplant — in the garden about two weeks before the expected last frost. But since even a nip of frost means death to them, be prepared. Use protective covers, as described later in this section, to keep them cozy.

- **Use a cold frame.** A *cold frame* speeds seed germination and shelters plants from frost. The frame is a bottomless box, usually constructed from wood. The structure has a slanting, tight-fitting top made of old windows or other transparent or translucent materials such as plastic or fiberglass. A typical frame is approximately 90 x 180 cm (3 feet wide and 6 feet long) with a 45 cm (18-inch-high) back sloping down to 30 cm (12 inches high) in the front. (See Figure 2-1.)

  Place the frame outdoors, over a garden bed or against the south wall of your home. Orient the frame so it slopes to the south. The sun warms the air and soil inside, creating a cozy environment for plants. Sow seeds for transplants directly in the cold frame. Or grow crops such as radishes, spinach, beets, and lettuce to maturity in the frame. We know a Zone 5 gardener who grows heat-loving peppers and eggplant to maturity in a 75 cm (2 ½-foot) high rectangular glass box made of old windows. It's open at the top, and the glass walls buffer breezes and warm the air. "A little pocket of Tropicana," he says.

Prop the top of your cold frame open during the day for ventilation and lower it at night to conserve heat. If you can't check the frame regularly, consider buying a thermostatically controlled vent opener as insurance against cooking or freezing your plants.

If you like the idea of a cold frame but want even greater temperature control, consider a *hot bed*. This device is essentially a cold frame with a heat source (commonly electric heating cable) to warm the soil. The cable usually includes a built-in soil thermostat preset for about 24°C (75°F), ideal for germinating most seeds. You can find cable with a thermostat and plug sold by wattage and length.

When tender plants are ready for the garden, you need to protect them from frost. Here's a rundown of useful frost guards:

- ✔ **Use hot caps.** These devices are individual covers that work like miniature greenhouses. Hot caps can be homemade or store-bought. To make your own, cut the bottom out of a plastic gallon milk jug. Anchor it in the ground with a stake and leave the cap off so the plant doesn't bake inside. Commercially produced hot caps are made of translucent wax paper, plastic, or fibreglass.

- ✔ **Set up a water-filled cloche.** A couple of different kinds are available: one has thin plastic, flexible walls and the other heavier, stiff walls. In both cases, you fill the walls with water. During the day, the water absorbs solar heat. As the water cools down at night, it releases heat slowly, protecting the plant inside from temperatures as low as 9°C (16°F). In some cases the water actually freezes, creating a little igloo inside. Use cloches to protect seedlings from late spring frosts.

- ✔ **Use row covers.** Drape lightweight synthetic fabrics, called *floating row covers,* over the plants. The covers let light and water pass through while protecting plants from temperatures as low as -4.5°C (24°F), depending on the fabric used. The fabrics are available in a variety of widths and lengths. (See Figure 2-2.)

  Row covers of slit plastic are cheaper but usually require more work because they need support from hoops or a frame. You also have to pull the plastic aside to water. Plastic covers create higher daytime temperatures than fabric, which may be advantageous when you're trying to give heat-loving plants like peppers a boost in cool weather.

- ✔ **Recycle junk from your house.** Every so often, an unexpected late spring frost catches you off guard. Usually, the frost prediction comes about the time green, tender, young plants dot the garden. To save plants, rummage around for anything that may protect them without crushing them. Cardboard boxes, old sheets, empty buckets, clay garden pots, paper grocery bags, or even newspaper spread over the plants lend a few degrees of protection. Just remember to remove the stuff the following day or the plants may bake.

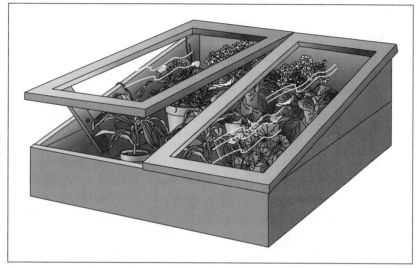

Figure 2-1:
Use a cold frame to protect young plants in early spring.

In addition to providing frost protection, serious cold-climate gardeners often warm the soil in early spring before planting. They spread a soil-warming, plastic-type mulch over the soil surface and cut holes in it for the transplants. After planting, they protect plants with floating row covers.

Clear plastic traditionally has been the mulch of choice for heating the soil, but weeds really thrive under it. Now you can use a new high-tech option called *IRT mulching film*. IRT stands for infra-red transmitting, and it's a plastic film manufactured in Canada by Arbortec Industries in Penticton, B.C. The green film heats up the soil as well as clear plastic, but blocks the portion of the light spectrum that supports weed growth. Black plastic is still the best to use if you want to *solarize* or heat the soil sufficiently to harvest earlier crops and improve yields. The IRT film is most effective in regions that have many consecutive hot, sunny days.

Gardening into autumn

Now that you have a jump on spring, consider these tips on foiling the first frosts of autumn:

- ✔ **Cover up again.** You often can face an occasional light frost before the first big killer. On those crisp, clear evenings when a light frost is forecast, throw a few bedsheets or floating row covers over tender crops. With a little effort, you can prolong the harvest of summer crops.

- ✔ **Spray on frost protection.** What if you forget — or are just too tired — to cover up crops on a chilly evening? Well, you have a second chance to save them. Turn on your garden sprinkler as soon as the temperature

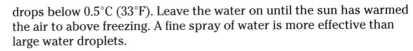

drops below 0.5°C (33°F). Leave the water on until the sun has warmed the air to above freezing. A fine spray of water is more effective than large water droplets.

✔ **Plant again.** Cool-season plants tolerate frost. You can plant a second crop of many flowers and vegetables in mid to late summer for a late autumn show or harvest. These plants grow quickly in the still-warm soil of summer and start maturing about the time tender crops are declining. Kale (both edible and ornamental), beets, chard, pansies, and lettuce are among the stars of the post-frost harvest.

If you want to reap every last tomato in autumn but don't want to hassle with protecting individual plants from frost, you have a couple of other options:

✔ Pick your barely blushing tomatoes as soon as you hear frost is on the way. Arrange them in a single layer on a shelf or table and cover them loosely with newspaper. Check frequently for ripeness and toss any that start to rot. Hard green tomatoes may never ripen, but you might pick them, too — fried green tomatoes are nice.

✔ When frost is predicted, cut or pull your plants and hang them upside down in a warm shed or garage. Drape with plastic. The tomatoes will continue to ripen.

One way to be sure you have strategy for getting ripe tomatoes, eggplants, peppers, and melons before the frost gets them is to grow *short season* or *early* varieties. These plants mature more quickly than their "long season" relatives. An Ichiban Japanese eggplant, for example, takes only 61 days to mature, whereas the Italian heirloom, Rosa Bianca, takes 75 days. In the melon family, Earlisweet cantaloupe is recommended by the Horticulture Science Department of the University of Saskatchewan and several cool-climate gardeners as a good early maturer.

Maximizing Winter Hardiness

You may be better off sticking with plants that are known to be hardy in your area. Then you don't have to fuss with various measures intended to help plants survive a cold winter or those damaging freeze-and-thaw cycles. But gardeners like to experiment, which is known as "pushing the limits" in gardening circles. To do this, you'll probably have to take some special steps to protect the plant against the cold.

Gardeners can, to some degree, help plants adapt to winter. For instance, reduce the amount of nitrogen fertilizer applied after mid-July and stop all fertilization by late summer. Do everything you can to ensure your plants enter the autumn season healthy but not growing too fast.

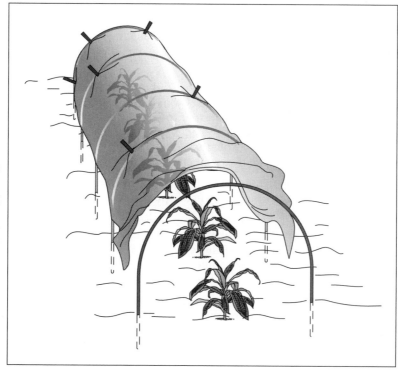

Figure 2-2:
Lay lightweight
row covers
directly over
seedlings or
support them
with wire
hoops. Plastic
row covers
develop more
heat and must
be vented.

Make sure the soil in which evergreens are growing is well-watered in mid to late autumn, before the soil freezes. If evergreens are planted in a dry site, in sandy soil, or under the overhang of a roof, make sure the soil is well-watered in mid-winter when — and if! — the temperature rises above freezing for a day or two.

Here are some other steps you can take to decrease the likelihood of winter injury to plants:

✔ **Plant on the north side.** Choose a location for marginally hardy plants with a northern or eastern exposure rather than south or southwest. Plants facing the south are more exposed to the sun on warm winter days and experience greater daily temperature variation.

✔ **Mulch.** Apply a layer of mulch, 7.5 to 10 cm (3 to 4 inches) deep, after the soil freezes to keep the soil cold rather than protect it from becoming cold. This practice reduces injury from plant roots' *heaving* (coming out of the soil) because of alternate freezing and thawing. Perennials, alpine, rock garden plants, strawberries, and other shallow-rooted plants benefit from this practice. A mulch maintains a more even soil temperature and retains soil moisture. If you live in an area of heavy snowfall, count yourself lucky — a good cover of snow acts as a mulch, especially if it lasts all winter. Whenever there's a heavy fall of snow, shovel some over your beds for extra protection.

Apply bark products, composts, peat moss, pine needles, straw, hay, or any one of a number of readily available materials from the local garden centre. You can prop pine boughs (or remains from Christmas trees) against and over evergreens to help protect against damage by wind and sun.

✔ **Wrap with twine.** Plants such as arborvitae, juniper, and yew often suffer damage from the weight of snow or ice. Prevent plant breakage by fastening heavy twine at the base of the plant and winding it spirally around and upward to the top and back down in a reverse spiral. This technique is more necessary as plants become larger and begin to open at the top. Be sure to remove the twine before the growing season.

✔ **Use a burlap screen.** Stretch a section of burlap around three stakes to protect young or not fully hardy plants from the south, west, and windward exposures.

A burlap wrap with stakes protects plants from the drying winter sun and wind, and drift from deicing salts applied to drives and streets. Wrap most of the plant, but leave some of the top of the plant exposed. Evergreens need light, even in winter. Remove the wrap by the end of March.

✔ **Prevent drying.** Narrow and broadleaf evergreens lose moisture through their leaves in winter. Roots can't absorb moisture from the soil in winter because it may be frozen, therefore the roots cannot replace the moisture the leaves lose. The foliage desiccates, turns brown, and may drop. This can be serious with evergreen azalea, holly, boxwood, and rhododendron. Make sure that evergreens are properly watered throughout the growing season and into the fall. Decrease watering slightly in late summer to encourage hardening off, and then water thoroughly for a few weeks in fall before the soil freezes.

✔ **Prevent animal damage.** Some landscape plants become a food source for rabbits, mice, or voles where there's an extended period of snow cover. When their normal food supply is covered with ice or snow, rodents turn to the bark and young stems of apple, flowering crab apple, mountain ash, hawthorn, euonymus, and viburnum, among other shrubs and trees. If the animals chew the bark completely around the plant and cause it to girdle, the plant may die. The all-important living cells of woody plants are just under the bark. If these cells are damaged or destroyed, the flow of water and nutrients between the plant's roots and leaves is impeded, or stopped completely. Partial girdling creates wounds where borers and disease organisms can enter, and weakens the plant itself.

Protect stems and trunks in late autumn with plastic collars cut in a spiral fashion so they can slip around tree trunks. Spray or paint trunks, stems, and lower limbs with rodent repellents. A number of these materials are available in most garden centers. Repeat the application at least once during a warm period in midwinter. Mixing the repellents with an antitranspirant often results in extended effectiveness of these products. If you use any kind of long-lasting wrap, be sure to remove it come spring.

Chapter 3

Planning Your Landscape

· ·

In This Chapter

▶ Taking inventory of your property

▶ Making your wish list

▶ Drawing up the plan

▶ Controlling costs

· ·

*W*hether your land consists of a new bare-dirt lot, an overgrown jungle of a garden, or any situation in between, your property is the canvas upon which you create your garden masterpiece — your place to relax, entertain, welcome visitors, watch your children play, hold backyard barbecues, and so on. The sum of your work on the grounds surrounding your home — including the hardscape (patios, decks, walks, and so on) and plantings — is your home's *landscape*. A good landscape not only adds value to your home, it can also solve problems such as bad views, noise, and lack of privacy.

We strongly recommend that you start your landscape with a plan. Most gardeners benefit from precisely planning a design on paper, but a loose mental plan may suffice. In any case, the goal is to figure out the best ways to maximize your outdoor space. Base your decisions on what looks good to you, how you plan to use the space, how much maintenance you want to do, and what you can afford. This chapter should give you enough information to assess the strengths and weaknesses of your site, create a plan for a landscape that suits your lifestyle, and accomplish your landscape as inexpensively as possible.

Your landscape is a large investment of your time and money, so you may want to call in a landscape architect or designer to give you advice or to draw up a plan for you. You can even show the professional your own plan and ask for suggestions or confirmation of your good sense. You can also pick up many more tips and tricks on the art and science of landscaping in *Landscaping For Dummies* by Philip Giroux, Bob Beckstrom, and the Editors of The National Gardening Association, published by IDG Books Worldwide, Inc.

Taking Stock of What You Have

The results of your landscaping work depends, to some extent, on what you have to work with, so you should begin your landscape plan by assessing the current condition of your property. This up-front *site analysis* is an integral part of planning a landscape. You should try to take into account issues such as the following:

- ✔ **Your property's strengths and weaknesses.** Does your property have good or poor drainage? Do you have a private area that catches the prevailing breezes in summer? Does your property have good soil, poor soil, or a combination? Do you want to accentuate or hide any views?

- ✔ **Problems that need solutions.** Do you want to cut off the view of nosy neighbours with a privacy hedge? Do you want to create an out-of-the-way area to make a compost pile to recycle your lawn clippings and raked leaves? (See Chapter 14 for more information on composting.) How much time and energy are you willing to put into maintaining your property?

- ✔ **Personal likes and dislikes.** Does your taste run to the calm and serene or to the colourful and wild? Do you want a brick patio with room for dozens of guests? Or would you prefer a vegetable garden with enough tomato plants to feed the neighbourhood all summer and still leave plenty to can or freeze? And, if you have children, where do you want them to play? View plenty of other landscapes to help determine your preferences: Go on garden tours, peek into neighbours' yards, visit arboretums, and look through books and magazines.

Start your site analysis by penciling in a rough drawing of your property on a large piece of paper (at least 8½ by 11 inches or 22 x 28 cm). Be sure to include important existing features of your property such as your house (including windows and doors), sidewalks, driveway, and permanent structures. Remember to add general compass directions to your sketch. The sketch doesn't have to be very precise at this stage.

Place your drawing on a clipboard and walk around your house and yard at different times of the day. Note the following:

- ✔ **Existing plants.** Draw in plants, such as large trees, that you may want to preserve.

- ✔ **Sun and shade.** Note areas that are sunny or shady and at what times of day. This information helps you match plants with appropriate light conditions, and it may also give you ideas about creating a more comfortable living space. Sunlight changes direction and intensity dramatically by seasons. For example, in midsummer, the south and west sides of the house are sunniest and warmest. If you live in a cool summer area, you may want to take advantage of the warmth in those areas, but if you live where summers are hot, these may be places where you want shade trees or arbours.

✔ **Views.** Note the good and bad views you may want to preserve or block. Good views are easy to recognize, but what about the neighbours' views of your yard or your view of theirs? And if you put in a raised deck, what will you see then? Are utility poles visible?

✔ **Prevailing winds.** Mark down strong winds that you may want to buffer or redirect.

✔ **Slope and drainage.** Draw in some arrows that give you a rough idea of the contour of the land. Sloping ground or uneven terrain can add interest to a landscape, especially if accentuated with walls or dry streambeds. But sloping ground also can present erosion or drainage problems that can threaten your house or yard. Record any areas that seem overly wet or where moss or algae grows. Watch where excess rainwater flows. Some plants not only live in wet or soggy soil, they thrive in it; these are the plants you find in bog and water gardens. Drainage problems are sometimes complicated; consider consulting with a landscape architect or engineer who has experience with water drainage problems.

✔ **Soil.** The soil in your yard provides nutrients, moisture, and support for plants. But soil types differ, sometimes even within the same property. Soils come in a huge range of textures and pH levels (the measure of acidity or alkalinity) and contain different amounts of organic matter, nutrients, and moisture. See Chapter 11 to find out more about soil characteristics so you can choose plants that will thrive in your garden.

✔ **Interesting natural features.** If you're lucky enough to have rock outcroppings or a small stream, use them as special landscape features.

✔ **Noise, smells, lights.** Open up all your senses and then write down anything else you notice — lights at night, noise from next door, and even unpleasant odours. You may be able to do something about them.

✔ **Views from indoors.** When you look out windows, what do you see: a nice view of the yard, or the neighbour's back porch? Who can see into your home via the windows from the street or next door? Does sunlight blaze through the windows, heating the house in the afternoon? Or is it pleasant light, cast on the kitchen table as you drink coffee in the morning? Do car lights, street lamps, or signs shine in the windows at night?

To help you organize the different areas of your yard, you can draw *goose eggs*. Drawing a goose egg doesn't mean you draw a complete blank (I just don't know what to do with this yard!); it refers to pencilling in somewhat circular areas you think work well for specific purposes, as shown in Figure 3-1. After you finish the first goose egg, draw several more to consider alternatives and decide which works best.

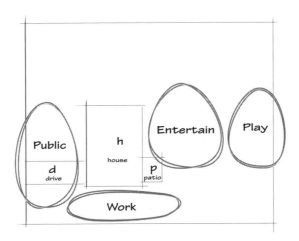

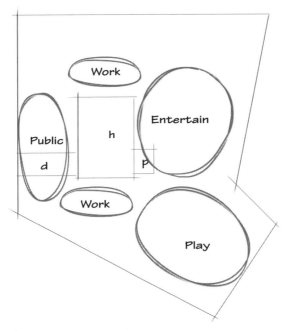

Figure 3-1:
The shape of your property doesn't determine how you use it. In these examples, two differently shaped properties are organized.

Most houses have a front yard, a backyard, and two side yards. To divvy up your list of outdoor wants and needs — eating, playing, sitting, and such — think of which activities you do in which areas.

Don't forget to use your property's natural strengths to your advantage. No doubt you already know the location of the best flat lawn for that pitch-and-catch area. You also know the most discreet place to hide the compost heap and trashcans. You know which neighbour will hate having a view of the dog-run from his bedroom window. You know where the sun beats down on late summer afternoons — perfect for the herb garden — and where the neighbour's oak tree casts a cool pool of shade.

Dreaming Up the Perfect Landscape

To get the most from your property, you need a design that meets the needs of your lifestyle. A good way to start is to develop a wish list of everything you want in the garden of your dreams. (Consider money to be no object; you can always come back to reality later.) Be sure to imagine members of your family enjoying the areas. Take a look at some of the things you can add to your wish list:

- Enough lawn for the kids to play catch
- A flower cutting garden
- A spacious deck or brick patio
- Lighting for night-time entertaining or for accenting special landscape features
- A gazebo, arbour, or pergola
- A lush vegetable garden or fresh herb plot
- A privacy hedge to keep out nosy neighbours
- A tool barn or potting shed
- A place where butterflies, birds, and cute little critters come to visit
- A private retreat with a bench or hammock where you can get away to read *Gardening For Canadians For Dummies*
- A fenced-in dog run
- A swimming pool or spa
- A pond for water gardening or fish
- A compost pile to recycle your lawn clippings and raked leaves
- A rose garden
- A fruit orchard
- A bulb garden where flowers announce the start of a new season
- A scented garden that comes alive with various fragrances
- A barbecue big enough to roast a pig

Who will use your yard?

Design your landscape so that it gets maximum utility and provides plenty of enjoyment. Make sure you think about issues like the following:

- ✔ If you have young children, safety, as well as fun, is a consideration. A swing set in a fenced backyard makes sense. You may also want to think about a storage area for all those toys.
- ✔ Older children can probably make use of the front lawn.
- ✔ Perhaps you can keep the back lawn smaller so you have room for a big vegetable garden.
- ✔ Do you barbecue enough to warrant a built-in grill placed as close to the kitchen door as possible? How about an outdoor sink?
- ✔ What about Fido? Better put in a dog run or who knows what he'll do to the new landscape.

When will you use your yard?

Think about the time of day and the time of year in which you plan to use your yard. Consider the following tips when planning your landscape and when you'll use it most.

- ✔ If you plan to be outdoors after work in the late afternoon, where will you be most comfortable at that time of day? Maybe that shady spot under the big oak tree out back. . . . On the other hand, if summer sunshine heats up the patio area, maybe you need an overhead structure for shade, or a few shade trees.
- ✔ If you like to use the garden at night, good outdoor lighting is a must.
- ✔ If you like to be outside during the rainy season, a covered patio would be nice.
- ✔ If bugs like the garden at the same time as you do, a screened-in patio cover can keep them at bay.

What's your neighbourhood like?

Most neighbourhoods have a certain character created by similar landscapes and homes. Large lawns and deciduous shade trees tie together many Maritime, southern Quebec and Ontario neighbourhoods. Graceful elms — where they remain disease free — unite neighbourhoods on the Prairies. In southwestern British Columbia, neighbourhoods with lush lawns and beautiful hedges are often nestled against wooded slopes with magnificent mountain views.

When you dream up your new landscape, remember to keep any regional or neighbourhood character in mind. Try not to be so different in your landscaping that you disrupt the overall continuity of the community, particularly in the front yards, which often tend to blend together. (You can probably go wild in the backyard.) This advice is practical, not a plea for conformity, because a new landscape that resembles what already exists in your neighbourhood looks best. On the other hand, if you have a vision and you're sure it's the look you want, deviating from the local style is perfectly okay (codes and covenants notwithstanding).

Then there's that thing called "resale value." Lots of people find themselves landscaping simply to enhance the street appearance of their home for potential buyers. If you're landscaping for resale, play it safe. Take cues from neighbouring yards.

Matching your garden to the historical or cultural heritage of your neighbourhood, house, or hometown is an easy jumping-off place. Consider an old-fashioned Grandma's garden for a charming small-town cottage, a naturalistic wildflower garden for a Prairies heritage home, or a lush English perennial border for a Tudor showplace.

How much maintenance are you ready for?

Landscape maintenance is an ongoing event that can guarantee success or failure. You can design low maintenance into a landscape, as follows:

- Create a yard with lots of hardscape and very little planting.

- Avoid overplanting or using fast-growing plants that get too large for their space. Such plants require heavier pruning or transplanting later.

- Use low-maintenance perennials or flowering shrubs instead of annuals. Annuals add brilliant colour, but you'll need to replant every year.

- Plant ground covers instead of a lawn if you're unwilling to mow your grass weekly. (But keep in mind that getting the ground cover thick enough to choke out weeds takes effort, too.)

- Use low-maintenance masonry rather than wooden landscape elements. If you plan to build wooden landscape elements like decks and fences, you'll have to paint or apply preservatives every two to three years. Consider using pressure-treated lumber for ground-contact situations or vinyl or plastic wood lookalikes for fences and decking.

- Set up an automated irrigation system (as explained in Chapter 14), which can water even when you're out of town. If you don't have an automated system, then you must water everything by hand or move sprinklers around your property.

What Goes Where: Designing the Plan

After adding the elements from the wish list to your sketch, you may want to create a more accurate and specific site analysis, drawn exactly to scale. (Check out this section's sidebar, "Making a scale drawing of your property.") You can get exact dimensions of your property from the lot plan or building plan developed when your house was built. If you can't find a plan, ask at your municipality's building or zoning department.

The lot plan shows the shape and size of your property as well as the location of your house. The plan saves you from having to fight your way through perimeter thickets to measure yard dimensions. Make a dozen photocopies of your original lot plan so you can try out different schemes and record your ideas.

Figure 3-2 shows a sample of what your site analysis might look like after you transfer the details of your inventory to the lot plan.

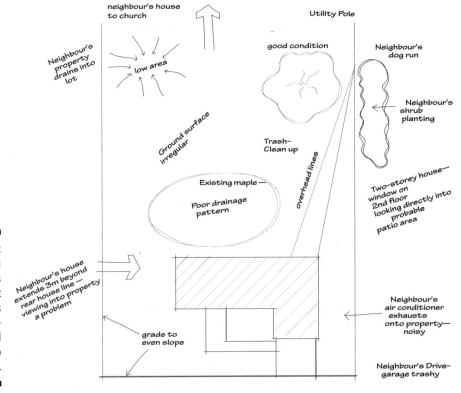

Figure 3-2:
A completed site analysis that includes topical features and problems to solve.

Using your space effectively

Make sure that you think of the whole outdoor property as living space. Overcoming the traditional approach — backyards are where we actually live, front yards are for show, and side yards are mostly ignored — can be difficult. Why not make your entire landscape your living area? The following are some off-the-beaten-path ideas that allow you to make good use of your front and side yards:

✔ **Front yard.** If you shield the front yard with walls of greenery or a privacy fence, then you can do what you like inside those walls. If that's a bit bold for you, consider at least moving some of your ornamental garden beds to the front instead of having only the boring, old-fashioned, look-good lawn. If you're inspired to plant a prairie or a naturalistic woodland out front, talk to the neighbours first so they know what you're doing, and keep paths well groomed so the landscape looks guided instead of frighteningly wild.

Many community home-owners' associations have restrictive covenants that very much narrow your landscaping options. Be sure to check before embarking on any do-it-yourself makeovers.

✔ **Backyard.** You don't always need to relegate your vegetable patch to the backyard. You can put your vegetable plants wherever the light, soil, and convenience are best. A well-tended patch, planted in an interesting design of diagonals or squares that intersperses veggies with flowers and herbs, has a lot of curbside appeal.

✔ **Side yard.** Side yards are often narrow, sometimes shady, and they're usually seen as nothing more than a passage from the front yard to the back. Give yourself reason to linger in your side yard by mounting a hammock or adding a bench. If your side yard is sunny, it can be the perfect place for a strawberry patch or a row of raspberries. Or add a surprise to be discovered — such as a whimsical garden ornament.

Defining areas and ways to move through them

Try to imagine decorating your living room if it had no walls. You'd have a hard time putting your furniture in the right place. Outdoor living rooms work the same way, except now you need to figure out where to put the flower bed instead of the sofa bed.

Structures and plantings can define the boundaries of your landscape, creating "walls" to set off different areas of your garden. For example, surround your herb garden with a hedge of lavender and install a gate at the entryway. Add a lattice screen to your deck or patio and grow flowering vines on it if you need a bit of privacy. See Chapters 8 and 10 for more suggestions on shrubs, trees, and vines to use for privacy.

Making a scale drawing of your property

If you don't have a lot plan, consider these tips for drawing your property to scale.

✔ **Start by using graph paper.**

The easiest kind of graph paper has five squares per inch of paper space, which allows you to easily record the garden in units of 5 and 10 — that is, 2.5 cm (1 inch) can equal 1.5 or 3 m (5 or 10 feet). Some kinds of graph paper come with four squares per inch, which requires more mathematical manipulating. In that case, 2.5 cm (1 inch) can equal 1.2 or 2.4 m (4 or 8 feet). Graph paper also comes in a variety of sizes. The standard 22 x 28 cm (8½ x 11-inch) paper may not be large enough to accommodate an entire landscape. You can find oversized graph paper, as large as 43 x 55 cm (17 x 22 inches), at better office or art supply stores.

✔ **Find a proportional scale that's suitable for your drawing and landscape complexity.**

If you want a simple landscape planted with trees and shrubs, you can make 2.5 cm (1 inch) of plan space represent 2.5 or 3 m (8 or 10 feet) of landscape space. But, if you want complicated flower, herb, and vegetable gardens, you can include more detail on your plot plan by making 2.5 cm (1 inch) represent 1.2 or 1.5 m (4 or 5 feet) — even less if necessary.

✔ **Always use a measuring tape to calculate distances.**

Eyeballing or estimating is not precise enough. At the minimum, you need a 15 m (50-foot-long) measuring tape.

✔ **Start your measuring in the front yard, recording the length and the width. Then measure the side yards and the backyard.**

The front yard ends at an invisible line that cuts across the width of your property and runs along the front of your house. Draw the front yard perimeters on the plan. For example, if you measure the front yard as 15 m (50 feet) long and wide and you use a scale of 1.5 m (5 feet) equals 2.5 cm (1 inch), then your front yard will be a 25 cm (10-inch square) on your plan. Do the same for the side yards and backyard.

After you establish the perimeters of your garden, turn your attention to the pathways. Make the walkways simple and practical. Your kids and your dog will want to get to the sandbox or the front door in a beeline. You'll also want an easy-access, straight-arrow path for getting to your car in the morning or for lugging in groceries after work. Plan a wide, flat, solid path to trundle wheelbarrows full of compost, manure, grass clippings, and other goodies.

Exercise your artistic side by planning pleasure routes through the rest of your landscape. Guests at your patio party can enjoy wandering along paths that go through flower beds and greenery. When you start playing with paths, you'll find they're a great design trick for making your garden seem bigger. Obscured by shrubs, ornamental grasses, or other tall plants, paths can double back, twist and turn, and proceed for much longer than you'd think in a limited space.

The width of paths affects the speed people walk them. Wide paths are not only practical for two people to stroll along side-by-side, the width encourages lingering. Narrow paths make our feet speed up.

Paths don't have to be made of paving materials. A swath of lawn that wends through garden beds is as much a path as that beautiful brick herringbone you lay through the herb garden.

If you plan to include fenced areas in your landscape, make sure they don't block access to other parts of the yard. Include gates where they make sense, or leave sections open for easier access.

The hardscape

Patios, decks, walkways, fences, trellises, gazebos and other "hardscape" elements of your landscape are just as important as the plants. Make your hardscape elements as attractive as your planting beds. Remember that you'll be looking at these structures unadorned in the off-season, when leaves are down and plants are dormant. Soften the hardscapes in all seasons by planting woody shrubs, vines, ornamental grasses, and trees nearby.

Shopping for hardscape materials is not for the budget-squeamish. Luckily, you can use some tricks to come up with a beautiful hardscape without breaking the bank. Scavenging materials is one of the finest arts in the home landscaping spectrum. Keep your eye out for demolition sites, dumps, and other likely bonanzas. (But don't assume that construction debris is headed for the dump. You run into lots of us recyclers these days. Remember to always ask permission before loading your pickup truck.) Most contractors are happy to give you their refuse so that they don't have to pay to put it in a landfill.

Frugal substitutes are fun to come up with and can give you even more satisfaction when you gaze upon your finished work. Jog your ingenuity with these starters:

- Instead of making a stone wall out of expensive fieldstone, stack chunks of old concrete sidewalk.
- Can't afford an all-brick walkway? Use a strip of brick (one or two bricks wide) along the sides and fill the centre with inexpensive concrete or pavers. Edge with landscape timbers for a finished look.
- Dress up plain grey concrete with dyes. Or use the small stones called *aggregate* in the mix so that the finished surface has a pleasant pebbly look.
- Customize your patio by making your own art pavers for corners and accents. Make handprints, press in and peel off leaves to make impressions, or stud with bits of coloured glass for a one-of-a-kind look.

✔ Visit architectural salvage dealers for real buys on fencing, arbours, iron-work, and neat decorative touches.

✔ Brick from buildings will deteriorate in the garden, but unless you're laying miles of paths, it can be a fine and frugal choice until you can afford the heavy-duty, high-fired exterior grade you want.

The plants

Plants come in a rainbow of sizes, shapes, and colours. (For information about how to use specific plants, see Chapters 4 through 10.) Some characteristics point out architectural highlights. Others are as handsome as sculptures. Some harmonize; others contrast. Consider the varying design characteristics of plants before you finish your design.

GARDENING TIP

Designing with repetition and unity

Unity refers to the overall feeling that a landscape creates a whole greater than the sum of its parts. In a unified landscape, the eyes and feet of visitors flow from one part to another. Clearly defined pathways are a first step toward unifying your landscape.

Repetition refers to a theme or element that crops up in different parts of your landscape. Repetition and unity go hand-in-hand — repeating elements often helps create a feeling of unity in your landscape.

Repetition of hardscape materials — including brick, wood, stone, concrete, wood chips, and fencing — is a simple way to give your garden a unified look, even if the areas are distinctly different. Man-made materials carry great weight in the landscape because they draw our human eyes like a magnet. If your hardscape materials match the style of your garden, you can quickly unify the various elements of your landscape. For example, you can use a single section of diagonal, framed lattice to support a climbing rose along the wall of your house. Attach a few sections to form an L-shape to shield the compost pile from view; or add three or four linked sections to serve as a privacy screen along the patio.

Repeating shapes helps pull elements together, too: curved outlines of beds, undulating paths, and mounds of plants; or yardstick-straight bed edges, spiky plant forms, clipped hedges, and vertical-board fences.

Repetition of plants themselves is another way to achieve unity. Sticking the same plants here and there is an easy trick. Simply repeat backbone plants that perform well most of the year — such as hostas, evergreens, ground covers, and shrubs — to tie your garden areas to each other.

Repeating colours also helps to unify your landscape. Plant clumps of yellow flowers in various beds, pots, or plantings across your backyard and you'll find that your eye travels from one patch of yellow to the next in a satisfying way. You can combine colours of plants with colours of the house or hardscape, too, for unity's sake.

✔ **Size.** The tallest trees can frame or shade your house or sitting area. Medium-tall plants, such as tall shrubs and small ornamental trees, can provide height in a small yard or function as screens. Medium-sized shrubs can help blend the house into the landscape. If you're planting shrubs around the foundation, stick with plants that are naturally dwarf, not growing much over 90 cm (3 feet) tall, so they don't overwhelm the site, block windows, or require regular pruning. Smaller plants — flowers, vegetables, low shrubs — can fill in openings between larger plants.

✔ **Form and shape.** Plants come in a variety of shapes that you can blend and balance for maximum beauty. A conservative way to start your landscape is to use a majority of rounded shapes, accented occasionally by other forms such as the following:

   • *Horizontally spreading plants,* such as junipers and native dogwoods, blend strongly vertical architecture — including the corners of your house — into the landscape.

   • *Upright or spiky plants,* such as columnar arborvitae, stand out like exclamation points. Avoid the cliché of using these on either side of your entry; choose low-growing plants instead.

   • *Low and spreading plants* such as creeping junipers and ivies cover the ground like a carpet, filling space with greenery to help tie the landscape together.

✔ **Texture.** Some plants, such as oak leaf hydrangea and sheared yew, have a bold, eye-attracting texture because of large leaves, dense branching, or a dark appearance. These plants are strong and can stand on their own or visually anchor a garden bed. But too many bold plants can look sombre or overwhelming.

Other plants, such as shasta daisies and spireas, have medium texture with moderate-sized leaves, average shapes, and a moderately loose growth habit. These plants look comfortable in the garden but, without other textures, can become boring.

Fine-textured plants, such as astilbe and flax, have small or finely cut leaves or open, fine-stemmed shapes that allow light to shine through. These plants can be intricate and invite a closer look but can also appear insubstantial and, in large quantities, chaotic.

✔ **Colour.** Plants provide colour with their foliage, flowers, berries or cones, or even stems, as in the case of red-osier dogwood. Choose a colour scheme that emphasizes one colour in addition to green. Make sure the colour looks good with your yard's hardscape — for example, maroon flowers are attractive near a red brick walk. And drop in small amounts of different colours as accents. You may have a small garden of blue or purple flowers with highlights of yellow. Hot colours, such as yellow, orange, and red, are strong and work well in a large garden or a faraway bed. Cool colours, such as blue and purple, recede and are best used in a small garden. They can make the property line seem farther away than it is.

✔ **Order.** Your garden needs dominant features with similar characteristics — plants of like shapes, sizes, textures, or colours — to create a sense of order. One way to achieve order is to mass identical varieties into natural-looking groups. But you also need some variety or accent, which you achieve by adding plants with different characteristics.

Creating a Final Plan

Think of your final plan as a tool to help determine the price tag of this project, to establish your priorities, and to ensure that all those separate parts of your landscape — the barbecue pit, the meditation pool, the children's area — are present and accounted for.

You can use copies of the lot plan to start your landscape design, sketching in existing landscape features that you intend to keep, using your site analysis as a reference point. If you can't find your lot plan, you need to measure your entire yard. Either way, make your plan to scale so that it gives a precise representation of your yard. See the sidebar in this chapter, "Making a scale drawing of your property," for tips on drawing to scale.

On paper, you can eliminate the existing features you no longer want — you'll create a blank slate on which to draw new features. You can adapt, change, and reorganize with a flick of an eraser. To help you visualize your new yard, make tracing paper overlays to show different scenarios for your landscape, moving the patio behind the garage or close to the kitchen door, for example. Set overlays on top of the original lot plan and secure them with masking tape so they're easy to move and change. Other overlays can show the colour of the garden as it changes by season or the size of trees and shrubs as they grow.

Follow these steps to create a final plan (assuming you have a lot plan).

1. **Take the graph paper and measuring tape out into the yard with you.**

   Note on the paper which directions are north and south and the scale you're using.

2. **Plot each landscape feature that you intend to keep.**

   Find its depth in the length of the yard by measuring from either the house or the street. Make a pencil mark to show its location. Then measure its distance from the side of the property. Move the pencil mark to indicate the correct spacing from the side property line.

   If the landscape feature is a tree, measure the limb spread of the tree and indicate it with a circle around the mark. If the tree is young, you may want to use a dotted line to show the ultimate shady, mature spread.

If you plan to eliminate existing features, don't bother to sketch them in. Not including them saves you time and trouble as you plan new developments for your yard.

3. **After you pencil in the entire yard, check the accuracy of the drawing.**

When you eyeball the plan and look at the yard, does it appear that everything is in the right place? Pull out your measuring tape and check several sample distances. Redraw as necessary.

4. **Add new features and plants.**

Draw in the plants and areas for all those special activities you will enjoy eventually. Add any paths you have planned, drawing lines to indicate their shape and width. Draw in fences, arbours, hedges, a patio or deck, and other elements you've chosen. After you have all the parts of the design in place, feel free to ink over your pencil lines with different coloured markers; you can see at a glance which lines are paths, which are fences, and so on.

Using your computer

A number of landscaping software programs are now available that can help you design your dream landscape. After you have your scale plan, input it in your computer and develop your design electronically.

Using landscaping software

- ✔ Saves you the time and trouble of drawing all changes and updates by hand.

- ✔ Lets you explore the way a landscape may look when viewed from different angles, at different times of the year, or at any time in the future.

- ✔ Helps your decision-making. The software may include a detailed plant encyclopedia. You may be able to indicate your landscape needs and have the program select suitable plants.

One example of landscaping software is *Complete LandDesigner 5.0* (Windows 95/ 98. Sorry, not for Mac) from Sierra Online. Phone 800-757-7707 or try www.sierra.com on the Internet. You can also write to Havas Interactive, Box 62900, El Dorado Jills, CA, 95762. This full-featured program includes 3D Landscape 2.0, Garden Encyclopedia 3.0, Photo LandDesigner 4.5 and 3D Deck.The package costs about $50 US, plus $5 shipping and handling. Keep in mind that these programs use the USDA plant hardiness zone numbers. Canadian zone numbers are not the same. See Chapter 2, devoted to Canada's zone system.

Field testing

If you want more of a real-life picture of what your landscaping will look like, go outside and play make-believe:

- Outline paths with a water hose or rope, or sprinkle a path of flour or ground limestone so you can see the direction paths take.
- Put lawn chairs where you want to add shrubs or young trees.
- Pound tomato stakes into the ground to show the future homes of roses or large perennials in your flower beds.
- Rake leaves or straw into the outlines of your new beds.
- Use a step ladder as a good fool-your-eye representation of an arbour.

Part II
Colour Your World

The 5th Wave   By Rich Tennant

In this part . . .

Of all the wonderful benefits that flowers bring to a garden, their vibrant and beautiful colours mean the most to us. We get excited just thinking about mixing and matching flowers of different colours to create striking effects, but actually seeing them is the real payoff.

Think of your garden as your canvas, and the colours of the various annuals, perennials, flowering bulbs, and roses as your palette. Now stretch out with your imagination: Can you see that little clump of yellow over there? Can you see those purple bunches here and there? How about splashes of red in the corners and there in the middle?

In this part, we tell you about our favourite annuals, perennials, flowering bulbs, and roses. Enjoy the colours!

Chapter 4

Annuals

• •

In This Chapter

▶ Understanding annuals and their needs

▶ Buying annual plants

▶ Using annuals' colour, shape, and fragrance in your garden

▶ Taking care of your annuals

▶ Looking at favourite annuals

• •

Annuals are the workhorses of the flower garden. If you want colour, if you want your garden to be bright and showy, and if you want your garden to look good right from the start, annuals are the answer.

What's an Annual?

Annuals are the shooting stars of the garden universe. They burn brightly indeed, but briefly.

To be technical for a moment, an *annual* is a plant that undergoes its entire life cycle within one growing season. You plant a marigold seed in May, the seedling sprouts quickly, it starts blooming in July, frost kills it anywhere from early September to late October, depending where you live, seeds scatter and (we hope) sprout the next spring to start the process again. Figure 4-1 shows the life cycle of an annual.

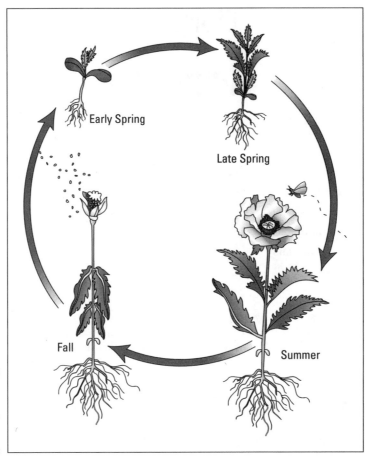

Figure 4-1:
The short,
happy life of
an annual.

Early Spring

Late Spring

Summer

Fall

In some instances, however, our definition of annual gets a bit dicey. Annuals and *perennials* (which we formally introduce in Chapter 5) have a way of overlapping — in definition, as well as in the garden. Some perennials act like annuals when you grow them in cold climates. Geraniums, for instance, may not survive the month of May in Saskatoon or another climate with late frosts, but will live for years in Southern California. You find perennials that act like annuals listed as annuals in this book.

Because annuals grow so easily and quickly — and are so popular — you can find an overwhelming number of varieties. Plant breeders have been busy with annuals for more than a hundred years, and look what they've done: A plant that in nature had yellow flowers with four petals may now produce a bloom with 16 white petals.

Many of the breeding efforts have gone into producing smaller, more compact plants (dwarfs). You can also find annuals developed to trail from hanging baskets (trailers). You can also find an amazing array of flower types, as described here:

- A *single* flower, the type most often found in nature, has a single layer of petals.
- A *double* flower has additional layers of petals.
- A *fully double* flower has many layers of petals.
- A *bicolour* flower has two prominent colours in its petals.
- A *star* flower has a colour pattern in the petals that is remarkably star-shaped.
- A *picotee* flower has petal tips in a colour different than the rest of the petal.

Getting Cozy with Annuals

Absorb a few facts about your area's climate and seasons, plus some of your own garden's idiosyncrasies, and you can make much wiser selections at planting time. Most important are some key dates, like when the danger of frost is past in spring and when frost is likely in fall. Such know-how is easy to get from your local nursery, Ministry of Agriculture and Food, or from the chapter about climates in this book, Chapter 2.

Some annuals are cool and some like it hot

Depending on their origin and what's been bred into them, annuals prefer one of two growing conditions.

- *Cool-season annuals* perform best in mild temperatures (about 70°F, or 21°C), cool soil, and when days are short. In most parts of Canada, these conditions are typical in early spring and early fall. These annuals also do well when temperatures are similarly mild all summer in mountain regions or along the coast and in areas to the far north.

   Cool-season annuals can withstand some frost. Some types are quite hardy and in some areas are actually perennials. Hot weather and long days cause cool-season annuals to set seeds, thus ending the bloom season. Examples of cool-season favourites are calendula, pansy, and snapdragon. Usually, you can safely plant cool-season annuals a few weeks before the average date of the last spring frost in your area.

✔ **Warm-season annuals** thrive in hot summer weather. Most of these annuals are tender — freezing temperatures can damage or even destroy them. Warm-season annuals include celosia, impatiens, marigold, vinca rosea, and zinnia. Plant warm-season annuals after the date of your last frost, when soil and air temperatures are warming up. These plants peak in midsummer.

Sun and shade

Most annuals are sun worshippers. After all, to grow and live as quickly as they do, their leaves need to collect all the energy they can, especially early in the season. This is particularly true in northern Canada, where the growing season is short. Fortunately, long hours of sunlight offset the disadvantage of late-spring frosts. For example, in Yellowknife — when the sun shines for twenty-one hours in June — annuals take off quickly, blooming abundantly in July and August. To find out how much sun your garden gets, watch how the sunlight falls on it and then use that information to decide which annuals to plant and where to plant them.

Most annuals need at least five to seven hours of direct sunlight during the middle of a summer day. If a spot in the garden gets its five to seven hours during the morning or late afternoon when the sun is not as intense, most annuals aren't going to prosper. On the other hand, if you live where the midday sun is particularly intense, even sun-loving annuals will benefit from some shade during that time. But for most of us, the best idea is to plant shade-lovers such as impatiens or begonias in those areas.

Watch the pattern of sun and shade in your garden. The patterns change with time and the seasons, as the sun moves higher and lower in the sky, as trees grow taller and develop and lose leaves, and as neighbours build or tear down buildings.

How to Buy Annuals

You have three choices when it comes to planting annuals.

✔ Sow seeds directly where the plants are to grow and bloom.

✔ Start seeds indoors in late winter and transplant seedlings to the garden later.

✔ Start with transplants of varying sizes (from small plants in four- or six-packs). Most often, buying transplants from local nurseries is the easiest approach. You can also buy transplants of annuals by mail and, in doing so, enjoy more choice.

Starting annuals from seeds offers a couple of big advantages:

✔ You save money if you're doing a lot of planting.

✔ You get a much bigger choice than with seedlings sold at the nursery.

A nice thing about buying transplants at the nursery is that many annuals can give your garden instant colour because they are already in bloom. Nursery transplants come in a wide assortment of package sizes, from four-packs to gallon size, as shown in Figure 4-2.

We describe techniques for each planting method — seeds in Chapter 11, and seedlings in Chapter 12 — so transplant yourself to those chapters for the scoop.

Many plants that bloom easily from seed, reseed themselves, and come back year after year on their own. Most annual wildflowers reproduce this way. Toward the end of the season, let annuals such as alyssum, calendula, cosmos, forget-me-nots, marigolds, pansies and violas, sunflowers, vinca, and zinnias go to seed for a garden full of *volunteers* next season. Such volunteers won't necessarily be exactly the same as last year, especially if they are seeds of hybrid varieties. For instance, the colours of the volunteers may fade or revert to the common colour. But unless you're a really expert gardener who wants a particular variety, these mongrel volunteers are just as good.

What You Can Do with Annuals

Inexpensive, fast-growing, and long-blooming annuals are perfect plants to have fun and experiment with. Try out wild colour combinations, carpet an entire bed, or fill pots to overflowing. Make a hideous mistake (perhaps red and lavender together makes your dog howl) and you may even have time to replant during the same growing season.

Annuals are versatile and just about foolproof. You don't need to be born with a silver trowel in your hand to achieve some beautiful effects in your yard:

✔ Plant entire beds and borders in swaths of colour.

✔ Create a combination of annuals for your pots and window boxes that blooms all summer long.

✔ Mix annuals into borders of trees, shrubs, and ground covers to add seasonal colour, fragrance, and texture.

Pulp pot

Gallon can

Inch pot

Six-pack

Figure 4-2:
Annuals
come in a
variety of
nursery
containers.

Playing with colour

Try different combinations of colour to find what you most enjoy in your garden. Experiment with mixing colours, and trust your own eye. One gardener's favourite combination, such as purple petunias with scarlet geraniums, may be another gardener's worst colour-clash nightmare.

Also remember that a great many plants now come with multicoloured-leaves (known as *variegated* in the trade), which creates a tapestry of colour and pattern even when the plant is not in bloom. Yellow-foliaged plants, or those with leaves splotched in cream or white, can brighten a dark corner as effectively as white flowers. Such foliage gives the effect of dappled sunshine on leaves. Coleus are the classic foliage plants, with leaves mottled in every colour from near black, to lime green, white, and bright fuchsia pink.

An easy way to deal with colour is to think of all colours as falling within the ranges of *hot* or *cool*. Hot colours, such as yellow, orange, bright purple, and red are lively and cheerful. Most cool colours, such as pink, blue, lavender, and cream, blend well together, creating a feeling of harmony and serenity.

Using shape, height, and structure

A plant's form is every bit as important as its colour and too often overlooked.

Need an almost instant privacy screen from neighbours? Annuals offer the perfect remedy. Annuals can add height to a garden, with towering sunflowers creating screening, or providing colour at the back of the border. As you hike in the woods, notice how nature layers plant heights: tall trees, small or *understorey* trees, large shrubs, ferns, and then ground cover plants that carpet the forest floor. Such complexity pleases the eye; you can blend annuals with other plantings to create this same effect in your garden beds. Use different heights, from a tall sunflower or ornamental corn to diminutive sweet alyssum.

No rule exists about planting the shortest flowers in front, with the taller in back. Tall, airy annuals, such as *Verbena bonariensis,* with its skinny branches topped with tiny purple flowers, work as *scrim* plants. The garden is meant to be viewed through airy scrim plants planted in the foreground, adding a new focus or perspective to the other plantings.

Texture adds another element to the garden. The droopy, chenille-like softness of love-lies-bleeding *(Amaranthus)* adds a striking note to a planting scheme, while the feathery foliage of love-in-a-mist *(Nigella)* can knit together varied plantings in the front of a border. Frilly China asters or the soft seed heads of annual grasses add fluff and interest. The spiky spires of foxglove or the candelabra-like heads of woodland tobacco *(Nicotiana sylvestris)* accent the more rounded forms of lower growing annuals, perennials, and shrubs.

Designing for fragrance

Of all the senses, smell most strongly evokes memory. The strong perfume of sweet peas, or the spicy smell of nasturtiums can bring back an acute longing for a favourite garden from the past.

The flower fragrances you prefer are as personal as the perfume or after-shave lotion you choose to wear. Plant generously so that you have plenty of flowers and leaves to pick for bouquets and bowls of potpourri. Even a few sprays of the unassuming common mignonette *(Reseda odorata)* can scent a room or front porch. As a rule, choose the more old-fashioned varieties of flowers, which usually tend to be more fragrant than modern hybrids; you may need to order seed packets to find the older, most strongly scented varieties.

The best way to find such old-fashioned, heirloom varieties is to study the catalogues of seed companies that make a specialty of them. Check Appendix B in this book and read the descriptions of the seed companies until you find the ones that include heirloom flowers.

Remember to add a few fragrant blooms to every pot, window box, or hanging basket. Concentrate sweet-smelling flowers near walkways, entries, patios, and decks so that you and your guests can enjoy them often. Some plants don't waste their scent on the daylight hours; they reserve their allure for night-flying moths and their pollinating ways. Many of these plants have white blooms. White alyssum is particularly sweet in the evenings, and even white petunias have a distinct perfume after the sun goes down. Flowering tobacco *(Nicotiana)* and the moonflower vine are also ideal additions to beds or pots near bedroom windows or on patios you use in the evening.

Here are some favourite easy-care annuals that add fragrance to the garden:

- **Heliotrope.** Dark, crinkly leaves show off vanilla-scented purple or dusky-white flowers.

- **Mignonette.** This little plant is easy to grow from seed and has an amazingly strong, sweet fragrance.

- **Nicotiana, or flowering tobacco.** The white flowers have a nearly tropical scent that is particularly strong in the evening.

- **Night-scented stock.** The flowers don't make much of a show, but this old-fashioned, early blooming favourite has a wonderful scent of cloves.

- **Scented-leafed geraniums.** Fuzzy, splotched, and streaked leaves come in a wide variety of scents, from chocolate, to cinnamon, lemon, and mint.

- **Sweet alyssum.** Masses of tiny scented flowers make this a favourite edging plant.

- **Sweet peas.** A childhood favourite for many people, the older varieties of sweet peas retain the sweetest of scents all day long.

- **Sweet William.** Gardeners have grown this plant since Elizabethan times for its spicy, sweet fragrance.

Getting annuals together

For the brightest blast of colour, plant annuals en masse. Low-growing types usually work best for this type of planting, and you can go with just one colour or mix a number of colours. The important consideration is to plant many annuals and plant them close (usually 15 to 20 cm, or 6 to 8 inches, apart). Buy four- or six-packs and space the transplants evenly in staggered rows. (See Figure 4-3.) The plants grow quickly and fill in the spaces to give you a solid bed of bright colour.

Figure 4-3: Plant annuals in staggered rows, evenly spaced, for a bed of colour.

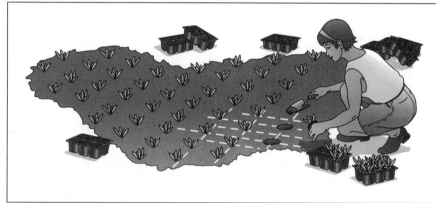

If you prefer a less-regimented look, try mixing many different types of annuals together in one bed. In general, keep the lower-growing plants in front and the taller ones in back, but no hard rules about plant placement exist. Keep to a particular colour scheme, such as mixing only complementary colours, or you can go with whatever colour scheme you like.

Low-growing annuals, such as Swan River daisy, *Brachychome iberdifolia*, and lobelia, are very useful as edgings. You can plant these low-growers along walkways or in front of other annuals, in front of perennials, or even in front of flowering shrubs, such as roses.

Containing annuals

Flowering annuals are especially at home in containers, making it easy for you to insert a touch of colour into visible, highly used areas. Match the plant's habits with the pot. Spreading annuals, such as alyssum, cascade over the sides of containers and look really nice in hanging baskets or window boxes.

Lower-growing, compact varieties usually are most suitable for container growing, but you can use taller types as well. By planting many pots with many different annuals, you always have some at peak bloom to put in your most visible spots, such as porches or patios. For details on growing plants in containers, see Chapter 19.

Taking Care of Your Annuals

Maintenance, especially proper watering, greatly affects how annuals behave. Unlike many plants, annuals aren't forgiving if they don't get the water they want when they want it. Fast, consistent growth is critical with annuals. If plant growth stalls, you may lose a good part of, if not all of, the blooming season.

Watering requirements vary with the weather, seasons, and garden conditions. (You knew we were going to say that!) Take a look at these ways to tell when your annuals need water:

- **Study your plants.** When an annual starts to dry out, the leaves look droopy, start to wilt, and may lose their bright green colour.

- **Dig in the ground.** Annuals grow so fast they don't have time to reach down deep in the soil. Most need water when the top 5 to 7.5 cm (2 or 3 inches) of soil dries out. Dig around with a small trowel or shovel to check how moist the soil is.

Fertilizer is also critical for first-rate blooming. For best flowering, you want to keep plants growing vigorously, never stalling. Here's a simple fertilizer program that works for most annuals in most gardens:

- When you are preparing the planting bed, spread a complete, granular fertilizer evenly over the bed at the rates recommended on the package. Use a fertilizer with a ratio of 10-10-10 or 5-10-10. Work the fertilizer into the soil along with a 5 to 7.5 cm (2- or 3-inch) layer of organic matter.

- Every four to six weeks during the growing season, fertilize again with a similar ratio of fertilizer but in liquid form.

The other essential step is deadheading: Cut or break off flowers as they fade. Doing so encourages the plants to produce even more blooms because the plant doesn't expend energy producing seeds.

Our Favourite Annuals

Everyone has his or her favourite flowers, and this section lists some of ours. We've left out some of the more well-know annuals, like geraniums, petunias, and impatiens, but the following choices are every bit as dependable and colourful. We divide the list into cool-season and warm-season types.

Cool-season annuals

Our favourite annuals able to withstand mild frosts in late spring and early fall include the following:

✔ **Snapdragon.** *Antirrhinum majus.* These plants produce wonderfully coloured spikes of white, yellow, orange, red, purple, and multihued flowers. The common name comes from the hinged blossom, which opens and shuts like jaws when you squeeze the sides. (Kids love that.) Varieties range from 30 to 90 cm (12 to 36 inches) high. Plant in full sun and use transplants.

✔ **Flowering cabbage or kale.** *Brassica* species. These relatives of the common vegetable look very much alike. Their value lies in their brightly coloured, ruffled, or frilly foliage arranged in a head like a cabbage. The foliage is usually green with purple, pink, or white markings. Spectacular in the fall garden, especially in containers. Plants grow 30 to 45 cm (12 to 18 inches) high. Plant in full sun from seed or use transplants.

✔ **Pot marigold.** *Calendula officinalis.* Yellow or orange (or sometimes white) daisy-like flowers highlight this easy-to-grow annual. Pot marigold is a nice cut flower. The compact plants reach 30 to 45 cm (12 to 30 inches) high. Plant in full sun from seed or use transplants.

✔ **Dusty miller.** *Centaurea cineraria.* One of the most valuable grey-foliaged plants, dusty miller, a perennial in mild climates,, makes other garden plants look better and brighter. The plants have finely cut leaves and a mounding habit; they grow to about 45 cm (18 inches) high. Plant in full sun from transplants. *Senecio cineraria* is another grey-foliaged plant that grows slightly taller (to about 75 cm, or 30 inches, high) than *Centaurea cineraria.*

✔ **Bachelor's buttons.** *Centaurea cyanus.* Tufted blooms usually in blue, but pink, white, and violet are also available. They grow 60 to 90 cm (24 to 36 inches) tall, in sun or dappled shade. Sow seed in the garden. Reseeds.

✔ **Larkspur.** *Consolida ambigua.* Delicate spikes of spurred flowers come in pastel shades of white, blue, pink, and purple. Larkspurs grow 30 to 120 cm (12 to 48 inches) high, depending on variety. The plants are easy to grow from seed sown in the garden and do best in light shade.

- **Chinese forget-me-not.** *Cynoglossum amabile.* Wispy clouds of tiny, deep blue, pink, or white flowers accent this classic for shady gardens. Chinese forget-me-nots grow 30 to 45 cm (12 to18 inches) high. The plants are easy to grow from seed and reseed readily. *Myosotis sylvatica,* the common forget-me-not, is very similar and is equally good in shady gardens.

- **California poppy.** *Eschscholzia californica.* The much-loved California wildflower grows easily from seed (and they reseed readily). California poppies bloom mostly in shades of yellow and orange (or sometimes white). The plants reach 25 to 60 cm (10 to 24 inches) high. Grow in full sun.

- **Godetia.** *Godetia grandiflora.* Also called *clarkia.* Lovely, showy, open-face flowers with large stamens. Grows 45 to 60 cm (18 to 24 inches) tall in white, pink, rose and purple. Tolerates some shade. Use transplants.

- **Sweet peas.** *Lathyrus odoratus.* Intensely fragrant blooms make this a much-loved annual. The vining plant comes in single colours and multi-colours — almost every hue except true blue and green. Sweet peas make a wonderful cut flower. Most varieties need support such as a fence or trellis. However, bushier, low-growing types, such as 'Little Sweetheart,' do not need supports. Plant in full sun from seed.

- **Stock.** *Matthiola incana.* Intense, spicy scents make stock one of the most deliciously fragrant annuals. Depending on variety, flower spikes reach 30 to 75 cm (12 to 30 inches) high in shades of white, pink, purple, and red. Stocks are best started from transplants. Grow in full sun.

- **Love-in-a-mist.** *Nigella* spp. And old-fashioned plant that was loved by Catherine Parr Trail. It has threadlike foliage and white, pink, rose, or blue flowers on erect branching stems. The fat seedpods are very decorative. Grows 20 to 40 cm (8 to 16 inches) tall. Sow seeds in a sunny part of the garden, or early indoors.

- **Primroses.** *Primula* spp. Primroses are perennials in many mild climates, but usually grown as annuals. Brightly coloured flower clusters rest atop straight stems that seldom reach more than 30 to 45 cm (12 to 18 inches) high. Many colours are available to choose from. Fairy primrose, *P. malacoides,* produces airy clusters of white, pink, and lavender blooms above hairy leaves. English primrose, *P. polyantha,* has brighter, often multicoloured flowers above deep green, crinkled leaves. Plant in full to partial shade and start with transplants.

- **Nasturtium.** *Tropaeolum majus.* This sprawling annual has neat, round leaves and bright orange, yellow, pink, cream, or red flowers. Nasturtiums grow about 38 cm (15 inches) high on the ground, but the plants can climb up to 3 m (10 feet) when given proper supports. Nasturtiums are easy to grow from seed; plant in full sun or light shade.

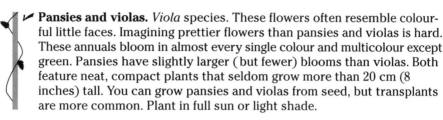

✔ **Pansies and violas.** *Viola* species. These flowers often resemble colourful little faces. Imagining prettier flowers than pansies and violas is hard. These annuals bloom in almost every single colour and multicolour except green. Pansies have slightly larger (but fewer) blooms than violas. Both feature neat, compact plants that seldom grow more than 20 cm (8 inches) tall. You can grow pansies and violas from seed, but transplants are more common. Plant in full sun or light shade.

Warm-season annuals

Ah, summertime . . . and the annuals are easy. Following is a list of summertime annuals that we like the best:

✔ **Bedding begonia.** *Begonia semperflorens.* These versatile annuals are most useful in shady gardens (although some types can take more sun). The flowers of bedding begonias come in shades of white, pink, and red. Leaves may be shiny green or bronze-red. Begonias with red flowers seem more sun-tolerant. Most varieties grow about 30 cm (12 inches) high. Bedding begonias are best started from transplants.

✔ **Madagascar periwinkle.** *Catharanthus roseus* (also known as annual vinca or vinca rosea). These cheery plants are workhorses in the summer garden. Compact with deep green leaves, Madagascar periwinkles produce an abundance of white, pink, red, or lavender blooms that often have a pink or white spot in the centre. These plants grow 30 to 50 cm (12 to 20 inches) high and perform best in full sun (but can take some shade). You can grow these plants from seed, but they are more easily grown from transplants.

✔ **Coleus.** *Coleus hybridus.* Grown for its intensely coloured foliage, coleus comes in a variety of colour combinations and different leaf shapes. This plant grows best in the shade and from transplants. You can also grow coleus as a houseplant. Pinch off the flowers to keep the plant compact.

✔ **Cosmos.** *Cosmos bipinnatus.* Bright green, airy plants bear brilliant blooms of white, pink, lavender, purple, or bicoloured daisy-like flowers. *C. sulphureus* has red, yellow, or orange flowers. Most types grow tall (upwards of 1.5 m, or 5 feet, high), but dwarf varieties stay more compact. Cosmos is easy to grow from seed or transplants, and the plants reseed. Plant in full sun.

✔ **Sunflower.** *Helianthus annuus.* Few annuals make a statement the way sunflowers do. Most sunflowers reach 2.5 to 3 m (8 to 10 feet) high, topped with huge, sunny, yellow blooms. But sunflowers also come in small-flowered forms in shades of red, orange, and white. Some dwarf varieties, such as 'Sunspot,' stay under 60 cm (2 feet) tall. All sunflowers have edible seeds. Plant from seed in full sun.

✔ **Lobelia.** *Lobelia erinus.* Deep to light blue blooms cover this low-growing (and often spreading) plant. Few blues are as bright as those of lobelia; white- and pink-flowering forms are also available. All lobelias reach about 10 to15 cm (4 to 6 inches) high. Grow lobelia from seed, but transplants are easier. Plant in full sun to light shade and add water regularly.

✔ **Flowering tobacco.** *Nicotiana alata* and *sylvestris.* Small, tubular, often fragrant blooms come in shades of white, pink, red, lime green, and purple. Flowering tobacco plants grow 30 to 90 cm (12 to 36 inches) high, depending on variety; *sylvestris* often reaches 120 cm (4 feet) and has long, tubular, incredibly fragrant flowers that open in the evening. Plant in full sun or light shade. Grow from seed or from transplants.

✔ **Sage.** *Salvia* spp. Tall spikes of bright white, red, blue, or purple flowers top these compact, sun-loving plants. Some types are perennials in mild-winter climates. Our favourites: clary sage, in clouds of pink and blue, and mealycup sage, *S. farinacea,* with spires of deep blue flowers. Sages range in height from 25 to 90 cm (10 to 36 inches). Plant in full sun and use transplants.

✔ **Marigold.** *Tagetes* spp. Marigolds are one of the most popular summer annuals, with blooms in the sunniest shades of yellow, orange, and red. Many varieties are available. Blossoms can be big or small, as can the plants. Plant in full sun. Easily grown from seed or transplants.

✔ **Verbena.** *Verbena hybrida.* Brightly coloured clusters of white, pink, red, purple, or blue flowers appear on low-growing, spreading plants. Verbenas grow 15 to 30 cm (6 to 12 inches) high. Plant in full sun. Start these plants from transplants.

✔ **Zinnia.** *Zinnia elegans.* A cut-flower lover's dream. Zinnias come in a huge range of flower colours (except blue), flower shapes and sizes, and plant heights. Small types, such as 'Thumbelina,' stay under 30 cm (12 inches) high. 'State Fair' grows up to 1.5 m (5 feet) high and has long stems for cutting. Plant in full sun. Easy to grow from seed or transplants.

Chapter 5

Perennials

- -

In This Chapter

▶ Getting to know perennials

▶ Using perennials in beds and for borders

▶ Putting perennials in the ground

▶ Digging into some can't-miss perennials

- -

*P*erennials are the phoenixes of garden plants: Every winter they die only to rise from the ashes the following spring, fuller and more beautiful than before. For that reason, perennials are good investments. In countries with frosty winters, like Canada, perennials have another advantage: They start growing early in the spring, and many begin flowering while the soil is still warming up enough to grow annuals.

Unlike annuals, which die after they've produced seed (the purpose of their life cycle), perennials return year after year. You need to replant annuals every year, but perennials increase in size and produce more blooms season after season.

Perennials include some of the best-loved flowering plants, such as daylilies *(Hemerocallis)*, phlox, and peonies. Generally, they have one main blooming season, usually for a few weeks in spring or summer, although many are at their best in fall. Spectacular foliage plants, such as ornamental grasses, hostas, and lamb's ears, are also perennials. We grow perennials for their beautiful flowers and for their foliage, and both have places in our gardens.

What's a Perennial?

A *perennial* is a plant that lives for several years, sprouting new growth in spring and making new blooms cyclically year after year. If you start a typical perennial, such as columbine, from seed in May, it spends its first summer growing foliage and developing a root system, and dies back to the ground for winter. The following spring it starts growing again, blooms in early summer, dies back again in the fall, and repeats the pattern of blooming and dying back.

When we say *perennials,* however, we're talking about a specific type: herbaceous perennials. These perennials have soft, fleshy stems — oak trees and lilac bushes, also perennials, have sturdier, woodier trunks and branches that don't die back for winter, even though the trees themselves lose their leaves. Herbaceous perennials live for several years under the right conditions, some — such as peonies — for 15 years or more. Others, likes lupines and dianthus, or pinks, are naturally shorter-lived and may thrive for only three to five years. And a perennial's life depends on more than its ability to survive the winter: The soil it has to grow in, the amount of space it has and the rainfall it receives, as well as the pests and diseases it has to cope with, also affect its longevity.

Most of the perennials we grow in Canada are *deciduous,* meaning that they lose their leaves at some point in the year, usually in winter, or they die back completely to the ground. Other perennials, such as *hellebores,* may remain evergreen in mild parts of Canada like southern British Columbia, and put out a new crop of leaves in spring. Thymes, candytuft and some sedums stay semi-evergreen in many parts of the country, and green up or send out new growth in spring. But it's not important to remember all this, unless you want plants that will have some presence, no matter how subtle, in your winter garden. What's important to know is whether the perennial you plant will survive the winter in your region, and for this information you should consult the plant tag or the nurseryman you buy the plant from.

If you read about a perennial that's described as tender — and many shown in British or American garden books and magazines are tender in our climate, even if they aren't described that way — you can be pretty sure it isn't hardy enough to last through a Canadian winter. You can still take a chance on these plants — within reason, of course! — or bring them into a cool basement under lights for the winter. Many plants we grow as annuals here — the lovely blue fan flower, *Scaevola aemula,* and the fuchsia are examples — grow as perennials in other countries.

Perennials are interesting for a variety of reasons. First, for the range of their flowers — from tiny fragrance-packed lavender to towering blue delphiniums. They're interesting in their sheer numbers and variety — thousands of kinds are available. They also interest gardeners because of the challenges they present: How do we divide them? Should we give them extra protection for the winter? Can we get a second burst of bloom from them in one summer? You don't just relegate perennials to the compost pile at the end of the season as you do with annuals.

Beds and Borders

Flower beds come in two basic configurations:

✔ **A border** is a flower bed located alongside a wall, fence or hedge, and is usually viewed from one side only. Some are placed along a sidewalk or driveway, and are seen from both sides. Borders are usually longer than they are wide, and they follow the contours of the backdrop.

✔ **An island bed** is a free standing flower bed surrounded on all sides by lawn, gravel, or pavement. The edges can be straight or curved. Island beds can be any shape or size.

The classic way to use perennials is to combine many of them in a large planting, or perennial border. A well-designed perennial border has something in bloom throughout the growing season. This type of border not only has a well-thought-out color scheme, but also relies on plant texture for visual interest. Designing a spectacular planting can take years of experience (even professional garden designers admit they're challenging), but a beginning gardener can create a workable, pleasing border, adding to it over the years as their knowledge increases.

For most gardeners, a perennial border is constantly evolving, which is part of the fun of creating it. If certain plants don't work, you can replace them with something else. If the border has some downtime when nothing is in bloom, you can plant some flowering annuals to fill in the gaps in the spring, or pop a container of annual blooms into a suddenly empty space later. Also consider some flowering shrubs, such as floribunda or polyantha roses, which bloom over a long season. When your border consists of a medley of flowering plants, including small trees, shrubs, bulbs, annuals, herbs, and even vegetables, you have a mixed border.

Designing a Perennial Border

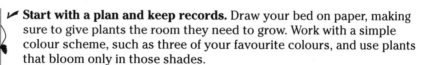

Even though individual experience is the best teacher, here are some pointers we've found useful in designing a perennial border:

✔ **Start with a plan and keep records.** Draw your bed on paper, making sure to give plants the room they need to grow. Work with a simple colour scheme, such as three of your favourite colours, and use plants that bloom only in those shades.

✔ **Plan for a succession of bloom.** Think seasonally, choosing plants that bloom in spring, summer and fall, so there's always — well, nearly always — something in bloom. Keep records of blooming times so that you know where the gaps are, and fill them the next season. And don't forget winter. Plant shrubs with colourful berries, attractive bark, or interesting shapes.

✔ **Prepare the soil carefully.** You won't be remaking this bed every year. Dig deep, add organic material and, most important, eliminate perennial weeds. For details on how to battle weeds, refer to Chapter 16 in this book.

✓ **Plant in groups.** One solitary plant gets lost in a crowd of other flowers. We find that grouping plants in odd numbers (3, 9, 15, and so on) has the greatest effect. But don't get hung up on rules. If you have room for only two of something, or if you want to try a plant and don't feel like investing a lot of money before you know whether it suits your garden, go right ahead and plant fewer than the guidelines suggest.

✓ **Don't forget the foliage.** Plants with dramatic foliage set off the flowers. Ornamental grasses or bold-textured shrubs make excellent focal points.

✓ **Use greys and whites.** Grey-foliaged plants (such as lamb's ears and artemisia) and plants with white flowers highlight other colours and tie everything together visually. These plants also reflect light and look great on nights when the moon is bright.

✓ **Consider the background.** A dark green background enriches the colour of most flowers. Consider planting a hedge (possibly of flowering shrubs or evergreens) at the back of the border.

Beyond borders

Don't feel that you have to limit perennials to beds and borders. Tuck in a few favourites wherever you have room — in front of an evergreen foundation planting, for example. Perennials are also great for cutting gardens.

Perennials in pots

Only where winters are sufficiently mild (with a few exceptions, Zones 7 and 8, which include parts of southern British Columbia and the tip of southern Ontario) are perennials at home all year in containers. In Zone 6, they sometimes survive winter if they're moved to a protected spot, like a garage. On the other hand, perennials sometimes surprise you and live a couple of winters in a container — it depends on the winter and the microclimate in your garden. Try protecting containers with a covering of leaves held in place around the pot with chicken wire. Or insulate the interior of large containers with 2.5-centimetre-thick (1 inch) slabs of foam insulation before you add the soil. Many gardeners grow perennials in a container for one season and then put it in the garden. A container is a good way to provide a plant with conditions not available in a bed (acid soil or shade, for instance).

For a good-looking arrangement, plant several perennials together in one container, varying the colour, shape, and size of the flowers. Make sure that you use a large container (at least 35 cm, or 14 inches, in diameter), and water it as often as daily or twice daily in hot weather.

Perennials for cutting

You can grow perennials specifically to cut them for indoor use — usually in rows or beds like a vegetable garden. Or work favourite bouquet-makers into your regular flower beds. Either way, the following perennials are long-lasting and striking as cut flowers:

- ✔ Yarrow (*Achillea*)
- ✔ Golden marguerite (*Argyranthemum frutescens*)
- ✔ Lilies (*Lilium*)
- ✔ Coral bells (*Heuchera*)
- ✔ Peonies (*Paeonia*)
- ✔ Black-eyed Susan (*Rudbeckia fulgida* 'Goldsturm')
- ✔ Pincushion flower (*Scabiosa*)
- ✔ Goldenrod (*Solidago*)
- ✔ Stokes' aster (*Stokesia laevis*)
- ✔ Speedwell (*Veronica*)

Planting Perennials . . . and Afterwards

Most nurseries sell perennial plants in four- or six-packs, 10-centimetre (4-inch) pots, or 4-to-8 liter (1- to 2-gallon) containers. Many mail-order suppliers sell a wide selection of bare-root plants; garden centres and nurseries occasionally do.

You can plant container-grown perennials any time you can work the ground. However, the best time to plant perennials — and especially bare-root plants — is in the early spring because the plants have time to get established before hot weather begins. Perennials planted in fall also do well as long the transplants have three or four weeks of good growing weather to develop roots before the first hard frost.

For more details about transplanting and planting seedlings, see Chapter 13.

Watering and feeding

How often you water perennials depends on the usual factors: Your climate and soil type, the sun and shade in your garden, and so on. Most perennials require water only when the top few inches of soil dry out but before the plants start to show symptoms of drought stress. Perennials from arid habitats generally benefit from a longer dry interval between waterings. Plants from wet places prefer never to dry out completely. You can find out a lot more about the whens, whys, and hows of watering in Chapter 14.

In regions with cold winters, which is most parts of Canada, start lengthening the intervals between waterings in late summer to toughen (harden off) your plants for winter. You don't want perennials to face the first frost with new growth that's easily damaged.

Fertilizing perennials is simple. One application of a complete fertilizer (see Chapter 14) to your perennial bed in early spring should be enough. If you think plants are lagging (weak or pale growth), follow up with another shot or two of the same fertilizer during the growing season.

Pinching and pruning perennials

Many perennials benefit from being cut back at various times during their growth cycles. To stimulate branching on lower stems and to make the plant bushier, for example, pinch out new growth at the top of the plant. (See Figure 5-1.)

Deadheading is the process of pinching or cutting off faded flowers while the plant is in bloom. Deadheading forces the plant to spend its energy developing more flowers instead of setting seed. The result of deadheading is usually a longer bloom cycle. (See Figure 5-2.)

Figure 5-1:
Pinching out new growth at the top of the plant helps it develop lower branches and become bushier.

Figure 5-2:
Deadhead
spent
flowers to
offset seed
production
and to divert
plant energy
to producing
new blooms.

Some perennials, such as coreopsis, delphinium, and gaillardia, rebloom if cut back by about one-third after the initial bloom cycle.

Once frost has killed the plant tops, you can cut back most perennials (some shrubbier types are an exception) to a height of 15 to 20 centimetres (6 to 8 inches) to make your winter garden look neat and to reduce your workload the following spring. Leave those with interesting seedheads, such as purple coneflower, to add architectural appeal to your garden. After the ground freezes, mulch plants with about 10 centimetres (4 inches) of organic matter such as straw, leaves, or shredded bark. If you use leaves, start with a deeper layer because over the winter they will pack down substantially. The mulch not only protects plants, it helps improve the soil.

Taller perennials, such as delphiniums, and bushy types, such as peonies, may need staking to prevent the flowers from falling over. Figure 5-3 shows two types of staking: thin metal wire loops (for bushy plants) and bamboo stakes ties (for taller perennials). Peony rings with divided sections also support plants well — insert the legs into the ground in spring to allow foliage to grow through the sections naturally.

If older plants become overcrowded or bloom poorly, rejuvenate them by dividing. In fact, division is a good way to increase plant numbers. (For more about plant division and other propagating methods, see Chapter 15.)

Figure 5-3:
Support
plants as
they grow
with either
metal loops
or bamboo
stakes and
ties.

Our Favourite Perennials

Everyone has a list of favourite perennials, so here is a look at ours. Some perennials are technically *biennials*, meaning that they grow mostly foliage the first year, bloom the second year, and then die.

- ✔ **Yarrow.** *Achillea* spp. Yarrow is a useful family of easy-care, summer-blooming perennials with ferny foliage and flat, upfacing clusters of yellow, white, and red and pink to peach blooms. They range from the low-growing woolly yarrow, *A. tomentosa,* and silver leaf yarrow, *A. clavenna,* to taller cultivars that grow up to 1.2 metres (4 feet), such as 'Coronation Gold'. Some tend to wander and many need support, but their long-lasting good looks are worth any cutting back and staking you have to do. Two favourites are *A. filipendulina* 'Moonshine', with fresh-lemon flower clusters atop 60 centimetre (2-foot) stems, and 'Salmon Beauty', a 75-centimetre (30-inch) plant with softly shaded pinky-peach blooms that fade to a delicate beige. Yarrow likes full sun and sandy soil. Most are hardy through Zone 3, some to 2. (See Figure 5-4.)

- ✔ **Artemisia.** *Artemisia* spp. These mounding, silver-foliaged plants are great as foils for hot-coloured flowers. One of the best is the hybrid 'Lambrook Silver', which fills a space 91 centimetres (3 feet) tall and wide; it benefits from a mid-summer shearing. 'Silver Mound' grows about 30 centimetres (1 foot) tall. Avoid the invasive 'Silver King' unless you have a large acreage. Plant in full sun. Hardy to Zone 5.

Figure 5-4:
Yarrow sizes
range from
ground
cover to
1.5 m (5 feet)
tall.

Yarrow (*Achillea* species)

✔ **Columbine.** *Aquilegia* spp. These widely adapted native perennials have fernlike foliage and beautiful, spurred flowers. Columbines bloom in spring and early summer in a single colours and multicolours — cream, yellow, white, blue, red, and mauve. Plants range in height from about 15 to 90 centimetres (6 inches to 3 feet). Columbines are easy to grow from seed, and they reseed. Plant in full sun to light shade, and keep moist. Hardy to Zone 3.

✔ **Aster.** *Aster* spp. Colourful perennials with daisylike flowers, mostly in shades of blue, purple, red, pink, and white with yellow centres. The native species, *A. novae-anglia,* grows in meadows and roadsides, and is sometimes called Michaelmas daisy. A few flower in early summer, but most are late bloomers, making them invaluable for the fall garden. *A. X frikartii* is a good garden plant, grows to about 61 centimetres (2 feet) and produces lavender-blue flowers with yellow centres. Other asters range from 15 centimetres to 1.8 metres (6 inches to 6 feet) high, depending on the species. Plant in full sun and any garden soil, and divide every two years to avoid mildew, a problem with some varieties. Hardy to Zone 4 or 5, depending on variety.

✔ **Basket-of-gold.** *Aurinia saxatilis.* Also called perennial alyssum. Brilliant gold flowers cover the grey foliage in spring on plants 30 to 38 centimetres (12 to 15 inches) high. Withstands drought and likes full sun, and spreads quickly. Use in rock gardens or as edging. Hardy to Zone 4.

✔ **Bellflower**. *Campanula* species. The much-loved family of mostly summer-blooming perennials produce bell-shaped flowers in blue, purple, or white. (See Figure 5-5.) 'Blue Clips' and White Clips' grow in well-behaved mounds about 13 centimetres (5 inches) high. The peach-leaved bellflower (*C. persicifolia*) grows to about 90 centimetres (3 feet) and has a sprightly, dainty presence in the garden. Don't accept any gifts of the creeping bellflower (*C. rapunculoides*): It may be beautiful, but it's far too aggressive.

Bellflower (Campanula)

Figure 5-5: Bellflowers get their name from their bell-shaped flowers.

The 60-centimetre (2 foot) clustered bellflower, *C. Glomerata,* has dense clusters of deep violet flowers. All prefer light or dappled shade, but can take sun. Hardy to Zone 4.

✔ **Bee balm**. *Monarda* species. Everyone should grow this native plant or one of the cultivars, if only to attract bees, who love its honey-lemon scented blooms. You will too. Also called bergamot or Oswego tea. The tufted flowers look like a jester's cap and come in lavender to deep pink. 'Marshall's Delight', bred in Morden, Manitoba, is mildew resistant. Plants grow 60 to 120 centimetres (2 to 4 feet), grow in clay to sand and moist to dry conditions. Hardy to Zone 3.

✔ **Chrysanthemum.** This very diverse, daisy-like group of perennials includes the familiar garden mums (*Dendranthema grandiflora,* Zone 4), so useful for autumn bloom. The group also includes the painted daisy, *Tanacetum coccineum,* Zone 4, and the shasta daisies, *Leucanthemum* *maximum,* Zone 3. All members of the family are wonderful cut flowers. Chrysanthemum plants vary in height, flower colour, bloom season, and hardiness. A special favourite is the lavender-pink, yellow centred 'Clara Curtis' fall blooming mum — it doesn't give up until a severe frost fells it. Most grow best in full sun.

✔ **Coreopsis.** *Coreopsis* species. Sunny yellow, daisy-like flowers top these easy-to-grow plants. The flowers appear from spring through summer. *C. verticillata* 'Moonbeam' is a beauty — filligree foliage topped with masses of pale lemon 5 centimetre (2 inch) blooms. Grows 30 to 60 centimetres (1 to 2 feet) tall. Most varieties hardy to Zone 3.

✔ **Dianthus.** *Dianthus* spp. This lovely family of usually fragrant, spring- and summer-flowering plants includes Sweet William, *D. barbatus,* a biennial that grows only foliage the first year and blooms the second, then dies. Cheddar pinks, *D. caesius,* is a favourite: hardy and easy to grow (to about 15 centimetres, or 6 inches), it has deep pink flowers and a wonderful spicy perfume. *D. allwoodii* virtually explodes in late June into masses of pink and crimson, single and double flowers. Cottage pinks are hybrids that have very fragrant, frilly, rose, pink, white, or bicoloured flowers on stems reaching about 45 centimetres (18 inches) high above a tight mat of foliage. Likes warm, sandy soil in full sun or light shade. Hardy to Zone 4.

✔ **Purple coneflower.** *Echinacea purpurea.* Tall purple or white, daisy-like flowers top this fine, long-lasting perennial, a native plant that's been adopted by the nursery trade. It attracts butterflies, especially the Monarch, and hummingbirds, and its cone-shaped seedheads look good in the winter garden. The downturned petals start out pale pink, and become deeper rosy purple as the centre cone grows larger and turns a glowing copper. *E. pallida* is a more subtle pink, with narrower petals. Plants grow 60 to 150 centimetres (2 to 5 feet) and accommodate full to partial sun, and average to dry soil. Hardy to Zone 3.

✔ **Bloody cranesbill**. *Geranium sanguineum.* This is one of the best of the species geraniums, a large group of perennials unrelated to the pot or bedding annual geranium, actually a *Pelargonium.* Dainty-looking, magenta, pink or white flowers appear in abundance above good-looking, deeply cut leaves that turn red in the autumn. Blooms spring to summer and mounds to 30 to 45 centimetres (a foot or more) high. *G. sanguineum striatum* has dark-veined pink flowers. Also look for taller varieties, such as the popular 'Johnson's Blue'. Plant in full sun to light shade. Hardy to Zone 5.

✔ **Daylily.** *Hemerocallis* spp. A dependable group of summer flowers, daylilies produce stalks of large, trumpet-shaped blooms and have become one of the most hybridized plants in recent years: hundreds of varieties are available. (See Figure 5-6.) Single and bicoloured blooms in yellow, orange, pink, red violet and nearly black last a day each, with new blooms appearing the next day. Some are fragrant. Attractive, grassy foliage grows 30 to 60 centimetres (12 to 24 inches) long. Flower stems can reach more than 90 centimetres (3 feet). Full sun to partial shade. Hardy to Zone 3.

✔ **Coral bells.** *Heuchera sanguinea.* This much-hybridized plant has been bred to produce beautiful lobed foliage, which can range from red, purple and bronze to copper, many with a metallic overlay or veining. The older, green-leaved vatieties are grown for their clusters of pink, white, or red bell-shaped flowers, held 30 to 60 centimetres (12 to 24 inches) above the plant and appearing in late spring. Plant in light shade or sun. Hardy to Zone 4.

✔ **Hosta**. *Hosta* spp. These bold and usually big foliage plants are a nice contrast to more delicate plants in a shade garden, and some have been bred to grow well in sun, too. Leaves are usually heart-shaped and often look like seersucker or puffy quilts; many are variegated, with creamy yellow or white centres or edges. Some new cultivars come in lime green, and many dwarf varieties useful for edging are also available. Mauve or white flower spikes appear in mid- to late summer. One long-time favourite is *H. sieboldiana* 'Francis Williams', which has 25- to 38- centimetre (10- to 15-inch), crinkled blue-green leaves with an uneven gold edge; it grows to about 91 centimetres (3 feet) high. Hardy to Zone 4.

✔ **Candytuft**. *Iberis sempervirens.* In early spring, snow-white flowers cover this dainty, compact plant. Grows 10 to 30 centimetres (4 to 12 inches) high and is great massed with thymes and other mounding plants in a tapestry planting. Full sun. Hardy to Zone 4.

✔ **Ornamental grasses**. Native grasses and cultivated varieties make stunning focal points among other plants, as well as beautiful, waving swathes of airy greens and golds on a larger property. The dried flowers often look good well into winter. Some are invasive, stealthily spreading with runners under the soil; others are the better-behaved clumping type. The huge selection includes these favourites: Blue fescue, *Festuca glauca,* 30- centimetre-tall (1 foot) bluish tuft suited to the front ot the border and hardy to Zone 3; Japanese blood grass, *Imperata cylindrica* 'Red Baron,' an upright tuft with deep red colouring, which grows to about 45 centimetres (18 inches) and likes moist soil, Zone 5; and the blue stem grasses, native to the prairies and also clump forming, also Zone 5. Little blue stem, *Andropogon scoparius* 'The Blues,' grows to 90 centimetres (3 feet) has bluish folage in summer and rich bronze fall colour with silvery tufts along the stems. Big blue stem, *Andropogon gerardii,* is dark green changing to reddish copper in fall, grows to 1.8 metres (6 feet), with flowers reaching 2.4 metres (8 feet), and looks best grown in a mass.

Figure 5-6:
Some
daylilies are
fragrant.

Daylilies *(Hemerocallis)*

Beware! Some ornamental grasses get very large and can become invasive.

✓ **Catmint**. *Nepeta fassenii*. These hybrids of the catnip that cats find so intoxicating are wonderful substitutes for lavender. The grey foliage and lavender-blue blooms combine beautifully with the chartreuse flowers of lady's-mantle or *Euphorbia polychroma*. Several cultivars to choose from in different heights. Cut back after the late spring bloom for a later smattering of flowers. Best in sunny dry sites, to Zone 5.

✓ **Beardtongue**. *Penstemon* spp. This family includes some of our loveliest wildflowers, mat forming and tall, many of which can be ordered as plants or seed from nurseries selling native plants. Cultivars are also plentiful. A good one is the recent introduction *P. digitalis* 'Husker Red', with deep burgundy foliage spring and fall, and pink tubular flowers on red stems; 45 to 90 centimetres (18 inches to 3 feet) tall. Hardy, although hardiness varies according to variety.

✓ **Phlox**. *Phlox* spp. A family that should be represented in any garden in one form or another. Moss phlox, *P. subulata,* grows dense mats of lavender, red, and pink flowers in spring. *P. stolonifera* and *P. divaritaca* produce longer stems of blue, white, or pink flowers that rise above the clumps of leaves in spring. The summer-blooming *P. paniculata* is the more common 60 to 120 centimetre (2 to 4 foot) garden phlox, often seen in magenta but also in nail-polish pink, white, salmon, orange, and many more, often with a contrasting eye. Powdery mildew and red spider mites can be a problem with *P. paniculata* — thin often to increase air circulation and keep watered during dry periods. Full sun. Hardy to Zone 4.

- **Black-eyed Susan**. *Rudbeckia fulgida* 'Goldsturm'. This is the most popular of all this family of black- or brown-centred golden daisies. It brightens the fall garden and the seedheads last well into winter. Grows anywhere, although it prefers sun to partial shade; 60 to 90 centimetres (2 to 3 feet) tall. Spreads easily, although not greedily, so you'll have plantlets for friends. Hardy to Zone 3.

- **Salvia.** *Salvia* spp. As well as the herb sage and the variety of annual salvias available, excellent hardy perennial salvias have been bred for the garden. They're mostly blues and purples, but pink is also grown. 'May Night' and 'East Freisland' are good choices. Most grow upwards to just over 30 centimetres (1 foot) tall, and like a dry, sunny site. (See Chapter 4 for annual salvias.) Hardy to Zone 5.

- **Lamb's ears**. *Stachys byzantina*. This is a lovely, low-growing foliage plant with soft, fuzzy, silver-grey leaves that grow 15 to 30 centimetres (6 to 12 inches) high. Insignificant purplish-white flowers in summer. A fabulous edging plant, and a great partner for blue flowers. Plant in full sun. Hardy to Zone 5.

Chapter 6

Bulbs

● ●

In This Chapter

▶ Understanding bulbs

▶ Caring for bulbs

▶ Dividing and propagating bulbs

▶ Taking stock of our favourite bulbs

● ●

*B*ulbs are a dream come true for many people, especially for those who have never had much luck growing any plants. Think of bulbs as flowering powerhouses: Plants that pack most of what they need for a season's worth of growth into some type of underground storage device. Plant it at the right time of year and at the proper depth, and you're almost guaranteed a spectacular bloom — true, you have to wait a few months, but the wait is worthwhile.

What Are Bulbs?

When you think of plant bulbs, you probably envision the spring-blooming types — daffodils, tulips or hyacinths, brownish things that look something like an onion. Those bulbs are true bulbs, and include the onion. But the term *bulb,* as used in gardening, refers to a great number of different types of plants with some kind of swollen root structure underground that stores food. In addition to true bulbs, other forms include corms, rhizomes, tubers, and tuber-corms. Each one of these types looks different. Some are underground stems surrounded by modified fleshy leaves, and others are swollen underground stem bases. Some are thickened, branching storage stems, and others are swollen roots.

All bulbs have a growing period and a resting time. But there the similarity ends. For one thing, bulbs don't all grow and rest simultaneously. Some early spring bulbs — the familiar tulips, daffodils, and hyacinths — blossom early in the year when nothing much else is growing and then die back and rest to rejuvenate themselves for the next season's bloom. Other bulbs — lilies, for example, and gladioli — bloom later and keep their foliage till fall, like most herbaceous perennials. Colchicums put out a lush growth of shiny green foliage, not unlike a huge romaine lettuce, in spring. It dies back for the summer, then the bulb unexpectedly throws up beautiful mauve, pink or white flowers, without foliage, in late summer and early fall, when just about everything else is going dormant.

And because bulbs are a family of their own, there are other differences: how they flower, when you should plant them, their hardiness and how they multiply all depend on what kind of bulb they are. Some are tender and must be brought indoors for winter — for example, the popular *agapanthus,* or lily of the Nile, the intoxicatingly fragrant freesia and tuberose, all of which are native to much warmer climates than Canada's. For the full nitty-gritty on plant bulbs, check out *Flowering Bulbs For Dummies*, by Judy Glattstein and the Editors of The National Gardening Association, published by IDG Books Worldwide, Inc.

Here's a quick rundown of the types of bulbs you can buy, and what to expect of them.

✔ **True Bulbs.** These contain the immature flower and foliage of next season's plant in the centre of the bulb, surrounded by scales and often covered with an onion-like skin. In fact, you can slice some bulbs open from top to bottom and make out the embryo flower and leaves inside, but that seems like a waste to us, unless you're teaching a class in botany. Once the plant has bloomed, the foliage of most bulbs dies back and their energy returns to the bulb to be stored for the next blooming period. Spring bloomers like daffodils, tulips, scilla, and hyacinths are true bulbs, as are alliums, lilies, and fritillaria. Most bulbs are hardy to Zones 4 or 5 (in fact, they need a cold period to rest in) although some lilies, like the oriental hybrids, can be touchy about cold winters. Species tulips and narcissi are hardy to Zone 3.

✔ **Tubers.** Tubers and tuberous roots are swollen underground stems that store food, but they don't have a flattish base plate from which roots grow, like corms and bulbs. Instead, fibrous feeder roots grow down from the ends of the tubers. During the growing season, new tubers and buds develop around the mother tuber. Tubers aren't winter hardy, but they can be stored for winter in a cool, but not freezing, spot, in a clump or divided into separate tubers. Dahlias, ranunculus, alstroemeria and the table potato are all tubers.

✔ **Corms.** Corms are actually swollen stems and don't have the scales true bulbs have. Leaves and flowers grow from two or more points on the top of the corm, and roots grow from the bottom; like other bulbs, the corm stores the food that produces the next season's flower and replacement corms, which grow from lateral buds on the original corm. Gladioli and crocuses are both corms.

✔ **Tuber-corms.** These are sometimes called tuber-stems, and are disc-shaped food storage organs, usually with concave or flat tops. Roots grow from underneath. Tuber-corms seldom produce offsets but increase in size with age. Examples are anemones, begonias, cyclamens, gloxinias.

✔ **Rhizomes**. These are bulbous stems that grow just under the surface of the earth, with thread-like roots on the underside. Many plants that grow from rhizomes, like daylilies and iris, are hardy in most parts of Canada, at least to Zones 4 and 5. The tender cannas and agapanthus are also rhizomes.

What You Can Do with Bulbs

Plant bulbs wherever you want to see them bloom: in the smallest little spot by the front door, in pots, in large swaths under trees, or among other flowering plants. Some bulbs, such as the early *Scilla bifolia* and *Chionodoxa,* or glory of the snow, look particularly good naturalized in shady woodland settings, while others, such as tulips, do well in formal gardens.

One of our favourite ways to use spring-flowering bulbs like crocus and species tulips and daffodils is in groupings of a dozen or more throughout a bed, over-planted with low-growing perennials such as iberis, thymes and aubretia. The bulbs come up through the other plants and create wonderful combinations. After the bulbs are through blooming, the perennials cover up the fading foliage of the bulbs.

Plan for a long season of colour from bulbs. Even though some of the most familiar bulbs (such as daffodils and tulips) bloom in spring, bulbs like lilies and dahlias bloom in summer and autumn.

If you really want to have fun, try forcing bulbs to bloom indoors. (See "Bulbs in Containers," in this chapter.)

When and How to Buy Bulbs

The best time to buy and plant bulbs depends on whether the bulb blooms in spring or summer.

Spring-blooming bulbs

Hardy, spring bloomers are the major-league bulbs most people know: Crocus, grape hyacinths, daffodils, hyacinths, and tulips are the most common. You plant the bulbs in fall and they bloom in spring. Plant all spring-blooming bulbs except tulips as soon as you have them in your hands in the autumn. Tulips prefer to be planted when the soil has cooled off a little, as late as November — even December in certain parts of the country — as long as the ground isn't frozen.

Nurseries get the bulk of their spring-blooming bulbs around the Labour Day weekend. Here are some tips to getting the pick of the crop:

- ✔ **Buy early, and buy everything you intend to get.** Supplies of a popular, sold-out item may or may not be replenished. Keep tulips — indeed, all bulbs, but especially tulips because you won't be planting them for a few weeks — in a cool, dry place until you plant them.

- ✔ **Make reservations.** If some bulbs are in limited supply, an early order reserves them for you. Orders are often shipped in rotation — early order, early shipping; later order, later shipping.

- ✔ **Specify a shipping date for mail-order suppliers.** Most, if not all, mail-order sources promise to ship at the appropriate time.

Summer-blooming bulbs

Most bulbs that bloom in summer are frost-tender types, such as dahlias, begonias, and agapanthus, which you plant in spring. Wait until close to tomato-planting time (after the last spring frost) if you intend to plant the bulbs directly in the ground. Space permitting, you can pot them up a month or six weeks before the last frost. Then plant outdoors once the weather is right. Early planting indoors gives them a good head start.

Nurseries, chain stores, and supermarkets often start selling summer-blooming bulbs while it's still winter. You can take advantage of these early sales with these harbingers of spring. Just follow these tips:

- ✔ **Don't wait.** Buy something you like as soon as you see it, as long as you can keep it growing in a sunny place or under lights. You should also buy dormant summer-blooming bulbs when you see them. If you wait to decide later, the bulbs may be gone. Just keep them in a cool, dry place until you can plant them. (The exception is lilies, which should be potted up as soon as you buy them.)

- ✔ **Aim for early blooms.** Pot up summer-blooming bulbs a month before frost-free weather arrives if you have the appropriate indoor space to grow them. Doing so gives you a jump-start on the season.

- ✔ **Cheat a little.** Once the weather is mild and settled, some tender bulbs may be available at the nursery as potted growing plants — dahlias, cannas and caladiums in particular. You can buy, plant, and enjoy all on the same day — no waiting!

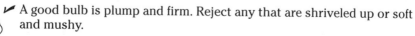

Shopping tips

Always purchase fine-quality bulbs — they give you more bang for your buck. Never forget that with bulbs, bigger is better. Larger bulbs, although more expensive, give you more bloom. Bargain bulbs are often poor performers. Avoid bulbs that are soft and mushy or have obvious signs of decay. Keep the following advice in mind as you shop:

- ✔ A good bulb is plump and firm. Reject any that are shriveled up or soft and mushy.

- ✔ A good bulb is healthy, with no mouldy patches growing on it. Judge a flowering bulb just like you would an edible one, like an onion.

- ✔ Size is relative — you'll never see a crocus corm as big as that of a gladiolus — but within a category, bigger is better. A large daffodil called *double-nosed* has more flowers than a smaller, single nosed or round of the same variety.

If you buy your bulbs through a mail-order catalogue, choose a reputable dealer. Mail order is the only way to buy bulbs not locally available. (Appendix B lists several companies that offer many varieties.) A specialty nursery can offer a wider selection of particular bulbs by mail than local nurseries can afford to stock. Take a look at some pointers for mail-order shopping:

- ✔ A good catalogue gives lots of information — more than just when a bulb flowers, its colour, and size.

- ✔ Be cautious about the truth of claims of fabulous displays that grow anywhere and everywhere. If it sounds too good to be true, it probably isn't true.

- ✔ If prices in one catalogue are significantly lower than in others, or in local garden centres, smaller bulb sizes might explain the difference. Undersize bulbs are inexpensive, and their flowering display is correspondingly small.

- ✔ Because you are buying the bulbs sight unseen, you have to trust the dealer to be reputable and send you good-quality bulbs. If they arrive mouldy or otherwise tainted, let the dealer know and send them back.

Ode to the Lily

Lilies are so popular and grow so well in almost every part of Canada that it's surprising the lily hasn't been named our national flower. Most thrive in

Zones 3 through 7, and some are hardy to Zone 2. They're a beautiful addition to any garden: tall and imposing, with exotic, mostly fragrant flowers. They're easy to grow and propagate, they make great cut flowers, and they're disease resistant and bothered by few pests. (The lily beetle, shiny scarlet on top and black underneath, can be a problem; pick them off and destroy them, or, as a last resort, use an insecticide containing malathion and Cygon 2. Insecticidal soap isn't effective.) But they won't tolerate poor drainage. A wet lily will soon be a dead lily — or at least a very sick one.

Daylilies and waterlilies, it must be noted, aren't really lilies. True lilies have six petals that grow in different shapes: trumpets, cups, stars, and bowls, some with recurving petals. They have luscious, prominent stamens loaded with pollen that ends up on your nose when you stoop to sniff the perfume.

Three families of lilies will take a garden through the summer. First to bloom, in late June and early July, are the cheerful, colourful *asiastics,* which grow to three or four feet (90 to 120 centimetres) tall with up-facing blooms in every colour but blue. Malta is a dependable, deep rosy pink; Roma is a vigorous grower with ivory flowers lightly spotted in chocolate.

Hard on the heels of the asiatics, sometimes overlapping them, are the *trumpets,* dignified and tall (some reach six feet/1.8 metres), perfuming the garden, in pastel cream and yellow through pink, apricot and copper. Pink Perfection and Black Dragon, the latter with white inside the petals and rosy-maroon on the outside, are two favourites.

In late July and August the *orientals* bloom; these flamboyant, fragrant blossoms with recurved or wavy petals are the least hardy of lilies and need a winter protection of mulch on the prairies. But they're generally hardy without protection to Zone 4. Depending on the variety, they grow 75 to 150 centimetres (2 ½ to 5 feet) tall, with most at about 105 centimetres (3½ feet). The tall 'Casa Blanca' has an enormous, nearly 25 centimetres (10 inch) pure white fuzzy bloom. 'Star Gazer', possibly the world's favourite oriental, has spotted crimson flowers with recurving petals; about 90 centimetres (3 feet) tall.

We wouldn't want you to overlook the species lilies. They like partial shade and include the beautifully perfumed early bloomer *Lilium regale,* commonly referred to as the Easter lily, and the martagons, or turk's cap lilies; they're shy about appearing the year they're planted, but worth the wait. Just don't forget where you planted them.

Lilies look best in groups, especially in drifts of blending colours. But one tall one in a bed of low plants makes a dramatic statement.

Planting Bulbs

Planting bulbs is easy, especially if you're planting only a few. You can break a serious sweat, however, if you're doing mass plantings. Either way, the two most important points that you should know about planting a bulb are

✔ Set the bulb at the correct depth.

✔ Make sure you place the bulb right side up in the hole.

The chart in Figure 6-1 shows the recommended planting depths and proper positioning for common bulb types. As a general rule, most bulbs should be planted at a depth equal to three times their diameter. For example, plant a 5 centimetres (2-inch) bulb 15 centimetres (6 inches) deep. Remnants of roots on the bottom of the bulb should tell you which side of the bulb points down. If you see no sign of root remnants, plant the bulb so that the most pointed, narrow part points up. If you have any doubts, ask your local nursery.

If you have heavy clay soil, try planting at one-half the recommended depth. The bulb won't have to expend as much energy struggling through the dense clay.

Figure 6-1:
Use this bulb-planting depth chart as a guide when you plant your own bulbs.

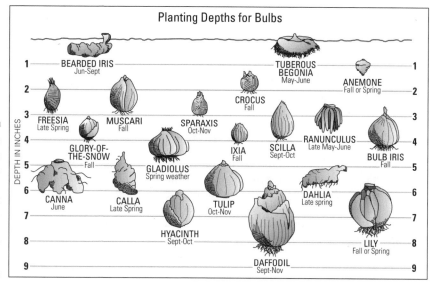

You can plant bulbs individually using a hand trowel or a bulb planter, which looks something like a small auger. If you're planting many bulbs, dig one big trench or hole and place the bulbs in the bottom.

Most bulbs require well-drained soil. (Bulbs can rot in soggy, overly wet ground.) Before planting your bulbs, mix a slow-release, complete fertilizer in the soil at the bottom of the hole, then top it with a little more soil so the bulb itself doesn't come in contact with the fertilizer granules. You can find appropriate bulb fertilizers in nurseries and garden centres. After planting the bulbs, water the ground thoroughly.

What's your style?

The design style you want to achieve — natural or formal — will dictate the planting method and type of bulb you choose. Some bulbs return dependably year after year in greater numbers; this is called naturalizing, or perennializing. Some species tulips are good naturalizers, as are some crocus and many daffodils (and many other bulbs). In naturalistic design, you do best to imitate the natural growth pattern of a particular type of bulb, and you choose bulbs that go on to multiply naturally on their own, thereby making the planting look more natural year after year.

In formal design, it's unlikely you'd need or want bulbs that come back every year because your planting is more structured and you'll want to repeat it or plan another pattern next year. It's also a good idea to plant in beds carefully excavated to one uniform depth to be sure the plants come up evenly and ensure identical bloom times.

Beware the creatures

A gardener can be pretty perplexed when the 200 bulbs he or she planted last fall make just a meagre showing in the spring. Yes, the reason could be inferior bulb quality or improper planting depth, but a likely culprit could be an animal. Chipmunks, voles, mice, deer, woodchucks, squirrels, and other animals forage for and feast on newly planted bulbs. But don't despair — you can grow beautiful flowering bulbs. Consider the following:

✔ Most critters leave daffodils and snowdrops alone — one big reason so many of these plants naturalize so well.

✔ Use bulb fertilizer or superphosphate instead of bone meal, which can attract some animals.

✔ If burrowing animals are a problem, plant in wire mesh bulb baskets

✔ Use traps, barriers, or scare tactics, like a loud radio or a hard spray of water from the hose.

✔ Once buds appear on bulb plants, spray them with an animal repellant spray. They have a very bitter taste animals don't like, and mostly stay away from. But be sure to spray it away from your face — you won't like it, either. Neither will kids or pets, so keep them out of the garden while spraying.

Caring for Bulbs

With many bulbs (especially those that bloom in spring), you won't have much else to do. Plant them and forget them. The bulbs grow, bloom, die back, and come back again the following year all on their own. Summer-blooming bulbs, like dahlias and begonias, however, need regular watering and fertilizing during their growth cycle. Most bulbs, in fact, benefit from a once-a-year application of nitrogen fertilizer during their growing season.

Pinch off faded blooms just as you would for most flowers (see Chapter 15 for the how-to on pinching.) Doing so steers the plant's energy into building food reserves rather than producing seed. After the bloom finishes, don't cut down the bulbs' foliage. The foliage provides the food for the bulb, preparing for next year's bloom. Let the foliage die down naturally and then trim off the withered leaves or just let them dissolve into the soil. In the same vein, don't braid or bundle up the leaves, either. Doing so impedes the food-gathering process and results in poor blooms the following year.

Digging and storing bulbs is necessary for tender bulbs such as canna and gladiolus. Wait until the foliage is almost dried out or frost-damaged and gently dig the bulbs up. (A spading fork works well.) Brush the dirt off the bulbs and allow them to dry for a week in a cool, dark place. After a week, discard damaged or rotting bulbs and dust the remaining ones with sulfur or another fungicide. Finally, pack the dusted bulbs in dry peat moss or perlite and store them in a cool, dark place until replanting time.

If digging and storing tender bulbs is too much work, treat them like annuals and plant new ones every year.

Dividing and Propagating Bulbs

Some bulbs, particularly smaller types such as crocuses and scilla, and the larger daffodils, can remain undisturbed for years. Such *'naturalizers'* just get better year after year. But other bulbs multiply so rapidly that they become too crowded and deplete the nutrients in the soil around them. And others, notably tulips, make smaller and smaller flowers over time. If your bulbs are vigorous and crowded, they need dividing. If they produce fewer and fewer blooms, dig them up and discard them.

Dividing occurs just after the foliage turns yellow and begins to die back. Dig up the clump using a garden fork, being careful not to injure the bulbs. Next, break off the individual bulbs, keeping the roots intact. Replant the bulbs immediately or store them in a dry place until autumn planting time. Water the area well and allow foliage to mature and die before removing it. The newly planted bulbs should bloom the following spring.

Larger bulbs (for example, lily) or corms (for example, gladiolus) develop small, immature offspring at the base of the bulb. Remove these *offsets* after the plant has bloomed and the leaves have died; then plant the offsets in an inconspicuous area where they can grow until they are big enough to blossom (usually a year or two).

You can use another method to divide and increase true bulbs, such as lilies. Bulbs of most true lilies resemble artichokes, with many swollen, scalelike sections. You can remove the individual *scales* of lilies and grow them to form new bulbs for planting the following spring. This process is somewhat involved, however, and best left to the more advanced gardener.

Bulbs in Containers

Forcing bulbs — bringing them indoors and getting them to bloom before their normal season — is easier to do than you probably think. Several spring bulbs — hyacinths, daffodils (especially the incredibly fragrant paperwhites, which will bloom in a few short weeks in a container filled with water and stones), and some tulips — are good choices for indoor flowering. Generally, the larger grades of bulbs are better for forcing because they produce more and bigger flowers. Avoid bargain bulbs.

In some areas of Canada, notably the west coast and parts of southern Ontario, you can also grow bulbs in containers outdoors for bloom at the usual time. It's also worth a try in colder areas, to Zone 6 or 5, if you give the containers some protection. Plant the bulbs in autumn, about the same time you'd plant them in the open soil. Move the container to an out-of-the-way location for the winter, such as a warm, protected alcove of the house, or a warm garage. You can also cover the pot with leaves or mulch held in place with chicken wire. Come spring, the bulbs will begin their growth. That's when you move the pot to the "display" location.

Then again, you might prefer our lazy-gardener's approach: Fill the bottom of a deep display container with earth or sand up to about 8 inches (20 centimetres) of the rim. As soon as forced bulbs in pots start appearing in your supermarket, buy enough to fill the container, stuff them in as tightly as you can and fill the spaces with sheet moss, sold at florist and hobby shops. Once the first lot of flowers fade, take the pots out and fill the container with new pots. You can keep up a good display for at least a couple of months this way. And there's a plus: Once the leaves of spent plants die down, you can harvest the bulbs and plant in them in the garden for bloom next spring.

Shallow clay or plastic pots called *bulb pans* are the best containers for forcing bulbs because they require less potting mix than ordinary pots and are less likely to tip over. The general rule for forcing bulbs is to have the pot at least twice as deep as the bulb is tall.

Any soilless mixture of peat moss and perlite or vermiculite works well. Don't bother buying expensive *bulb bark,* a special mix for forcing bulbs. In the autumn, fill the chosen pot ¾ full with the soilless mix and place the bulbs, 1.25 centimetres (½ inch) apart, on top of the mix, with the bulb's pointed end facing up. When forcing several kinds of bulbs together in one container, place the largest bulbs in the center and fan out the smaller bulbs around them. Gently press the bulbs into the mix so the tips are level with the rim of the pot. Then fill the pot with more of the soilless mix and add water until the soil is evenly moistened.

Set the potted bulbs in a cool (4°C to 7°C or 40°F to 45°F), dark place for 8 to 15 weeks to allow the bulbs to grow roots. Smaller bulbs may need a little less time; larger bulbs may need slightly more time.

You can use your refrigerator for this cool phase, if it has the space. If you use the refrigerator, cover pots with a slightly open plastic bag, and keep apples and other fruits away as the ethylene gas they produce will abort the bulb's flowers.

After the required cooling period, check your pots. You should begin to see evidence of shoots emerging from the soil mix. To gradually reintroduce the pots to light and warmth, place the pot in a cool room with indirect sunlight. By the end of one week, move the pot into direct sun with temperatures to 18°C (65°F). Within a month of being brought into warmth, the bulbs should begin to flower. As the foliage dies back, add a weak solution of 20-20-20 fertilizer every other watering, then save bulbs for planting in the garden once the soil warms up. Some may not bloom a second time, but many will.

Favourite Bulbs

Whether it's stately lilies, fragrant hyacinths, or cheery daffodils, everyone has a favourite bulb. Following is a list of a few of ours. For more information, consult some of the bulb catalogues that appear in Appendix B.

✔ **Allium.** *Allium* spp. Late spring bloom. Zones 4-5. The lovely balls of tiny florets and the decorative seed heads of this relative of the onion are favoured by flower arrangers. Bees and butterflies find the flowers irresistible, bugs give them a wide berth, and gardeners love their range and versatility. They grow in purple, blue, pink, rose, yellow and white, in heights from 30 centimetres (1 foot) to 120 centimetres (4 feet), on strong stems and with long, strappy leaves. *A. sphaerocephalon,* like little drumsticks of deep purple, look great scattered through a natural garden. *'Globemaster',* which has huge heads of mauve-violet florets, makes a stunning clump of five or more. *A. moly's* sunny yellow balls of bloom carried on 30 centimetres (1 foot) stems bring cheer to a rock garden.

✔ **Begonias.** *Begonia tuberhybrida;* summer bloom. Tender. To our eye, begonias look like roses or gardenias, and their lovely colours complement shade plants like ferns and hostas. Many varieties to choose from, some with large flowers (up to 20 centimetres /8 inches across), others with smaller blooms borne on "weeping" plants. Few begonias grow more than 20 to 45 centimetres (12 to 18 inches) high. Begonia flowers come in almost all shades except blue and green. Foliage is good-looking and succulent. They make ideal container plants and grow best in light shade. Dig up and store the bulbs over winter.

✔ **Canna.** *Canna* spp.; summer bloom. Tender. A tropical looking upright plant with large leaves and showy flowers in shades of yellow, orange, salmon, pink, and red; some are bicolour. The varieties with variegated leaves, some in yellow, red and green, are spectacular. Some cannas grow to 1.5 metres (5 feet) high, but many are shorter. Full sun. Dig and store over winter.

✔ **Colchicum.** *Colchicum* spp. Zone 3 to 5. We think everyone should have clumps of these fall-blooming, seldom-seen crocus-like plants in their gardens. They glow in colours of rose, pale amethyst, and white in the golden fall light, and look wonderful in clumps of green plants, like low-growing ground covers or hostas. Just don't let the adjacent plants drown them — colchicums grow 15 to 30 centimetres (6 to 12 inches) high. They throw up a lettuce-like growth of leaves in spring, which dies down before the blooms (without foliage) suddenly appear in fall. 'Waterlily' has the most presence, with rosy mauve foot-tall double flowers. Colchicums perennialize well —one bulb becomes a nice clump in about three years. That's good, because they're not cheap.

✔ **Dahlia.** *Dahlia* spp.; summer bloom. Tender. A diverse family of hybrids that offers an incredible array of flower form — from cupped, formal-looking petals to rolled or shaggy shapes — and sizes. Some blossoms are tiny balls; others are huge, dinner-plate blooms more than 20 centimetres (8 inches) across. Available in almost every colour but blue, dahlia plants range from 15 cm (6 inches) high to more than 1.5 metres (5 feet). Plant in full sun and water regularly. Dig and store tubers over winter. Small varieties are often grown as annuals.

Fritillaria. *Fritillaria* spp. Hardy to Zone 5. Another family of plants that spans several forms. The most dramatic is the exotic 60 to 90 centimetres (2 to 3 foot) *F. imperialis,* with large leaf-tufted, bell-shaped flowers in yellow, red, and orange, hanging from strong stems. They're sure to stop conversation in your garden. Other, more subtle forms include the recently popular *F. meleagris* with nodding bells in purple, grey, brown, and white on 30 centimetres tall (1 foot) plants. The bulbs have a skunky odour that squirrels don't like.

Snowdrops. *Galanthus* spp.; very early spring bloom. Zone 4. Lovely, drooping, bell-shaped white flowers punctuate this plant. Snowdrops naturalize nicely and grow from 20 to 30 centimetres (8 to 12 inches) high. Plant in full sun or partial shade, especially under trees, where they perform beautifully. The giant snowdrop, *G. elwesii,* is the earliest and largest.

Gladiolus. *Gladiolus* spp.; summer bloom. Tender. This much-loved cut flower bears tall spikes of trumpetlike flowers. Blossoms come in almost all colours except blue. Most grow to 1.2 to 1.5 metres (4 to 5 feet) high, but smaller types are available. Plant in full sun and treat as annuals or dig up bulbs for winter storage. Baby gladiolus, *G. colvillei,* grows lower and is hardier.

Hyacinth. *Hyacinthus orientalis;* early spring bloom. Zone 4 to 5. Wonderfully fragrant spikes are composed of white, red, pink, yellow, blue, or purple bell-shaped flowers. Because of their tight form, hyacinths are ideal for formal plantings in their first year; after that, the flowers grow in looser clusters. Most grow to about 30 centimetres (12 inches) high. Full sun or light shade.

Iris. *Iris* spp.; spring to summer bloom. Zone 5. A huge group of elegant plants to choose from. Favourites include the bearded iris, which has huge blooms with tight, upfacing cups and gracefully arching falls, petals that grow downward. *I. siberica* is flatter and more open. The wonderful *I. reticulata* is one of the first flowers to bloom in spring, and 'Harmony' is our favourite: A clear, strong blue with yellow markings. Irises come in many colours, especially blues and violets to nearly black, and reach from 15 centimetres to 1.2 metres (6 inches to 4 feet) high. Plants spread freely. Full sun or light shade.

Grape hyacinth. *Muscari* spp.; spring bloom. Hardy to Zones 3 to 4. These miniature hyacinth look-alikes quickly form carpets of fragrant, mostly blue flowers and grassy foliage. Grow from 15 to 30 centimetres (6 to 12 inches) high and naturalize freely. Full sun or light shade. Some foliage appears in late summer and early fall, and plant blooms with more foliage in mid-spring.

✔ **Daffodils and Narcissus.** *Narcissus* spp.; spring bloom. Hardy to Zone 3. Carefree bloomers flower year after year, even in mild climates. If you plant only one type of bulb, this should be it. Narcissus generally bears clusters of small, often fragrant, flowers. Daffodils have larger blooms. You can choose from many daffodil and narcissus varieties (mostly in white and yellow shades), with trumpet cups or flattish faces in double and single forms. Favourites are 'Thalia', a fragrant white trumpet with several flowers per stem, and the early, foot-tall 'Jetfire' with a red trumpet and yellow, flared back perianth. But you can't beat 'King Alfred', a rich gold trumpet 45 centimetres (18 inches tall). Full sun to light shade.

✔ **Ranunculus.** *R. asiaticus*; spring to summer blooms. Tender. Bright-coloured very double flowers come in shades of white, yellow, orange, red, and purple. Some are multicoloured. Grow 30 to 60 centimetres (12 to 24 inches) tall and have deeply cut leaves. Full sun or light shade. Dig and store bulbs in autumn.

✔ **Tulips.** *Tulipa* spp.; spring bloom. Hardy to Zone 3. These much-loved bulbs with the familiar cup-shaped flowers come in almost all colours, even multicolours, including mauves that verge on blue and purples that deepen to almost black. There are so many varieties, from the early, short species to the tall, late blooming Darwins, that we can't do them justice here. A couple of our favourites: the early 20 centimetre (8-inch) lilac pink, yellow-centred *T. saxatilis,* and the late May, early June *'Marilyn',* a lily-flowered variety with pointed, reflexed petals in white striped with strawberry. Tulips grow from 25 to 60 centimetres (10 to 30 inches) high and like full sun.

Chapter 7

Roses

• •

In This Chapter

▶ Speaking the language of roses

▶ Choosing varieties for you

▶ Landscaping with roses

▶ Buying and planting

▶ Pruning and other mysteries

▶ Facing up to rose problems and quirks

• •

*F*or a gardener, falling in love with roses is easy. As if their sumptuous petal colours and shapes weren't enough, many roses seduce with an intoxicating scent designed precisely, it seems, to snag a susceptible gardener. But even from the most pragmatic gardener's point of view, there's much more to the allure of a rose.

Roses are charter members of that club of plants that grow just about anywhere. That's why you see roses and rose gardens in Victoria, St. John's, Bonn, and Bejing — often the same varieties. While all over the world large-flowered and long-stemmed roses on 1.2 to 2.1 metres (4- to 7-foot) plants are favourites, the diversity of roses means there's almost surely one to fit your needs and to suit your taste, no matter where you live or how you define beauty. Do you prefer roses short or tall? Do you like your flowers simple, with 5 petals, or complicated, with 60? Is scent more important or less important than colour and shape?

Now don't get us wrong. Roses really aren't that complicated. And you can find a lot of information about them in books, magazine articles, advertisements and catalogues, along with thousands of different rose varieties from which to choose.

We want to guide you through this maze of information. Let us boil things down a bit. If you want to grow roses successfully, there are a few things you should know before you begin.

✔ Roses come in many varieties. Before you go out to shop, read up on roses — and these pages are a good place to start. Don't buy a rose just because you like its picture — it may be a tall shrub when you want a short bush. It may not be hardy in your zone, or it may bloom once in late spring, when you want a repeat bloomer.

✔ Most roses in Canada are *grafted*. This means that the varietal upper portion of the plant is grafted to a root of another variety, which isn't a problem if the root is a hardy *Rosa multiflora*. But most of our roses are imported from the U.S., where many are grafted onto a variety called 'Dr. Huey'. Unfortunately, the good doctor often doesn't last through a Sudbury or even a Mississauga winter. So ask what the graft is, and if no one can tell you, go somewhere else. *Caveat emptor* rules. Roses raised in Canada are a better bet, and roses grown on their own roots are the best, but even hardy Explorer or Parkwood roses (see "Canadian originals," later in this chapter) are often grafted because it's quicker for a grower to grow a nice bushy plant on a grafted root than to root a cutting. It's not the grafting, but the plant used for the graft, that counts.

✔ There are some rules to rose care. Proper planting, with the bud union (or graft) at the right depth, is crucial (see "Planting Roses," later in this chapter). Pruning is easier than you think, but it's important, too. Same thing is true for fertilizing. It's a fact that some roses require more care than your typical landscape plant, so also be prepared to deal with common maladies.

Kinds of Roses

You can choose from literally thousands of kinds of roses, short to tall plants, with big to little flowers, with fragrance or nearly scentless — you name it. But most of the roses found in garden and home centres, and available by mail-order, are "modern" roses, which means they're one of the following: hybrid tea, floribunda, grandiflora, climber, or miniature. Many more kinds of roses are available (see the section "Old garden roses" in this chapter), but this is a good place to start.

The entire Northern Hemisphere came equipped with several hundred species of roses, some of them dating back to the time the dinosaurs disappeared from this Earth. In recent centuries, growers have selected, crossed, and recrossed those species to form numerous types, or classes, of roses. If you aspire to become a rabid rose hobbyist, you need to learn about polyanthas and noisettes and other historical strains; but if you just want to grow some roses, jump right into the following pool of varieties in this section.

Trying out hybrid teas

The blossoms of *hybrid tea roses* look like the roses that come from a florist, yet usually smell much better. The plants are upright and rather angular, and their distinctive flowers and buds on long stems have come to typify what a rose is for most people. The hybrid tea is the latest development in the history of the rose and is by far the most popular rose today. The big plus of hybrid teas is that they're ever-blooming, meaning they bloom all summer. (But that's a bit optimistic. Though some varieties come close to being in bloom all season, most bloom in waves every six weeks or so beginning in spring and peaking again in fall.) The minus is that most are less hardy than other types of roses and require considerable care to win a blue ribbon at the rose show or look like they belong in the florist's window.

Hybrid teas look good as specimen shrubs in mixed flower beds, or grouped in a special rose bed. The following cultivars are recommended by The Canadian Rose Society.

- ✔ **'Ingrid Bergman'.** Large, bright red velvety blooms. Zone 7.
- ✔ **'Double Delight'.** White blushed with red and very fragrant. Zone 3.
- ✔ **'Garden Party'.** Ivory with tinges of pink and yellow. Mild fragrance. Zone 5.
- ✔ **'Olympiad'.** Velvety red, perfect, lightly scented blossoms. Zone 5.
- ✔ **'Chicago Peace'.** Ivory blushed with pink and yellow. Pink darkens as flower opens. Zone 4.
- ✔ **'Pascali'.** White high-centred bloosoms, lightly fragrant. Zone 2.
- ✔ **'Tiffany'.** Soft pink, strongly scented. Zone 5.
- ✔ **'Fragrant Cloud'.** Coral-orange, high centred, intoxicating citrus fragrance Zone 7.

Sub-zero roses

These long-stemmed, high-centred roses that resemble hybrid teas were developed by Dr. Walter D. Brownell in the northern U.S. in the 1930s and they're still coveted today. Look for them in mail-order catalogues. Hardy to Zone 5. Protect in colder areas by mounding with earth and covering with snow.

- ✔ **'Arctic Flame'.** Fragrant, 13-centimetre (5 inch) fiery red blooms that open from high, pointed buds. Long stemmed.
- ✔ **'Carlotte Brownell'.** Yellow buds open to blush-pink flowers. Moderately long stems.
- ✔ **'Curly Pink'.** Long-pointed rosy red buds open to outward curled deep-rose flowers. Heavy bloomer. Stems can be 45 centimetres (18 inches) long. Bush 90 centimetres (3 feet) tall.

Fun with floribundas

Floribunda roses, which are crosses of the cluster-flowered *polyantha roses* with hybrid teas, were developed in an attempt to bring larger flowers and *repeat bloom* (bloom early in the season, stop, and then bloom again later) to winter-hardy roses. Roses in the floribunda class have blossoms shaped like those of hybrid teas, but the flowers are usually smaller and often are grouped in loose clusters. Yet floribundas are comparatively rugged and make great specimen shrubs or hedges.

All the following are fantastic floribundas. Those with superior fragrance are noted.

- ✔ **'Trumpeter'.** Orange. Zone 7.
- ✔ **'Europeana'.** Deep red. Zone 2.
- ✔ **'Iceberg'.** Pure white. Zone 2.
- ✔ **'Sea Pearl'.** Light pink petals, reverse apricot yellow. Zone 2.
- ✔ **'Sexy Rexy'.** Light pink. Zone 2.
- ✔ **'Lavaglow'.** Burgundy red. Zone 5.
- ✔ **'Tabris'.** Pink blend. Zone 5.
- ✔ **'Sunsprite'.** Dark yellow. Zone 2.

The experts' choice

Here are The Canadian Rose Society's 10 all-time favourite roses, in order of preference:

- ✔ **'Sexy Rexy',** floribunda. Zone 2.
- ✔ **'Tropicana' (also known as 'Super Star'),** hybrid tea. Zone 5.
- ✔ **'Chicago Peace',** hybrid tea. Zone 4.
- ✔ **'Graham Thomas',** Austin rose. Zone 5.
- ✔ **'Bonica',** shrub rose. Zone 5.
- ✔ **'Peaudouce' (also 'Elina'),** hybrid tea. Zone 5.
- ✔ **'The Fairy',** polyantha. Zone 3.
- ✔ **'Mister Lincoln',** hybrid tea. Zone 5.
- ✔ **'Tiffany',** hybrid tea. Pink, strong fragrance. Zone 5.
- ✔ **'Folklore',** hybrid tea. Zone 5.

Hail to the queen

The class called *grandiflora* was invented to describe the stately, clear pink 'Queen Elizabeth', which came about as a cross between a pink hybrid tea and a red floribunda. The flowers have the size and form of hybrid teas but are more freely produced, singly or in clusters, on taller, exceptionally vigorous plants. Subsequent breeding efforts to expand the grandiflora class have yet to produce roses as fine as the queen herself, with the possible exception of 'Gold Medal', a colossal yellow rose.

Additional top-rated grandifloras include:

- ✔ **'Shining Hour'.** Bright yellow. Zone 5.
- ✔ **'Love'.** Petals are bright red on top, silver beneath. Zone 5.
- ✔ **'Mt. Hood'.** White. Zone 5.
- ✔ **'Just Joey'.** Orange blend. Zone 5.
- ✔ **'Solitude'.** Brilliant orange-yellow. Zone 5.
- ✔ **'Tournament of Roses'.** Two-toned pink. Zone 2.

Climbing high with roses

Climbing roses are very long-branched roses that you can tie on to (or weave into) a support structure so the roses look as though they're climbing. Climbing roses can be old-fashioned roses, hybrids, or chance variants of hybrid teas. The supporting structure can be anything from a chain-link fence to a fancy iron archway. Tie climbing roses gently with pieces of stretchy cloth or old pantyhose.

Some great climbers are

- ✔ **'Alchymist'.** Yellow-apricot, very double. Zone 4 with winter protection.
- ✔ **'New Dawn'.** Pale, creamy pink, double. Zone 4.
- ✔ **'Mrs. John McNabb'.** White, pink at the centre. Very double. Zone 2.

"Honey, I shrunk the roses!"

Miniature roses have small leaves, short stems, and small flowers; they usually grow less than 60 centimetres (2 feet) tall. Miniatures fit easily into small beds and make great edging plants. Awesome in containers. You'd think these little beauties would be tender, but they're surprisingly hardy, although hardiness for all varieties isn't established yet. We'd try them to Zone 3, but provide some winter protection — small plants also have small roots, and they grow close to the surface.

- **'Glowing Amber'.** Velvet red inside petals, deep yellow outside. 38 to 45 cm (15 to 18 inches)
- **'Ellamae'.** Rich apricot, all-season bloom. (46 to 60 cm, 18 to 24 inches)
- **'Sweet Chariot'.** Clusters of lavender, lilac, and purple nearly continuous blooms. (46 cm, 18 inches)
- **'Cupcake'.** Frosted clear pink. (30 to 40 cm, 12 to16 inches)
- **'Opening Act'.** Single, dark red flowers, yellow stamens. (46 cm, 18 inches)
- **'Jeanne Lajoie'.** All-season two-tone pink blooms on 'tall' miniature that can be used as a climber. (1.8 to 2.4 m, 6 to 8 feet)

When a rose is a tree

Another fun trick rosarians have played on the hapless rose is turning it into a tree. These trees are called *standards,* and you can buy almost any kind of popular rose this way. Imagine a regular rose, but on stilts. Standards cost more because it takes more time and effort to create one, but they're worth it. The secret? Growers graft desired roses on top of a tall trunk. We like standards because they raise the flowers to nose height.

Shrub roses

We can't think of any reason at all to confine roses to the rose garden. While growing roses for their charm alone has many rewards, hundreds of kinds of roses serve as colourful landscape shrubs, ground covers, and vines. Shrub roses didn't just evolve; growers have hybridized them by crossing modern and old roses. They combine some of the best traits of the toughest roses with the most beautiful. Ideal features of shrub roses are:

- Profuse and nearly continuous bloom, plus fragrance
- Pest and disease resistance
- Cold hardiness in most regions
- Minimal pruning needed
- Attractive plant shape
- Good fruit, or hips, for winter interest

David Austin or English roses

David Austin (or *English*) *roses,* created by rose breeder David Austin, were the first to mix the blossom shapes and scents of almost-forgotten old garden roses with the disease resistance and ever-blooming qualities of newer types. More than 60 varieties are currently available in Canada. Most are strongly scented. Varieties differ regarding plant size and hardiness, but most are reliably cold-tolerant through Zone 5 (some, such as 'Heritage', are hardy to Zone 4b), but a garden's microclimate seems to have a big influence on their survival through winter. Here are some of our choices, but we suggest you look in Appendix B for a rose catalogue, obtain it, slaver over its contents, and order a rose appropriate for your garden's conditions.

- ✔ **'Gertrude Jekyll'.** Strongly fragrant shell-pink blossoms. (1.2 by 1.2 metres, 4 by 4 feet)

- ✔ **'Glamis Castle'.** White, deeply cupped, myrrh scented flowers. Free bloomer. (90 centimetres by 90 centimetres, 3 by 3 feet)

- ✔ **'Golden Celebration'.** Pinkish buds open to shockingly fragrant large golden-yellow blossoms on a plant that likes to sprawl. (1.2 metres by 1.2 metres, 4 by 4 feet)

- ✔ **'The Prince'.** Rich crimson aging to royal purple. Deep fragrance. (90 centimetres by 90 centimetres, 3 by 3 feet)

- ✔ **'Heritage'.** Extremely well-behaved pink rose with a citrus scent; perfect as a specimen shrub in a mixed border. Bushy, repeat bloomer. Slightly more hardy than most Austin roses. (1.2 by 1.2 metres, 4 by 4 feet).

- ✔ **'Tradescant'.** Velvety wine-crimson with rich old-rose scent; slender and arching growth. (60 centimetres by 75 centimetres, 2 by 2½ feet). In warm areas, it could grow tall enough to be used as a climber.

Ground-cover roses

Ground-cover roses produce long, wide spreading canes, but grow no higher than about 61 centimetres (2 feet). They make good covers for slopes. Plant 1.2 or 1.5 metres (4 or 5 feet) apart. Use them in containers where they can spill over the sides, or plant them wherever you'd like to have a trespass-preventing barrier. All are vigorous, cold hardy (many to Zone 2), and produce many flowers; they grow 30 to 45 centimetres (12 to 18 inches) high with a slightly wider spread.

Here are eight of the best ground-cover roses:

- ✔ **'Flower Carpet' series.** Rose pink, apple-blossom pink, and white blossoms on plants hardy to Zone 2 with winter protection. (60 centimetres, 2 feet)

- ✔ **'Pavement' series.** An unfortunate name for a handful of handsome and hardy (to Zone 2) plants with semi-double flowers. Dark pink, scarlet, white and pale pink. (60 centimetres by 90 to 120 centimetres, 2 feet by 3 to 4 feet)

- ✔ **'The Fairy'.** Cluster of small pale pink flowers from July to hard frost. Zone 4. (60 by 120 centimetres, 2 feet by 4 feet)

- ✔ **'Young Cale'.** Eye-catching vermilion-orange blooms on a low, arching bush 45 centimetres (18 inches) tall. Also good in hanging baskets.

- ✔ **'Red Meidiland'.** Clusters of red-cupped flowers with a white centre. Repeat bloomer. Zone 4 to 5. (60 by 120 centimetres, 2 by 4 feet)

- ✔ **'Sea Foam'.** Creamy white clusters of bloom on a plant 60 to 90 centimetres by 1.5 to 1.8 metres (2 to 3 feet by 5 to 6 feet).

- ✔ **'Bonica'.** Delicate pink double flowers with deeper pink centres. Bright orange fall hips. (90 to 120 centimetres by 1.2 to 1.8 metres, 3 to 4 feet by 4 to 6 feet)

Patio roses

The Brits created the *patio* classification for roses taller than miniatures but shorter than floribundas, with flowers larger than the miniatures but smaller than the floribundas. Got that? All you have to remember is that they're great for edging, hedging, planting around larger bare-legged roses and, yes, for patio pots. Hardy to Zone 5. Protect containers or store in a cool garage for winter in climates below Zone 7. Some to look for:

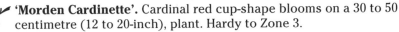

- ✔ **'Heaven Scent Pink'.** All-summer soft-pink blooms. (Upright plant 40 by 30 centimetres, 16 by 12 inches)

- ✔ **'Morden Cardinette'.** Cardinal red cup-shape blooms on a 30 to 50 centimetre (12 to 20-inch), plant. Hardy to Zone 3.

- ✔ **'Gourmet Popcorn'.** White flowers with yellow centres smother the ever-blooming plant. Remove hips for continuous bloom (40 by 40 centimetres, 16 by 16 inches)

Spinosissima hybrids

If you like simple roses with single to double rows of petals and pronounced fragrance, these are for you. (They're also called *Pimpinellifolia hybrids,* and the parent species is commonly known as the *Scotch briar rose,* or *Burnet rose.*) They're tough, thorny, and reliable, and grow almost anywhere, as befits a species whose natural habitat is the windswept seashore.

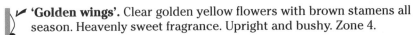

- ✔ **'Golden wings'.** Clear golden yellow flowers with brown stamens all season. Heavenly sweet fragrance. Upright and bushy. Zone 4.

- ✔ **'Prairie Maid'.** Double cream flowers bloom intermittently. (1.2 by 1.2 metres, 4 by 4 feet). Zone 2.

- ✔ **'Stanwell Perpetual'.** Double, quartered blush pink flowers all season. Prickly arching shrub about 1.2 by 1.2 metres, 4 by 4 feet. Zone 3.

Canadian originals

If you were to ask our personal opinion, we'd suggest you eschew hybrid teas or any rose that demands an undue amount of care and grow only the Explorer or the Parkland roses. Of course, not all rose fanciers agree, so we leave the decision to you. But by all means, try at least one of these hardy and beautiful roses, bred in Canada for Canadian conditions but known around the world for their hardiness and disease resistance. Most grow to 1 to 1.5 metres (3 to 5 feet), and many can be trained as climbers.

Explorer roses

The breeding program started in the 1960s at Agricultural Canada's Ottawa Experimental Farm (later transferred to the station at L'Assomption, Quebec) and concentrated on developing plants with long or continuous bloom and resistance to black spot and mildew. Many are named for the explorers of Canada, and there are now dozens to choose some; here's a handful of favourites.

- **'Captain Samuel Holland'.** Medium red, fragrant, trailing (train as climber). Zone 3.
- **'Champlain'.** Velvety deep red blooms that continue to hard frost. Low bush. Zone 3 to 4.
- **'Frontenac'.** Deep-pink shrub. Zone 3.
- **'David Thompson'.** Red, fragrant, climber. Zone 3.
- **'Henry Hudson'.** Waves of snowy white flowers, semi-dwarf. Zone 2.
- **'John Davis'.** Clear vibrant pink. Sprawling bush good as a climber. Zone 2.

Morden series

These were developed at the Morden Research Station in Manitoba starting in the 1940s for the prairies and similar climates. They're not as resistant to black spot or mildew as the Explorers, but spring back with vigorous growth after winter die-back and are free bloomers.

- **'Morden Amorette'.** Continual carmine blooms, shrub. Zone 3.
- **'Morden Blush'.** Ivory with blush pink centre, sometimes semi-quartered. Long bloom, low bush. Zone 2.
- **'Morden Fireglow'.** Flaming orange-red. huge blooms. Repeats. Good resistance to mildew and black spot. Zone 3.
- **'Prairie Dawn'.** Pink, shrub. Zone 3.
- **'Cuthbert Grant'.** Semi-double deep red flowers resembling a hybrid tea, all season. Low bush. Zone 3.

Hybrid musk roses

Hybrid musk roses are large, 1.8 to 2.4 metre (6- to 8-foot) nearly ever-blooming shrubs or climbers. They descend in large measure from the musk rose, *Rosa moschata.* Flowers are typically pink, and many produce bright orange hips in the fall. Compared to most roses, hybrid musk roses grow well in light shade. Hardy to Zone 6, Zone 5 with winter protection.

Some of the best varieties are

- **'Buff Beauty'.** Light apricot
- **'Ballerina'.** Pink and white single bloom
- **'Mozart'.** Deep pink with white eye.
- **'Penelope'.** Shell pink
- **'Robin Hood'.** Cherry red

Old garden roses

When we talk about an *old garden rose*, we usually mean old in the sense that the rose was popular among Victorians. And some types, such as the *centifolias,* have been grown for centuries. The plants you buy are, of course, only a couple of years old, same as any rose you purchase. Here are a few old roses:

- **Alba.** All descended from *Rosa alba,* the White Rose of York, and made famous during England's 15th-century War of the Roses. They make tall, vigorous, and thorny plants; flowers are fragrant and usually pale-coloured. Some have autumn colour. Blooms once per season. Varieties include 'Alba Semiplena', 'Great Maiden's Blush', and 'Königin von Dänemark'. Zone 3.

- **Bourbon.** Tall, vigorous plants. Blooms more than once per season. The first Bourbons in the early 1800s were hybrids of *R. chinensis and R. damascena* 'Semperflorens'. Many forms evolved, shrubs to climbers, and most were very fragrant. One of our favourites is the pink-flowered shrub/climber 'Souvenir de la Malmaison'. Also consider the red and fragrant 'Madame Isaac Pereire'. Zone 5.

- **Centifolia.** Favored by Dutch painters of the 1700s, all are varieties of *Rosa centifolia.* All have flowers with so many thin, overlapping petals that early on they were compared to a head of cabbage (thus the name "cabbage rose"). Centifolias have arching, thorny stems. Fragrant flowers come in spring only. Pink 'Rose des Peintres' is typical. Zone 4.

- **China.** Descendents of *R. chinensis,* these are the roses that came back to Europe from China via the tea trade in the early 1800s. Their capacity to bloom more than once in spring quickly created a sensation, and the genes of these plants helped create most modern roses. The originals are delicate plants with lots of twiggy growth. Zone 7.

✔ **Damask**. These roses descend from *R. damascena,* the rose of the perfume industry. Damask roses have thorny, arching stems. Flowers are usually pink and very fragrant. Most bloom only once per season. One variety, *R. d.* 'Semperflorens' (also known as the 'Rose of Castile') blooms twice. Zone 4.

✔ **Gallica**. Many varieties of *R. gallica* exist. They were grown by the Persians in 12 BC and by Empress Josephine at Malmaison. Plants are mostly a compact, 90 to 120 centimetres (3 to 4 feet high) with arching stems. Fragrant roses come in clusters once per season. Varieties include *R. g. officinalis* and the 'Apothecary Rose'. Zone 4.

✔ **Hybrid perpetual**. Just prior to the advent of the modern roses in the early 20th century, these were the garden rose to have. Oversize 2.4 metre (8-foot) plants produce huge and often strongly fragrant flowers, some as large as 18 centimetres (7 inches) in diameter. Cold hardy through Zone 4 with protection; plant deeply.

✔ **Moss**. Roses with moss-like fur over their flower stems and buds are called moss roses. Two species of roses produce moss roses: *R. centifolia* (softer moss) and *R. damascena* (stiffer moss). Flowers are white, pink, or red and often very fragrant. Some bloom once per season; some varieties repeat bloom. 'Chapeau de Napoleon', or crested moss (pink) is typical. Red 'Henri Martin' blooms more than once a season. Zone 4.

✔ **Portland**. These small shrubs are also known as Damask perpetuals. They were among the first hybrids to combine the new China roses with the old European types, in this case *R. damascena* 'Semperflorens'. Fragrant flowers are typically pink. The original variety from about 1800, 'Duchess of Portland', had bright scarlet flowers. Also consider bright pink 'Jacques Cartier'. Zone 4.

Here are The Canadian Rose Society's three favourite old roses, which means they were grown before 1900.

✔ *R. centifolia* 'Fantin-Latour'

✔ *R. damask* 'Mme Hardy'

✔ *R. gallica* 'Rosa Mundi'

Rugosa roses

These roses are all descendants of *Rosa rugosa,* a species of roses noted for its hardiness to cold and sea spray. The deeply quilted pattern in their leaves is also distinctive. Though the native species blooms only once, in spring, these hybrids will bloom a second time. Fragrance is light, but at best spicy. Most have gold or burgundy fall foliage. Plants produce large hips that are well suited to jams and jellies. Don't expect much top growth the first year — rugosas put down root systems first.

✔ **'Blanc Double de Coubert'.** Snow white, fragrant. (1.5 by 1.2 metres, 5 by 4 feet).

✔ **'Frau Dagmar Hastrup'.** Pointed pin buds open to single phallic-shape blooms with prominent golden stamens. Blooms till frost. (90 by 120 centimetres, 3 by 4 feet). Zone 2.

✔ **'Therese Bugnet'.** Old-fashioned pale pink flowers, June to frost. Very hardy. (1.8 metres or 6 feet tall). Zone 2.

As you jump into the world of roses, be sure to check in with The Canadian Rose Society. (Insiders refer to it as the CRS.) If you're searching for a particular rose, or for more information on any rose subject, write to CRS secretary at 10 Fairfax Cresc., Scarborough, ON M1L 1Z8. phone 416/ 757-8809; Fax 416/ 757-4796; `graber@netcom.ca`. Web site: `www.mirror.org/groups/crs/` Annual membership in the CRS, which includes *The Rose Annual*, published each September, and three issues of *The Rosarian*, costs $25.

Got a rose question? Get an answer quick via the American Rose Society's Consulting Rosarians Online. Find the one nearest you at `www.ars.org/cronlinr.html` on the Internet.

Landscaping with Roses

Roses in formal rows are a typical sight in public gardens, but the plants are a lot more versatile than that. You can use roses in many more ways in your own garden.

You can put several roses together in a special rose bed, plant a group of the same kind of rose in a line to create a hedge, or work your roses into a mixed bed or border with other flowers. In all three of these situations, you soon discover that roses are not beautiful all the time. Solve this problem by using companion plants that look great while your roses aren't blooming. In most climates, your roses look less than attractive three times during the year — winter, early spring, and midsummer.

✔ **For winter allure.** Keep the scene lively with small evergreen shrubs, ground cover junipers, or ornamental grasses.

✔ **For spring excitement.** Punctuate your rose planting with small clumps of daffodil, muscari, or crocus bulbs; or incorporate mounds of creeping phlox (or perennial candytuft) or an edging of pansies.

✔ **For midsummer colour and contrast.** Choose one or more of these as possible partners: perennials such as geraniums, blue salvias, dwarf daylilies, and dwarf lady's mantle *(Alchimella mollis);* and foliage herbs, like rosemary, thymes, artemisias, and lamb's ears *(Stachys).*

Buying Roses

The best selection of roses hits the garden centres in early spring, when plants are sold bare-root (see Figure 7-1) out of beds of sawdust or shavings, or with their roots tightly wrapped in plastic. Such roses look dead, but they're merely dormant, or sleeping. At other times of year, roses are available in containers; treat and plant them like you would any other shrub you bring home from the nursery. (See Chapter 13 for details on how to plant.)

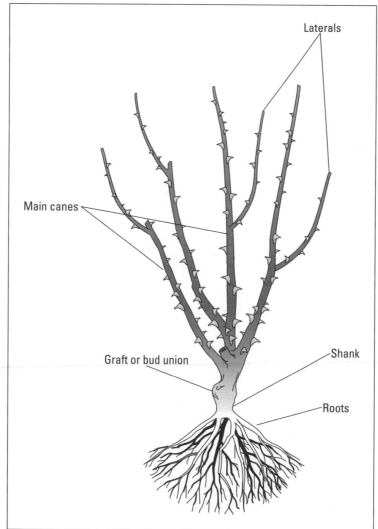

Figure 7-1:
When you buy a bare-root rose, familiarize yourself with its parts: bud union, shank, roots, main canes, and laterals.

Laterals

Main canes

Graft or bud union

Shank

Roots

What do you want your rose to do?

- **Formal beds and borders:** Floribundas; hybrid teas

- **Hedges:** Shrub roses; old roses; grandifloras

- **Perennial and shrub borders:** All classes, but especially floribundas or shrubs

- **Edging and low borders:** Miniatures; small shrub roses; patio roses

- **Formal rose garden:** Hybrid teas or sub-zero roses, floribundas, grandifloras, and others

- **Cutting:** All roses

- **In arrangements:** All classes, but especially hybrid teas for long stems

- **Fragrance:** Many new and old roses

- **Walls or trellises:** Tall climbers, hybrid musks

- **Low fences:** Short climbers

- **Low-care gardens:** Modern shrub roses

- **Long-flowering:** Hybrid teas; floribundas; grandifloras; shrub roses; most miniatures

If you want your roses to hit the ground running, spend the little extra money for top-grade plants, which have more stems and roots than less-expensive second-grade plants. Whether bare-root or in a container, a top-grade hybrid tea or grandiflora should have three fresh, moist (green, not shriveled) canes that are at least 18 inches (46 cm) long. Most roses are really two plants — the first plant is the hardy, vigorous root, and the second plant is the fancy rose grafted onto that root. The graft or bud union should look like a solid bulge just above the roots, and the plant should have at least three main canes reaching for the sky. Make sure the root is a hardy *Rosa multiflora,* especially if it's been imported form the U.S., as are many of the roses on the Canadian market.

Other tips for choosing healthy and strong rose plants:

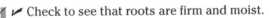

- Check to see that roots are firm and moist.

- Look for plants with canes that are 3 to 4 cms (½- to ¾-inch) thick, and ask if they're at least two years old.

- If buying roses in containers, choose a plant that has deep green leaves that are free of pests, and stems that show many flowers or flower buds.

The latest and greatest roses are usually patented. Having patents is fair because if the rose is successful, a royalty from the patent rewards the hybridizer who invested years of cross-breeding into its development. By the same token, you can look for nonpatented roses. The plants are just as healthy and vigorous, and you save a few dollars.

Planting Roses

Roses are sun-loving plants, so place yours where they can get at least six hours of sun each day, away from tree roots and roof overhangs. In cool, cloudy climates, roses grow best with all-day sun. On the prairies, afternoon shade gives them a much-needed break. Only one type of rose, the hybrid musks, are notable for shade tolerance and even these *prefer* six hours of sun a day.

Roses need sufficient air circulation to help their leaves dry quickly whenever they get wet — don't crowd the plants in close quarters. Also, make sure that you can reach your roses easily when the time comes to cut flowers, trim, and prune them.

Like most other plants, roses need good soil drainage. They prefer a near-neutral soil pH of 6.5 to 7.0 (see Chapter 11 for details on testing and adjusting your soil pH). They're not particularly picky about the kind of soil in which you plant them, but it never hurts to improve the soil excavated from the planting hole with generous amounts of well-rotted manure, compost and a smaller portion of damp peat moss.

To plant a bare-root rose, first soak the roots in a bucket of water for 12 hours or overnight. If you can't plant right way, bury the plant in moist earth in a slanted position till you can. Just before planting, cut back damaged roots and tops to healthy tissue. Dig a hole wide enough to allow roots to spread out. Spread the roots over a low cone of soil in the centre of the planting hole. (See Figure 7-2.) Backfill with the soil removed from the hole, firming it with your hands. Finally, water thoroughly to settle soil and eliminate air pockets.

In Zones 2 to 5, be sure the bud union or graft is set at least 10 centimetres (4 inches) below the surface of the earth. In Zone 6, it should be buried 5 centimetres (2 inches) below the surface. In Zones 7 and warmer, you can plant with the bud union at the surface.

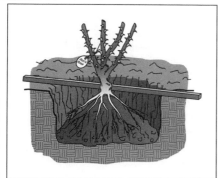

Figure 7-2:
Spread the bare roots over a cone of soil.

When planting container-grown roses, remove the pot, even if it's a fibre type. Tease the mass of roots apart to loosen them and allow them to spread somewhat in the planting hole, but try not to damage them. In most cases, you should plant at the depth they were growing, unless the bud union is showing above the soil. Gently spread roots and backfill as above. Roses grown on their own roots can be planted at the same depth they were growing before transplanting. (More Canadian growers are adopting this practice because it ensures hardier roses.)

The most important element in the life of a newly planted rose is water. It needs frequent watering to get established. But don't let water puddle in clay soil, or the roots will be kept too wet and the plant won't be able to get sufficient oxygen.

To plant a rose in tight clay or porous sand, dig a roomy planting hole about 45 x 60 centimetres (18 x 24 inches) square and put the excavated soil in a wheelbarrow. Mix the excavated soil with 25 percent peatmoss and 25 percent bagged compost, and a couple of handfuls of an organic fertilizer, such as composted manure. Partially refill the hole, spread out the roots of your rose, add some more soil, and water well. Then finish dumping in your enriched soil.

Non-grafted or own-root roses are a better bet if you live in Zones 2-5. When the part of the rose above the graft of a grafted rose dies, you've lost the rose you purchased. But when the top of an own-root rose dies, it can regrow from its roots the following spring. Many of the shrub and Canadian-bred roses mentioned in this chapter are own-root rose, although some are grafted on hardy roots to speed up the propagation process.

Roses planted in early spring in Zones 7 and warmer can suffer some damage if the graft union should fall prey to an unexpected frost and freeze hard. Cover the graft union with a mound of extra soil when you plant; then remove the extra soil after all danger of frost has passed.

Fertilizing and Watering

Although the secret to growing great roses is building the quality of the soil with compost and well-rotted manure, most roses need frequent applications of fertilizer to keep them growing vigorously and blooming repeatedly. To keep the process simple, go to the nursery and buy fertilizer labeled "Rose Food" and follow the directions on the package. Any granular or water-soluble fertilizer with a ratio of about 1-2-1 is fine. For example: 10-29-10, 5-10-8, 6-12-8. Don't fertilize newly planted roses until after their first bloom. The normal pattern is to fertilize established plants in early spring, then just before their

June blooming period, and a third time in July. Later applications aren't recommended so plants can harden their wood before winter. The exception is Zone 7 and up; plants in these warmer areas can be fertilized until two months before the first expected frost.

Watering is the other key to productive roses. Of course, all kinds of variables (your climate, soil, and much more) can affect how you water. Consider a few major guidelines:

- Roses need more water more often in hot weather than in cool weather.
- Even if it rains often where you live, rainfall alone may not provide enough moisture for your roses. Make sure each plant gets about 8 litres (2 quarts) of water a week.
- When you water, do it deeply enough to wet the entire root zone — to a depth of at least 18 inches (46 centimetres).
- If you want to be sure that the root zone is wet enough, dig into the soil. If the top 2 to 4 inches (5 to 10 centimetres) are dry, you probably need to water.
- To reduce disease problems, water the soil, not the leaves, by using soaker hoses or drip irrigation.
- Mulch to conserve moisture in the soil.

For more tips and ideas about watering, see Chapter 14.

High-powered rose fertilizer

If you want to grow prize-winning roses, take some advice from a rose guru friend of a friend of ours:

1. A week after plants leaf out, use a 20-20-20 soluble fertilizer at the rate of 1 tablespoon (15 mL) per gallon (3.8 litres) and 2 gallons (7.5 litres) per rose plant.

2. One week later, scatter 1/2 cup (125 mL) of Epsom salts around each plant and water it in.

3. The third week, apply fish emulsion, also at the rate of 1 tablespoon (15 mL) per gallon (3.8 litres) and 2 gallons (7.5 litres) per plant.

4. Week four, apply a liquid fertilizer with an approximate 16-4-2 ratio and which also includes a soil penetrant and chelated micronutrients, again at 1 tablespoon (15 mL) per gallon (3.8 litres), 2 (7.5 litres) gallons per plant.

5. Week five, start all over again.

We can't guarantee this regimen to work for every rose gardener, but our friend's friend has won hundreds of awards for his perfect roses.

The Mystery of Pruning

The following sounds hokey, but when it comes to knowing exactly how to prune a rose, you must discuss the matter with your plant. The first year with any rose is like a blind date — you don't know what the rose thinks of you; you don't know what you think of it. Here are some things to look for when you think that your rose is subliminally telling you that it wants to be pruned:

- **Long, skinny canes with a tuft of leaves at the end**: Carefully examine the canes for tiny, pinkish, pointed bumps called leaf buds. Find a good leaf bud that faces away from the center of the plant and is no more than halfway down the cane. Prune about 7 mm (¼ inch) above that bud.

- **Branches that come up out of the ground below the graft union**: Gently dig down to where these guys begin and cut them off with a sharp knife. These branches are shoots from the rootstock, usually an ultravigorous but unattractive type of rose. If you don't cut them out, they can take over the rose plant. (If your rose is not grafted, you might want to keep canes from below ground.)

- **Sickly looking branches where most of the leaves show black, circular freckles**: This combination of symptoms indicates a common disease called black spot (see Chapter 16). Prune off badly affected branches to keep black spot from spreading out of control.

- **Dead canes**: Prune them out.

Hybrid teas require somewhat more pruning to bring out their best performance. The rule is to cut back farther (leaving canes 30 to 45 centimetres, 12 to 18 inches) for fewer but larger flowers; cut back less (leave canes 2-3 feet, or 60-91 centimetres) for more but perhaps smaller flowers.

In early spring, cut back vigorous hybrid tea canes to the height of the other canes on the plant. Make cuts at a 45° angle, about 7 millimetres (¼ inch) above a bud. If you see brown tissue in the centre of the cane, cut back farther until the cane is creamy coloured and healthy all the way through. (Daub some white glue on the cut tips to prevent cane borers.) Remove suckers and any dead or crowded branches. All this effort keeps the centre of the plant open, meaning free of twiggy growth, and allows sunshine to reach all parts of the plant. See Figure 7-3.

You also need to prune off dead blossoms. If your rose blooms very heavily and then looks as if it's ready to die, prune the whole plant back by one-third, fertilize lightly, and water it well. Within two weeks you should see lots of new branches budding all over the plant, and within a month you should once again be smelling a rose.

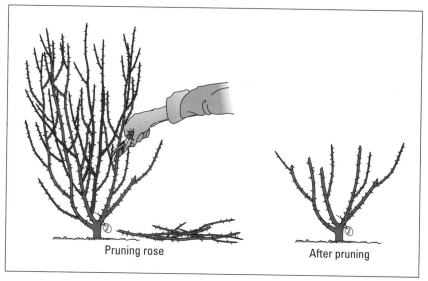

Pruning rose

After pruning

Other Rose Quirks

How perfect do you want your roses to be? That determines the extent of your pest- and disease-control program. We recommend a common sense approach. Live with a few bugs. But if they begin to wipe out your plants, take some steps to control the problems. However, use only products that have the least impact on the environment. See Chapter 16 for details on insecticides.

You can do a number of things to keep potential pest and disease problems to a minimum:

- ✔ **Grow healthy plants**. Feed, water, and prune on a regular basis.

- ✔ **Plant problem-free varieties**. As you shop, pay attention to the descriptions that cite resistance to diseases, especially black spot.

- ✔ **Encourage beneficial insects**. The good guys include lady beetles, green lacewings, and parasitic nematodes.

- ✔ **Keep your garden clean**. Doing so reduces the number of hiding places for pests and diseases.

- ✔ **Apply a dormant spray**. A combination spray (horticultural oil and fungicide) smothers insect eggs and kills disease organisms. The best time to apply is right after you prune in early spring.

> ✔ **Spray with a fungicide every 10 days to 2 weeks** from the time new shoots are 10 to 15 centimetres (4 to 6 inches) long until frost. Use materials formulated for black spot and mildew, such as Funginex with benomyl or folpet (Phaltan).

Be prepared for the inevitable. No rose is totally immune to insects that typically prey on them: Aphids, cucumber beetles, Japanese beetles, June beetles, caterpillars, rose midges, rose chafers, rose stem borers, spider mites, and thrips. Typical diseases are black spot, mildew, and rust. For descriptions and controls about these pests and diseases, see Chapter 16.

Helping Roses Survive Winter

Roses are damaged most from freezing and then thawing and then freezing all over again. Too much of this, and the plant won't survive even what seems to be a mild winter. It's better for them to freeze and stay that way over winter.

In general, you should cut canes back when the plant seems to be nodding off into dormancy, and then protect the leaf buds on the bottom of each cane with a mulch of some kind. Here are The Canadian Rose Society's tips for winter protection of roses in Canada.

✔ In Zones 2-4, cut canes back in early October to about 60 centimetres (30 inches) so that they won't whip about in the wind. Pull away dead leaves from the bed. When the ground is partially frozen, place a collar of cardboard or plastic around the bush and fill with dry soil and peat moss to a depth of 40 to 50 centimetres (16 to 20 inches). Water the plant well, cover with straw, wood chips, or similar material. This will make the bushes freeze and keep them frozen till the spring thaw, even in areas where the chinooks blow.

✔ In Zones 5 and 6, cut canes back to about 1 metre (40 inches). Remove dead leaves and plant material from bed. Add new soil around the plant to a depth of about 30 centimetres (1 foot). Once the ground is frozen, put leaves or branches over the soil for further protection.

✔ In Zones 7 to 9, plants require almost no protection. Again, cut canes back to 1 to 1.2 metres (3 to 4 feet) to prevent wind damage, and remove debris from bed. If you have very tender cultivars, mound extra soil around the base of the plants to about 30 centimetres (1 foot) high.

You know you've chosen good roses for your climate and are giving them suitable care if the plants get bigger and stronger with each passing year. But a certain amount of trial and error exists in growing roses. If at first any rose does not succeed, you can always try again.

Part III
Sculpting with Plants

The 5th Wave   By Rich Tennant

"Something's about to die in your cactus container."

In this part . . .

We live in a three-dimensional world, so naturally you want your garden to be interesting and functional in all dimensions. For example, give your garden a sense of perspective — and a feeling of privacy — by using trees, shrubs, and hedges. Or go horizontal with lawn and ground covers, which also are the best way to protect and enhance your garden's soil. And get out of the rut of looking at eye-level: Use vines to put your garden up over your head!

This part brings your garden into fine perspective while also dealing with such pragmatic matters as afternoon shade and erosion control. You'll find our favourite trees, flowering shrubs, grasses, ground covers, and vines here, so you can do a little sculpting of your own.

Chapter 8

Trees and Shrubs

· ·

In This Chapter

▶ Seeing what a tree can do

▶ Choosing the right tree for you

▶ Looking at our favourite trees

▶ Getting close to shrubs

▶ Digging into our favourite shrubs

· ·

*T*rees and shrubs are the most fundamental types of plants. They may not be the most exciting or colourful in your garden (although they can well be), but they're the ones you typically count on the most — for shade, scale, background planting, property dividing, screening, and all sorts of other landscape functions (not to mention tree houses). Think of trees and shrubs as the skeleton of the landscape — the bones that you build beauty around by using other plants like flowering annuals and perennials. Take a look at how Mother Nature uses trees and shrubs: Her plantings are layered, with trees and shrubs blended in a backdrop for wildflowers and ground covers. This is what you can aspire to in your gardens.

But don't limit trees and shrubs to workhorse-duty. As you discover in this chapter, these plants can add beauty and interest to any garden.

What Trees Can Do for You

No home or neighbourhood should be without trees. Trees bring a home into scale with the surrounding landscape and give a neighbourhood a sense of place. Deciduous or evergreen, trees provide protection from the elements by buffering strong winds and blocking hot summer sun. In our crowded world, trees can also provide privacy by screening you from neighbours or unpleasant views. And planting trees can increase your property value — studies have shown that homes with large trees usually sell for more money than similar properties without trees.

However, more than anything else, trees offer beauty: beauty in flowers held high among the branches, or simply beauty in their leafy green canopy. Beauty in colourful berries and seed pods dangling among the limbs. Beauty in dazzling hues created by autumn leaves. Even beauty in winter, when the texture of their bark and the structure of their branches add strength and permanence to the landscape. Beauty in diversity, too — after all, without trees, where can the birds perch or the squirrels dash?

In our fast-paced world of concrete, asphalt and hazy urban skies, trees are the great equalizers. They shade our streets and cool our cities and neighbourhoods, they absorb dust and air pollution, and their roots hold the soil in place and prevent erosion.

Lower heating and cooling expenses

Providing cooling shade is one of a tree's greatest assets, especially in regions where summers are long, hot, and dry. If you plant *deciduous* trees (trees that drop all their leaves and are leafless for a period of time) on the warmest side of your house (usually the southwest or west side, but the east side can also be warm), the shade they provide keeps your house cooler in summer and reduces your air-conditioning expenses. The best shade trees spread wide and tall enough to shade a one- or two-storey home.

Of course, you don't have to worry about deciduous trees cooling your home in winter: Trees lose their leaves (right when you need them to) so the warm sun can shine through, thus reducing heating costs.

You can save energy by planting trees as windbreaks. Planted close together and at right angles to prevailing winds, upright, dense-growing trees can reduce the chilling effects of winter winds and lower heating bills. (Energy conservation aside, planting trees is just a good way to create a comfortable and inviting place in the garden.)

Make you look marvelous

After you decide on the kind of tree you need in terms of size, shape, and adaptation, you have a wealth of ornamental characteristics to choose from. Consider the following points.

  ✔ **Seasonal colour.** Most flowering trees, including fruit trees, bloom on bare branches in early spring. Others, such as the linden (with fragrant, if inconspicuous, flowers) bloom in early summer or even midsummer, like the catalpa.

We are blessed in Canada that we have such a wealth of trees to choose from for exciting fall colour. The sugar maple is the obvious choice, but many trees and shrubs take on various hues of red, pink, orange, yellow, and gold. They offer a whole palette of colours to choose from.

✓ **Colourful fruit.** Trees such as crab apples and hawthorns follow their blooms with colourful fruit, which can (if the birds don't eat it) hang on the tree into winter after the leaves have fallen.

Don't overlook trees that produce edible fruit when you're making your choices. Many fruit and nut trees are exceptional ornamentals and have the added bonus of bringing food to the table.

✓ **Attractive bark.** The white bark of birch trees is familiar to most people, but many other trees have handsome peeling or colourful bark.

Choosing the Right Tree

People who know trees like to say there is no perfect tree, and they're right. You have so many trees to choose from that many of them can probably do the job for you. But as with people, every tree's personality has its good and bad aspects. Before you plant one, you need to learn everything you can about it, both the good and the bad. Most trees get big and live a long time (possibly longer than you), so if you make a mistake and plant the wrong one in the wrong place, it may be very costly to remove or replace. Removing it may even be dangerous to people and property. Figure 8-1 shows the general shapes trees grow in.

Get to know a tree before you commit to it.

✓ How fast does it grow?

✓ How tall and wide will it get?

✓ Is it adapted to your climate and the sun, soil, and water conditions at the proposed planting site?

✓ Does it have any common problems — invasive roots, weak limbs, insects, diseases?

✓ Does it need any special maintenance, such as pruning?

✓ How does the shape of the tree fit into your overall landscape?

✓ How messy is it? Does it drop excessive amounts of flowers, fruits, or leaves?

A local nursery is a good place to find out how a tree performs in your area; so are city or provincial parks departments. Extension offices can help you with information about trees; and parks and university campuses often have fine plantings to study. Botanical gardens and arboretums are especially good places to observe a wide variety of trees.

Columnar

Cone

Fastigate

Globe

Horizontal Spread

Open Irregular

Figure 8-1:
Choose a
shape that
suits your
landscaping
needs.

Vase

Weeping

Informal Globe

Contact your municipal planning or parks department before planting trees on property that belongs to the city, such as the boulevard beyond the sidewalk or, if you live in the 'burbs, the part of your lot nearest the road. You may need permission. The people there may have a list of suitable street trees — if they let you plant at all. If you plant something not on their list, they may make you remove it.

To help get trees planted in the public areas of your community or in forests damaged by fire or abuse, contact Global ReLeaf. For more information, write Tree Canada Foundation, 220 Laurier Ave., W., Ste. 500, Ottawa, ON K1P 5Z9; or call 613-567-5545. Visit the Web site at `www.amfor.org/`.

Don't Try This at Home

The following sections point out some things you should *not* do when planting a tree, for practical and aesthetic reasons. (See Chapter 13 for more about planting trees.)

- **Planting too close to buildings.** Even smaller trees should be planted at least 3 metres (10 feet) away from the side of a house or building. Larger trees should be even farther away. Otherwise, the trees don't have room to spread and develop their natural shape. Also, aggressive roots can damage the foundation; falling limbs can damage the house.

- **Planting a tree that's too big at maturity.** Some trees can get huge — more than 30 metres (100 feet) tall and almost as wide. These trees belong in parks and open spaces where they can spread out. But even smaller trees can be too big for a planting site, eventually crowding houses or shading an entire yard. For example, horse chestnut and weeping willow can overwhelm a small garden in only a few years. Choose a tree that, when mature, will be in scale with your house and won't crowd out the rest of your garden. See Figure 8-2 for an illustration of how large some trees get at maturity.

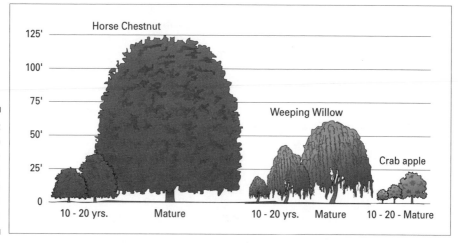

Figure 8-2: Be sure to consider the mature height of the tree you plant.

✔ **Planting trees where they will grow into power lines or utilities.** Pruning such trees is dangerous and costly and results in misshapen trees, and fallen limbs can cause power outages. Also, don't plant a big tree in a small yard. Not only will it look cramped, but branches overhanging the house and walkways can be hazardous.

✔ **Planting too close to paving.** Some trees are notorious for having shallow roots that, as they grow, buckle sidewalks and raise patios. Actually, almost any tree, especially larger species, will cause problems if planted too close to paving. Leave at least 1–1.2 metres (3 or 4 feet) between the trunk and the paving. If you live where trees require watering to supplement rainfall, apply water slowly, as a trickle from the hose and for long periods, so it can soak deeply into the soil. This practice encourages roots to grow deep and not near the surface.

✔ **Planting a messy tree in the wrong place.** All trees shed some leaves at one time or another, but certain species are messier than others. Don't plant trees that drop wet fruit or excessive flowers near patios or sidewalks. They not only make a mess (and more work for you) but can also make the surface slippery, causing a passerby to fall.

✔ **Planting too many fast-growing trees.** Fast-growing trees are valuable for providing quick shade, but they are often also weak-wooded and short-lived. Consider planting a mixture of slow- and fast-growing types and then removing the less desirable trees when the slower ones reach functional size.

Our Favourite Trees

We divided the following lists of trees into two main groups: *deciduous* and *evergreen*. Evergreen trees include both conifers, such as pine and fir, and broadleaf evergreens, such as the west-coast arbutus. To make your final choice, you need more information than we can provide here — see Appendix A for gardening books that discuss trees; or consult the experts at nurseries that specialize in trees (see Appendix B).

Unlike *deciduous* trees, *evergreens* retain their leaves or needles for more than one growing season. Which type of tree you want is your first decision. Then you have to make sure the tree you plant will survive year to year where you live, and that raises the question of hardiness zones.

To see what zone you live in, refer to Agriculture Canada's Hardiness Zones map in the colour section of this book. To learn more about your zone and how to best use zone information, see Chapter 2.

Crisp air, squirrels hunting for acorns, and the crunch of leaves underfoot . . . that's autumn! Here's our list of favorite deciduous trees.

Choosing a healthy tree at the nursery

The easiest way to have tree problems down the road is to purchase and plant one that's unhealthy to begin with. Here are some tips for buying a healthy tree:

✔ Avoid trees that have been in a nursery container for too long or are unhealthy and growing poorly — they'll probably be disappointing once in the ground.

✔ Examine the top of the root ball. Avoid specimens that have large, circling roots near the surface, a sign the tree has been in the container too long.

✔ Avoid trees that are the smallest or largest of a group. Select ones that are well proportioned from top to bottom.

✔ Select trees that can stand on their own without being tightly tied to a stake. (Tightly tied stakes can be like crutches, preventing a tree from developing a strong trunk).

✔ Ideally, pick a tree that has an evenly tapered trunk from bottom to top.

✔ Look for healthy, even-coloured foliage.

✔ Pick a tree that's free of insects and disease. (See Chapter 16 for more about common pests and diseases.)

✔ **Maple.** *Acer* spp. Of the more than 100 species of maples around the world, 13 are native to North America, 10 of them to Canada. And in our gardens we grow both native and introduced species, so there are plenty to choose from. We like them best for their autumn leaf colour, which is a splendid seasonal spectacle in eastern North America every year. The most coveted maple is the sugar maple, *A. saccharum,* Zone 4, from which you get maple syrup, as well as high-quality wood for things like furniture and cutting boards. (It's also the leaf on the Canadian flag.) At 12 metres (40 feet), 'Legacy' is a shorter cultivar than the native species, which can reach 20 metres (70 feet). Various cultivars of red maple, *A. rubrum,* Zone 4 to 5, also become brilliant red in fall; look for 'Red Sunset' or 'Red Embers'. Douglas maple, *A. glabrum,* Zone 5, is a shrubby, often multi-stemmed western variety useful in small gardens because of its size (up to 10 metres, 33 feet) and dark red fall colour. The tall silver maple, *A. saccharinum dasycarpum,* Zone 4, grows to 20 metres (70 feet) and has leaves with silver undersides that become yellow in fall. The Norway maple, *A. platanoides,* Zones 4 to 5, of which there are many cultivars, is a European tree introduced to Canada 200 years ago for use in urban landscaping. It's escaped to the wild and is now choking out native trees in ravines, floodplains, and woods in southern Ontario. It has many greedy roots near the surface and bombards lawns and gardens with its fruit keys, which quickly grow into thousands of seedling trees. In other words, it's not your best choice of tree. We'd avoid even the handsome 'Crimson King'. As for the Manitoba maple, *A. negundo*, Zone 2, also called box elder and ashleaf maple, it grows anywhere its seeds land, so why would you put it in your garden? We do concede that the cultivar 'Flamingo', which has white and pink leaf variegation, is less of a problem, but it's hardy only to Zone 5.

✔ **European white birch.** *Betula pendula.* Loved for its papery white bark, the European white birch has multiple trunks and yellow autumn colour. The tree is hardy to Zone 2, but is often grown in Zones 7 or 8 as well. Avoid planting it where summers are hot and dry, or where birch borers are prevalent. Call your provincial agriculture and food office or local nursery to find out about birch borers. Grey birch, *B populifolia,* native to the Maritimes, but with extended range, is similar. The native white birch, *B. papyrife,* is an excellent choice. It grows across Canada, doesn't have borer problems, and is very ornamental.

✔ **Redbud.** *Cercis canadensis,* the eastern redbud, has densely packed pink blooms growing along leafless branches in spring, and yellow fall foliage. It reaches 6 to 9 metres (20 to 30 feet) high and spreads almost as wide. Hardy to Zone 6. 'Alba' has white flowers; 'Forest Pansy' has maroon foliage. (Check with your nursery to be sure plants are northern-grown from northern seeds.)

✔ **Flowering dogwood.** *Cornus florida., C. alternifolia, C. Kousa.* The key attributes are the horizontally branching, deep-red autumn colour and large white or pink mid-spring flowers followed by bright-red fruit. These are fine small (6 to 9 metres, 20 to 30 feet) trees. Hardy to Zones 4 to 6, depending on variety. Flowering dogwood is not well adapted to hot, dry climates but often can grow successfully in partial shade. Pacific dogwood, *C. nutalli,* Zone 8 and B.C.'s provincial flower, has spectacular floral bracts and red berries, often appearing at the same time. Anthracnose and borers can be serious problems. Hybrids 'Rubra', 'Constellation', 'China Girl', and 'Stellar Pink' are less prone to anthracnose disease.

✔ **Hawthorn.** *Crataegus* spp. These small trees (most are 6 to 7.5 metres, or 20 to 25 feet high) offer a long season of colour: White, pink, or red flowers in mid-spring, bright-orange-to-red fruit in autumn and winter, and usually orange-to-red autumn leaf color. Hardiness varies by species, but many are hardy to Zone 4. 'Toba' (double deep-red-rose flowers) and 'Snowbird' (white flowers) were developed at the Morden Research Station in Manitoba and are hardy through Zone 3. Fireblight and rust can be a serious problem.

✔ **Russian olive.** *Elaeagnus angustifolia.* This tough, single- or multi-trunked tree has narrow, silvery leaves. Spring flowers are fragrant but not showy and develop into small, yellow fruit. Russian olives form an excellent hedge or screen in difficult, dry situations but can be weedy where summers are wet and positively invasive in natural areas. Grows 9 to 10.6 metres (30 to 35 feet). Hardy through Zone 2.

✔ **Tricolour beech**. *Fagus sylvatico* 'Roseo Marginata'. The beech is a large family of stately, slow-growing trees of great beauty, and this is our favourite member. An upright, oval-shaped tree with purple foliage edged in pink and white. It stands out in the garden. 15 metres (50 feet) at maturity. Zone 6.

✔ **Ash**. *Fraxinus* spp. These are mostly large, spreading-to-upright trees, with many reaching well over 15 metres (50 feet) high. They're good, fast-growing, tough shade trees that can thrive under a variety of conditions. Most grow throughout Zones 4 to 9. Many have excellent autumn colour. Though ash trees have many virtues, a variety of pests and problems, such as anthracnose disease and borers, plague them. Sometimes trees develop a dieback called ash yellows, probably caused by climate-induced stress. The best advice is to only plant named varieties, which in most every case are an improvement over unnamed, seedling trees.

✔ **Ginkgo**. *Ginkgo biloba*. The oldest tree in the world, they say: It's been dated back to the dinosaur era, when several genera and species grew. Only one variety is left; it has pretty, bright green fan-shaped leaves that turn yellow in fall, and a tapering form that almost becomes a point at the top. An herbal memory remedy is made from its seeds — incidentally, choose a male tree to plant; the seed coats on the female tree have a disagreeable smell. Zone 4.

✔ **Goldenchain tree**. *Laburnum anagyroides*. These are small trees reaching about 4 metres (13 feet), native to Europe and hardy here to Zone 6. Common cultivar is *waterii* 'Vossi'. Leaves grow in groups of three leaflets and yellow blooms hang in long pendulous clusters.

✔ **Magnolia**. *Magnolia* spp. Highly regarded trees that offer a spectacular display when in flower. Huge flowers sometimes more than 25 centimetres (10 inches) across bloom on bare branches in shades of white pink, purple, and yellow. Leaves are large and leathery. Trees grow 4.5 to 7.5 metres (15 to 25 feet) tall and are often multi-trunked. Easy to grow in sun or partial shade and relatively pest free, but they're shallow-rooted and should not be disturbed by cultivation. The saucer magnolia, *M. soulangiana,* has large cup-shaped flowers with white on the inside, purple outside. Zone 5. *M. acuminata* 'Yellow Bird' has pure yellow tulip-shaped flowers, Zone 5. The Little Girl hybrids are all erect, shrub-like plants 2 to 3.5 metres (6 to 12 feet) at maturity.

✔ **Flowering crab apple.** *Malus* spp. Crab apples differ from apples in that the fruit measures less than 5 centimetres (2 inches) in diameter. You have many species and varieties to choose from, ranging in tree size and shape, including weeping varieties Spring flowers come in white, pink, or red. Colourful red, orange, or yellow edible fruit often hang on the bare branches into winter. Most are hardy through at least Zone 4 (some varieties can be grown into Zones 3 and 2). Subject to severe diseases, including fireblight, powdery mildew, and scab (see Chapter 16). Ask for disease-resistant varieties. 'Dolgo' has white flowers and large red fruit great for making jelly. 'Profusion' has rose-pink blossoms, bronze leaves and red fruit. Columnar Siberia crab apple is an upright form about 1 metre (3 feet) wide with white flowers and small bright red fruit. Great for an alley.

✔ **Ornamental pear.** *Pyrus calleryana.* The best known and most widely planted of this group is 'Bradford', followed perhaps by 'Aristocrat'. These and all varieties have white flowers in early spring. Shiny green leaves turn bright orange, red to purple in fall. Height is 9 to 13.7 metres (35 to 45 feet). 'Bradford' is a good tree but has been overplanted and tends to split catastrophically. Other good varieties include 'Capital' (very narrow and upright), 'Earlyred', and 'Redspire'. All are hardy to Zones 5 to 6. 'Redspire' to Zone 4.

✔ **Mountain ash**. *Sorbus decora, S. americana.* Showy small trees with delicate pointed leaves on a central stalk and white flowers followed by clusters of shiny orange to red fruit in late summer. Fruit is an important source of food for local wildlife. Zones 2 to 5, depending on type.

✔ **Oaks.** *Quercus.* This is an extensive family of strong-wooded, long-lived trees, many of them very large and suitable for open areas only. Some have good autumn colour, and others have leaves that stay on the tree for the winter in a dried, papery form. The red oak, *Q. rubra*, Zone 3, has a spreading rounded form and grows to about 25 metres (85 feet); the green foliage turns brilliant red in fall. Pyramidal English oak, *Q. robur* 'Fastigiata', Zone 5, has a columnar habit and leaves that become crisp and copper coloured in fall and stay on the tree till spring. Oaks prefer well-drained acid soil in full sun, but pin oak tolerates wet soil.

And here are our favourite conifers. To be honest, this is such a large family of pines, junipers, spruces, firs, hemlocks, and cedars, it's nearly impossible to pick favourites. They make terrific windbreaks, and the sound of the breezes playing in their needlelike leaves is music to the ears. Most are large trees, but dwarf forms have been developed. Check with your nursery for those adapted to your climate.

✔ **Balsam fir**. *Abies balsam.* This 20-metre (70-foot) tree has dark green soft needles with a sweet, resinous aroma. It has a narrow, even triangular form, making it the most popular Christmas tree. It's native to northern Saskatchewan, Alberta, Ontario, and Quebec, and survives in central Labrador. Zone 2.

✔ **Bristlecone pine**. *Pinus aristus.* A slow-growing pine with an attractive irregular form. It has blue-green foliage with flecks of white resin. Grows to 6 metre (20 feet) and is tolerant of rocky, dry soil. Zone 2. An old-man of a tree that lives up to 5,000 years, so choose the right location for yours.

✔ **Norway spruce**. *Picea abies.* A great conifer for windbreaks because it's fast growing; 20 metres (70 feet). Zone 2.

✔ **Fat Albert spruce**. *Picea pungens glauca* 'Fat Albert'. Okay, you see a lot of it around, but it's a great little evergreen for small gardens. Dense, pyramidal shape, bluish foliage and at most 3 metres (10 feet) tall. Zone 3.

✔ **Colorado blue spruce**. *Picea pungens* var. *glauca*. This is one of the first evergreens people get to know by name. In fact, it's many selected variations of spruce with good blue colour. It's also hardy, with a dense conical form, and grows 20 metres (70 feet) tall. Looks wonderful in a group of conifers of varying shades of green. 'Hoopsi' is a more controlled variety that grows to 10 metres (33 feet). Both Zone 2.

✔ **Austrian pine**. *Pinus nigra*. This attractive evergreen with the slightly irregular form and longish needles has become almost a cliche, it's used so much on highway plantings. But that's because it tolerates a wide variety of soil conditions and exposures. It's just as forgiving in your garden, and looks good in groups of 3 or as a single specimen. Zone 4.

✔ **White pine**. *Pinus strobus*. Graceful and magnificent when full grown (about 30 metres, 100 feet). It has long, soft, blue-green needles. Zone 3.

✔ **Eastern larch or tamarack**. *Larix laricina*. Larch is the only deciduous conifer, which means it drops its needles in fall. They're tall, slender trees, with straight or sinuous trunks reaching to an almost pointed top. They grow in every province and territory in Canada. Blue-green needles become yellow in fall before dropping off; grows 15 metres (50 feet) tall. Zone 1 — survives right to the tree line just south of Inuvik.

All evergreen trees aren't conifers. It just seems that way in Canada because there are so few hardy broadleaf evergreens. British Columbia is the place to grow them.

✔ **Arbutus or Pacific madrone**. *Arbutus menziesii*. These lovely trees are restricted to a narrow belt on the east coast of Vancouver Island and the west coast of British Columbia's mainland. It has oval leaves, white urn-shaped flowers with a strong honey scent, and clusters of orange-red fruit. The peeling bark and reddish undersurface are additional features. Grows up to 20 metres (70 feet) tall; Zone 8.

✔ **Eucalyptus**. *Eucalyptus* species. This large group of fast-growing, mostly drought-tolerant plants are native to Australia. Most are valued in dry-summer and mild-winter climates; few can be grown in areas colder than Zone 8b. Beyond B.C.'s coastal areas, they're an iffy survivor, but here are three highly recommended by an acquaintance who lives in Delta, B.C. Jonama snow gum, *E. debeuzevillei*, sports mottled gray and white bark, snow-white young branches and steel-blue leaves. It grows to 7.5 metres (25 feet) — 2 metres (8 feet) in one season, and will survive an occasional light frost. Alpine cider gum, *E. archeri*, is a dwarf eucalyptus that grows to 4 metres (15 feet) but can be kept smaller by pruning. The bluish leaves — often cut and used in wreaths — have a pleasant minty fragrance when brushed, so it's great for planting beside a path. Alpine

snow gum, *E. niiphophila,* boasts "snake-skin" bark in bright grey, cream and green and silvery white leaves that grow on snow-white branches. It grows from 4.5 to 7.5 metres (15 to 25 feet) and is the second hardiest eucalyptus in Canada. All eucalyptus are shallow-rooted, so don't plant in a windy area.

✔ **Holly.** *Ilex* species. English holly, *I. Aquifolium,* is the holly we associate with Christmas, sporting shiny leaves and bright red berries that remain on the trees till late winter. Holly is commonly planted in southwestern B.C. where it grows to 15 metres (50 feet) and is occasionally naturalized. American holly, *I. opaca,* is similar, but its leaves are larger. Both are hardy to Zone 7.

Rub-a-Dub-Dub, What's a Shrub?

Both versatile and hardworking, shrubs are the backbone of the landscape. They tie the garden together, bringing unity to all the different elements, from tall trees to low-growing ground covers.

The term *shrub* covers a wide variety of plants. They can be deciduous or evergreen, and they provide a variety of ornamental qualities, from seasonal flowers to colourful fruit to dazzling autumn foliage colour. But equally important, shrubs offer diversity of foliage texture and colour, from bold and dramatic to soft and diminutive. As the backbone of the landscape, shrubs are always visible, whether or not they're in bloom. So you should always consider the foliage and form of the plant when selecting shrubs and deciding how to use them.

Technically, a *shrub* is a woody plant that branches from its base. But that's actually too simple a definition. Shrubs can range from very low-growing, spreading plants that are ideal ground covers (see Chapter 9) to tall, billowy plants that you can prune into multitrunked trees. In general, shrubs cover themselves with foliage from top to bottom. Try to pigeonhole all shrubs into an absolute size range, and you run into many exceptions. For our purposes, most shrubs range from 30.5 centimetres–4.5 metres (1–15 feet).

What Shrubs Can Do for You

Like trees, shrubs are large and long-lived plants, so it's essential to select ones that can thrive in your region and at your specific site. Consider the advice offered in Chapter 2 regarding climate and hardiness and also be mindful of soil types and quantity of light or shade.

So many shrubs are available that you are sure to find several that can thrive no matter what the condition of the soil is in your garden. However, if you make even modest improvements in your soil, such as improving the drainage of heavy soils or the moisture retention of sandy soils, adjusting pH, or increasing the fertility of poor soils, the number of shrubs that can grow well dramatically increases. You can read more about improving your soil in Chapter 11.

You can buy shrubs in containers, bare root, or balled-and-burlapped. The majority are sold in containers. Examine your choice carefully to be sure it's not damaged. Slide out the root ball — this is easy to do if the shrub is in a plastic pot. Look for young, white roots — these are essential for efficient uptake of water and nutrients. Older, darker roots function primarily to stabilize the plant. See the section on choosing container-grown trees and shrubs in Chapter 13 for more information.

Design considerations

Shrubs serve so many functions in gardens that categorizing them is useful. As you consider your garden design, use these following categories to understand how to best use shrubs.

- ✔ **Foundation plantings.** Traditionally, one of the most common uses of evergreen shrubs is to plant them around the base of a house to conceal the foundation and to soften the transition between the lawn and the building. This use of shrubs also gives the landscape winter appeal.

   However, using too many of one species of plant leads to monotony and an unnatural look. Try mixing groups of plants with different sizes and textures. And don't plant too closely to the house. Bring the plantings out some distance to gain a smoother transition and to give the shrubs more growing room.

- ✔ **Unity.** Repeating small groupings of plants in different parts of a landscape ties everything together and gives the yard a feeling of order and purpose. Similarly, shrubs serve well when planted among shorter-lived perennials in border plantings. Because shrubs are usually larger and more substantial, they provide a foundation for the more extravagant perennials and a structure for the garden when the perennials are dormant. For more about perennials, see Chapter 5.

- ✔ **Accent.** Some shrubs, such as azaleas and rhododendrons, are spectacular bloomers. Others have stunning berries or autumn colour. Just a plant or two in a special place can light up a whole yard. And don't forget the foliage — a bold hydrangea with large leaves can make a stunning statement among plants with smaller leaves, like azaleas.

As you select shrubs for your garden, be sure to note the season of the shrub's peak interest. For example, many shrubs produce flowers in early spring, but others — such as several of the hollies and some cotoneasters — are showy in winter, particularly against a backdrop of snow. By mixing shrubs with different seasons of peak interest, you can be sure to have plants worth admiring in your garden any time of the year.

✔ **Hedges, screens, and ground covers.** Many types of shrubs can form hedges or screens when you plant them close together and maintain them as such. For example, you can clip some shrubs, including box-woods and euonymus, into the rigid shape of a formal hedge to give a garden a very organized look. Let other types grow naturally to create screens for privacy. Many prostrate (low-growing) shrubs make excellent ground covers. For more information about ground covers, see Chapter 9.

✔ **Background and barriers.** Shrubs can be the perfect backdrop for flower beds. A consistent, deep green background is one of the best ways to highlight blooming plants. If you want to keep pets (or people) out of a certain area, plant a line of thorny pyracantha. The interlopers will get the "point."

Organizing shrubs by height

When planting a mixture of different shrubs or when planting shrubs with other plants (such as flowering perennials), consider the mature height of the shrub. You can follow the old gardening axiom: Place low growers in front, medium-sized plants in the middle, and tall plants in back. With that approach, nothing gets blocked out and you can see all the plants.

Our Favourite Shrubs

The following shrubs are just about foolproof. All are widely available, and most are broadly adapted. Regarding specific soil needs, please refer to Chapter 11 to see how to adjust soil as needed for certain plants. Likewise, see Chapter 16 to read more about the pests to which some shrubs are prone. For more about hardiness zones, see Chapter 2 and the colour maps that show Agricultural Canada's Hardiness Zones.

We organize our favourite shrubs by botanical name; however, we list the common name first.

- **Glossy abelia.** *Abelia grandiflora.* Evergreen in warm climates, but not in Canada. This handsome, arching plant grows to 3 metres (10 feet) and has bright green, glossy foliage. New growth is bronzy red. Small, fragrant, white or pink flowers are bell shaped and appear in summer. Can be grown as a hedge. Plant in full sun or light shade. Attracts butterflies and hummingbirds. Hardy to Zone 7.

- **Japanese maples**. *Acer palmatum.* One of the most popular small trees for the garden, but large and small shrub choices abound. For years they've been hybridized and selected for form, shape, and colour. They come in dramatic weeping and cascading forms with finely cut or dissected leaves in green, maroon, purple-black, cherry red, and more. Many change colour in the fall. Most are hardy to Zone 6. 'Waterfall' has a flowing habit with bright green foliage that becomes golden yellow tinged with red in fall; 1.8 to 3 metres (6 to 10 feet). Zone 6. 'Red Pygmy' grows to about 1.5 metres (5 feet) and has long, narrow maroon foliage all summer. It needs some protection from winter winds and shouldn't be allowed to dry out. Red and purple varieties need sun to maintain colour.

- **Barberries.** *Berberis* spp. Evergreen and deciduous. These shrubs are known for their thorny stems, red berries, and tough constitution. They're invasive, particularly the deciduous Japanese *thunbergerii,* and are the alternate host of black stem rust, so should never be grown where wheat is a crop. Some have showy yellow flowers and colourful foliage. However, you have many varieties from which to choose, varying in height and foliage colour. Most have good autumn colour. 'Atropurpurea' has reddish-purple foliage during the growing season. It is hardy in Zones 4 to 9. Evergreen barberries include *B. mentorensis,* a compact, dense plant growing 1.8 to 2.1 metres (6 to 7 feet) high. It is hardy in Zones 5 to 8. *B. darwinii, B. julianae, B. verruculosa,* and *B. gladynensis* are rust resistant and popular in B.C. Most barberries can grow in sun or partial shade and thrive under a variety of growing conditions.

- **Butterfly bush.** *Buddleia davidii.* Deciduous. The much loved, summer flowering shrub has long, arching clusters of lightly fragrant flowers that attract butterflies. Most varieties bloom in shades of purple, but you can often find selections with pink or white flowers. Buddleias grow very fast, reaching up to 3 metres (10 feet) high in areas with long summers. Cut back almost to the ground in early spring to keep the plant compact and attractive, and for bloom — it blooms on new wood grown the same year. Full sun. Zone 5.

- **Boxwoods.** *Buxus* spp. Evergreen. The boxwood is one of the finest plants for a tightly clipped, formal hedge. Small, dark green leaves densely cover the branches. 'Green Mound' and 'Green Velvet' both Zone 5 and growing just over 90 centimetres (3 feet), stay a rich dark green all year. 'Winter Beauty' is blue-green in summer and turns bronzy in winter. 'Green Mountain' is an upright variety that's often clipped in a pyramidal form. Also Zone 5. Sun or part shade. Many named varieties are available.

✔ **Siberian pea tree**. *Caragana arborescens*. These small trees or shrubs are native to eastern Asia and hardy here to Zone 2. A member of the bean family, they have pea-like leaves and bright-yellow pea-like flowers. New wood is bright green. We know one prairies gardener who clipped a thick stand of caragana to look like bamboo — it was very effective. Weeping cultivars are also available as small trees. Caragana is easy to grow and puts up with almost any condition of soil, salt or wind but likes full sun.

✔ **Bluebeard**. *Careoptyris* spp. Like butterfly bush, these shrubs attract butterflies as well as bees and should be pruned almost to the ground in spring. Attractive arching stems with pointed leaves; grows to about 1 metre (40 inches). The showy 'Worcester Gold' grows to 60 centimetres (2 feet) and has bright yellow foliage and light blue late summer flowers. 'Dark Night' has dark green foliage and purple-blue blooms August to frost. Full sun. Zone 6.

✔ **Flowering quince.** *Chaenomeles.* Deciduous. Among the first shrubs to bloom in early spring, flowering quince are tough, reliable plants that never let you down. The flowers are borne on bare stems in shades of mostly red, orange, and pink, but also white. Plants range in size and shape depending on variety, but generally grow 5 to 10 feet high, are upright and have thorny branches. Some grow low enough to be used as ground covers. You can clip flowering quince as a hedge, and they usually look best with regular pruning. Bring cut branches indoors in late winter to force into early bloom. Many named varieties are available, differing mostly in flower colour. Plant in full sun. Zone 5.

✔ **Cotoneaster.** *Cotoneaster* spp. Evergreen and deciduous. You can choose from many types, which range from low-growing ground covers to shrubbier kinds. Most have a profusion of white spring flowers followed by red berries and are tough, widely adapted plants. Deciduous kinds often have good autumn color. Cotoneasters like full sun. Fireblight disease can be a problem. Ground-cover types of cotoneaster are described in Chapter 9.

✔ **Dogwood**. *Cornus* spp. Good foliage, flowers, and fall berries on a group of shrubs hardy from Zones 2 to 6. Mottled tatarian dogwood, *C. alba* 'Gouchaulti' has yellow and green variegated leaves and dark red stems that stand out in winter. *C. a. sibirica* has vivid red stems, as does red osier. Part shade. All three hardy to Zone 2.

✔ **Euonymus.** *Euonymus* spp. Evergreen and deciduous. Euonymus are workhorse foliage plants. Deciduous kinds, such as winged euonymus, *E. alata,* are hardy in Zone 3, and often have stunning red autumn colour. The European spindle tree, *E. europaea* (Zone 4) grows to about 17 feet (5 m) and produces showy red and pink fruit in autumn. Evergreen euonymus, such as *E. japonica* (Zones 8 and 9) and *E. fortunei* (Zones 4 to 5) come in numerous named varieties: 'Emerald Gaiety' (silvery-white with green) and 'Emerald 'n' Gold' (bright green and gold with a pinkish tinge in winter) are very popular. 'Coloratus' can be used as a ground cover or climbing vine. Euonymus range in height from 1.8 to 6 metres

(6 to 20 feet) and make fine hedges. Sun or light shade. Many are susceptible to scale, so ask at your nursery for a resistant variety.

✔ **Hydrangea.** *Hydrangea* spp. Deciduous. The big, bold leaves and huge
summer flowers of these unique plants put on a great show in shady gardens. The bigleaf hydrangea, *H. macrophylla,* hardy to Zone 6, comes in
two types: lacecap or mophead. The large flower clusters are white or
light to deep blue in acid soil (add peat moss or aluminum sulphate),
pink to red in alkaline soil (add horticultural lime and a 15-30-15 fertilizer). Plants usually grow 1.2 to 2.4 metres (4 to 8 feet) high and flowers
grow from buds formed the previous year. Cut back to the top pair of
buds in spring to encourage compactness and heavy bloom. Plant in
full sun.

Smooth hydrangea, *H. arborescens,* 'Annabelle', hardy in Zone 2, has
large, round heads of white flowers. Prune stems to 30 centimetres
(1 foot) in early spring.

Panicle hydrangea, *H. paniculata*, is a hardy upright shrub that blooms
in late summer, when other plants are fading. Hardy to Zone 4. 'Peegee'
is probably the best known, with white flowers that turn pinkish and
then tea rose late in the season.

The oakleaf hydrangea, *H. quercifolia,* is notable for fall colour. Several
varieties, such as 'Snowflake' and 'Snow Queen' are available. Zone 6.

H. serrata is hardy to Zone 5 and has saw-tooth leaves and earlier flowers. 'Blue Bird' and 'Preciosa' (rose red) both have lacecap flowers.

✔ **Hollies.** *Ilex* species. There are many kinds of hollies and all are notable
for the red berries they produce in fall. Because holly plants are either
male or female, both types must be present in order for female plants to
produce berries. Plant in part shade.

Hollies are deciduous or evergreen. Grow deciduous kinds, such as the
native winterberry *(I. verticillata)* if you live in Zone 3 and up. 'Afterglow'
is a compact female variety with orange-red fruit, 1 metre (3 feet).
'Winter Red' is a taller female at 2.5 metres (8 ½ feet).

Evergreen hollies are notable for their bright-red berries and clean-
looking, spiny, often multicoloured leaves. Many make excellent hedges. *I.
meserveae*, Zone 5, is a good breed similar to the less-hardy English holly
and grows to about 2 metres (6 ½ feet). 'Blue Princess', Blue Girl', and Blue
Maid' have bright red berries. 'Golden Girl' has, can you believe it, yellow
ones. (Use male-named counterparts as pollinators.) 'Little Rascal' is true
to its name and is both a dwarf variety and a good pollinator.

✔ **Junipers.** *Juniperus* species. Evergreen. The low- and wide-spreading
growth pattern of most junipers makes them most useful as ground
covers and some are hardy to Zone 2, although 3 is more common. (See
Chapter 9.) However, many more upright, shrubby types exist, including
forms of the Chinese juniper, *J. chinensis,* such as 'Pfitzeriana' and 'Blue
Pacific'. Columnar varieties are also available, such as 'Skyrocket' and

'Spartan'. Vase- or globe-shaped varieties include 'Blue Star', *J. squamata*, and 'Buffalo' *J. sabina*. Full sun. Hardiness varies; most are reliable to Zone 4.

✔ **Photinia.** *Photinia fraserii.* Photinia encompasses several species that show bronzy-red new growth in spring followed by clusters of small, white flowers and sometimes by berries, but only *fraserii* is available in Canada, and then only in B.C., unfortunately for the rest of us. *P. fraseri* reaches 3 to 4.5 metres (10 to 15 feet) high and is popular because of its resistance to powdery mildew, but it does not have berries. Full sun. Hardy in Zones 8 and 9.

✔ **Mugho pine.** *Pinus mugo.* Evergreen. This neat, compact pine rarely exceeds 1.2 to 2.4 metres (4 to 8 feet) in height. Mugho pines are easy to care for as a specimen or in group plantings. New growth appears as attractive candle shapes at the ends of the branches in spring. Snap off half of each candle to prune the plant. Full sun. Zones 1 to 3.

✔ **Bush cinquefoil.** *Potentilla fruticosa.* Deciduous. These are handsome little shrubs with bright green, fine-textured foliage and small but colourful, wild-rose-like blossoms. Plants bloom from late spring into autumn in shades of red, yellow, orange, and white. Yellow varieties, such as 'Gold Drop', are most popular, but some pretty pinks and dark reds are available. Heights range from just under 60 centimetres (2 feet) up to 1.5 metres (5 feet). Full sun. Zone 3.

✔ **Ornamental fruit.** *Prunus* spp. Many valuable shrubs belong to this large family of plants, which includes some of our most popular fruit, such as peaches and plums.

The purple-leafed sand cherry, *P. cistena,* is a very hardy deciduous flowering fruit tree. It makes white spring flowers, purple leaves, and produces small edible plums. The sand cherry grows to about 3 metres (10 feet) high and is hardy in Zones 3 to 7. Likes full sun but tolerates light shade.

The Manchu cherry, *P. tomentosa,* grows about 3 metres (10 feet) high and spreads to about 4.5 metres (15 feet). White flowers appear very early in spring and are followed in fall by scarlet fruits. Full sun. Zone 2.

Dwarf flowering almond, *P. glandulosa* 'Sinensis', is a small flowering shrub densely packed with blossoms in spring that grows to just over 90 centimetres (3 feet) high and is hardy to Zone 2. Full sun.

✔ **Firethorn.** *Pyracantha* spp. Colourful and dependable, firethorn are evergreen to semi-evergreen shrubs with stiff, spiny branches and an open habit. However, they can be pruned to grow upright against a wall as well. All cover themselves with clusters of small, white flowers in spring followed by showy, orange-to-red berries that last into autumn and winter. Good cultivars include 'Gnome' and 'Yukon Belle'. Fireblight can be a serious problem; hybrids 'Mojave' and 'Teton' are fireblight-resistant. They grow to about 3.6 metres (12 feet) high, with orange-red and yellow-orange berries, respectively. Plant firethorn in full sun. Most are hardy to Zone 6; a few to Zone 5.

✓ **Azaleas and rhododendrons.** *Rhododendron* species. Evergreen and deciduous. This is a huge family of much-loved flowering shrubs. You can choose from many types, but all grow best in acid soil. Most prefer moist, shady conditions and soil rich in organic matter. Some can take full sun. There are plenty of winter-hardy varieties to choose from.

Azaleas are generally lower-growing, compact plants that cover themselves with brightly coloured spring flowers in shades of pink, red, orange, yellow, purple, and white. Some are bicoloured. Favourite evergreen types include 'Boudoir' (pink), 'Elsie Lee' (purple) and 'Pleasant White'. Hardy to Zone 6.

Deciduous azaleas lose their leaves in autumn and are more tolerant of winter than evergreen kinds. The Northern Lights series is hardy to Zone 4 and comes in lovely soft colours like apricot-orange, mauve-purple, yellow, and white with yellow. The cultivars are easily identified by their names, such as 'Orchid Lights', 'Spicy Lights', and 'Northern Highlights'.

Rhododendrons are usually taller, with larger flower clusters. They come in basically the same colour range. Lepidote hybrids, Zone 5, are hardier than the Elepidotes, which have larger, smooth leaves and are hardy to Zone 6; some of the well-known catawbiense types are Elepidotes. For hardier rhodos, look for Lepidotes with P.J.M. on the label. These have smallish leaves that become rich mahogany purple in fall. Finnish hybrids are among the hardiest of all, and the names reflect their heritage: 'Hellekki', violet-red; 'Peter Tigerstedt', white with violet specks; and 'Elvira', bright red. Zone 4.

✓ **Roses.** *Rosa* spp. Deciduous. Many roses are outstanding landscape shrubs. Among the best are the hardy rugosa roses, which are notable for the "quilted" look of their leaves. They flower in spring and produce large, edible rose hips in autumn. There are so many roses for so many garden situations, we've set aside an entire chapter for them (the one just before this one), Chapter 7.

✓ **Sumac.** *Rhus* spp. Deciduous. The native staghorn and smooth sumacs are associated with large natural landscapes, brilliant fall colour and lovely, felty cone-shape "flowers." But although the native plants are fine at cottages or country properties, and especially used for erosion control, they spread so rapidly via suckers they aren't practical in an urban garden. Still, we can appreciate their fine-cut foliage and breathtaking fall foliage in our gardens with a couple of varieties that require elbow room but won't eventually take over the beds and borders. 'Dissecta' grows to 2.5 metres (8 ½ feet) and branches low, with a spreading, sweeping habit. Zone 3. 'Gro-Low' is a fragrant, bushy variety that grows to to about 75 centimetres (2 ½ feet) and spreads to 2 metres (6 ½ feet). Zone 4.

✓ **Spirea.** *Spiraea* spp. Deciduous. You have many types of spireas to choose from. Many are mounding, fountain-like shrubs with an abundance of tiny, white flowers in mid-spring to late spring. Included among these is the graceful, arching 'Bridalwreath', *S. vanhouttei,* which grows to about 1.8 metres (6 feet) high and at least 2.4 metres (8 feet) wide. Its small, dark green leaves turn red in autumn. Other spireas, like *S. bumalda* 'Anthony Waterer', have clusters of pink-to-red blooms later in summer. 'Goldflame' has bright green-bronze foliage and is frequently seen in corporate landscapes combined with purpleleaf sand cherry. Full sun. Many hardy to Zone 3, some to Zone 2.

✔ **Common lilac.** *Syringa vulgaris.* Deciduous. Wonderfully fragrant clusters of spring flowers make lilacs a favourite wherever they grow. Most bloom in spring in shades of lavender and purple, but some are white or rosy pink. Plants usually grow 2.4 to 4.5 metres (8 to 15 feet) high and have dark green leaves. Plant in full sun. Powdery mildew can be a problem. The Canadian-bred Preston hybrids are the hardiest, to Zone 2; French hybrids are hardy to Zone 4.

✔ **Viburnum.** *Viburnum* spp. The viburnums represent a large family of evergreen and deciduous plants that vary in size from dwarf to large shrubs and small trees. They're wonderful additions to the landscape, with great variety of form and function, colourful flowers, bright berries and, often, autumn colour. They grow in sun or partial shade. Favourite varieties include Korean spice *(V. varlesii),* a dense and compact shrub with scented creamy pink flowers in May; Zone 5. Witherod *(V. cassinoides),* Zone 2, has lustrous green foliage, white flowers that darken to red, then blue fruit that eventually becomes black; as well, it boasts highly coloured fall foliage. European snowball *(V. Opulos* 'Roseum') is a popular shrub with large greenish flowers that become pure white. Zone 2. The highbush cranberry, a 2 to 3 metres (6 ½ to 10 foot) native shrub, is also a viburnum *(V. trilobum).* It has white flowers clusters in spring and large, edible red berries in fall. Zone 2.

Shrubs for multi-season colour

If it's colour you're after, certain shrubs provide it in abundance through a combination of flowers, fruit, fall leaves, and winter berries. In other words, these are shrubs that provide more than one season of interest. Here are some of our favourites:

✔ **Azalea.** Flowers, fall colour

✔ **Cotoneaster.** Flowers, fruit in fall through winter

✔ **Euonymus.** Fruit, colourful fall foliage

✔ **Firethorn.** Flowers, fruit that lasts through winter

✔ **Flowering fruit.** Flowers, colourful foliage

✔ **Evergreen holly.** Winter berries, colourful foliage

✔ **Hydrangea.** Flowers that dry on the branches and last into early winter.

✔ **Photinia.** Flowers, colourful spring foliage

✔ **Roses.** Flowers, rose hips in winter

✔ **Spirea.** Flowers, fall colour

✔ **Viburnum.** Flowers, fruit, colourful foliage

Hedge viburnum (*V. opulus* 'Nanum') is a rounded dwarf shrub that almost never flowers and is suitable for clipping as a hedge. Zone 2.

✔ **Yucca**. *Yucca filamentosa, Y. glauca.* A great native broadleaf evergreen some might not consider for the shrub border, but in fact it's a good focal point among the softer, more common shrubs. It also adds a touch of the southwest, and does well in hot, dry gardens. The spikes of large, fragrant white flowers are head-turners. Spanish bayonet *(Y. glauca)* is hardy to Zone 3 and has narrow, rigid silver-gray leaves and creamy white flowers in July. The various cultivars of Adam's needle *(Y. filamentosa)* such as 'Ivory Tower' and 'Garland Gold' (gold leaves with green margins) are hardy to Zone 4. Both grow about 1 metre (3 feet) tall.

Native shrubs for your garden

Some of the favourite shrubs in this chapter are native to Canada. Here are some others we haven't mentioned. Native plants thrive in the conditions they're native to and usually adapt well to similar climates, soil, and exposures in other parts of the country. In the interests of preserving both our environment and the plants that grow in it, native plants are well worth seeking out at your local nursery.

✔ **Bog rosemary** *(Andromeda polifolia):* A low-growing broadleaf evergreen that spreads to over 90 cm (3 feet) and needs moist soil. Pink flowers in June. Zone 3. Shade.

✔ **Oregon grape holly** *(Mahonia aquifolium):* The holly-like glossy green foliage turns bronze in winter. Yellow flowers in June, then blue fruit. Grows to 1.5 m (5 feet). Zone 5. Grows in full sun to full shade.

✔ **Downy serviceberry** *(Amelanchier canadensis):* A hardy, shrubby tree with white flowers in early spring followed by sweet, edible purple fruit. Birds love it.

Leaves are yellow-orange in fall. Tolerates moist soil. Full sun to part shade. Zone 4.

✔ **Summersweet** *(Clethra alnifolia):* Long, pointed clusters of scented white flowers bloom on an upright shrub in July. Likes acidic soil. Full sun to full shade. Zone 5.

✔ **Dwarf fothergilla** *(Fothergilla gardenii):* A 90 cm (3-foot) shrub with white sweetly scented white flowers in May and red fall colour. Zone 6.

✔ **Witch hazel** *(Hamamelis virginiana):* Small, fragrant yellow flowers in late fall, after everything else has flowered, plus yellow foliage. Likes moist soil but does fine in regular soil. Cultivars that bloom in very early spring have also been developed. Native plant grows to 4.5 m (15 feet). Shade or sun, but protect from winter sun scald. Zone 5.

✔ **Blue elderberry** *(Sambucus cerulea):* A large, leafy shrub that grows to 3 m (10 feet). White spring flowers and clusters of edible blue-black berries. Zone 2.

Chapter 9

Lawns and Ground Covers

• •

In This Chapter

▶ Deciding on size and grass variety

▶ Planting seeds

▶ Planting sod

▶ Taking care of your lawn

▶ Considering the virtues of ground covers

▶ Choosing the right ground cover

• •

For most people, a landscape isn't complete without at least some lawn. The lush colour and smooth, uniform look complement our homes, trees, shrubs, and other plantings. It's tough to beat a grassy area as a place for family and pets to relax and play. Many grasses can handle heavy foot traffic, and some even thrive in moderately shady areas; so lawns solve certain landscaping problems.

The utility of a well-kept lawn is undeniable. That's why, for decades, putting in a lawn was the first thing people did when they bought a new home. But recently, many people have started to question the amount of time, money, and resources lawns demand. You should do the same as you decide on the type and size of lawn you want — or whether you even want a lawn.

If foot traffic is not an issue, you may decide to plant ground covers instead of a traditional lawn. Ground covers can offer your landscape a natural look and are relatively low maintenance. The selection of good ground cover plants is so broad that you can find several to fit any landscape situation and climate.

Lawn Decisions

Putting in a lawn is a lot of work. There's soil preparation, perhaps installing a permanent underground irrigation system, and the actual planting. But the sweating doesn't stop there — you must maintain it year after year. A lawn also uses resources — water, fertilizer, and pesticides — that may be in short supply in some areas, or can be sources of pollution if not used correctly.

Do a little homework before you run down to the local garden centre and purchase 23 kilograms (50 pounds) of seed. First, figure out how much space you need for a lawn. Then determine which type of grass does best in your area. After this research, you're ready to plant and you have more choices — mainly whether to plant from seed or sod.

How big?

If you have a newly built home and you're starting from scratch with the landscaping, think seriously about how much weekend time you want to spend pushing the lawn mower (or sitting on the riding mower) and the appropriate water use for your part of the country. You also want to think about the costs of water, an irrigation system, fertilizer, and things like paying someone to mow and maintain your grass.

The one easiest way to save money in the long run is to plan for and plant a smaller lawn. For instance if you have about 93 square metres (1,000 square feet) where you can plant a lawn, you can reduce long-term costs by 40 percent by planting only 56 square metres (600 square feet).

Where summers are dry, as they can be on the Prairies and, indeed, in many parts of Canada, conserving water is another factor to consider. Most families need only 56 to 74 square metres (600 to 800 square feet) of grass — enough for a small play area or lounging space.

Where summer rainfall is common and water conservation isn't a factor, you might want a larger area of lawn. If your plans include lawn games like badminton or croquet, you need a rectangle measuring 14 x 24 metres (45 x 80 feet), or 334 square metres (3,600 square feet).

Which grass is for you?

Growing the appropriate variety of grass for your area is critical. Your decision makes all the difference between a thriving lawn and one that doesn't survive the winter or languishes in the heat of your climate.

Turfgrasses (grasses specially bred for use as a lawn) fall into two broad groups: cool-season and warm-season grasses. *Cool-season grasses* grow best between 16°C and 24°C (60°F and 75°F) and can withstand cold winters. Warm-season grasses grow vigorously in temperatures above 27°C (80°F). In Canada, we grow only cool-season grasses for lawns, even in the warmer parts of British Columbia, where various varieties of tall and fine fescues are favoured.

Each type of grass has its named varieties, many of which have been bred for improvements like tolerance of drought, shade, or sheer ruggedness. Your local agricultural office or garden centre can recommend varieties for your area.

For much more detail about lawns and kinds of grasses, check out *Lawn Care For Dummies* by Lance Walheim and the Editors of The National Gardening Association (IDG Books Worldwide, Inc.).

You can start a new lawn in a couple of ways: from seed or from sod. Some types of grass are available only as sod, which is a faster way to grow a lawn. Keeping weeds out of the bare soil of a seeded lawn until the grass fills in is critical.

Turfgrass short list

The following section describes grasses suitable for most parts of Canada. Use these descriptions to help you decide which type of grass is best for you.

Types of grasses

When most North Americans picture a perfect lawn, they're seeing a cool-season lawn grass, particularly one that is predominantly Kentucky bluegrass. When Canadians go south in winter to places like California, Arizona or Florida, we tend to feel slightly superior because lawns there aren't as fine textured as ours, just as we like to put our noses in the air about our superior medicare system (but you know what they say about pride coming before a fall!). Tropical and subtropical grasses, like Bahia and Bermuda grass, have stiffer, wider leaves; they love heat and wouldn't survive here anyway.

The peak growth seasons for the cool-season grasses more suitable in our country are spring and fall.

It's important to remember that all grasses go dormant if they don't get enough water. This usually happens in midsummer, when they tend to look dried out and beige. If you irrigate during arid seasons, your lawn will stay green, but this can be both expensive and ecologically unsound. It also means you have to anticipate the weather: Once dry conditions have set in and your lawn goes dormant, there's not much point in overwatering it in an attempt to green it up again. Let it happen naturally — which it will when the weather becomes cooler and rainier.

The four kinds of cool-season turfgrass you should know are:

- ✔ **Fine fescue.** The *fine* in their name refers to their needlelike blades, so narrow and pointed that, if they were stiff enough, they'd serve as a sewing needle. There are various kinds of fine fescue: chewings, red, sheeps, and hard fescue. All are quick to germinate and become established, and all grasses do well in less than ideal growing conditions. Fine fescues are the most shade-tolerant of the northern grasses, and they grow better than other cool-season grasses in the presence of many tree roots. But let's face it — all grasses need sun, even fescues; they may hang on longer in a shaded area, but they still need a minimum of 2 or 3 hours of sun a day. Compared to other cool season grasses, they require little fertilizer. Newer varieties offer insect resistance.

  Hard fescue is a good low-maintenance lawn in humid regions such as southern Ontario. Varieties like 'Frankin', 'Jasper', 'MX86', and 'Southport' have minimal fertilizer needs.

- ✔ **Kentucky bluegrass.** The most common lawn grass, bluegrass is relatively slow to form a turf, but once established, it spreads and fills in nicely. Its soft, fine texture and rich green colour is the look most gardeners prefer. Kentucky bluegrass is very hardy and comes in many disease-resistant varieties, but it requires somewhat more fertilizer than many other grasses. A few of the current top-rated varieties of Kentucky bluegrass include 'Baron', 'Eclipse', 'Limousine', 'Nuglade' and 'Regent'.

  Varieties that combine natural Kentucky bluegrass good looks with more Spartan maintenance needs include: 'Colbalt', 'Midnight' and 'Ram-2'.

- ✔ **Perennial ryegrass.** This is a fine-textured, fast-growing grass. It can produce a walkable, mowable turf in as little as one week. Compared to Kentucky bluegrass, it's not as cold hardy; in fact, it's iffy even in Zone 6 and warmer, where an exceptionally cold, icy winter could kill it off. It also doesn't mow as cleanly. And although it's somewhat shade tolerant, it doesn't match fine fescue on this score. Newer varieties, such as 'Imagine' and 'Wizard' offer insect and disease resistance. 'Yorktown II', 'Palmer III', and 'Fiesta II' have the best heat, shade, and cold tolerance.

- ✔ **Turf-type tall fescue.** Casual observers may have a hard time distinguishing this grass from rye or Kentucky bluegrass, but compared to them, its leaf blades are wider and the colour is not quite as dark a green. This grass makes an attractive and practical lawn grass for coastal areas like British Columbia and Nova Scotia where Kentucky blue and fine fescues suffer in summer's heat. New varieties are resistant to everything: heat, drought, diseases, and insects. Look for 'Bonsai', 'Crossfire', 'Jaguar II', 'Watersaver', and 'Rebel Jr.' 'Shenandoah' and 'Tribute' contain high levels of a natural pest repellent called *endophyte*.

For best performance, lawns should contain different species of grass. If one develops a problem, the others usually compensate for it and continue to grow. For a lawn in the shade, the best ratio is 40 to 60 percent creeping red fescue; 30 to 35 percent bluegrass; and 15 to 25 percent perennial ryegrass. In sun: Use half bluegrass, 25 percent creeping red fescue, and 25 percent perennial ryegrass.

For the very latest information about top-performing grasses, check the Web site of the Guelph Turfgrass Institute, `www.uoguelph.ca/GTI/`. Another Canadian Web site, `www.agric.gov.ab.ca/pests/diseases/turfgras.htm/`, shows photos of diseased turfgrass in western Canada.

Putting in a New Lawn

The most common and economical way to plant grass is by spreading seed. Proper soil preparation and follow-up care are the keys to success here.

The fastest way to put in a new lawn is by *laying sod* — setting large sections of fully grown turf in place on the soil. The idea of an instant lawn certainly has its appeal; however, sod is an expensive option, and you still have to prepare the soil as thoroughly and maintain the newly planted area as carefully as you would for a lawn from seed.

The first step in preparing the area to be sown is to test your soil to see whether it's fertile and has the proper pH to grow grass. Turfgrasses prefer a nearly neutral soil pH of 6.5 to 7.5. If your soil is acidic, you may need to raise the pH by applying ground dolomitic limestone. To lower the pH of alkaline soil, you apply elemental sulfur. See Chapter 11 for more on testing soil and adjusting the pH. The results of your soil test will indicate how much of these soil amendments to use.

Grasses aren't picky about soil, but if you don't have reasonably fertile soil that can be worked to a depth of 15 to 20 centimetres (6 to 8 inches), purchase a load of topsoil — rich soil that's high in organic matter.

Spread the topsoil smoothly over the area to be seeded, mixing some of it in with the native soil below to prevent a water barrier. Make the topsoil layer 2.5 centimetres (1 inch) below the final level of the lawn if installing sod or 7 mm (¼ inch) below if sowing seed, and have it slope slightly away from the house for proper drainage.

Planting Lawn from Seed

The best time to seed a new lawn is just prior to the grass's season of most vigorous growth. For cool-season grasses, that means cooler weather — late summer to early fall. Early spring is the second-best time.

Shopping for seed

Your lawn is a landscape feature you'll have for years to come, so skip the cheap stuff. How do you recognize fine-quality seed?

- ✔ A variety name on the label, such as 'Nuglade' Kentucky bluegrass instead of generic Kentucky bluegrass indicates a good-quality grass. However, variety names are not always mentioned on labels in Canada because there are no laws requiring it. Even the best companies use generic names because sometimes one variety has to be substituted for another, for one reason or another. The essential rule is: You get what you pay for.

- ✔ The highest-quality seed is nearly free of weed and other undesirable crop seed. But all grass seed will have some weed seeds in it. Rely on a high-quality product from a reputable supplier.

- ✔ The *germination percentage* means the percentage of seeds in the bag that will sprout and begin to grow. It should be 85 percent or greater for Kentucky bluegrass and above 90 percent for all other grasses.

How much seed to buy

To determine how much seed you need to purchase, start with a pretty close estimate of the size of the area you aim to plant. For example, a rectangular lawn that is 6 x 15 metres (20 x 50 feet) is 93 square metres (1,000 square feet) in area. Most lawns aren't so convenient to measure, and if yours is one of these, don't worry. For one thing, your measurement needn't be precise. You can also measure the area by dividing it into separate, discrete shapes and then adding them all together.

Measure with your stride: An adult stride is usually around 1 metre (3 feet). Measure yours with a yard stick until you know what a 1-metre (3-foot) stride feels like before heading out on your lawn. If your lawn measures in acres rather than feet, consider renting one of the distance-measuring tools available at local rental yards.

If you buy a seed mix for home lawns, the label will most likely specify how much area the package will cover. If you aren't buying packaged seed, use the size of your area and Table 9-1 to figure out how much seed to buy.

Table 9-1	How Much Seed to Sow	
Grass Name	*Kilograms of Seed/93 sq. m.*	*Pounds of Seed/1,000 sq. ft.*
Fine fescue	2 to 2¼ kg	4 to 5
Kentucky bluegrass	½ to 1 kg	1 to 2
Perennial ryegrass	2 to 2¼ kg	4 to 5
Turf-type tall fescue	2½ to 4½ kg	6 to 10

Planting day

When you're ready to plant, assemble all the tools, materials, and equipment you need, including:

- ✔ **Soil amendments.** These include lime or sulfur if a soil test has indicated they're needed; also fertilizers and 5 to 8 centimetres (2 to 3 inches) of organic material such as compost if you live in a new subdivision. In established areas you likely don't have to add anything. Grass will grow well even in ordinary topsoil.

- ✔ **Rototiller.** You need one of these to mix the amendments into the soil. Various machine sizes are available to rent.

- ✔ **Grass seed.** Refer to Table 9-1 to find out how much to sow.

- ✔ **Lawn spreader.** This tool scatters seed evenly as you roll it over the soil — also called a mechanical spreader.

- ✔ **Board scraper.** A board that you drag over the soil surface.

- ✔ **Rake.** You need a stiff-tined rake to level soil after tilling.

- ✔ **Lawn roller.** A large, heavy drum with a handle that you roll over the scattered seed to press it into the soil. You can fill the drum one-third to one-half full with water to increase the weight.

- ✔ **Mulching material.** Use straw or other organic material to lightly cover the seed and keep it moist.

If you don't own large tools, you can rent them for the day. When you have all your materials together, follow these steps:

1. **Spread any amendments required to correct the pH over the soil and apply a complete fertilizer recommended for new lawns. Follow the directions given on the fertilizer bag.**

   Chapter 11 has more information about soil and pH levels.

2. **Rotary-till the soil a few inches deep to loosen it.**

   Don't overcultivate — leave small lumps and cracks to catch seed so that it sprouts quickly. Remove stones and sticks.

3. **Level the soil with a board scraper or rake.**

   Leveling the soil eliminates high spots where the mower would cut the grass too short, as well as depressions where it may miss spots or where water may collect.

4. **Roll the seedbed with the empty roller to firm the soil as shown in Figure 9-1.**

   Make sure the soil is dry before you roll; otherwise, it compacts, preventing seeds from sprouting.

5. **Sow the seed as shown in Figure 9-2.**

   Don't be tempted to oversow; if you do, the plants won't develop properly. Although a mechanical spreader helps spread the seed uniformly, spreading seeds by hand is also practical, especially with larger seeds, such as ryes and fescues. Whichever way you spread the seed, coverage will be more even if you apply half the seed moving one direction across the lawn area, and the other half moving the opposite direction.

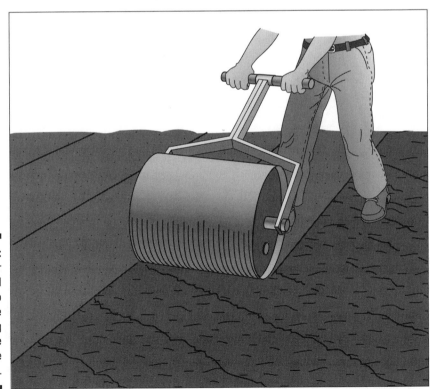

Figure 9-1:
Roll over
tilled and
raked soil to
firm the
planting
surface
before
seeding.

Figure 9-2:
Spread seed
with a drop
spreader
or with a
hand–held
broadcast
spreader.

6. **Rake the surface lightly, barely covering about half the seed and leaving the rest exposed.**

7. **Roll once more with the empty roller to press seeds in contact with the soil. (Refer to Figure 9-1.)**

8. **Lightly mulch the seedbed to cover and protect seeds and to keep the soil moist until the seeds germinate. (See Figure 9-3.)**

   The mulch keeps rain from washing the seeds away, provides protection from the drying sun, and prevents birds from getting a free meal.

9. **Give the newly seeded area a thorough initial soaking, shown in Figure 9-4, and then keep it well watered until the grass is established.**

   Water more deeply but less frequently as the grass becomes more established.

   Each watering should penetrate the soil to a depth of several inches to promote good root growth.

Figure 9-3:
Spread
mulch to
keep the soil
moist.

Planting Lawn from Sod

Sod has two important advantages over seed: Climate permitting, you can plant a sod lawn almost any time of the season, and the layer of sod covers existing weeds as long as you don't have an infestation of deep-rooted weeds, which means you start out with an almost weed-free lawn.

Even though you can lay sod just about any time during the growing season, your results are better if you plant during the ideal season: Early fall or early spring for most parts of Canada, late fall for warmer areas of British Columbia. But if you can water enough to keep a newly sodded lawn healthy through a summer drought or heat spell, you can plant anytime.

Figure 9-4:
Give the
newly
seeded
ground
a good
soaking.

Buying sod

Sod is expensive, so buy from a quality supplier. Look for sections that are about 2 to 3 centimetres (1 inch) thick , with no brown patches or dried-out edges. Have the sod delivered on planting day so that it doesn't sit in a pile and heat up (a stack of fresh sod will literally cook itself to death, just like a compost pile). And to help prevent drying out, keep the sod in a shady location until you plant it.

Laying sod

When you're ready to lay the sod, assemble all the tools and equipment that you need: soil amendments, rototiller, board scraper or rake, and a lawn roller. Prepare the planting area as you would for a lawn from seed. (Check out Steps 1 through 3 in the "Planting day" section of this chapter.)

Next, follow these instructions for laying sod:

1. **Roll out a piece of sod and press it into position. Fit the next section against it tightly but don't overlap, as shown in Figure 9-5.**

2. **Continue laying sections, staggering them like bricks.**

   Lay a board across the sod so that your feet don't break through the sod, as shown in Figure 9-6. Trim odd-shaped sections with a heavy utility knife, as shown in Figure 9-7, and fill gaps with small cut sections, as shown in Figure 9-8.

Figure 9-5:
Roll out sod
so that
pieces don't
overlap.

3. **Use a roller over the newly laid turf, as shown in Figure 9-9, going back over it a second time at right angles to the first pass.**

4. **Rake the new lawn lightly to lift up the flattened grass, and keep the soil moist until the sod is well established.**

Figure 9-6:
Use walking boards to avoid damaging sod.

Figure 9-7:
Trim sod with a heavy knife until it fits curves, odd shapes, and around obstacles.

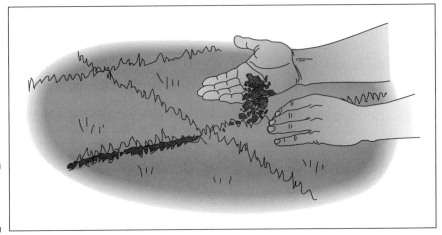

Figure 9-8:
Filling gaps in sod.

Figure 9-9:
Rolling the sod with a roller.

Care and Feeding of Lawns

It's no secret that your lawn requires some regular maintenance to keep it looking its best. Basic lawn care consists of weeding, mowing, fertilizing, and watering. Take care of those things and you may avoid more complex chores like pest and disease control. The following sections give you some tips on performing the basic chores. For more advanced lawn maintenance techniques, check out *Lawn Care For Dummies* by Lance Walheim and the Editors of The National Gardening Association (IDG Books Worldwide).

Weeding

The best technique for keeping weeds under control in your lawn is to grow the right kind of grass and take good care of it. Weeds can't get established in a thick patch of healthy turf.

If you want to yank out the prime offenders, you can find tools for this purpose at most garden centres. But you don't need to be obsessive — a few weeds won't spoil the overall look or purpose of the lawn.

Garden centres offer an array of herbicides, sometimes mixed with fertilizers, that you can spray or spread over your lawn. We are not thrilled by most of these herbicides simply because they tend to wash off the lawn and make their way to streams, rivers, and lakes where they can cause harm. (See Chapter 16 for more about weed control and herbicides.) If you don't like herbicides either, keep grass cut to 5 to 8 centimetres (2 to 3 inches) tall, fertilize regularly, and water when needed. You may have a few weeds, but the lawn will be healthy and look green.

Mowing

The mowers available today make the inevitable task of mowing the lawn easier and more enjoyable. If you're in the market for a new mower, read about some of your options in Chapter 17.

Here are some tips to keep your grass healthy and well manicured:

- Keep grasses at a height of 6 to 7.5 centimetres (2½ to 3 inches). Cutting too short also inhibits root growth, affects the roots' search for nutrients in the soil and reduces the nutrients manufactured by the leaves. Be sure you mow late in the season so your grass goes dormant at 2 to 3 inches high.

- Mow when the grass is ⅓ higher than its recommended height. Letting the lawn grow long and then shortening it by half its height all at once weakens it.

- Mow when the grass is dry.

- Mow in a different direction each time — north-south one week, east-west the next. You can even mow at a diagonal. Changing the mowing pattern prevents soil compaction and helps the grass grow upright.

- Leave clippings in place as long as they aren't longer than an inch or so or piled up in small mounds — they add nitrogen to the soil as they break down.

Fertilizing

Fertilizing lawns has grown into a whole science, and you really don't need to know about it unless you're the head greenskeeper at Glen Abbey — in which case, we're surprised and flattered that you're reading this book.

Remember that a well-fertilized lawn is healthier, denser, and more weed-free than a poorly managed one. Most grass varieties need regular fertilizing.

When to fertilize depends on your type of grass. Grasses need nitrogen and other nutrients during their seasons of active growth; fertilizing grass when it's dormant is useless. The most important time to feed grasses is in the fall and early spring. Fall fertilizing promotes deeper rooting and greater tolerance of winter stress, but don't use a slow-release product. You want one that acts before the grass stops growing for the season. Apply one low in nitrogen and higher in potassium and phosphorus. You want to promote root growth, rather than leaf growth. (See Chapter 14 for more information on fertilizer labels.)

To know how much to apply, read the label directions. Most lawn fertilizer products specify exactly how much, even how to adjust various commercial spreaders to apply the right amount. Above all, don't use too much. Grasses can't absorb more than the recommended amount, and the excess will dissolves in the ground water and could eventually affect municipal water supplies.

Organic fertilizers and manures have advantages and disadvantages compared to commercial lawn fertilizers. Organics contain less nitrogen per pound, meaning that you need to apply more for your lawn to gain an equivalent benefit. You usually end up paying much more (per unit of nitrogen) and doing more muscle work to fertilize your lawn. On the other hand, organic fertilizers deliver a host of nutrients and benefits to soil that commercial fertilizers can't.

Most lawns need between 1 to 3 kilograms (2 to 6 pounds) of actual nitrogen per year, obtained from fertilizer or grass clippings, for good growth.

For more details about fertilizers, see Chapter 14.

Tune-ups and face-lifts

You've got too many thin spots, weeds have gotten the upper hand, or the wrong type of grass is struggling to survive: What do you do? Relax — you probably don't have to tear out the whole thing and start over. As long as your lawn is at least 50 percent grass (as opposed to weeds), you can give it a face-lift by seeding an improved grass variety right on top. (The process is called *overseeding*.)

The best time to overseed is in autumn. Here's how:

1. **Mow your lawn closely to a height of about 5 centimetres (2 inches), and thoroughly rake out the mat of dead grass and stems, called *thatch*.**

   Loosen compacted soil with a *coring machine*, a piece of power equipment that cuts out small plugs of soil to improve air and water circulation around the grass roots and also gets rid of some of the thatch.

2. **Adjust the soil pH if necessary and fertilize.**

3. **Sow seed at the rate recommended on the package, or see the table in this chapter "How much seed to sow."**

4. **Sprinkle a light layer of mulch, such as hay, over the lawn (called *topdressing*) and water thoroughly.**

Ground Covers instead of Lawns

Perhaps you don't want a lawn, maybe you have an area too shady for grass, or maybe you want something in addition to lawn: You may be considering a lawn alternative for one of many reasons. That's where ground covers come in. *Ground covers* (low-growing, spreading plants) come in hundreds, maybe thousands, of varieties, and they fill in enough to give solid coverage when planted close together. Some ground covers are less demanding than lawns, but others aren't as tough or as forgiving as a lawn. And rarely can you walk or play on a ground cover like you can a lawn.

Ground covers range from very low-growing plants that are just a few inches high to more shrubby types that are several feet high. Some of the lowest-growing ground covers, such as chamomile and creeping thyme, can take a little foot traffic; you can plant these types between stepping-stones or in other areas where people occasionally walk.

Ground covers have an artistic side, too. You can create a nearly infinite variety of contrasts with ground covers, and you can mix in other shrubs, vines, annuals, and perennials for a variety of effects. Foliage textures can range from grassy to tropically bold, and colours can range from subtle shades of gray to vibrant seasonal colours. Ground covers provide a naturalistic appearance, so look to the local wild areas for ideas. Choose plants that mimic what you see in wooded areas, in unmown fields, in meadows, or on steep slopes.

Planting Ground Covers

Plants sold as ground covers usually come in cell-pack containers or in nursery flats, depending on their growth habits. Cut plants in flats into individual sections before planting.

The spacing between ground covers is very important. If you space them too far apart they take a long time to fill in, which gives weeds more time to gain a foothold. If you plant them too close the plants may quickly become over-crowded. Recommended plant spacings are included in the plant descriptions given later in this chapter. For even results, plant ground covers in rows, as shown in Figure 9-10. Staggering the rows gives more complete coverage.

Figure 9-10:
Plant rows of ground-cover seedlings to achieve maximum coverage.

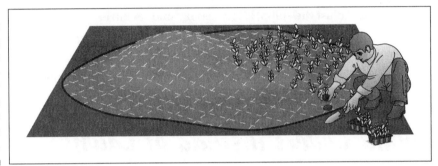

To plant small plants from pots or packs, dig a hole just deep enough for the root ball. For larger container-grown plants, taper the hole outward at the base and create a mound for the root ball.

If starting from flats, prepare the whole planting area as if you were planting a lawn (see "Planting day" earlier in this chapter). As with all plantings, you need to attend to soil needs (see Chapter 11) before introducing your plants to your landscape. Newly set out plants need adequate watering to help get them established; after the plants are growing well, many types need only minimum maintenance.

If you're planting a ground cover on a steep slope, set each plant on its own terrace (with the top of the root ball slightly above the soil level) and provide a watering basin behind the plant.

Control weeds between plants until the ground cover is established. We like to use an organic mulch or, for shrubby ground covers, landscape fabric (see Chapter 16) to control weeds. One advantage of organic mulches is that they also protect the plants in winter.

An occasional shearing can rejuvenate or freshen up many spreading, non-woody ground covers such as English ivy, St. John's wort, and vinca. (Shearing also prompts various suburban critters like roof rats and voles that have set up housekeeping in your ground cover to promptly relocate!) Cut the plants back to several inches above the ground in spring and then fertilize them. Within a few weeks, the plants will regrow and look full, clean, and healthy.

If you have a lawn or weed mower that you can set to cut high enough, use it to shear and rejuvenate your ground cover.

Top Ground Cover Choices

Although the number of possible candidates is nearly infinite, the following common ground cover plants have proven themselves in a multitude of situations and environments.

- **Woolly yarrow.** *Achillea tomentosa.* This tough, spreading, evergreen ground cover reaches 15 to 23 centimetres (6 to 9 inches) high. Small yellow flower clusters top its ferny, gray-green leaves in summer. Woolly yarrow can take some foot traffic but also can be invasive. Plant 15 to 23 centimetres (6 to 9 inches) apart in full sun. Hardy to Zone 3.

- **Bearberry, also called kinnikinnick.** *Arctostaphylos* 'Vancouver Jade'. A plant native to the Pacific northwest, but with a wide range, this cultivar has bright, glossy green leaves, pink flowers in spring, and bright red berries in fall and usually over winter. It likes sandy soil and grows in sun or partial shade. It grows to 40 centimetres (16 inches) high and is hardy to Zone 4. *Arcostaphylos uva-ursi* 'Massachusetts' is 15 centimetres (6 inches) high and is hardy to Zone 3. Plant both 30 to 40 centimetres (12 to 16 inches) apart.

- **Carpet bugle.** *Ajuga reptans.* Evergreen. This plant forms a low-growing, spreading (sometimes to the point of invasiveness) ground cover with attractive dark green or purplish-green foliage reaching 5 to 15 centimetres (2 to 6 inches) high. Spikes of blue flowers in late spring. Plant in partial to full shade (some types with coloured foliage can take more sun), 15 to 30 centimetres (6 to 12 inches) apart. Hardy to Zone 4.

- **Wild ginger.** *Asarum canadense.* Its single, three-lobed maroon flower in late spring is insignificant, but that's made up for by the broad, heart-shaped leaves, which make a lovely ground cover in woodland gardens. In moist, humusy soil it spreads rapidly and grows to about 15 centimetres (6 inches) high. Plant new plants about 30 centimetres (1 foot) apart in a largish bed to allow them room to spread. Zones 3 to 4.

- **Heather**. *Calluna vulgaris.* Evergreen ground cover that grows in mounds from 15 to 35 centimetres (6 to 14 inches) tall and looks lovely planted in groups of blending colours. Pink to purple-pink flowers loved by bees bloom at various times according to variety, sometimes almost all summer. Avoid windy sites and drought, and don't over fertilize. **Spring heath,** *Erica carnea,* a close relative, blooms in spring and early summer, grows to about 30 centimetres (one foot) tall in pink, red and white. Both thrive in 100 percent peat moss. Plant about 45 centimetres (18 inches) apart. Both hardy to Zone 6.

- **Chamomile.** *Chamaemelum nobile.* Chamomile's fine-textured, aromatic evergreen foliage can take some foot traffic. The plant has small yellow flowers in summer. Chamomile stays low and compact in full sun, rarely getting over 15 centimetres (6 inches) high; plants grow taller in partial shade. You can mow chamomile or plant it between stepping-stones. Plant in full sun, spacing plants 15 to 30 centimetres (6 to 12 inches) apart. Zone 5.

✔ **Cotoneaster.** *Cotoneaster* spp. Evergreen and deciduous. This large family of shrubs includes many dependable ground covers known for their bright-green foliage, small flowers, and red berries. Favourites include the evergreen bearberry cotoneaster, *C. dammeri* (which grows only 20 centimetres (8 inches) high and spreads up to 3 metres, or 10 feet; Zone 4); the deciduous rock cotoneaster, *C. horizontalis* (which grows 60 to 90 centimetres, or 2 to 3 feet, high and has orange-to-red autumn colour, Zone 5), and the evergreen rockspray cotoneaster, *C. microphyllus* (which rarely exceeds 60 to 90 centimetres, or 2 to 3 feet, in height, Zone 5). Plant at least 3 feet (90 centimetres) apart in full sun. (Some of the widest-spreading types should be spaced 1.5 metres, or 5 feet, apart.)

✔ **Rose daphne.** *Daphne cneorum.* A low-mounding evergreen with fragrant pink flowers in spring. Great in rock gardens, as well as mixed with other plants in a garden of ground covers. Grows to about 50 centimetres (20 inches) tall and spreads to 90 centimetres (3 feet). Zone 5. Likes sun but tolerates partial shade.

✔ **Winter creeper.** *Euonymus fortunei.* This very hardy evergreen plant comes in many fine ground-cover varieties. 'Colorata', the purpleleaf winter creeper, has bright green foliage that turns purple or bronze in autumn and winter. 'Colorata' grows about 61 centimetres (2 feet) high. 'Ivory Jade' has green leaves edged with white and also grows about 60 centimetres (2 feet) high. 'Kewensis' grows only 5 centimetres (2 inches) high and makes a very dense ground cover. Plant winter creeper in full sun, spacing the plants from 30 to 90 centimetres (1 to 3 feet) apart. Most grow well throughout Zones 5–9, and in Zone 4 with a good snow cover.

✔ **Blue fescue.** *Festuca glauca.* Silver-blue foliage highlights this mounding, grassy ground cover. It grows 10 to 25 centimetres (4 to 10 inches) high and gets by on little water. Plant in full sun, spacing the plants 15–30 centimetres (6 to 12 inches) apart. Hardy to Zone 4.

✔ **English ivy.** *Hedera helix.* With its dark green, lobed leaves, English ivy is one of the most popular ground covers. This semi-evergreen grows well under many conditions, including sun or shade. Many varieties, such as 'Thorndale' and 'Baltica' (differing in leaf size, texture, and colour) are available. Can be invasive, especially in Western Canada, climbing into trees and over structures if not kept under control. Space plants 30 to 45 centimetres (12 to 18 inches) apart. Hardy to Zone 6, occasionally to Zone 5.

✔ **Aaron's-beard; creeping St. John's wort.** *Hypericum calycinum.* These adaptable, evergreen ground covers thrive under a variety of conditions. They grow 30 centimetres (12 inches) high and have bright-yellow flowers in summer. The plants spread rapidly and can be invasive. They prefer full sun but will take partial shade. Space 30 to 45 centimetres (12 to 18 inches) apart. Hardy to Zone 5.

✔ **Junipers.** *Juniperus.* Many prostrate junipers (differing in height and foliage colour) are available. Junipers are tough evergreens that get by with little care but must have well-drained soil. *J. sabina* 'Broadmoor' has a spread over 125 centimetres (4 feet) a dense growth habit and bright green foliage; Zone 3. *J. horizontalis* 'Bar Harbor' grows about 30 centimetres (1 foot) high and spreads up to 3 metres (10 feet); the shaggy grey-green leaves turn bluish in winter; Zone 2. *J. chinensis* 'Paul's Gold' has bright golden foliage and is a good rock garden plant with a spread of 60 centimetres (2 feet); Zone 3. Plant junipers in full sun. Most should be spaced 60 centimetres to 1.5 metres (2 to 5 feet) apart, depending on the variety. Hardy in Zones 3–9.

✔ **Mondo grass or lily turf.** *Liriope* or *Ophiopogon.* Mondo grass and lily turf are two similar, grasslike plants that make attractive evergreen ground covers in shady situations. *Liriope spicata,* creeping lily turf, is one of the most adaptable, growing 15 to 25 centimetres (6 to 10 inches) high. *L. muscari* grows up to 60 centimetres (2 feet) high and has blue summer flowers that are partially hidden by the foliage. Some varieties have variegated leaves. *Ophiopogon japonicus* is a common mondo grass with dark green leaves; the plants grow 20 to 25 centimetres (8 to 10 inches) high. Space these plants 15 to 45 centimetres (6 to 18 inches) apart, depending on height. The popular 'Ebony Night' or *nigrescens* black mondo grasses grow up to 30 centimetres (1 foot) tall, usually shorter, and are dramatic with bright green moss or grey-green foliage plants. The hardiness of both species varies, but most can be grown in Zone 6; Zone 5 depending on the microclimate in your garden.

✔ **Japanese spurge.** *Pachysandra terminalis.* Japanese spurge is an attractive, spreading foliage plant for shady, moist conditions. This evergreen features rich green leaves on upright 25-centimetre (10-inch) stems, with fragrant white flowers in summer. Plant in partial to full shade and space them 15 to 30 centimetres (6 to 12 inches) apart. Hardy in zones 3–9.

✔ **Spring cinquefoil.** *Potentilla neumanniana* (alternatively *P. tabernaemontanii* or *P. verna*). This evergreen plant's dark green, divided leaves form a soft-textured cover 8 to 15 centimetres (3 to 6 inches) high. It has small clusters of yellow flowers in spring and summer and can take some foot traffic. Plant in full sun to partial shade and space the plants 25 to 30 centimetres (10 to 12 inches) apart. Hardy in Zones 4–9.

✔ **Creeping thyme.** *Thymus praecox arcticus.* A low-growing, creeping evergreen herb especially useful between stepping-stones or in a tapestry planting of various varieties. It can take foot traffic and can even be grown as a lawn alternative. Creeping thyme grows 8 to 15 centimetres (3 to 6 inches) high and has white, pink, and mauve flowers in early summer. Plant in full sun and space 15 to 25 centimetres (6 to 10 inches) apart. Hardy to Zones 4-5.

✔ **Foamflower.** *Tiarella cordifolia.* Its spikes of white, long-lasting star-like flowers in early spring dazzle the eye in a mass planting. It likes part to full shade and rich soil. Foliage resembles the maple leaf. Because it's shallow rooted, it does well at the base of trees. To retain moisture and provide soil enrichment, mulch liberally with dead leaves, and plant about 15 centimetres (6 inches) apart. Grows to 15 to 30 centimetres (6 to 12 inches) tall. Zones 3 to 4.

✔ **Dwarf periwinkle.** *Vinca minor.* This spreading, deep green ground cover is good for shady conditions. The evergreen grows from 15 to 30 centimetres (6 to 12 inches) high and has violet-blue flowers in spring and summer. It can be invasive. Space the plants 15 to 20 centimetres (6 to 8 inches) apart. Hardy in Zones 4–9.

Over in the Meadow

Using native grasses like little bluestem, side oats grama, and northern sea oats along with flowering prairie and meadow plants such as blazing star, culver's root, and wild asters instead of a conventional lawn has caught on like a spring burn on the prairies in the last couple of years. These plants create meadow-like landscapes that attract birds, bees, butterflies and other insects and heed the balance of nature.

Native grasses are superbly adapted to their native ranges and are often well adapted to other areas, too. Most native grasses can survive on less water than traditional lawn grasses and are left unmown, therefore they require little maintenance. Don't expect a lawn like you neighbour's, however — your grass will be longer and more showy, with attractive seedheads and a graceful growth habit that often allows it to ripple in the wind. Sheep fescue is one native grass you can cut, but you should leave it alone until the seedheads have matured, to allow thick growth. It grows 30 centimetres (1 foot) tall and looks especially attractive and cared-for in casual gardens with gravel paths and benches. Little blue stem grows to about 60 centimetres (2 feet).

Long-grass prairies varieties grow up to 1.5 metres (5 feet) tall, with flower and seedheads that grow from 90 centimetres to 1.5 metres (3 to 5 feet) tall. Mixed-grass prairies varieties grow 60 to 90 centimetres (2 to 3 feet) tall with flowers up to 90 centimetres (3 feet).

Common types of native grasses include wheat grass (a very drought-tolerant native grass of the Rocky Mountains), blue grama grass, little blue stem, and big blue stem, and all are native to the prairies. You can buy seed or plugs (small rooted sections of grass, which will give you quicker results). Prairie Habitats, Box 1, Argyle MB R0C 0B0, 204-467-9371, sells seeds and wildflowers. Prairie Originals, 17 Schreyer Cresc., St. Andrews, Man., R1A 3A6 204-338-7517, sells wildflowers and grass plugs. Otter Valley Native Plants, Box 31, RR1, in Eden, Ont., N0J 1H0, is a great source for native grasses. Also consult Appendix B.

Chapter 10

Vines

. . . .

In This Chapter

▶ Understanding how vines work . . . and work for you

▶ Getting to know some vine do's and don'ts

▶ Providing necessary support

▶ Looking at our favourite vines

▶ Exploring a few annual vines

. . . .

*V*ines can be a garden's beautiful prima donnas — visualize a morning glory in full bloom — or a gardener's nightmare: Imagine that same morning glory smothering your backyard shed.

Vines can do some amazing things: cool a blazing hot patio, beautify a blank wall, or create privacy with a wall of foliage. You should become acquainted with them — for their beauty and for their usefulness.

In this chapter, we help you understand how vines work and how to put them to work for, not against, you. Then we share some of our favourite vines — permanent types as well as fast-growing annuals.

Let's Do the Twist

Vines need to grow on something, either another plant or a trellis you provide. Before deciding what kind of support to provide for your favourite climbers, you need to know exactly how the climbers hold on. Vines fall into several groups, according to the way they climb.

✔ **Clinging vines**. Examples are English and Boston ivy. These vines have specialized growths — like little suction cups or claws — along their stems that can hook onto any surface they touch.

✔ **Sprawling vines**. An example is a climbing rose. These vines are often just very vigorous, spreading plants. In order for them to climb, you need to support them with a trellis or other type of structure.

✔ **Twining vines.** These vines come in two types. Some, like bittersweet, wrap around anything that falls in their way. Others, such as grapes, have small, twining tendrils at the bases of their leaves. The tendrils grab and wrap around anything they can reach.

Using Vines Effectively

Like other plant groups, vines offer a variety of ornamental characteristics, including seasonal flower colour, bright berries, and autumn colour. Because most grow vertically, you can use them in tight spots where few other plants would fit. And they are versatile — vines can create privacy, provide shade, and conceal unattractive landscape features.

Because of their rapid growth rate and the way they attach to structures, some vines can cause problems as they mature. The following sections give you tips on avoiding problems with vines.

Don't let vines grow where they shouldn't

Clinging vines, such as ivies and Virginia creeper, can attach so firmly to walls and fences that getting them off without damaging the structure becomes almost impossible. And sometimes the attaching parts of the plant work their way into cracks and crevices. As the vines enlarge and grow, they can lift shingles and damage even the sturdiest materials, such as concrete and brick.

Letting a vine attach directly to the walls of your house usually isn't a good idea unless the house is made of brick or stone — and the type of vine also makes a difference. And even then you can have problems. Instead, build a trellis a few feet away from the side of the house and let the trellis support the vine. That way, you can also paint the wall when you need to.

Don't let vines climb into the tops of trees. The vigorous vine almost always compromises the health of the tree, covering its canopy and shading its foliage. You can allow some deciduous vines, such as clematis, to grow into trees. Their delicate, open habit seldom harms the other plant.

Provide sturdy support

As vines grow, the branches enlarge and the plant gets heavier. If the supports aren't strong enough, they can buckle under the weight. Build supports that are sturdy and long-lasting. Two-inch galvanized pipe and pressure-treated 90 x 90 millimetre (4 x 4) lumber are both good choices. (See the section "Choosing a Vine Support" later in this chapter for more information.)

Prune for healthy vines

Pruning prevents vines from getting out of control, becoming too heavy, or growing into places where they're not wanted. Prune with vigour to keep the vine healthy and attractive. (For more information on pruning, see Chapter 15.)

Winter is a traditional time for pruning, but you can prune in any season to keep a rampant vine in check. Prune flowering vines, such as wisteria, immediately after the plants drop their blooms. The best time to do your major pruning of vigorous-growing fruiting plants, such as grapes and kiwi, is during their dormant season (late winter or very early spring). But you can nip back plants of any kind whenever they begin to grow out of the bounds you've set for them.

Lean on Me

You have many ways to support a vine, from arbours to lath trellises to wires strung between secure anchors. The important thing is to plan the supporting device in advance, make it strong, and design it to fit the growth habit of the vine.

Heavy fences or the walls of outbuildings are another place to plant climbers, and these supports require little work from you. And then there is the whole world of trellises, arbours, and other special supports for vines.

Although the chief purpose of supports is to hold up climbing plants, trellises and their kin also add height to the garden and maximize ground space. These structures can be decorative, as well as practical, when they turn a plain wall into a vertical garden, frame a view, or create a privacy screen.

The most important guideline for choosing a structure is that it be large and sturdy enough to support the plant when fully grown. Choose a simple garden structure that harmonizes with your home and existing garden features. And remember that some climbing plants naturally cling to their supports, but others must be trained and tied.

Recycled nylon hosiery, cut into strips, is one of the very best materials for tying plants to their supports. Nylons are strong, yet stretchy, so they don't bind and cut plant stems.

Choosing a Vine Support

You can grow most types of vines on one or more of the supports described here. (The exception is vines with adhesive disks, which grow best on stone or brick walls.) When choosing a structure for your garden, first consider the type of plant you are growing and how it will fit and look on the structure. After that, your choice is a matter of personal taste, maintenance considerations, and budget. (See Figure 10-1.)

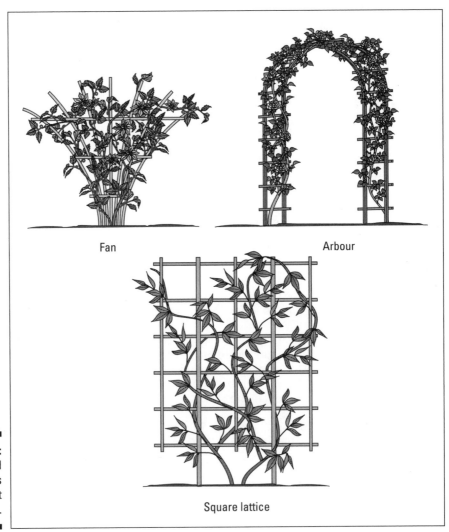

Fan

Arbour

Square lattice

Figure 10-1:
You can find
a trellis
to suit
every need.

Bamboo teepees

Perhaps you remember bamboo teepees from your childhood. Bamboo teepees have long been popular in vegetable gardens for supporting climbing green beans. Teepees are quick and easy to make, and you can reuse the bamboo stakes for many garden seasons.

To make a teepee, arrange three or four 3.7-metre (12-foot) bamboo stakes around a 90- to 120- centimetre (3 to 4 foot) circle. Space the stakes at least 46 centimetres (18 inches) apart. Push each stake into the ground at least 30 centimetres (12 inches) deep. Lash the top of the stakes together with twine.

Plant beans (or other annual climbers) at the base of each stake. As the beans start to grow, direct them up the stakes; once started, the plants don't need additional training or tying. At the end of the season, clean off the bamboo and store it indoors.

Teepees can serve double-duty when they provide support for climbers and create shade beneath for plants, such as lettuce, that prefer cooler temperatures.

Mini-teepees of 0.5- or 1- centimetre (¼- or ½-inch) diameter bamboo canes (often dyed green and sold at garden centers) are useful supports for annual climbers in containers. Try planting sweet peas or climbing nasturtiums at the teepee's base.

Chain-link fences

Okay, so the bare metal chain-link fence is not the most attractive plant support, but such fencing is strong and durable. Chain-link's industrial appearance practically screams to be cloaked in greenery. For an attractive barrier or privacy screen, plant a climbing rose at the base of a chain-link fence. (The links provide both air circulation and spaces for tying branches.) Or cover the fence with a dense climber (such as one of the cultivars of evergreen winter creeper, *Euonymus fortunei*) or an annual vine (such as morning glory).

Chain-link fencing covered with black vinyl, relatively new on the market, virtually disappears into the background, so if you're putting in a new fence, choose it. If you have an existing metal-finish fence and lots time on your hands (as well as patience), you could always paint it.

Metal trellises

Chic, freestanding metal trellises come in many shapes and sizes. Such trellises are whimsical to formal in design and are made from a variety of materials, including copper tubing, epoxy-coated wrought iron, and galvanized steel (with a hardened oil finish). Metal trellises are sturdy and easy to install (simply push their feet into the soil), but they're not very wide (most are less than 2 feet, or 60 cm, wide). Metal trellises look most attractive when placed in front of simple walls, and then draped with a single vine. Expect to pay $50 to $100 (or more!) for each trellis.

For an impressive selection of decorative metal trellises, check the catalogues in Appendix B.

Latticework trellises

Premade lattice trellises are usually constructed of wood, although trellises made of plastic are also available. Lattice is designed for mounting on walls or fences; or attach it to fence posts to make inexpensive screens. Look for lattice at lumber yards and home-building centres.

When securing lattice directly to a solid surface, extend connecting supports several inches beyond the solid surface so that the trellis does not lie directly upon the surface. This extra space improves air circulation around the plant, which helps reduce pest and disease problems.

To make house painting or other maintenance easier, fasten the latticework to hinges at the bottom so you can lay the trellis back for easy access to the wall. Use metal hooks and eyes to attach the lattice to the wall at the top. Many vines are flexible enough to bend as you raise and lower the lattice.

Sturdy lattice can also be attached to the top of a wooden fence; it adds height to the fence and extends the growing area. Clematis looks great peeking through the lattice, although on a solid wood fence it will need support to reach the lattice.

Fan trellises

Made from wood or plastic, store-bought fan trellises come in many sizes. Each fan trellis generally supports a single climber. You can use fan trellises in much the same way as you would use lattice. A fan trellis also can support a climber in a container. Try to secure the fan trellis to the inside of the container before planting in the container. (This task is easiest to accomplish if you use a wooden trellis and a wooden container.) Grow annual vines, such as sweet peas or black-eyed Susan vine.

Plastic netting

Lightweight plastic netting (often in an unobtrusive green) is a quick fix for vining vegetables like pole beans, peas, and cucumbers. Plastic netting is easy to install: Just suspend it between vertical posts. Although some types of plastic netting are resistant to ultraviolet radiation and can last for years, you need some patience to remove old vines and tendrils without cutting or ripping the mesh.

Pillars

Simply put, a pillar is a sturdy, rot-resistant wood or metal post set in the ground. (Perhaps you have a lamp post just waiting for a vine?) Pillar dimensions can vary, but the pillar's base should be buried at least 2 feet (61 cm) deep. Climbing roses are a traditional pillar plant. Examples of good pillar roses are 'Dortmund' (cherry red with white eye), 'Climbing Iceberg' (white), 'Sombreuil' (white), and 'John Hudson' (rose pink). You need to use ties to train roses up a pillar.

An obelisk is also a pillar. These are more open structures of varying heights (choose a tall one for a perennial vine like a clematis or a rose), mostly made of metal (although they can easily be constructed of wood), and they are not only popular, they're useful. (The bamboo teepee mentioned earlier more or less falls into this category.) The metal ones aren't cheap, but they last forever and become bits of garden architecture even after the vine has died.

Wall-mounted supports

If you have masonry walls, you can create a sturdy support system with galvanized wire. Attach eye bolts to the wall with expanding anchors and then thread and tie 14- or 16-gauge wire through the eye bolts. Arrange the wires horizontally, vertically, or in a fan shape, depending on the space and the plant to be grown. This system is sturdy and supports heavy climbers like roses and honeysuckles.

As an alternative, simply attach plant ties (any flexible material used for tying plants — your nursery sells several types) through the eye screws and eliminate the wires. Either way, extend the eye screws a few centimetres beyond the wall to provide air circulation.

Arbours

Decked with wisteria, porcelain vine or clematis, an arbour raises the garden to new heights. Arbours may be works of art in their own right, or they may have simple designs that highlight plants without competing with them. A heavy-duty arbour anchors the landscape, creating a feeling of permanence as well as a feeling of comfort. Placed over a path at the garden's entrance, an arbour becomes a welcoming doorway.

Arbours may be homemade, custom-made or prefabricated. Above all, they must be sturdy. To avoid damaging the growing plant while working, put the trellis or support in place before planting.

Vines We Love

You can choose from dozens of vines to adorn the sides of buildings or fences as well as ramble through your shrubs and trees. If your space is limited, look for vines that offer more than one benefit, such as handsome foliage as well as beautiful flowers or delectable fruit. Some vines provide handsome bark in winter, and others offer superb autumn colour.

Following are a few of our favourite vines:

✔ **Variegated porcelain vine.** *Ampelopsis brevipedunculata* 'Elegans'. Zone 6. We regret that people who live in zones colder than 6 aren't likely to be successful with this vine. Its lovely green, pink, and white foliage makes it pretty enough all summer, but it's when those beautiful turquoise blue berries appear that it achieves conversation status. Needs support, and some protection from the hot afternoon sun.

✔ **Clematis.** *Clematis* spp. This diverse, mostly deciduous family of eye-catching flowering vines is available in hundreds of selections. Large-flowered hybrids, with summer blooms up to 25 centimetres (10 inches) in diameter in shades of white, pink, red, blue, and purple, are the most popular. But the early species, which have smaller, nodding blooms, and the later fall varieties, in dramatic yellow or with sweetly scented clusters of white bloom, are well worth growing. The plants have delicate stems that can twine more than 3 to 4.5 metres (10 to 15 feet) high. Plant where the roots are cool and shaded but where the top can grow into full sun. For example, set the plant at the base of a large shrub and let it ramble through to the sunny top. Or plant clematis anywhere and cover the roots with a thick mulch. Clematis have different pruning needs — some should be cut back to the ground in spring because they bloom on new wood, others should be left till after blooming because they flower on old wood. Always keep your tag so you know which variety you have. Many are hardy from Zones 4 to 10.

✔ **English ivy.** *Hedera helix.* Evergreen, fast-growing, tenacious and adaptable, English ivy comes in many varieties differing in foliage size, shape, and colour. The species has deep green, heart-shaped leaves and is very vigorous. It clings with small aerial rootlets and takes over open areas in a minute. English ivy can damage all but the hardest surfaces. 'Baltica', whose leaves are a mixture of white and green, and 'Thorndale' are valued for their winter-persistent foliage and ability to thrive in deep shade. Generally hardy to Zone 6.

✔ **Dropmore honeysuckle.** *Lonicera* X *brownii* 'Dropmore Scarlet'. This vigorous twining vine bred in Canada for harsh conditions has terminal clusters of slender scarlet flowers from June to September, sometimes later, depending on the area. But there is one drawback: Unlike most honeysuckle plants, this one is not fragrant. It likes sun, as do most blooming plants, but can take dappled shade, and is hardy right down to Zone 2.

✔ **Virginia creeper**. *Parthenocissus quinquefolia.* A deciduous vine known for its fiery red autumn colour. Its leaves are divided into five leaflets, and it produces clusters of blue-black fruit in the fall, which birds love. Sun or shade, fairly moist soil. Also good as a fast ground cover. Grows to 18 metres. Zone 2.

✔ **Climbing roses.** *Rosa* spp. You can use many types of vigorous roses the same way as vines. (See Chapter 7 for more details on roses.)

✔ **Grape.** *Vitis* spp. The sprawling grapevine is one of the best choices for covering an arbour or trellis. In addition to interesting gnarled trunks, good-looking leaves, and autumn colour, you also get edible fruit. This deciduous plant is hardy from Zones 3 or 4 to 9, depending on the type of grape.

✔ **Wisteria.** *Wisteria sinensis* and *W. floribunda.* The former is the Chinese wisteria, the latter the Japanese version. About the only difference is the length of the flower — the Japanese bloom may reach 45 centimetres (18 inches) whereas Chinese blooms are shorter, up to 30 centimetres (12 inches), although still showy because the clusters bloom from top to bottom at once, unlike the Japanese variety, which opens more slowly. Whichever variety you choose, wisteria is surely elegant — dangling clusters of fragrant purple blooms among bright green, divided leaves in spring. The twisting, twining shoots keep growing almost indefinitely. As the shoots mature, they take on the classic "muscular" appearance, and so need a strong support, such as a wooden arbour. This vine requires annual pruning to look its best and to bloom prolifically— keep it to three strong stems from the ground, and don't let the green arms take over. Plant in full sun. Funny, a lot of people think it's hardy only in the south but it grows profilically in Zone 6, Zone 5 in a protected area.

Annual Vines

Want a really fast — but temporary — vine? Consider an annual vine. Like a petunia or other annual flower, it grows quickly and blooms in one season, which may be just fine for screening off a summer eyesore. (We're talking about permanent eyesores, not your neighbour mowing his lawn with his shirt off.) An annual vine can also provide glorious summer flowers.

Here are half a dozen favourite annual vines that are easy to grow:

- **Canary creeper.** *Tropaeolum peregrinum.* This fast-growing vine can reach 4.5 metres (15 feet) in one season. The name comes from the 2.5-centimetre (1-inch), bright yellow flowers that look like they have wings. (Some call it nasturtium vine.) Plant near a fence or trellis, or provide stakes for support — it's not a dense vine that will hide the neighbour's trash heap. Actually, it does well in containers, supported by wooden fan trellises, or in hanging baskets. Sow seeds directly in the ground in full sun or part shade after all danger of frost has passed. Thin seedlings to stand 12 inches (30 cm) apart. Canary creeper does best in cool-summer climates. Keep roots cool with an insulating mulch of organic matter.

- **Hyacinth bean.** *Dolichos lablab.* This is another one of the family of beans that look as good as they taste, maybe better. This one has purple-pink flowers and deep purple stems and flower buds. The lustrous burgundy bean pods stay on the pod for the rest of the season once they appear. Best started indoors a few weeks before setting out in warm weather. Vines reach 2.5 metres (8 feet) and keep blooming and producing beans till frost. They show off best on a low fence, rather than a taller trellis.

- **Morning glory.** *Ipomoea imperialis.* This is the standard for fast-growing, big-leafed, free-flowering summer vines. Varieties can climb as much as 4.5 metres (15 feet) in one season. Trumpet flowers up to 10 or 13 centimetres wide (4 or 5 inches) come in a rich range of blues, pinks, and purples. Newer varieties stay open for longer, not just the "morning" suggested by the name. Plant near a trellis, fence, or arbour, and let vines climb. Sow seeds directly in the ground in full sun in spring after all danger of frost has passed. Space 30 centimetres (12 inches) apart. The seeds have a hard coat and don't sprout easily. Help them germinate by notching seeds with a knife or file, or soaking for a couple of hours in warm water before planting.

- **Moonflower.** *I. alba,* is the morning glory's evening-flowering cousin. The flowers are big, round, and white, and have a sweet, heady scent that attracts moths. Blooms open just after sunset and wilt by afternoon the next day, but more are ready to open. Plant them in pots on a patio or under a bedroom window. The large leaves form a dense screen. May-planted seedlings usually start flowering in early August.

✔ **Bottle gourds.** *Lagenaria siceraria.* Here's a vine that will easily hide your neighbour's trash heap by July. The squash-like fruit has many uses in other countries, and has for centuries: In South America they're carved to make souveniers for tourists; in Africa they're dried and turned into bowls. In this country, we often use them, dried and painted, as bird houses or table decorations. Like other members of the squash family, the plant has large leaves and requires a good support, like a sturdy wood trellis, and often has to be tied at intervals — the fruit is, after all, rather heavy. Start the seed indoors if it's the gourds you want; outdoors in the ground if the foliage is what matters. If plants are started too early, the leaves get ratty looking in the middle of August. Mature vines can reach 6 metres (20 feet).

✔ **Nasturtium.** *Tropaeolum majus.* Nasturtiums make themselves right at home in a casual garden. Edible, bright flowers in orange, yellow, cream, red, or pink bloom abundantly through the summer (or winter and spring in mild climates). The bright green, round leaves can make a thick low carpet that's attractive in its own right. Climbing varieties, which trail up to 2 metres (6 feet), can be trained on a trellis or as a ground cover. After soaking seed overnight, sow them directly in the ground in full sun or part shade in spring after all danger of frost has passed. You can also start them four weeks early indoors. Thin seedlings to stand 30 centimetres (12 inches) apart. Nasturtiums are easy to grow in well-drained soil, and are quick about it. Best in cool-summer climates, they live through winter in mild climates and can reseed themselves — the nicest sort of "weed" if you like a wild look.

✔ **Sweet peas.** *Lathyrus.* If you appreciate old-fashioned charm and heady fragrance, find a sunny spot for sweet peas. The tall climbers are the most familiar , and although they don't grow tall enough to be considered a screen, they vine to 1.5 metres (5 feet) or so, and are wonderful cut flowers. Colours include blue, orange, pink, purple, red, and white. Sweet peas need a support, such as chicken wire or strong netting. They can't stand heat and do best in cool climates. If you live in a typical cold-winter, hot-summer climate, plant early in spring as soon as the soil can be dug so blooming can take place while weather is still cool. In warmer climates, make sure you choose varieties labeled as heat-resistant. Sweet peas perform best when seeds are planted directly where they are to grow. Choose a spot in full sun with a climbing surface — a trellis, net, wire fence, or other kind of support. To hasten seed germination, soften the seed coat by soaking seeds in water for at least a few hours before planting.

Part IV
At Ground Level

In this part . . .

This is the part where you get your hands dirty. (If you have an aversion to getting a bit of soil on your hands, now is your chance to take up stamp collecting.) Even though it's the stuff that happens above ground that draws all the ooohs and aaahs, most of the important action that determines whether your plants will flourish takes place below ground.

Here you find out how to improve your soil so that your garden has its best chance to succeed, how to plant seeds, and how to transplant seedlings and saplings.

Chapter 11

Understanding and Improving Soil

In This Chapter

▶ Clearing a site

▶ Understanding and testing your soil

▶ Improving your soil

▶ Digging and tilling

▶ Making raised beds

*P*reparing your soil is probably the most important step toward bringing your garden to life. The reason? *Roots*. This underground lifeline makes up half of every plant — sometimes more. You may often forget about roots, however, because you don't see them — except for the occasional maple root that the lawn mower keeps hitting. But the roots are there, spreading, digging, and questing for nutrients and moisture.

Before you plant, take some time to get acquainted with your soil. (It's more interesting than you think!) Chances are you'll find out you need to make some improvements — typically by adding organic matter (a process called *amending the soil*) and a perhaps a few other goodies, as well. Your goal, as you discover in this chapter, is to create an airy soil, rich in oxygen and nutrients that enable your plants to thrive.

Clearing the Site

The perfect spot for your garden may already be occupied. Whether it's a beautiful sweep of lawn or a patch full of weeds and brush, you need to clear your site of existing vegetation before testing and improving the soil. Follow these steps for clearing a site where you intend to place your garden:

1. **Outline the area where you'll go to work.**

   If you're developing a square or rectangular area, you can establish straight lines by stretching a string between two sticks. Leave the string in place or mark the line with a trickle of white ground limestone, spray paint, or flour. For curved portions of the garden, use a garden hose or rope to lay out the line. Adjust the hose position until the curve looks smooth.

2. **Use a flat spade to dig a small trench that establishes the outline of the garden plot.**

3. **Clear the surface by removing plants, sod, brush, and rocks.**

4. **Mow the site to clear the rough ground.**

5. **Cut down woody plants and dig out the roots.**

6. **When the vegetation is down to a manageable level, you can remove the sod and other low vegetation.**

You can use several techniques for clearing the site. If the garden is currently lawn, strip off the turf, roots and all, by using a flat spade or sod cutter. This method is hard work but does a thorough job.

Stripping sod

Your site-clearing process may very well involve getting rid of natural sod. Here's how:

1. **A couple of days prior to digging, water the area you want to clear.**

   Stripping sod is easier when the soil is lightly moist.

2. **If you haven't done so already, mark the edges of the plot.**

3. **Starting at one side of the plot, slip your spade under the grass and slide it under the sod.**

   Don't dig too deep; you want to remove merely the sod and an inch or two of roots.

   Another approach is to precut the sod into square or rectangular sections and then loosen each section with the spade.

4. **Pivot the tool up, letting the sod flip up over the spade.**

5. **Slice off the sod section and toss it into a wheelbarrow to take to the compost pile.**

6. **Gradually continue in this manner until the garden is free of sod.**

Many garden experts get rid of grass by spraying it with a nonselective herbicide, such as Roundup or Finale. When the grass is completely dead, they till it into the soil, adding organic matter to the soil in the process. However, our feeling is that most gardeners are better off avoiding herbicides, even considering the promise of saving time and energy. To use herbicides or not is a decision you have to make for yourself.

If you have a large area of sod to clear, consider renting a sod cutter. These machines are the size and weight of full-size rototillers, so you need a pick-up truck or trailer to get one home. (Some rental yards deliver and pick up heavy equipment, but of course they charge extra.)

After stripping the sod, stack the strips like bricks into a 1- or 1.2- metre (3- or 4-foot) pile and let it become compost. Or create a berm, or small hill, on a flat lot by piling the sod upside down in a gradual slope and planting it with ground covers. You might want to wait a year to let the sod break down and settle before planting. At that point, you could add to the hill with more soil.

Other soil-clearing methods

You can use other ways to clear a garden: Cover it with black plastic or layers of newspapers, or simply use repeat cultivation.

- **Black plastic.** After a month under black plastic, existing plants die from lack of sunlight. Spread the plastic over the entire garden area, securing the edges with spare rocks, bricks, or boards. Overlap neighbouring pieces of plastic by several inches so that no light can penetrate. Come back in a month, remove the plastic, and rototill the dead plant matter into the soil. Wait about 10 days for errant weeds to sprout. (Because you haven't removed weed seeds, you're sure to get some growth.) Cut down or pull out any weeds that emerge.

- **Newspapers.** To use newspapers, spread a layer five to six sheets thick over the entire area in the fall. Overlap the sheets about 12.5 centimetres (5 inches). Use black and white newsprint only — coloured ink may contain lead or other heavy metals. Cover the newspaper with straw or other mulch and leave it alone for one season. After a few months, the sod, newspaper, and other material will have decomposed enough to till under. You've recycled the newspapers and the decomposed sod adds nutrients.

- **Repeat cultivation.** If you have plenty of time or if your garden is too large for the other site-clearing methods to be practical, then consider the *repeated tilling method*. This process adds good organic matter to the soil and kills existing weeds but takes much of the growing season to complete.

1. **In spring, rototill the garden area and broadcast seeds of a cover crop such as buckwheat, Sudan or sorghum grass or black-eyed peas.**

2. **After the cover crop gets to be about 6 inches (15 cm) high, till again to work it into the soil.**

3. **Let the cover crop decay, which takes a couple of weeks during warm weather. Then till again and prepare to plant.**

Meeting Your Soil

Taking time to create a healthy underground environment before you plant goes a long way toward ensuring a healthy, productive garden. You need to know only a few basics and perform some easy tests to determine the characteristics of your soil, and you're ready to start improving your soil like an expert!

To understand your soil, keep in mind what plants need from soil: moisture, air, and nutrients.

Soil texture

Soil comprises air spaces, organic matter, and, mostly, mineral particles. Soil minerals come in three types: sand, silt, and clay. Sand is the largest particle in most garden soils. Silt particles are smaller than fine sand and larger than clay. Clay is the smallest particle. The relative proportions of these particles in the soil determine its texture.

The ideal soil texture is *loam*. Loam soils have all three mineral types in roughly equal proportions — enough sand to allow good water drainage and air circulation, but enough clay to retain moisture and nutrients. (See Figure 11-1.)

Most garden soils are best understood as either sandy, clay, or loam. (Silty soils occur where ancient glacial lakes deposited significant amounts of dust, along rivers that frequently overflow in spring, or where dust storms have deposited soil. The state of Oklahoma considers silt to be its official soil, and it's found somewhere in every Canadian province.)

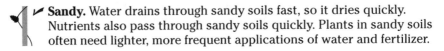 **Sandy.** Water drains through sandy soils fast, so it dries quickly. Nutrients also pass through sandy soils quickly. Plants in sandy soils often need lighter, more frequent applications of water and fertilizer.

✔ **Clay.** Soils dominated by clay particles are heavy and tend to pack tightly. Clay soil sticks to your shoes and shovel when it's wet, and cracks when dry. Water enters and drains slowly from clay soils, which can make them difficult to manage. On the other hand, clay soil's ability to retain moisture and nutrients makes them very fertile.

✔ **Loam.** Loam soils come in many types, but all combine the properties of sand, silt, and clay. A "perfect" loam soil contains 40 percent sand, 40 percent silt, and 20 percent clay. Loam soils have such a good reputation because they are ideal for most plants. But many plants grow well in non-loam soils.

A quick test for texture: Ribbons and bows

You can use two methods to identify your soil's texture: the *ribbons-and-bows method* and the *jar method.*

Get a general idea of your soil's texture by taking a handful of moist soil, squeezing it into a ball, and working it out in a ribbon between your thumb and your forefinger. Stand the ribbon straight up in the air.

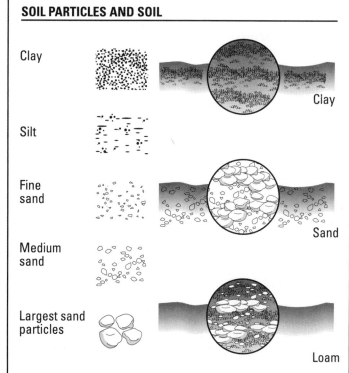

SOIL PARTICLES AND SOIL

Clay

Silt

Fine sand

Medium sand

Largest sand particles

Clay

Sand

Loam

Figure 11-1: The size of the mineral particles determines a soil's texture. Loam is the ideal soil for most plants.

✔ If you can't form a ribbon, the soil is at least 50 percent sand and has very little clay.

✔ If the ribbon is less than 5 centimetres (2 inches) long before breaking, your soil has roughly 25 percent clay in it.

✔ If the ribbon is 5–9 centimetres (2–3½ inches) long, it has about 40 percent clay.

✔ If the ribbon is greater than 9 centimetres (3½ inches) long and doesn't break when held up, it is at least 50 percent clay.

A more accurate test for texture: The jar method

For most gardeners most of the time, knowing the exact texture of your soil is not so important. But once you do know, that information can help explain much of what goes on in your garden. You can then tailor your soil management for maximum effect. Allow several days to carry out the following test.

1. **Put 2.5 centimetres (1 inch) of dry, non-lumpy garden soil in a tall litre (quart) jar.**

2. **Fill the jar ⅔ with water and add 5 millilitres (1 teaspoon) of a dispersing agent, such as a liquid dish detergent or table salt.**

3. **Shake the jar thoroughly and let the contents settle.**

4. **Measure the depths of the different layers of soil.**

✔ When the sand settles to the bottom (in about a minute), measure the depth of that layer.

✔ Silt settles in four to five hours. You should see a colour and size difference between the silt and sand layers; if not, subtract the sand depth from the total to determine the silt depth. The clay takes days to settle, and some of the smallest particles may remain permanently in suspension.

By measuring the depth of each layer, you can figure out the approximate percentages of sand, silt, and clay in your soil. For example, you have loam soil if the 5 centimetres (2 inches) of soil settles down like this: The sand and silt layers are about 2 centimetres (¾ inch) each, and the clay layer is less than 13 milimetres (½ inch).

Soil structure

The way in which sand, silt, and clay particles combine or cluster is called the *soil structure*. Structure modifies the influence of texture. Most often, gardeners use additions of organic matter — compost, peat moss, mulch, and so on — to improve soil structure.

No matter what kind of soil you have, adding organic matter improves the soil structure. Organic matter helps form *humus,* which enables small clay or silt particles to stick together to form larger aggregates; in sandy soils, humus acts like a sponge to catch and hold moisture and nutrients. For more details about humus, see this chapter's section, "Exactly what do you add?"

Two methods of determining your soil structure are the *percolation method* and the *metal-rod method,* which we explain in the following sections.

A quick test for structure: Percolation

The percolation do-it-yourself test evaluates *water drainage* — the ability of water to move through the soil, which is called the *percolation rate.* To evaluate drainage:

1. **Dig several holes 30 centimetres deep to 60 centimetres wide (1 foot to 2 feet) in various places in your garden.**

2. **Cover the holes with sheets of plastic to let the soil dry out.**

3. **When the soil is dry, fill each hole to the top with water and record the time it takes for the water to completely drain.**

   The ideal time is between 10 and 30 minutes.

   • If the water drains in less than 10 minutes, the soil will tend to dry out too quickly in the summer. Amend the soil with moisture-retaining matter such as peat moss and humus.

   • If it takes 30 minutes to 4 hours to drain, you can still grow most plants but you have to water it slowly to avoid runoff and to allow the water to soak in deeply.

   • If your soil takes longer than 4 hours to drain, you may have a drainage problem. In sandy soil, dig 30 to 60 centimetres (a foot or two) deep to see whether a hard layer is blocking water movement. If so, break it up in the area you want plants to grow. You may have to dig down with a post-hole digger, though in some cases the impermeable layer is too deep even for that. You can also use a nozzle on the end of a pipe to make a water jet bore through an impermeable layer.

   If your soil is clay, create a raised bed and use purchased soil or a homemade soil mix for planting. The goal is to get plant roots up out of the soggy soil and into well-drained, elevated soil rich with organic matter.

Another test for structure: The metal-rod method

In some regions, particularly ones that receive little rainfall, a concrete-like layer lies just under the soil. This layer, which is known as *caliche,* prevents normal water movement and root growth.

In addition to caliche, some soils suffer from a layer of dense clay soil called *hardpan.* Though not as hard as caliche, this dense layer also prevents good plant growth. (See the section "Improving Your Soil," in this chapter.) The simplest way to see whether your soil has a hardpan or compaction layer below the surface is to take a metal rod and walk around your property sticking it into the ground. If you can't easily push the rod into the soil at least 15 to 20 centimetres (6 to 8 inches) deep, you need to improve the soil's structure. If you push it down and consistently meet resistance at a certain depth, you may be hitting a hardpan layer.

One more big thing: Soil pH

Just to intimidate the rest of us, chemists use a chemical symbol to represent the relative alkalinity (sweetness) or acidity (sourness) of the soil. This symbol, *pH,* represents the "negative logarithm of hydrogen ion concentration." (Better make a note. You'll be tested on this later.)

Soil pH is rated numerically on a logarithmic scale of 1 to 14, but you'll almost never see a soil with a pH of 2 or 13. In practice, soil with a pH of 4.5 is strongly acidic and a pH of 9.5 is strongly alkaline. Most soils in the world range between a pH of 5 and 9. An absolutely neutral pH is 7.0.

The correct pH for your plants is important because certain nutrients are available only to plants within a specific pH range. The ideal pH for most plants is from 6.0 to 7.0. A few plants (such as acid-loving rhododendrons and blueberries) prefer more extreme conditions. Usually, areas of high rainfall have a low pH, and areas of low rainfall have a high pH.

Kits for testing pH are available in many garden centres. You can also figure out your soil's pH by using a professional soil test (see section below). For a quick check of your soil's pH, try the following fizz tests. These tests are not very accurate, but can be fun to watch!

✔ To check whether your soil is severely alkaline, take a tablespoon (15 mL) of dried garden soil and add a few drops of vinegar. If the soil fizzes, the pH is above 7.5. (The "free carbonates" in the soil react with the acid at a pH of 7.5 and above.)

✔ To check for acidity in the soil, take 15 millilitres (a tablespoon) of wet soil and add a pinch of baking soda. If the soil fizzes, the soil is probably very acidic (pH less than 5.0).

Your soil, in detail

For the definitive word on your soil's chemistry and makeup, a professional test is the next step. Your local agricultural office may be able to test your soil. Some provincial and private labs are listed in Appendix B. The results of these tests can tell you about soil nutrient levels, soil structure, and pH. You also get suggestions on how to make your soil even better.

Keep in mind that the reliability of any soil test depends on the accuracy of the soil sample. Avoid contaminating soil samples with residue from tools, containers, or cigarette ash, for example. The small sample that you send to a lab must also be representative of your garden. Gather soil from several places and mix it together to form a composite picture of the plot. However, don't mix soil from different garden areas where you'll be growing plants with different needs or with soil near foundations or walls where construction residues may remain. Follow the directions from the soil lab or agricultural office for best results.

Improving Your Soil

If your soil is a nice, fertile blend — one that grows good grass — you may not need to do anything special to it to grow most garden plants. But beefing up the organic content never hurts, because organic matter is constantly being broken down. *Organic matter* — such as decaying leaves, hay, grass clippings, compost, and decomposed cow or horse manure — releases nutrients and other chemicals that make soil fertile and productive. Organic matter is especially valuable for adding richness to sand and lightness to clay. The organic material makes good gardens great and poor gardens better by making any soil more like the ideal loamy soil. Be careful not to use cat or dog droppings, because this waste can contain parasites.

Before planting in reasonably good soil, dig in 2.5 or 5 centimetres (1 or 2 inches) of organic matter, such as compost, peat moss, decayed livestock manure, shredded leaves, or decayed lawn clippings. Then, each year, mulch planted areas with an inch or more of compost or organic mulch.

Amending your soil before planting is not always necessary, especially if you're planting long-lived trees and shrubs and if your soil is reasonably good, if not perfect. On the other hand, if you find that your soil is not what it needs to be for the kinds of plants you want to grow, try to correct the problem before you plant. Be prepared to amend the entire planting area so that plant roots can grow freely without encountering a bewildering range of different soil blends. Dramatically different soil types can stop root growth cold. Apply a layer of organic matter, at least 5 to 10 centimetres (2 to 4 inches), and till it into the soil.

Plan to maintain your improved soil by adding several inches of organic material each year — even more in particularly difficult soils. Here are some tips to improve tough soils:

✔ Add a 5- to 10-centimetre (1- to 2-inch) deep top dressing of compost to compacted soils in perennial beds annually. No need to rake it into the soil.

✔ Break up a compacted layer and build extra-deep top soil in annual gardens by double digging (see the section "Double digging" in this chapter) or by deeply tilling the soil below the hardpan layer and mixing in generous amounts of organic matter.

✔ Build a raised bed if the thickness of the hardpan layer doesn't allow for planting. (See "Simple raised beds" in this chapter.) Build the bed about 20 centimetres (8 inches) high — or even higher if you install a retaining wall. Cover the existing soil with commercial topsoil that's preblended with about 20 percent compost.

Exactly what do you add?

Organic matter that you can add to your soil comes in so many forms and varieties that this book couldn't possibly list them all. Nursery and garden centres offer many kinds, often in 10- or 20- kilogram (20- or 40-pound) bags. But if you have really big plans, consider buying your organic amendment by the truckload. By the bag or by the truckload, here are some of the tempting tidbits that you'll find can do wonders to improve the texture of garden soil:

✔ **Compost.** When different kinds of dead plant material get piled together, dampened, and stirred or turned every week or so to keep air in the mixture, they become compost after a few months (or a year). Products labeled as compost can originate from all sorts of stuff, but enterprising people who have tapped into the yard-waste stream usually create them. Fallen leaves, shredded Christmas trees, and wood chips left from tree-trimming crews often find their way to compost-manufacturing facilities. Compost ingredients can also include sawdust from lumber mills, peanut hulls from peanut processing plants, and hundreds of other agricultural by-products.

One place to get lots of compost cheap is from your own city. Many municipalities offer free compost and mulch. Some charge a modest fee for it. The only caveat is quality. Some cities compost industrial by-products that you might not want to have in your garden. Check with your local parks department.

Expect to find little bits of sticks and other recognizable things in a bag of compost, but mostly judge quality by the texture of the material, which should be soft and springy. If you plan to buy a large quantity of compost, compare products packaged by different companies to find the best texture. A 7.5-centimetre (3-inch) layer of packaged compost, worked into the soil, is a liberal helping that should give instant results. To estimate how much you need, figure that an 18 kilogram bag (40 pound) (that may actually weigh more or less, depending on how it's been stored) covers 0.84 metre^2 (one square yard) of bed space.

✔ **Composted manure.** In addition to its soil-improving properties, composted or "aged" manure also contains respectable amounts of nitrogen and other important plant nutrients. Nutrient content varies with the type of manure. Composted chicken manure is very potent, whereas steer manure is comparatively lightweight. Packaged sheep manure is quite popular among gardeners, and you may eventually encounter some truly exotic renditions based on the waste from zoo animals, bats, and even crickets.

The amount of manure you should use depends on your soil type. With bulky manure from large animals (cow, horse, goat, sheep, elephant), start with a 2.5-centimetre (1-inch) layer, or about 18 kilograms (40 pounds), per 2.5 metres^2 (3 square yards). Follow package application rates when using stronger manure from rabbits, chickens, and other birds.

✔ **Humus.** Bags labeled as *humus* are the wild cards of the soil-amendment world. Anything that qualifies as organic matter for soil, or any soil-organic matter mixture, can be considered humus. Unlike compost, which is supposed to be "cultured" under controlled conditions, humus can come from more humble beginnings. For example, humus may be 2-year-old sawdust and wood chips from a lumber mill mixed with rotten leaves and dark topsoil. Or, it could be rotten hay mixed with soil and sand. You just don't know what to expect until you buy a bag and open it up. If the humus has a loose, spongy texture and dark colour, and you like the way it feels and smells, go for it. A 5 to 7.5 centimetre (2 to 3 inch) layer (18 kilograms per 1.7 metres^2, or 40 pounds per 2 square yards) is a good estimate.

✔ **Topsoil.** Breaking into bags of topsoil to see what's inside is always interesting. Sometimes the soil is exactly what you might find in bags of humus or compost, and other times it may look more like unbelievably black soil. Whatever the bag contents include, topsoil is almost always cheap. You can use bagged topsoil as a soil amendment, or use so much of it that your flower bed is filled with mostly imported topsoil and only a little of the native stuff.

✔ **Peat moss.** Peat moss is a very spongy acidic, brown material harvested from peat bogs in Canada, Michigan, and a few other places. On the plus side, peat moss absorbs and holds huge amounts of water and nutrients while frustrating soil-borne fungi that can cause plant diseases. Peat moss is more beneficial in sandy soil as opposed to clay soils. In sandy soils, the water-holding power of peat is put to good use. Clay soil retains water, so adding peat moss is overkill.

On the negative side, some gardeners are concerned about the sustainability of peat moss harvesting. Peat bogs that are damaged by over-harvesting may require a thousand years to regenerate. Because of this, you might want to limit your use of peat moss to situations where it's most valuable, such as creating special soil mixtures for container-grown plants, or for planting shrubs that really like it a lot, like azaleas and rhododendrons. We think most, but not all, of the peat moss in nurseries and garden centres is harvested responsibly and sustainably. Gardeners in some areas use shredded coco-bean fibre as a substitute.

Changing pH

If you're growing pH-sensitive plants, or if you're dealing with very acidic or very alkaline soils, you can adjust pH with specific soil amendments. To make soil less acidic, add ground limestone. To increase alkalinity, add soil sulfur. But rather than commit to the ongoing need to adjust pH, consider choosing landscape plants that grow well in your native soil with its existing pH. Amending soil with many kinds of organic matter gradually lowers pH. (Some animal manures tend to have an alkaline effect so should not be used to acidify.) Likewise, most nitrogen-containing fertilizers, natural or manufactured, acidify soils — some a great deal, others only slightly. But if your soil pH is significantly too low or too high for the kinds of plants you want to grow, you need to add ground limestone or soil sulfur. To increase or decrease your soil pH, do the following:

- ✔ **Add limestone to raise your soil pH from 5.0 to 6.5.** To each 93 metres^2 (1,000 square feet) of sand, add 18.6 kilograms (41 pounds); to each 93 metres^2 of loam, add 35.4 kilograms (78 pounds); and to each 93 metres^2 of clay, add 69 kilograms (152 pounds).

- ✔ **Add sulfur to lower your soil pH from 8.5 to 6.5.** To each 93 metres^2 (1,000 square feet) of sand, add 20.8 kilograms (46 pounds); to each 93 metres^2 of loam, add 25.8 kilograms (57 pounds); and to each 93 metres^2 of clay, add 31.3 kilograms (69 pounds).

Adding nutrients

If your soil is low in nutrients, which you can determine by having it tested or by seeing that plants grow poorly, add extra nutrients. If your soil has been tested, add amendments and fertilizers according to the lab's recommendations. If you haven't tested the soil, add a complete granular fertilizer according to package directions. A *complete fertilizer* is one that contains nitrogen, phosphorus, and potassium, the major nutrients that all plants need. For general purposes, use a balanced fertilizer with a ratio of 10-10-10 or 20-20-20.

Green manure crops and cover crops

One easy way for gardeners to add organic matter and nutrients to the soil is to grow *green manure crops*. These are plants grown to be chopped and tilled or spaded into the soil when they are still green (before they blossom and produce seeds). The succulent plant material breaks down quickly, adding nutrients and improving soil texture. These crops are usually grown during the main gardening season — between crops or just after harvesting a crop. In many climates, green manure crops remain standing over the winter and get plowed into the soil before spring planting.

Cover crops are often the same plants that are used for green manure crops. However, the primary purposes of a cover crop are to prevent soil erosion and to choke out weeds, usually when the soil is bare of crops before and after the harvest.

The plants used as green manure and cover crops can be divided into two broad categories: *legumes* and *nonlegumes*. Legumes have special nodules on their roots that house nitrogen-fixing bacteria of the genus *Rhizobium*. Examples of legumes are soybeans, vetches, cowpeas, and clovers. If you till the legumes back into the soil, succeeding crops benefit from the nitrogen that the legumes and its *Rhizobium* absorbed from the air.

Although nonlegumes don't add as much nitrogen to the soil as legumes do, many nonlegumes are very useful as green manure and cover crops simply for the organic matter that they add to the soil.

Loosening the Soil

The depth and techniques you use to loosen the soil depend on which plants you intend to grow and the condition of your soil. For your average garden of annual flowers and vegetables, for example, you can use a process called *single digging* to break up the top 20 centimetres (8 inches) of soil by using a spade or rototiller.

In existing gardens with light, fluffy soil, you may be able to turn the bed with a spade without too much difficulty and minimize organic matter loss. If you prepare the soil in autumn, let frost help break up the soil clumps. Then spade again in spring and finish up with a rake.

When to work the soil

Have you ever grown your own mouth-watering melon, checking it daily to see whether it's perfectly ripe? Preparing the soil is similar. You need to wait until the soil is in the right condition — lightly moist, but not wet. If too wet, clays can dry into brick. If too dry, soil can turn into dust and blow away, leaving beneficial soil life to perish. If your soil tends to be wet and clammy in spring when you're ready to plant annual flowers, you can avoid this frustration by preparing your beds in the fall, when dry conditions often prevail.

Fortunately, the right soil condition is easy to evaluate. Take a handful of soil and squeeze it in your fist. Tap the resulting ball with your finger. If it breaks up easily, the soil is ready. If it stays in a sodden clump, the soil needs to dry out more. If it doesn't cling at all, the soil is dry: Water the area, wait a day, and try again.

Begin digging by removing a section of soil the width of the bed and the depth of your spade. Place excavated soil in a garden cart or wheelbarrow, or simply pile the soil to the side temporarily. Soon, you'll have what looks like a shallow grave. Next, slice down into the adjacent portion of soil with the spade and roll that soil into the trench you just made. Continue this process until you have covered the garden width (or length). Finally, haul the soil excavated from the first trench and place it into the last space.

After your first pass with the shovel, break up the clods and add the soil amendments and fertilizer. Then dig through the bed again, rake vigorously to break up clods and to mix in the amendments. Use a garden rake to comb through the soil and remove rocks, clods, and any chunks of vegetation or plant roots that you missed previously. Smooth the soil over the entire bed by raking, and you're ready to plant.

Time for a tiller

Digging a small flower bed is a good exercise program, but preparing a large one by hand in one day is almost impossible without the help of a tiller. If you need to cultivate more than 93metres^2 (1,000 square feet), consider renting, borrowing, or buying a tiller. (Of course, exactly how much is too much to do by hand depends on your strength and ambition.) Lightweight minitillers are sufficient for many tilling chores. For larger jobs, look to either front- or rear-tined tillers. Professional growers usually favour the latter.

Another option is to have someone else till your garden. No matter where you live, you can usually find someone in your community who does this for a living in the spring. Look in the classified ads in the newspaper or call local garden centres to find this most valuable resource person. Before the person arrives to churn up your soil, have all the soil amendments on hand that you intend to use. After you or your hired person has tilled the area and raked out the weeds, spread out your soil amendments and fertilizer, and have your tiller till it again.

Rototillers are a handy tool for occasional use. Beware, however, that repeated use of tillers can create a hardpan layer (known as *plough pan* or *pressure pan*). Tillers promote faster breakdown of soil organic matter because of how they stir and mix the soil; and tillers cultivate soil to only one depth, so the soil beneath the tilled layer becomes compacted from repeated pressure from the tiller.

Double digging

Double digging works the soil more deeply than single digging and is useful for deep-rooted plants or areas where drainage needs improvement. This process takes a lot of work, but the effects last for years.

1. **Mark out a bed 90 centimetres to 1.2 metres (3 or 4 feet) wide and up to 7.5 metres (25 feet) long.**

2. **Across the width of the bed, remove a layer of the topsoil to create a trench 15 to 20 centimetres (6 to 8 inches) deep and 30 to 60 centimetres (1 to 2 feet) wide. Place the soil in your wheelbarrow.**

3. **With a digging fork, break up the subsoil at the bottom of the trench to the full depth of the tines — about 15 to 20 centimetres (6 to 8 inches). Mix in plenty of soil amendments.**

4. **Step down into the bed and dig the topsoil from the adjacent strip, moving it onto the exposed, loose subsoil of the first trench.**

5. **Break up the newly exposed subsoil with the garden fork, and add amendments.**

6. **Continue in this fashion until you break up upper and lower layers across the entire bed. The soil from the first trench, held in the wheelbarrow, goes into the last trench.**

7. **Spread soil amendments over the entire bed and rake it into the top 15 to 20 centimetres (6 to 8 inches) of soil.**

After you finish, the earth is mounded up high in the bed. Walk on the adjacent ground rather than on the raised bed. When you go to prepare the bed in subsequent planting seasons, you'll be amazed at how little work it takes to loosen the ground.

Simple raised beds

Raised beds are an ideal way to loosen the soil of the garden and define planting areas. To make a raised-bed garden, outline the beds with string. For vegetable gardens, a 90-centimetre (3-foot) wide bed is best; for ornamental plantings, choose a size that best fits your design. After you define the beds, loosen the soil by using a shovel or a garden fork. Then shovel soil from the adjacent area onto the bed. Figure 11-2 shows a basic raised bed and one edged with wood.

Roses, carrots, parsnips, and other deep-rooted plants grow best when you loosen the soil 30 centimetres (12 inches) deep or deeper. This requirement calls for building a raised bed over the existing garden or for double digging.

Figure 11-2:
Create raised beds by first (A) drawing soil from the perimeter of the bed onto loosened soil. (B) Leave the edges as they are. Or (C) finish the edges with untreated wood or other materials.

Chapter 12

Raising Plants from Seeds

• •

In This Chapter

▶ Shopping smart

▶ Sowing right in the ground

▶ Top choices for direct sowing

▶ Starting seeds indoors

▶ Top choices for indoor sowing

• •

Starting some plants from seeds can't be simpler. On a warm June day, say, you poke a big fat sunflower seed into moist ground, stand back, and — almost before you know it, a towering 3-metre (10 feet) plant is looking down on you. But, as you may expect, some plants are not so easygoing — like that Australian annual that comes with directions to "first scorch the the hard shell of the seed with a blowtorch."

Naturally, we're going to stay closer to the sunflower camp. The plants that are easiest and most rewarding to start from seeds are annuals (marigolds, zinnias, and many more) and vegetables (squash, corn, and many more).

Why start flowers and vegetables from seeds when so many different kinds of seedlings are available at the nursery?

✔ With seeds, you have a greater variety of choices than you'd find with small plants in a garden centre. One seed catalogue may offer dozens of different marigolds, whereas a garden centre could have just six or eight.

✔ Seeds can save you money. One pack of seeds, which can produce hundreds of plants, can cost less than a six-pack of the same variety of small plants.

✔ Some plants do better or just as well when started as seeds in the spot where you want them to grow to maturity.

✔ Sowing seeds is satisfying and fun. Do we need to explain why?

What Those Needy Seeds Need

Flower seeds come in all shapes and sizes, from begonia seeds the size of dust grains to nasturtium seeds the size of peas. Larger seeds are the easiest to handle, and they often grow into comparatively large seedlings. Be forewarned that tiny seeds usually take longer to grow into big plants.

Growing flowers from seeds is pretty straightforward. You plant them in soft soil, add water, and keep them constantly moist until they sprout. Here are the basic necessities for growing seeds:

- ✔ **Moisture** triggers the germination process and softens the hard outer covering of the seed, called the seed coat, so the sprout can emerge.

- ✔ **Soil temperature** affects the speed of the germination process. For most seeds, the warm side of 21°C (70°F) is just about right.

- ✔ **Light** is critical for seedlings from the moment the sprout breaks through the soil. If you want to grow healthy seedlings indoors, you need a greenhouse or some sort of supplemental light; tabletop fluorescent fixtures that hold both a warm and a cool light tube are perfect for this because together the tubes provide nearly 100 percent full-spectrum light, like daylight. You can also buy full-spectrum fluorescent bulbs especially for seed-starting, but one costs more than a warm and a cool tube.

Seedlings grow roots as rapidly as they grow leaves, and some annual flowers put a huge amount of energy into roots right off the bat. Flowers that spend their infancy developing long, brittle taproots often are difficult or impossible to transplant, so they are best sown in their designated garden spot. This is the reason you don't often see larkspur or Shirley poppies, for example, sold as bedding plants.

Smart Shopping

Every garden centre and home supply store puts big seed racks where you can't help but see them. Those packets usually contain good quality seeds. Just to be sure, though, look beyond the beautiful picture on the front of the packet to find other information that reveals much more important data:

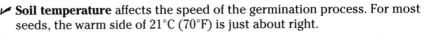

- ✔ Species and/or variety name
- ✔ Mature height
- ✔ Packing date (Don't purchase if the seeds are more than one year old.)
- ✔ Special planting instructions

Some seed companies also put the expected germination rate on their seed packets, which should always be above 65 percent. This number indicates the percentage of seeds in the packet that you can realistically expect to sprout. If no germination rate is available, you can usually assume that the seeds meet or exceed the germination standards for that species. All reputable seed companies discard bad seeds rather than sell them.

Mail-order seed companies can maintain huge selections, and they tend to be meticulous about storage conditions. However, because they display and guarantee their seeds in their catalogues, the actual packets often give little information beyond variety name and the approximate number of seeds inside. As soon as your seeds arrive, read over the packet labels and write the year on the packets if the date isn't stamped on there somewhere. Doing so reminds you just how long ago it was that you bought that seed, and you can get a fresh supply when you need it. For a list of mail-order seed suppliers, see Appendix B.

Sowing Seeds Right in the Ground

Direct sowing means planting seeds outdoors in the soil in the place where they are to sprout and mature. This method is the best way to grow many flowers and vegetables that don't transplant well (for example, larkspur, poppies, sweet peas, beans, beets, carrots, peas, and radishes) and a very good way to grow many other plants.

Follow these guidelines for successful seed sowing in open soil:

- ✔ **Use the recognition factor.** Plant seeds of plants you will recognize or that have a distinctive appearance. Otherwise, you can easily mistake a seedling for a weed.

- ✔ **Give seeds a head start.** Moisten large seeds by leaving them overnight in a tray or bowl with moist vermiculite or perlite, or between layers of a moist towel. But once the seeds are moist, be sure they don't dry out prior to planting. This moistening process really speeds things along when you are sowing hard-coated seeds like sweet peas.

- ✔ **Sow seeds at the right season.** Some direct-seeded annuals are best planted in fall or first thing in the spring; others do best planted in warmer soil in early summer. Plant seeds in soil that's warm enough for the particular plants you're working with. For example, peas germinate nicely when the soil is about 16°C (60°F), but basil needs soil that is 21°C (70°F) to sprout well.

- ✔ **Prepare the planting bed thoroughly.** (See Chapter 11.) Take extra care to rake smoothly — lumpy soil and clods interfere with germination.

✔ **Sow seeds in a definite pattern.** Some seeds are best sown in rows, while you can scatter others. (If you like, mix seeds with sand to help you broadcast them more evenly.) When you see a pattern of little sprouts in your soil that look the same and germinated at the same time, you know those baby plants are flowers or vegetables and not weeds.

✔ **Read the label.** Pay attention to directions for best planting depth. If you plant deeper than indicated on the packet, the seeds may not contain enough energy for seedlings to reach the surface. A light layer of sifted compost may be sufficient coverage; or just press seeds into the soil with the back of a hoe.

✔ **Water carefully and gently.** Keep soil damp until seeds sprout. The best way to water is with a soaker hose or drip irrigation. These systems are ground-hugging tubes that let moisture trickle out without splashing or compacting the soil. (See Chapter 14 for more information about watering systems.) You can water from overhead as long as you do it gently with a fine spray from a hose, sprinkler or watering can.

✔ **Weed early and often.** If you have trouble weeding around small seedlings, use a table fork to gently pull out awkward little weeds. For more about dealing with weeds, see Chapter 16.

✔ **Create some elbow room.** When the seedlings have developed two sets of true leaves, thin out seedlings that stand too close together. (The first leaves a seedling produces are called seed leaves or cotyledon, which are followed by the true leaves.) To *thin out* seedlings, gently pull extra seedlings without disturbing the ones you want to keep; or snip them off with scissors just above the soil line.

You have a choice of planting patterns to use. Here are some tips on arranging your garden:

✔ Plant small vegetables — carrots or lettuce, for example, or flowers that you want to transplant later — in beds a couple of feet wide. Many gardeners find that beds 90 centimetres (3 feet) wide are an ideal size for vegetable gardens because they adapt well to trellises and "season extenders" (such as row coverings) and allow easy access to plants from either side of the bed.

✔ If you like a neat, exact garden, use a wire grid of hardware cloth to calculate your spacing. With carrots, for example, use wire mesh with inch-square openings. Lay the wire mesh across the bed and press a few seeds down into the soil through each opening. Thin (remove excess seedlings) when the seedlings come through the soil so that each carrot has at least 7.5 centimetres^2 (3 square inches) of space. For larger plants, such as lettuce, you can plant a seed every four or five squares to eliminate overcrowding.

You can also plant carrots the way most gardeners do: Scatter the seeds as evenly as possible over the planting area, as shown in Figure 12-1a. Sometimes this method means having to do a bit more thinning than otherwise might be necessary, but some gardeners like the insurance of sowing the extra seeds.

✔ Larger plants need more space. You can plant seeds in wide beds, alternating two or three across the bed in a diamond or triangle. Another method is to place seeds of larger plants in single rows, as shown in Figure 12-1b. To make the rows straight, tie a string between two stakes. Following the string line, run a hoe through the soil to dig a trench of the proper depth for the seeds you're planting. Set the seeds in the trench at the proper spacing. Then cover the seeds with soil.

✔ In a decorative annual-flower garden, you can plant in rows, as shown in Figure 12-1c, but wide beds with clusters or drifts of flowers have a more informal air. Use a trickle of ground limestone (or gypsum if your soil pH is alkaline) to mark the places where you want a mass of seed-grown flowers, such as zinnias or nasturtiums. Set the seeds within that space as you would for a wide bed.

A Dozen Easy Annuals to Direct-Sow

These plants are easy to grow from seeds sown directly in carefully prepared beds:

✔ **Alyssum.** *Lobularia maritima.* Some gardeners scorn this popular little plant because it's so common, but it has many virtues. It's incredibly easy to grow in sun or shade, it blends well with other plants, and it willingly acts as a groundcover to disguise dead spaces or fill holes between paving stones. It also has a lovely sweet scent, especially in the evenings. Sprinkle the tiny seeds over fine soil and thin seedlings to about 7.5 centimetres (3 inches). Self-seeds prolifically.

✔ **Bachelor's buttons or cornflower.** *Centaurea* spp. An old-fashioned, frost-tolerant favourite that often seeds itself. The smallish fluffy flowers are held on slim stems, so it's best not to grow them in a windblown location. Comes in pink and white as well as the favourite blue. Sow seeds where they are to grow as soon as soil can be worked in spring.

✔ **Catchfly.** *Silene* spp. This foot-tall plant gives an impressive show of bright magenta five-petalled flowers in early summer. If allowed to go to seed in long-season parts of Canada, it may produce a second crop of plants late in summer. Broadcast seeds in a sunny place in spring, even before the last frost. Self-seeds the next summer if left alone.

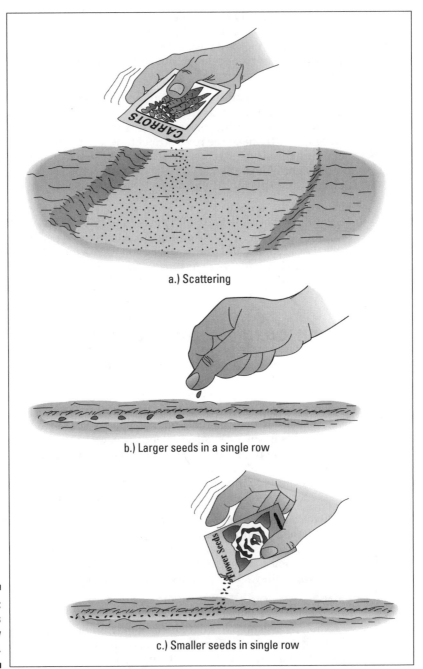

a.) Scattering

b.) Larger seeds in a single row

c.) Smaller seeds in single row

Figure 12-1:
Three ways
to sow
seeds.

- **Calendula, or pot marigold.** *Calendula officinalis.* Its cheery yellow, orange, or copper flowers love cool weather but may wilt in very hot conditions. Otherwise, the flowers last a long time in the vase or the garden. The plant is sturdy enough to survive several frosts, so you may even have fresh cut flowers for Thanksgiving. Sow seeds after the last frost in warm soil. Germination takes three days to a week.

- **Clary sage, also called tricolour sage.** *Salvia viridis, S. horminum.* The pink-, purple-, blue-, or white-veined flowers are not actually flowers but leaf bracts, but that doesn't take away from their beauty. Easy to grow, self-seeding, and not seen in every garden. Sow seeds after the last frost in full sun or partial shade. Thin seedlings to about 30 centimetres (1 foot) apart. The plants create a massed effect, with foliage right down to ground level.

- **Cleome, or spider plant.** *Cleome* spp. A tall, dramatic plant with spiky, showy blooms. Sow in late spring after the last frost has passed, in a sheltered sunny place. Seeds should be 60-90 centimetres (2 to 3 feet) apart. Germination, which takes a week or two, may improve if the seeds are kept in the fridge for a week before planting. Cover the soil after planting to keep seeds moist.

- **Cosmos.** *Cosmos* spp. Sow plenty of seeds in late May, and you'll have a good stand of cosmos by the end of July — you can even sow in July for a new crop before fall. Germination takes about a week. Cosmos are excellent for cutting and come in a wide range of colours from reds and oranges to white, pink , rose, and crimson, and heights from 38 centimetres (15 inches) to 90 centimetres (3 feet). Usually self-seeds.

- **Hyacinth bean.** *Dolichos lablab.* This big purple bean looks like an ornamental pole lima. Its red stems and fragrant white or purple flowers add to its decorative qualities. To boot, the beans, flowers and young leaves are edible. Soak the big seeds before planting them in a warm, sheltered place. When the plants are a few inches tall, add mulch around them to keep down weeds; train the vines up a fence or arbour.

- **Marigold.** *Tagetes patula.* You can grow a very nice border of little French marigolds from one packet of direct-sown seeds. They tolerate temperatures of 16°C (60° F) for both germination and flowering.

- **Morning glory.** *Ipomoea* spp. This must be the most popular climber in the country, and justifiably so. Its almost rampant growth quickly covers a trellis with big, heart-shape leaves and gorgeous trumpet flowers, usually in the favourite 'Heavenly Blue'. But they can't stand frost. After the last spring frost, soak the seeds overnight or file the hard coat to penetrate it a bit, then sow seeds a couple of inches apart where they are to grow. Thin seedlings to about 20 centimetres (8 inches). Germination takes a week or more.

✔ **Nasturtium.** *Tropaeolum majus.* Carefree and easy to grow. Nasturtium leaves look like little flat umbrellas, the cream to orange, peach and mahogany spurred flowers like bright faces. Both the flowers and leaves are edible, and the seeds can be pickled like capers. Soak seeds overnight and sow a couple of weeks before the last expected frost in soil that isn't too rich.

✔ **Poppies.** *Papaver* spp. Although the papery, fragile flowers don't last long, some poppies can be deadheaded for return bloom. Corn poppies and Shirley poppies have feathery green foliage, while the taller opium and peony-flowered types have strong grey-green leaves, straight stems, and spectacular double blooms. The low, yellow and orange four-petalled California poppy looks great massed in an informal garden. Broadcast seed where plants are to grow in fall or early spring, and press down on soil to firm seeds. Don't bother trying to move the plants — they hate being disturbed. But be sure to thin out plants to allow for proper growth. Most self-seed prolifically.

✔ **Sunflower.** *Helianthus annuus.* Sunflowers are now available in a rainbow of hot colours. The large leaves shade out weeds, and the plants often reseed themselves. Some dwarf varieties grow to less than 60 centimetres (2 feet) tall. Sow 1.25 centimetres (½ inch) deep in fertile soil in a sunny place and thin plants later to 30 to 60 centimetres (1 or 2 feet), depending on mature growth of plant.

✔ **Sweet pea.** *Lathyrus odoratus.* Sweet pea seeds benefit from soaking for a full day before planting. Sow in early spring while the soil is still quite cool. In mild-winter areas, you can sow in fall. Sweet pea seedlings easily survive spring frosts and plants like cool, moist roots. Keep well watered and support with string.

Starting Seeds Indoors

Annual vegetables and flowers tend to be the quickest and easiest to grow from seed indoors. When you start seeds for these plants in late winter or early spring, they can be ready for the garden by the earliest possible planting dates for your region. In addition, many plants get off to a better start when they are sown indoors in containers and later transplanted in the garden.

Here are the basic seed-sowing methods that work for us:

1. Choose a soil container with drainage holes.

You can plant in purchased flats or recycled containers. Store-bought containers usually come as a solid-bottom rectangular plastic pan with optional 4- or 6-section cell packs that fit inside. Or you can plant directly into a flat with small drainage holes. We like the cell packs/solid-bottom flat because it's easier to water without getting drips all over the floor, and requires less transplanting of seedlings later. If you use recycled containers such as fast-food containers, foil pans, yogurt containers and plastic cups, punch a couple of small holes in the bottom so seedlings won't rot away.

2. **Buy a commercial planting mixture specifically formulated for starting seeds.**

   Garden centres offer several kinds of these; they usually say "seed starting mix" on the bag and are soilless mixtures of peat moss, perlite or vermiculite and compost. Pour some in a bucket and thoroughly moisten it.

3. **Fill the container to 13 millimetres (½ inch) from the top with the mixture and level it, as shown in Figure 12-2.**

   If you're using cell packs in the flat, fill each section evenly to the top.

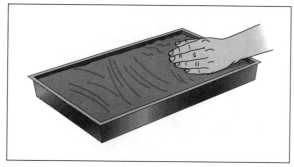

Figure 12-2:
Level the soil about 2.5 cm (1 inch) from the top of the container.

4. **Plant the seeds.**

   • **Small seeds.** Broadcast over the soil surface and cover with a fine layer of the moistened planting mix.

   • **Large seeds.** Plant in shallow furrows (trenches) scratched or pressed into the soil surface, or poke each one into the soil individually, as shown in Figure 12-3. Cover seeds as recommended on the seed packet, usually to a depth equal to twice the seed diameter. Press the mixture gently yet firmly to make sure seeds are in contact with the planting mix.

Figure 12-3:
Poking holes to contain larger seeds.

5. **Water the seeds gently.**

Use a gentle mist from a watering can, or use a poultry baster to carefully moisten the soil without washing the seeds away. Another watering method is to place the flats with drainage holes or the recycled containers in a larger tray. Add 2.5 to 5 centimetres (1 to 2 inches) of water to the larger tray, as shown in Figure 12-4. The plant container uptakes as much water as needed through the drainage holes. With solid-bottom flats containing cell packs, add water to the flats under the packs.

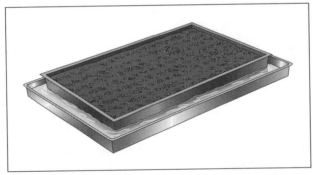

Figure 12-4:
Water the seeds.

6. **Cover the container with a plastic bag, as shown in Figure 12-5, to conserve moisture and keep light out. (Check the seed packet — a few types of seeds need light to germinate.)**

Place the container in a warm spot (ideally 24° C or 75° F), such as the top of a refrigerator, or the top of your fluorescent plant-growing fixture, if there's space. Or place near another heat source.

7. **Start checking for growth in about three days.**

As soon as seedlings emerge, remove the plastic and move the container to bright light. Water as needed to keep the planting mix moist.

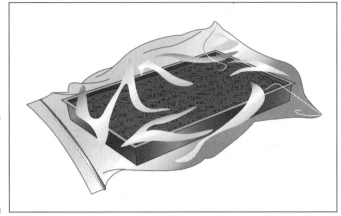

Figure 12-5:
Cover the container with a plastic bag.

You can buy plant-propagation fixtures that are specifically designed to provide plants with ideal light for growth, as shown in Figure 12-6. Make sure it comes with full-spectrum fluorescent bulbs, or one cool and one warm tube, which gives nearly the same result. Adjust the height of the lights so that they're nearly touching the seedlings (raise the lights as the seedlings grow) and leave lights on for 16 hours per day.

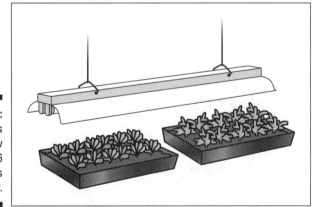

Figure 12-6:
Leave plants under grow lights for 16 hours per day.

8. **When the seedlings have a second pair of true leaves, it's time to transplant them to small, individual pots filled with moist planting mix.**

Use a narrow spatula, popsicle stick or similar tool to help scoop the plants from the flat or recycled pot. If necessary, gently separate the seedlings — hold the plants by the leaves rather than by their fragile stems — then replant in pots. Space them 5 or 7.5 centimetres (2 or 3 inches) apart in larger containers if you have too many for individual pots. Use the same method with cell-packs, leaving one seedling to grow on in each section.

9. **Place the container in bright, indirect light and keep the planting mix moist.**

   In most homes, the seedlings should receive the brightest light available as soon as they emerge. Leave as many as you can under the fluorescent growing lights, 2.5 or 5 centimetres (1 or 2 inches) below the tubes and for 16 hours a day, and set others on sunny window sills. They won't receive as much light there as they should, so it's a good idea to exchange plants frequently for optimum light. Begin feeding seedlings with liquid fertilizer. Follow label directions or, to be safe, begin feeding at half the recommended rate.

10. **One or two months after transplanting, you can harden off most plants and plant them in the garden.** (See this chapter's sidebar entitled "Hardening off seedlings to their new environment.")

A Dozen Easy Annuals to Start Indoors

Here are a dozen easy annuals well worth the trouble of planting early indoors.

- **Basil.** *Ocimum basilicum.* Everyone who likes to cook should grow basil for pesto and drying or freezing as well as for use fresh. It grows easily from seed started indoors about 6 weeks before the last expected frost. Once seedlings have been moved to larger pots and have four or five sets of true leaves, pinch tops to encourage branching. The trimmings are a fragrant taste of summer in late spring salads.

- **Bells of Ireland.** *Moluccella laevis.* The plants develop tall spires studded with little green seashell-like structures that fade to pale beige. The seeds are large and easy to grow. Start about 4 weeks before the last frost.

- **Cup-and-Saucer Vine.** *Cobeaea scandens.* This lovely 20-foot climber needs no trellis to support it, just a rough wall such as brick on which to trace its network of stems. The pale lilac flowers look like small cups and saucers, and are followed by a dark green fruit. The plants need a long season to bloom, so start indoors in early March.

- **Celosia.** *Celosia cristata, C. plumosa.* The plume types are lovely additions to any garden, but some people really like the cockscomb types, with rippled flower heads that look like brains. Start 4 weeks ahead of the last frost; they'll be in bloom in a couple of months. Don't let them get pot-bound indoors.

Hardening off seedlings to their new environment

Seedlings and cuttings raised in comfortable indoor conditions need gradual adjustment to the more strenuous outdoor environment. This process of acclimatizing plants to the wind, strong light, and cooler temperatures outdoors is called hardening off.

1. **One week before you begin hardening off your plants outdoors, cut back the amount of water you give them, stop fertilizing them, and, if possible, keep temperatures slightly cooler by lowering the thermostat.**

2. **Starting about 10 days before transplanting into the garden, place plants outdoors in bright, indirect light for a couple of hours.** Protect the plants from strong winds and be sure to keep them watered, because plants dry out more quickly outside.

3. **Each day, increase the time the plants are left outdoors and gradually expose them to more intense light and wind and a range of temperatures.**

4. **The last few days before transplanting, you can leave them outdoors overnight if weather permits.**

A cloudy, windless, warm day is the best time for easing the plants into their new home outdoors.

✔ **Globe amaranth.** *Gomphrena globulosa.* Flower arrangers covet the little globes, which look like tiny hedgehogs, for both fresh and dried uses. Start about six weeks early and set out seedlings late in spring, after the last frost is long gone.

✔ **Heliotrope.** *Heliotropium arborescens.* Popular in Victorian times, the fragrant heliotrope — also called cherry pie plant — is coming back in nurseries but is also easy to grow from seed indoors. It has broccoli-like heads of purple or white blooms, and textured, dark green foliage. Start indoors 2 to 3 months before the last frost. Keep evenly watered.

✔ **Nicotiana.** *Nicotiana sylvestris.* This old-fashioned strain of flowering tobacco produces wonderfully fragrant, down-facing white trumpet flowers on tall spikes that open at night. Good at the back of the border. It's becoming more popular in nurseries but has been difficult to buy as started plants, so to be sure of having them, start seed indoors 8 weeks before the last frost — seeds are tiny and need time to grow.

✔ **Mexican sunflower.** *Tithonia rotundifolia.* Tall, heat-loving neon-orange tithonia lights up the background of a sunny garden. Looks good with dark green foliage, yellow, orange-red or blue flowers. Start seeds in late spring and use the plants as replacements for others that wear out in hot weather.

✔ **Moonflower.** *Ipomoea alba.* Like its namesake, the flowers appear just before sunset and closes by noon the next day. The sweet heady scent emitted by the 15-centimetre (6-inch) white blooms attracts night-flying moths. Leaves are large and heart shaped. Soak seeds before planting three or four months before the last frost date.

✔ **Tomatoes.** *Lycopersicum esculentum.* Here is the annual that's most often started indoors — in some prairie gardens they remain indoors, in greenhouses, because they thrive in the sun and heat. Sow seeds in moist soil six to eight weeks before the last spring frost in your area. Every couple of days, for 30 seconds or so, some gardeners brush their hands gently over the seedlings to make plants sturdy. Well, it can't hurt, unless you do it so vigorously you break the small stems.

Chapter 13

Choosing and Planting Seedlings, Trees, and Shrubs

In This Chapter

▶ Planting seedlings

▶ Working with container-grown trees and shrubs

▶ Knowing what to do with bare-root plants

▶ Getting balled-and-burlapped trees and shrubs into the ground

*N*urseries in the same geographic location tend to sell certain types of plants during certain seasons and in certain ways. (Think of fruits and vegetables in a grocery store: Some are available only during specific seasons, and different types may be packaged differently, each requiring a specific type of cleaning and preparation prior to eating.) Understanding when to shop for your plants and how to plant different plant types is a useful and important gardening skill.

Most annuals and vegetables are available as seedlings or transplants — the little guys that come in packs or small pots.

Larger, permanent plants — shrubs, trees, and vines, for example — come typically in containers of gallon size to 4 to 60 litres (15 gallons) and larger. You can buy container-grown plants throughout the growing season in most areas of Canada.

Plants are also available in two other, more seasonal forms: bare-root and balled-and-burlapped. Each has its own reasons for being, and its own special planting techniques.

Of course, you can use other ways to get plants started — like bulbs (see Chapter 6). And roses are so popular that we give special planting directions for them in Chapter 7.

Buying and Planting Seedlings

In this section, we talk mostly about annuals and vegetables sold in plastic cell-packs of various sizes and in small pots (usually 7.5 or 10 centimetres, 3 or 4 inches wide). Of course, the same planting advice also applies to seedlings you have grown yourself, as described in Chapter 12.

Exactly when plants are available locally depends on your climate. Early in spring, expect to find seedlings that grow best in cool conditions. Plants that require warmer weather arrive later on and keep coming as long as customers keep buying.

As you shop, look for seedlings that are a vibrant green colour and are relatively short and stocky. Also look around at the display. Has the retailer simply lined everything up in the blazing sun or gone to the trouble of placing shade lovers like coleus and impatiens under benches or shade-cloth? Most bedding plants, including those that grow best in full sun, hold better in small containers when kept in partial shade.

Plants grown in small containers cost less than those in larger ones. Larger plants with more extensive root systems have a head start over smaller plants; however, larger, more developed bedding plants may have one disadvantage. In any container, a plant's roots tend to grow into a thick spiral. If the root system is extremely crowded, the roots may refuse to spread outward after transplanting.

At the nursery, don't be shy about tipping the plant out of its pot or pack and inspecting its roots. Avoid plants with thick tangles of root searching for a place to grow — like out the bottom of the container's drainage hole.

If you buy plants already in flower, pinch off the blossom when you set out the plants. This preemptive pinching encourages the plants to grow more buds and branches.

Figuring Out Spacing for Transplants

Flowering annuals vary in how much space they need to grow. Plant spacing tends to be very tight in window boxes and containers, but in open beds your best strategy is to space plants so that they will barely touch each other when they reach full maturity. Space very small annuals like sweet alyssum and lobelia only 10 to 15 centimetres apart (4 to 6 inches), whereas big coleus and celosia may do better 46 centimetres (18 inches) apart. Most other annuals grow best planted 25 to 30 centimetres (10 to 12 inches) apart, more or less. The plant tags stuck into the containers of purchased bedding plants usually suggest the best spacing.

Instead of setting your annuals in straight lines, stagger them in a concentrated zigzag pattern so you have two or more offset rows of plants. Better yet, plant different annuals in natural-looking teardrop-shaped clumps (called drifts). The clump approach also makes many flowers easier to care for. A closely spaced group of plants that needs special care is much simpler than a long row when you need to pinch, prune, or water and feed.

You can estimate spacing by eye if you like, and simply go over the prepared bed, making little holes where you intend to set the plants. Or, you can mark the planting spots with craft sticks or lightly dust each spot with plain, all-purpose flour. If you purchased plants in individual containers, place each one where you intend to plant it, and move them around as needed until you are happy with the arrangement.

Planting Seedlings, Step by Step

Whether you buy seedlings at the nursery or grow your own from seeds, follow these steps to ensure a seamless transition from nursery to garden.

1. **A day or two before transplanting, water the planting bed so it will be lightly moist when you set out your plants.**

2. **At least one hour before transplanting, water your seedlings thoroughly. Doing so makes them much easier to remove from their containers.**

   Ideal transplant time is any time temperatures are moderate, neither too hot nor cold or too windy. If weather is particularly hot when seedlings are ready, plant in the evening or wait for a cloudy day. Transplanting under the hot sun causes unnecessary stress to the little plants.

3. **Check to see if small roots are knotted around the outside of the drainage holes.**

   If you find roots knotted in such a manner, break them off and discard them before trying to remove the plants.

4. **Remove the plant from the container by tapping the container bottom so the entire root ball slips out intact, as shown in Figure 13-1.**

   If the root ball doesn't come out easily, squeeze the bottom of the container, if it's a thin plastic cell-pack, or use a table knife to gently pry the roots out, the same way you might remove a sticky cake from a pan. For stubborn trees and shrubs, carefully use a strong utility knife to slice through the container. Pull on the top of the plant only as a last resort.

Figure 13-1:
Carefully
remove
the plant
from the
container so
that the root
ball slips out
intact.

5. **Use your fingers or a table fork to loosen the tangle of roots at the bottom of the root ball.**

   Loosening the roots is important! Otherwise, the roots may make little effort to spread out into the soil.

6. **Make final spacing decisions, and then dig small planting holes slightly wider than the root balls of the plants.**

7. **Set the plants into the holes at about the same depth they grew in their containers.**

   You may need to place a few handfuls of soil back in the hole and then set the plant in place to check the height.

8. **Lightly tamp down the soil around the roots with your hands so that native soil comes in contact with the root ball, as shown in Figure 13-2.**

   Tamping down the soil helps remove some pockets of air, which can dry out roots. Keep a watering can handy to help settle soil around roots.

Figure 13-2:
Firming the
soil removes
pockets of
air around
the roots.

9. **Mix a batch of balanced or high-phosphorous water-soluble fertilizer and give each plant a good shot (high-phosphorous fertilizers have a large middle number, such as 5-10-5).**

   If you mixed in fertilizer while preparing the planting bed, you shouldn't have to fertilize more now. Generally not essential, high-phosphorus fertilizers promote strong roots and good flowering. For more about fertilizers see Chapter 14.

10. **Water the entire bed until it is evenly moist.**

11. **After a few days, check to make sure soil has not washed away from the top of the plants' roots.**

    If the root ball is exposed, use a rake or small trowel to add more soil, making sure the root ball is covered.

12. **As soon as new growth shows, mulch around plants with an attractive organic material such as shredded bark, pine needles, or shredded leaves.**

A 5- to 7.5-centimetre (2- to 3-inch) layer of mulch greatly discourages weeds and radically reduces moisture loss from the soil due to evaporation. It also prevents the soil from forming a crust by cushioning the impact of water drops from rain and sprinklers.

Container-Grown Trees and Shrubs

Most shrubs and trees you buy these days are in containers made of plastic or fibre. These containers have several advantages: The plants are easy to move around, and you don't have to plant them right away. (Be sure to continue to water until you are ready to plant.)

Planting your own trees and shrubs saves costs, but planting larger plants requires stamina. Start with smaller, container-grown shrubs that are not too heavy and that can be planted any time the weather is mild. Large balled-and-burlapped trees are heavy and may require a crew of several strong people. Select your plants carefully and calculate placement and hole width and depth in advance so that you don't have to attempt last-minute corrections.

Choosing container-grown trees and shrubs

You want plants that look healthy — with sturdy branches, dense foliage, and other signs of vigorous growth, depending on the type of plant. Inspect the root system as well as you can. You don't want a plant that has spent too little or too much time in the container. If recently planted, the root system may not have developed enough to hold the soil ball together; soil may fall off the roots as you plant. If the plant has been in the container too long, it may be root-bound — when roots are so tangled and constricted they have a tough time spreading out into the soil and growing normally.

Look for these classic root-bound symptoms:

- ✔ Roots stick out the container's drain holes.

- ✔ Roots bulge out above the soil line.

- ✔ Plants are spindly (tall but with few leaves), poorly proportioned in relation to the container, or have a lot of dead growth.

Avoid root-bound plants; or, failing this, at least gently loosen and untangle the roots without shattering the ball of soil at planting time.

If a plant is extremely root-bound, slice right through the bottom of the root-bound ball, going up a little more than halfway. Spread open the two flaps over a mound of soil and plant as usual. Or using a sharp knife, slice through the outer roots is several places. This causes the roots to branch out and form new growth.

Transplanting trees and shrubs from containers

Follow these steps for planting container-grown trees and shrubs:

1. **Dig a hole as deep as the original root ball (use a stick to determine depth) and three times as wide.**

   Slant the walls of the hole outward and loosen them with a shovel or garden fork to allow easy root penetration. In heavy clay soil, ensure good drainage around the plant by digging the hole 1 or 2 inches (2.5 to 5 cm) shallower than the depth of the original root ball.

   If you have average or better soil, don't bother to amend the soil you use to refill the hole; roots may not grow beyond the amended area if you do. If your soil is especially poor, work compost or other organic matter into the excavated soil that will go back into the hole.

   Locate any underground wires, cables, or pipelines before you begin digging and proceed around them carefully. You can easily cut through a wire with a sharp spade or fork.

2. **Remove the plant from its container.**

   Most plant containers are plastic and plants slip right out. If they don't, trim away any roots protruding from drainage holes and water the plant thoroughly. Tap the bottom or knock the rim of the containers on a hard surface, and then tip it upside down (or onto its side, for large plants) and slide out the root ball.

   Many nurseries are happy to take back empty plastic containers, either for recycling or reuse.

3. **Place the plant in the hole, at the right depth, and fill around the root ball with soil, as shown in Figure 13-3.**

   Stand back and check the plant's position to be sure it's oriented the way you'd like, and then begin backfilling. Once you've replaced about half the backfill, tamp down with your hands or the flat side of a shovel. Water the hole and let it drain before continuing to fill to the soil level (which is usually the same as the root-ball level).

4. **Water the plant well by letting a hose trickle into the planting area until the area is soaked.**

   To help direct irrigation and rainwater to the new roots, shape loose surface soil with your hands into a water-holding basin. Make it 7.5 to 10 centimetres (3 to 4 inches) high just outside the root ball.

Figure 13-3:
A cutaway
view of a
container-
planted tree.

Continue to water any time the soil begins to dry out for the next six months to a year. Don't count exclusively on sprinklers or rain to water new plants. To see if soil is dry, dig down 10 to 15 centimetres (4 to 6 inches) with a trowel. If it's hard to dig, and if the soil is very dry, the root ball needs water.

5. **Mulch the plant.**

   Cover the excavated soil and several inches beyond (the larger the plant, the wider the circle) with 5 to 7.5 centimetres (2 to 3 inches) of mulch. After spreading the mulch, pull it an inch or two away from the main stem of the plant. (Sometimes mulch there will promote disease problems.)

6. **Stake, if necessary.**

   Some trees in some situations need support for a year or two until they can support their own weight. A stake is recommended if the trunk is very narrow or if you've planted in a very windy situation. Otherwise, most trees are better off without stakes.

To stake a tree, drive one or two stakes into the soil on either side of the tree beyond the roots. Attach ties to the tree at the lowest point at which the top remains upright. Tie loosely so that the tree can move in the wind and gain trunk strength. Figure 13-4 shows how to stake a tree with a single stake and with two stakes.

If using guy wires, establish the lowest point on the trunk where the tree needs support. Use cable or heavy twine to connect the tree from that point to stakes in the soil, as shown in Figure 13-5.

Whatever kind of staking you use, be sure to check once or twice a year to see if it's still necessary. Remove the stakes as soon as practical. Stakes left in place beyond their usefulness are a common cause of tree problems.

Bare-Root Planting

The tried-and-true method of bare-root planting offers benefits to the plant and to the gardener. During the dormant, leafless season, nursery workers dig up deciduous (leaf-shedding) plants and remove the soil around the roots. Bare-root plants are easy to transport and handle — which allows for a lower price than the same plants sold in containers. Bare-root is also a good way for plants to get off to a good strong start; roots can follow their natural direction better than they can in the confines of a container.

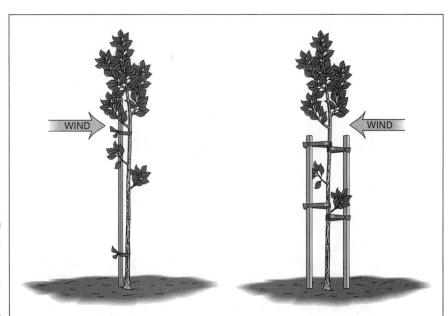

Figure 13-4:
Staking a tree with one stake or two stakes.

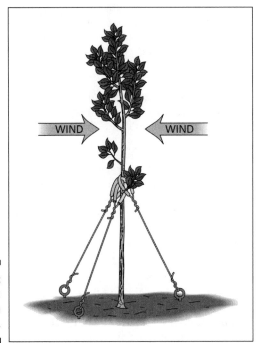

Figure 13-5:
Staking a
tree with
guy wires.

Choosing bare-root plants

The most important factor to look for are roots that are fresh and moist, not dried out and stringy. Check for damaged, soft, broken, mushy, or circling roots. Inspect the top growth for broken branches and damaged buds. Ask a nurseryperson about proper preplanting pruning for the specific plant. Most roots should be trimmed back to healthy, firm growth. Don't let the roots dry out; soak them in a bucket of water before planting, if necessary.

Planting bare-root plants

Plant bare-root plants by using the same procedure for container-grown plants described in the section "Transplanting trees and shrubs from containers." The only difference between the two procedures is in the shape and depth of the hole you dig.

For bare-root planting, set the base of the roots on a cone of soil in the middle of the hole, as shown in Figure 13-6, adjusting the cone height so that the first horizontal root is just below the soil surface. Spread the roots in all directions and refill the hole gradually, watering and tamping down the soil so no air pockets are left around roots.

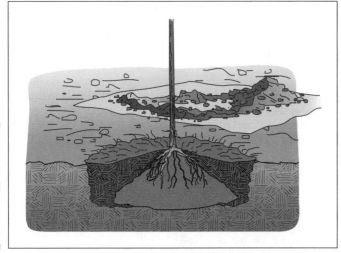

Figure 13-6:
Spread the roots of a bare-root plant around a central cone of soil.

Burlap-Wrapped Root Balls

Another time-honoured method for distributing plants, particularly evergreen shrubs and trees such as spruce, pine, and fir, is the wrapped root-ball method. During fall and winter, nurseries dig these plants from growing fields and wrap the root balls in burlap (sometimes also wrapping both burlap and root ball in a wire cage for extra support).

Choosing balled-and-burlapped plants

When looking at balled-and-burlapped plants, be sure to check for major cracks or breaks in the root ball. Make sure the trunk doesn't rock or move in the soil ball. Keep the root ball moist if you can't plant right away; cover it with organic matter such as ground bark, and moisten thoroughly. Keep the plant in a shady spot until you plant it.

Planting balled-and-burlapped plants

Dig a hole with a circumference twice as large and a depth equal to the root ball. The root ball should sit on firm soil to avoid settling. Set the root ball into the hole; check the position of the plant, and then remove all burlap, nails, and any twine or wire to prevent interference with the plant's future growth. If you can't remove all the burlap, use a sharp knife to cut off everything except for what is directly underneath the ball. (See Figure 13-7.)

To get balled-and-burlapped planting heights just right, open the root ball and remove some soil from the top until you find the first *root flare* or horizontal root. That root should be positioned just below the soil surface. Many trees are planted too deeply because they have too much soil over the roots in the burlap wrap.

Like many things, burlap isn't quite what it used to be. Don't assume it will decay in a season or two, so it would be fine to leave in the soil around the root ball. Nowadays, "burlap" is often a coarsely woven synthetic that can take years to dissolve in the soil, if ever.

Figure 13-7:
Remove any
metal,
burlap, and
twine to
avoid
inhibiting
growth.

Part V
Caring for Your Plants

The 5th Wave® By Rich Tennant

IT WAS A MOMENT FROZEN IN TIME WHEN A LONE MOLE TOOK A STAND FOR ALL OF MOLEDOM THAT SUNNY AFTERNOON ON TIANNAMEN'S LAWN.

In this part . . .

Yippee! You made a garden! Or maybe you just inherited one.

Do you need water? How much? What about fertilizer? And what about weeds . . . and pruning or feeding? Oh yeah, and what about pests? What tools do you use to care for your garden?

We answer all these questions in this part. Garden care may sound like a lot of work, but it's really not. And anyway, it's fun. Garden maintenance is a misnomer of sorts — there's nothing janitorial about it.

Caring for your garden is, in fact, the essence of gardening.

Chapter 14

Feed Me, Seymour! Watering, Feeding, and Composting

....

In This Chapter

▶ Looking at the whys of watering

▶ Figuring out the hows of watering

▶ Understanding plant nutrients

▶ Fertilizing your plants

▶ Mulching around

▶ Dabbling in the art and science of composting

....

*W*hat's the most important thing you can do in your garden? The answer depends on who you talk to and where the gardener lives. A Winnipeg gardener may say nothing is more important than watering (unless it's keeping the mosquitoes at bay). Someone with a lot of container plants will put fertilizing first. If you have horrid soil, nothing, we mean nothing, is more essential than composting.

So, what do we say? Our answer, of course, is . . . all of the above. But the amount of watering, feeding, and composting (the Big Three of your support system for healthy plant growth) you do depends on where you live, what you grow, and all sorts of other local conditions. But take our word for it — each of the three is extremely important.

Watering Basics

How much water your plants need to stay healthy depends on a number of factors:

✔ **Climate.** If you live in an area like Vancouver, where rainfall is regular and reliable, watering isn't a constant chore except in prolonged dry spells or periods of drought. In drier areas like the prairies, watering is something that gardeners need to squeeze into their schedules almost on a daily basis.

✔ **Weather.** The average weather where you live on a season-to-season, year-to-year basis determines climate. Weather is what's happening outside right now. Out-of-the ordinary weather can wreak havoc on your plants. Hot, dry winds can fry plants even when the soil is moist.

✔ **Soil types.** Different soil types also affect how often a garden needs water.

  • **Sandy soil** holds water about as effectively as a sieve. Water penetrates sandy soils readily and deeply but tends to filter right on through. Adding organic matter, like compost, leaf mould, peat moss, or shredded bark helps sandy soils retain moisture.

  • **Heavy clay soil** is the exact opposite of sand — the dense particles in clay cause the soil to crust over and deflect water drops. Water applied slowly and in stages soaks in deeply; water applied quickly just runs off. Saturated clay holds water very well — sometimes so well that the plants rot. Adding plenty of organic matter helps break up the soil and improves drainage.

✔ **Location.** In general, shady gardens need less water than those receiving direct sun. However, in places where trees cast the shadows, their roots may greedily hog all the water, leaving little for the flowers. In such cases, applying enough water to satisfy both the trees and the flowers without causing disease or other problems may be almost impossible.

✔ **Genetic disposition.** Most plants need a consistent supply of moisture to remain healthy and free-blooming. Some types, however, can get by on less water than others.

Getting water to your garden

The best watering method for you may depend on the size of your garden. For example, with just a small bed of marigolds, you may find that watering with a hand-held watering can or hose is not only effective but rewarding. If, however, you have a 19-square-metre (200-square-foot) mixed flower bed, watering effectively by hand is not only impractical, it's impossible.

In some areas, certain watering techniques become a matter of necessity instead of practicality. Where droughts are common or water supplies are unpredictable, conservation is the order of the day. You need to water in ways that hold every drop precious. Where foliage diseases like powdery mildew are common, you want to keep water off the plant leaves and apply the water only to the roots.

The following sections describe many fundamental watering methods.

Hand watering

If you want to stand among your heliotrope with a hose and water the plants by hand, that's fine. Hose-end attachments soften the force of the spray and help apply the water over a larger area. You can control the amount of water each plant gets and even do some pest control at the same time — blast that blanket flower to wash away aphids! Hand watering, however, takes time— a lot of time, especially in large gardens — and most of us aren't patient enough to stand there with the hose the entire time it takes to supply enough water.

Sprinklers

Hose-end sprinklers come in a wide range of styles and sprinkler patterns. You've probably used a few of them. The problem with watering with sprinklers is that you have to drag the hose around and move the sprinkler every so often. Also, most hose-end sprinklers don't apply water very evenly. If you forget to turn off the sprinkler, you waste a lot of water.

If you need help remembering to turn off the sprinklers, check out the various timers that are available. Some fit conveniently between the faucet and hose and so help prevent wasting water when watering the lawn.

One other possible problem with sprinkler watering is the wet foliage that results. In humid climates, overhead watering can spread disease and turn flowers into a mouldy mess. On the other hand, in hot dry climates, wetting the foliage rinses dust off the leaves, cools the plants, and helps prevent spider mite infestations.

Furrow irrigation

Furrows are shallow trenches that run parallel to your rows. Usually you dig the furrows with a hoe at planting time and then plant a row of flowers or vegetables on either side of the furrow. Ideally, the bed should slope just the tiniest bit so that water runs naturally from one end of the furrow to the other. (See Figure 14-1.) When you want to water, you just put a slowly running hose at the end of the furrow and wait for the water to reach the other end.

Furrow irrigation, unlike sprinkler watering, keeps the foliage dry and doesn't promote disease. However, you do have to move the hose around frequently, and furrow watering doesn't work well on fast-draining, sandy soil. (The water soaks in too quickly and never reaches the other end of the furrow.)

Drip irrigation

Drip irrigation is a very effective and efficient way to water plants. Most drip irrigation systems are made up of a black plastic header hose to which is attached, at intervals, sections of emitter hose, equipped with tiny holes through which water drips. Sometimes the system comes with little gadgets called drippers, which are attached to the ends of feeder tubes placed to match your plantings, and the feeder tubes are then attached to a poly header pipe. (Incidentally, don't confuse these systems with the green plastic soak-or-spray hose, depending on which side you placed up, that's been around since we wore diapers.) The header hose or pipe connects to a water supply, filter and, often, a pressure regulator, which helps regulate the flow on uneven surfaces. The emitter sections weave among and around the plants, applying water directly to the base. You can lay the pipe on top of the soil and cover it with a mulch, or bury it a few inches deep. Most people like to keep the pipe close to the surface so they can check it for clogs or fix breaks.

Drip emitters wet an entire planting bed from one end to the other at each watering. You can either snap the emitter hoses into the header hose to suit the placement of your plants, or buy the header hose with the emitters already installed. If you're doing the installation, space the emitters 30 centimetres (12 inches) or no more than 45 centimetres (18 inches) apart along the length of the header hose, as shown in Figure 14-2. The moisture radiates sideways and underground, and slowly wets the soil between the holes.

Drip systems usually have to run for at least several hours to wet a large area. Watch the soil carefully the first few times you water. Dig around to see how far the water has traveled over a given time and then make adjustments to how long you water in the future.

Figure 14-2:
Drip
irrigation is
an efficient
watering
solution.

Most nurseries sell drip irrigation systems. You can also purchase them through the mail (see Appendix B). Emitters are available with different application rates, varying by the number of gallons applied per hour. Pressure-compensating emitters apply water consistently from one end of the line to the other regardless of pressure changes due to uneven ground. You can also buy punctured hoses made of recycled tires or other non-degradable materials; they leak water along their entire length, but apply water unevenly if the ground is not perfectly level and may become clogged with earth.

To prevent your drip irrigation from bursting in winter, don't leave it outside. Instead, drain the water, roll up the tubing, and store it in the garage.

Automated watering systems

Automated watering systems can be real time-savers and can give you the freedom to safely take a vacation in the middle of summer. You can find an interesting choice of timers at your local irrigation supplier or in mail-order catalogues. (See Appendix B.) Some timers hook between hose bib and hose; others connect to valves and underground pipes that supply sprinklers. You can even build a moisture sensor into an automated system so the water comes on only when the soil is dry. You can automate both drip and sprinkler systems.

Grass lawns have their own special water requirements as well as a world of irrigation methods. See Chapter 9 for specifics.

Determining the amount and frequency of watering

A plant's water needs vary with the weather and the seasons. Even an automated system needs adjusting to water less in spring than in summer. You need to learn to be a pretty good observer and make adjustments accordingly.

Irrigation hardware is useless if you don't have a clue as to how much water your plants need. The answer is to water just enough, but not too much.

Plants lose moisture through their foliage because of transpiration, and the soil gives up water by evaporation. This is called *evapotranspiration*. In some parts of North America where irrigation is a fact of life, a recommended watering rate based on the amount of evapotranspiration that's taken place in a week or month is printed in newspapers. In Canada, you usually can rely on the old-fashioned rule: an inch to 2.5 to 4 centimetres (1 inch to 1½ inches) per week.

Here are a couple of simple and fairly obvious ways to tell when your plants need water:

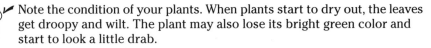

- ✔ Note the condition of your plants. When plants start to dry out, the leaves get droopy and wilt. The plant may also lose its bright green color and start to look a little drab.

- ✔ Your goal is to water before a plant gets to the wilted and pale point, so it's a good idea to dig in the ground around the plant if you haven't had rain for several days to a week. Most plants need water when the top 5 to 7.5 centimetres (2 to 3 inches) of soil are dry. Eventually, through observation and digging, you'll develop a sense of when your plants are thirsty.

The next challenge is to figure out how much water to give your plants. As stated, the general rule is 2.5 to 4 centimetres (1 inch to 1½ inches) per week. There are formulas based on your water pressure and hose circumference for figuring out how long you need to run the sprinklers to deliver a particular amount of water, but the simplest way is to place containers in important locations throughout your sprinkler's spray pattern. Be sure the containers have straight, vertical sides — canned fish tins work well. Run the sprinkler for a specific length of time, such as an hour. With a metal ruler, measure the depth of water in each can. Use the can with the least amount of water as the standard (let's hope it's not too different than the others), because even the area that receives the least must get enough.

Conserving water

Water shortages are a reality in almost any climate or region. Following are a few things you can do when water is scarce or limited, when you want to reduce your water bill, or when you just want to conserve the precious resource of fresh water.

- ✔ **Use a timer.** Don't tell us you've never forgotten to turn the water off and flooded half the neighbourhood. Just set an egg timer or an alarm clock to let you know when it's time to shut off the water. Or get even more high-tech and use one of the automated timers mentioned under automated watering systems in this chapter.

- ✔ **Install drip irrigation.** This watering method applies water slowly without runoff. Drip is definitely the most frugal watering system you can use.

- ✔ **Mulch, mulch, and mulch some more.** Several inches of compost, shredded fir bark, leaf mould, or other material cools the soil and reduces evaporation, thus saving water. And as the mulch breaks down, it improves the soil. For more on mulches, see this chapter's section "A-Mulching We Will Go . . ." and Chapter 11.

- ✔ **Pull weeds.** Weeds steal water meant for your plants. Pull out weeds regularly. For more on weeds, see Chapter 16.

- ✔ **Water deeply and infrequently.** Shallow sprinkling does very little good. Water to a depth of 20 to 25 centimetres (8 to 10 inches), then let the soil dry out partially before you water again. This method encourages plants to develop deep roots, which can endure longer periods between waterings.

- ✔ **Water early**. Water early in the day when temps are cooler and it's less windy. That way, less water evaporates into the air and more reaches the roots.

- ✔ **Use rainwater.** Put a barrel or other collector where the drain pipes from your roof empty out. Then use that water on your garden.

- ✔ **Measure rainfall.** Keep track of how much rain you get. An inch is usually enough to let you skip a watering.

- ✔ **Plant at the right time.** Plant when your plants have the best chance of getting fully established before the onset of very hot or very cold weather.

Providing a Balanced Diet for Your Plants

Before you head for the nursery to pick up a bag of fertilizer, remember that understanding the nutrients plants need and how they use them will help you make the right purchase.

Sixteen elements are known to be essential for healthy plant growth. Plants particularly need carbon, hydrogen, and oxygen in large quantities. Plants also need energy from sunlight for photosynthesis, the process by which green plants take carbon dioxide from the air and water from the soil to produce sugars to fuel their growth. Apart from watering plants, gardeners can trust nature to supply these big basic requirements.

Plants also need nitrogen, phosphorus, and potassium in relatively large quantities. These three elements are often called *macronutrients,* or *primary nutrients.* Plants take up these three nutrients from the soil. If they are not present in the soil, you can supply them by adding fertilizers. The percentages of these nutrients are the three prominent numbers on any bag or box of fertilizer, and the nutrients always appear in the same order. For more on fertilizer, see this chapter's section "Don't Compromise, Fertilize!"

- **Nitrogen (N).** This nutrient, represented by the chemical symbol N, is responsible for the healthy green colour of your plants. It is a key part of proteins and *chlorophyll,* the plant pigment that plays a vital role in photosynthesis. Plants with a nitrogen deficiency show a yellowing of older leaves first, along with a general slowdown in growth.

- **Phosphorus (P).** Phosphorus is associated with good root growth, increased disease resistance, and fruit and seed formation. Plants lacking in phosphorus are stunted, have dark green foliage, followed by reddening of the stems and leaves. As with nitrogen, the symptoms appear on the older leaves first.

- **Potassium (K).** This nutrient promotes vigorous growth and disease resistance. The first sign of a deficiency shows up as browning of the edges of leaves. Older leaves become affected first.

- **Calcium, magnesium, and sulfur.** Plants need these three *secondary nutrients* in substantial quantities but not to the same extent as nitrogen, phosphorus, and potassium. Where the soil is acid (areas of high rainfall), calcium and magnesium are important to add to acidify the soil. Doing so maintains a soil pH beneficial to plants and supplies the nutrient that the plants need. Where the soil is alkaline (areas of low rainfall), adding sulfur to the soil is similarly beneficial. For more about pH, see Chapter 11.

- **Iron, manganese, copper, boron, molybdenum, chlorine, and zinc.** These seven elements are the *micronutrients,* meaning plants need only minute quantities for good health. These nutrients are often not lacking in the soil, but they may be unavailable to plant roots. The cause of this problem is usually a soil pH that is too acid or too alkaline. In this case, rather than adding the nutrient, adjusting soil pH is the remedy. Too much of any of these nutrients can be harmful.

Don't Compromise, Fertilize!

After you decide to feed your plants, you'll face myriad fertilizers at the nursery. How do you know which kinds to buy?

When you buy a commercial fertilizer, its analysis appears on the label with three numbers. These three numbers are helpful because they let you know the amounts of nutrients (N-P-K) that are in a particular fertilizer.

- ✔ The first number indicates the percentage of nitrogen (N).
- ✔ The second number, the percentage of phosphorus (P_2O_5).
- ✔ The third, the percentage of potassium (K_2O).

A 43-kilogram (100-pound) bag of 5-10-10 fertilizer consists of 5 percent nitrogen (2.3 kilograms, or 5 pounds); 10 percent phosphate (4.6 kilograms, or 10 pounds); and 10 percent potash (4.6 kilograms, or 10 pounds). Altogether, the bag has 25 pounds of plant-usable nutrients. The remaining 34 kilograms (75 pounds) usually consists of only *carrier,* or filler; a small amount of the filler may contain some plant-usable nutrients.

Any fertilizer that contains all three of the primary nutrients — N-P-K — is a *complete fertilizer.* The garden term *complete* has its basis in laws and regulations that apply to the fertilizer industry: It does not mean that the fertilizer literally contains everything a plant may need.

Common fertilizer terms

You don't need a degree in botany to have a lovely garden. But when looking for the right fertilizers, you do need to understand some of the terminology.

Take a look at some of the fertilizing terms you may encounter:

- ✔ **Chelated micronutrients.** The word *chelate* comes from the Latin word for *claw,* and that's a useful way to understand how these micronutrients function. These compounds bind to certain plant nutrients and essentially deliver them to the plant roots. Nutrients that plants require in minute quantities — such as iron, zinc, and manganese — are often available in chelated form. The chelated fertilizer you buy may be a powder or liquid.

- ✔ **Foliar.** As the name implies, foliar fertilizers are liquids that you apply on a plant's leaves. These fertilizers contain nutrients that plant leaves can absorb directly. Although a plant's roots also can absorb the nutrients in most foliar fertilizers, those absorbed via leaves have a quick effect. Don't apply foliar fertilizers in hot weather because leaves can become damaged.

✔ **Granular.** These fertilizers are the most common and most often sold in boxes or bags. Most granular fertilizers are partially soluble. For example, a 10-10-10 granular fertilizer is best applied to the soil about a month prior to planting in order for the nutrients to be available at planting time. You also can get special formulations, such as rose food or azalea food. These specialized fertilizers supply nutrients over a longer period of time than liquid or soluble fertilizers but not as long as slow-release kinds. (See Figure 14-3.)

Figure 14-3:
Use a
spreader
to apply
granular
fertilizer.

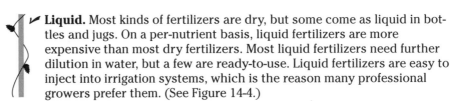

✔ **Liquid.** Most kinds of fertilizers are dry, but some come as liquid in bottles and jugs. On a per-nutrient basis, liquid fertilizers are more expensive than most dry fertilizers. Most liquid fertilizers need further dilution in water, but a few are ready-to-use. Liquid fertilizers are easy to inject into irrigation systems, which is the reason many professional growers prefer them. (See Figure 14-4.)

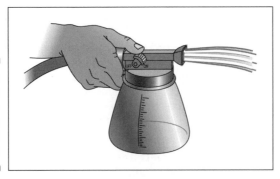

Figure 14-4:
Applying a
liquid fertil-
izer with a
hose-end
sprayer.

✔ **Organic.** These fertilizers are often made from dead or composted plants and animals. Examples are blood meal, fish emulsion, and manure. Usually, organic fertilizers contain significant amounts of only one of the

major nutrients; for example, bone meal contains only phosphorus. Nutrients in organic fertilizers are made available to plant roots after soil microorganisms break down the nutrients. Activity of these microorganisms is fastest in summer when soils are warm. As a general rule, half the nutrients in organic fertilizers are available to plants the first season.

✔ **Slow-release.** These fertilizers release the nutrients they contain at specific rates in specific conditions over an extended period. For example, Osmocote fertilizers release nutrients in response to soil moisture. The nutrients inside the tiny beads "osmose" through a resin membrane. Soil microorganisms slowly act on another type, sulfur-coated urea, until the nutrients release. Some fertilizers can release their nutrients for as long as eight months. Slow-release fertilizers are very useful for container plants that otherwise need frequent fertilizing.

Kinds of fertilizers for various plants

Different kinds of plants need different kinds of fertilizers, and Table 14-1 lists our recommendations. Of course the best advice before using any fertilizer is to have your soil tested. For more about soil testing, see Chapter 11.

Table 14-1	Fertilizing at a Glance	
Plant	*Fertilizer*	*Comments*
Annuals	Granular	Apply before planting and supplement with soluble fertilizer.
Bulbs	Granular 8-8-8 or similar	Apply at planting time.
Fruit trees	Granular and/or organic	Apply as necessary in spring only.
Hanging baskets	Slow-release or liquid soluble	Apply every two weeks.
House plants	Slow-release or liquid soluble	
Lawns	Granular and/or organic 28-7-14 or similar, preferably slow-release; or an organic, high-nitrogen fertilizer	
Perennials	Granular and/or organic	Apply in autumn; supplement with liquid soluble.

(continued)

Table 14-1 *(continued)*

Plant	Fertilizer	Comments
Roses	Granular and/or organic	Apply in spring and autumn for good growth.
Trees and shrubs	Granular and/or organic	Apply in autumn; supplement with complete granular (10-10-10 or similar) if spring growth is poor.
Vegetables	Organic	Apply in autumn or at least one month prior to planting. Continually enrich soil with organic fertilizers; supplement with granular 5-10-10 first two gardening seasons.

Organic fertilizers

Organic or natural fertilizers such as manure and composts are more cumbersome and possibly more expensive than synthetic fertilizers, but nothing quite takes their place. These fertilizers provide some nutrient value and, when you incorporate them into the soil, improve soil structure, which increases the soil's ability to hold air, nutrients, and water.

Plants take up nutrients in specific forms, regardless of whether the source is organic or synthetic. You can supply all the nutrients that plants need by using only organic materials, but you need to use some care and effort to ensure that sufficient amounts of nitrogen, phosphorus, and potash are available to the plants throughout the season.

Because the nutrients in organic materials are tied up in more complex molecules, these nutrients often take longer to become available to the plants, which can result in temporary nutrient deficiencies, especially in the spring.

Fresh manure can "burn" plants (damaging leaves and growth from excess application) just as surely as any chemical fertilizer, whereas woody materials (wood chips, sawdust, leaf piles, and so on) can cause a temporary nitrogen deficiency until they are sufficiently decomposed. The microorganisms that help the decay process may use up all the available nitrogen to break down the woody material. You can counteract this effect somewhat by applying a little extra nitrogen in the spring. A rule of green thumb is that when the material starts to resemble soil, it is ready for the garden.

Piling onto the Compost Bandwagon

As we visit the gardens of friends and neighbours around the country, a stop at the compost pile is a must in almost every garden tour. Meeting a gardener who shows off a rich, dark, earthy compost as eagerly as towering dahlias is not at all unusual.

Not so long ago, we gardeners hid our compost piles. In privacy, we would witness the magic of composting, the transformation of garden and yard waste into sweet-smelling black gold. We feared that others (especially neighbours) would judge our passion as a waste of time and space.

Attitudes have changed. Landfills are filling up, and composting is now widely recognized as an easy, effective way to reduce solid waste at home. Many municipalities collect yard waste with garbage collections and make their own compost, which is used in public parks and sold or given away to residents.

More to the heart of gardeners is the fact that compost is a valuable, natural soil amendment. Adding compost to garden beds and planting holes enhances nutrients and improves soil texture. Compost helps loosen heavy clay soils, and it increases the water-holding capacity of sandy soils. (See Chapter 11 for more about soils.)

A *compost pile* is a collection of plant (and sometimes animal) materials, combined in a way to encourage quick decomposition. Soil microorganisms (bacteria and fungi) do the work of breaking down this organic material into a soil-like consistency.

These organisms need oxygen and water to survive. Turning the pile over provides oxygen, and an occasional watering helps keep it moist. If the pile is well made and the organisms are thriving, it heats up quickly and doesn't emit any unpleasant odours. In hot weather, finished compost that looks and feels like dark, crumbly soil can sometimes take as little as six weeks to produce.

From refuse to riches

Whether you make your compost in an elaborate store-bought bin (one that closes tightly) or simply in a freestanding pile, the essentials of good composting are the same. To get fast results, follow these steps:

1. **Collect equal parts, by volume, of dried, brown, carbon-rich material (like old leaves or straw) and fresh, green, nitrogen-rich material (fresh-cut grass, green vegetation, and vegetable kitchen waste).**

A few materials should *not* be used in an open compost pile. Although farm animal manures are a safe source of nitrogen for the pile, dog and cat waste can spread unhealthy organisms. Meat, fats, bones, and cooked foods decompose slowly, may be smelly, and may attract animal pests — add these only to compost bins that close tightly. Avoid chemically treated lawn clippings and diseased plant material. Finally, keep out tenacious weeds that spread by runners and roots, such as Bermuda grass.

2. **Chop or shred the organic materials into small pieces, if possible.**

   Pieces that are 2 centimetres (¾ inch) or smaller are ideal because they break down quickly.

3. **Build the pile at least 1 metre x 1 metre x 1 metre *(1 cubic metre or 1 cubic yard)*, alternating layers of the carbon-rich material with the green material.**

   Layer a thin covering of soil for every 45 centimetres (18 inches) of depth. The soil carries more microorganisms that aid in decomposition.

4. **Wet the pile as you build it.**

   Keep the material moist, not soaked. (It should be about as moist as a wrung-out sponge.)

5. **After the temperature begins to decrease, turn the pile, wetting it as necessary to keep it moist.**

   A well-built pile heats up in approximately a week, peaking between 49°C to 71°C (120°F and 160°F). If you don't have a compost thermometer, use a garden fork to turn the pile every week or so the first month.

Bin there, done that!

A compost pile cares not whether it's caged or freestanding. An enclosure, called a compost bin, mostly keeps the pile neat and can help retain moisture and heat. Depending on its design, a compost bin also keeps out animal pests. For these reasons, especially in urban settings, a bin is a good idea. (See Figure 14-5.)

To build or to buy?

Bins are available by mail order and, increasingly, through nurseries, garden centres, and even discount stores. You can spend up to $400 or more for a commercial compost bin, or you can make your own with scrap materials.

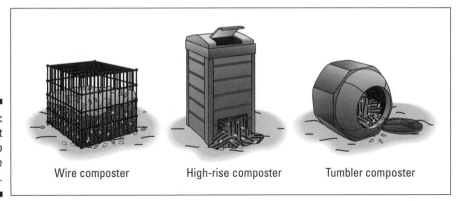

Figure 14-5:
Compost
bins keep
the pile
neat.

Wire composter

High-rise composter

Tumbler composter

A *wire bin* is perhaps the easiest type to make. You need a 3.5 metre (11-foot) length of 90 centimetre-wide (36-inch), welded reinforcing wire with a grid of about 5 x 10 centimetres (2 x 4 inches). Simply bend the wire to form a hoop and tie the ends together with strong wire. Lining the wire mesh with land-scape fabric helps prevent the pile from drying out excessively. This bin holds about a cubic yard when full.

To use the bin, fill it with the appropriate balance of organic material. When the pile is ready to turn, lift off the wire mesh and set it next to the pile; then, turn the material and fork it back into the enclosure.

Another option is a *wooden compost bin,* made with wooden pallets, wooden scrap boards, and wire or — for the more elaborate model — 5 x 10 centime-tres (2 x 4) and 5 x 15 centimetres (2 x 6) lumber. The Cadillac of the wooden compost bins uses three bins arranged side by side, as shown in Figure 14-6. Though this bin can be time-consuming to construct, some gardeners prefer the convenience of a three-box bin. Each bin is for compost at a different stage of maturity. For example, fresh material is added to the far-left bin, turned into the middle one after a few weeks, and then turned into the bin at the far right to finish.

Commercial bins come in four basic flavours:

✔ **Containers for hot compost.** Usually made out of recycled plastic, these bottomless boxes or cylinders are designed to be used in much the same way as the wire bin. You completely fill the bin with the right blend of materials and let the pile heat up. To turn the compost, when the bin is full, you lift off the top section of compost and place it on the ground (the section on top now becomes the section on the bottom). Then you reach in with a fork and lift some of the lower compost, making it the top section of compost, and so on.

✔ **Bins for a static pile.** With these plastic units (which usually have air vents along the sides), you make a compost pile by putting a balance of waste materials in the top of the bin and letting the mixture sit. As the waste decomposes, you remove the finished compost from the bottom of the bin and add more waste to the top.

This type of bin is the most commonly available bin, although not necessarily the best. You don't need to do any turning, and you can add waste at any time; however, decomposition is slow, and you get only small amounts of compost at a time. Because the pile does not get very hot, weeds, seeds, and plant diseases may survive.

✔ **Tumblers.** With a tumbler, you place your compost inside the container and then turn the entire bin to toss the compost inside. Some tumblers have crank handles for turning. One tumbler system is designed to roll on the ground, tumbling the compost inside as it goes.

With these units, you make a hot compost by balancing the waste materials and turning the bin frequently. Tumblers are generally the most expensive type of bin, but the ease of turning and the fast results may be worth the money. Choose one with at least a 1-cubic-metre (1-cubic-yard) capacity and test it for ease of loading and turning before you buy.

✔ **Anaerobic containers.** These sealed, closed-to-air compost bins require no turning or aerating. You simply fill the container with organic material, close the lid, and wait, sometimes up to six months.

Although no maintenance is required, this type of bin often has insect and odor problems. The decomposed product is slimy and requires drying before use, and shoveling the compost out of the bin is difficult. We give this product low marks for home gardeners.

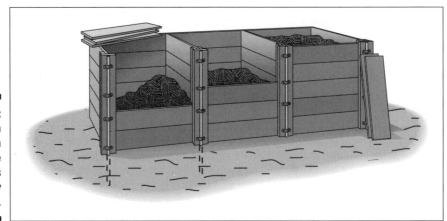

Figure 14-6:
A wooden compost bin with three bins allows for easy turning.

Composting aids . . . who needs them?

You don't need to have any store-bought gadgets to make compost. With or without accessories, you can create a perfect pile. A few supplies, however, do make composting faster, more exacting, and perhaps easier. Here's a rundown of these handy items for your consideration. All are available through mail-order garden supply catalogues. (See Appendix B.)

✔ **Compost starters.** Manufacturers say these products, sometimes called *inoculants* or *activators,* accelerate the composting process and improve the quality of the finished compost. We say you don't really need them, and that adding a little garden soil for every 30- to 45-centimetre (12- to 18-inch) layer of yard waste will accomplish the same thing. At most you might want to add a little soybean meal, but only then if the materials are mostly brown (high in carbon).

As an alternative to buying a commercial starter, make a thin layer of rich garden soil when you first build your pile.

✔ **Compost thermometer.** This thermometer consists of a face dial and a steel probe (about 50 centimetres, or 20 inches, long). You use this tool to accurately monitor the temperature of compost. The instrument measures temperatures from –18°C to 104°C (0°F to 220°F) and enables you to know when your pile is cooking and when it is cooling down and ready to turn. After you insert the steel probe into the pile, you can see the temperature reading on the face dial. If the compost gets hot, meaning up to 60°C to 71°C (140°F to 160°F), most of the bad players — weeds, diseases, and insect eggs — get killed.

✔ **Compost aerating tool.** You push a galvanized steel tool, which is about 90 centimetres (36 inches) long, into the compost pile. As you pull the tool out, two paddles open, creating a churning action that enables oxygen to enter the pile.

✔ **Compost sifter.** Because different materials decompose at different rates, you may end up with some large chunks of not-yet-decomposed material in compost that is otherwise ready for the garden. The sifter separates out the large pieces, which you can then toss back into a new compost pile to further decompose.

You can save a few bucks by making your own sifter. To do so, use 2 millimetre (¼-inch) window screen stapled or nailed to a wooden frame made of lumber. Make the frame large enough so that you can position it over a wheelbarrow and sift compost through it.

✔ **Pitchfork.** This long-handled tool, with tines about 25 to 30 centimetres (10 to 12 inches) long, is the best instrument to use for turning compost.

Heapin' it on

So what else can you put in your compost pile besides the obvious? The following list describes several other materials found around the home and garden that make good additions to any compost pile:

- ✔ Ashes from the wood stove (sprinkle them lightly between layers; *don't* add them by the bucketful)
- ✔ Chicken or rabbit manure
- ✔ Coffee grounds and tea leaves
- ✔ Eggshells (crush them before adding)
- ✔ Flowers
- ✔ Fruit and vegetable peels, stalks, and foliage (everything from salad leftovers to old pea vines)
- ✔ Fruit pulp from a juicer
- ✔ Grass clippings (mix them thoroughly to prevent clumping)
- ✔ Hedge clippings
- ✔ Shredded leaves (whole leaves tend to mat down and block air)
- ✔ Pine needles (use sparingly; they break down slowly)
- ✔ Sawdust
- ✔ Sod and soil
- ✔ Wood chips (chipped very small for faster decomposition)

A-Mulching We Will Go . . .

Mulch is any material, organic or not, placed over the surface of soil to conserve moisture, kill weed seedlings, modify soil temperatures, or make the garden look more attractive — or all four at once. Mulch was traditionally thought to mean natural, organic materials such as leaves, wood chips, and sand. Now a multitude of plastic-based films or woven materials are available.

A common goal of mulching is to reduce weeding, so it makes little sense to use mulch that is chock-full of weed seeds. Instead, use seed-free organic mulches or inorganic mulches such as the following:

- ✔ Grass clippings (from a weed- and pesticide-free lawn)
- ✔ Leaves (shredded or composted)
- ✔ Newspaper (shredded or flat)
- ✔ Pine needles (for acid-loving crops)

    ✔ Salt hay (a generally weed-free plant from oceanside meadows)

    ✔ Sea weed

    ✔ Shredded bark

    ✔ Wood chips. Use fresh chips from a local arbourist, or better, composted wood chips from a soil or amendment supplier.

Inorganic mulches

Inorganic mulch holds in moisture and stops weeds but doesn't add fertility to the soil. Use this mulch around perennials, shrubs, or trees that are naturally adjusted to your soil and don't require additional fertilizer. Examples of infertile mulch include gravel, landscape fabric, sand, and stone.

Fertile mulches

Double your gardening pleasure by using fertile mulch, which controls weeds *and* provides small amounts of nutrients. All organic mulches made of plant material fit this group. Some organic mulches quickly rot (decompose) and dissolve nutrients into the soil; these are green, fresh, and not too woody. The mulches that quickly decompose are useful in annual flower and vegetable beds. When sprinkled with water, or in rainy-summer areas, organic mulch that decomposes fairly quickly also leaches some nutrients while sitting on top of the soil.

Other organic mulches are slow to decompose and release few nutrients; these are usually dry, woody, and very low in nitrogen. Bark mulches are slowest to decompose because bark is naturally rot-resistant. Use these for pathways, or around trees and shrubs. Chips of tree sapwood may be fresh or composted. The latter is preferable, if available. Fresh wood chips can make an excellent mulch, but you should apply a little extra nitrogen fertilizer over the mulch so that it doesn't take all the nitrogen at your plants' expense.

Fertile mulches that quickly decompose but have weed seeds include cow, rabbit, goat, sheep, and horse manure; hay; some poultry bedding; sewage sludge; and straw. Fertile mulches that also quickly decompose but have no weed seeds include clean grass clippings, leaves, and salt hay.

Newspaper, shredded bark, and wood chips add little fertility to the soil and decompose slowly because they are high in carbon; they have no weed seeds.

All the mulches we mention are just part of a nearly infinite selection of local specialties. Rice hulls, cocoa shells, ground corncobs, peanut shells, and grape pomace are a few you may encounter, depending where you live.

Woven plastic materials (called *landscape fabric*) act as a seedling barrier as well, but these effective materials are not attractive enough for some situations. Also, sunlight deteriorates these mulches, so covering them with a weed-free organic mulch to block the sun's ultraviolet rays is a good idea. The fabric lasts longer and your garden looks better.

A well-read mulch

Newspapers provide the ultimate organic herbicide, a simple and cost-effective way to mulch out weeds. A thin layer of five to ten sheets of newspaper suppresses all sprouting weed seeds, stops some resprouting taproots, and makes life difficult for runner roots. Use newsprint that 's plain black and white or has colour. (We used to discourage the use of glossy, coloured paper because of the chemicals, such as cadmium and lead, in the inks. This is less a problem now that most printers have switched to less toxic inks.) The newspapers are best used around woody perennials, shrubs, and trees, but once you're familiar with the process, you can use them around flowers or vegetables.

To apply the newspaper, moisten the sheets so they don't blow around as you lay them out among the plants. Cover the papers with a thin layer of a weed-free, attractive mulch. The mulch helps the newspaper last for 6 to 18 months, depending on whether you have wet or dry summers, respectively.

Cardboard works even better than newspaper for the really tough weeds.

Chapter 15

A Snip Here, a Snip There: Pruning and Propagating

In This Chapter

▶ Pruning smart

▶ Mastering the basics

▶ Gearing up for pruning

▶ Taking stem cuttings

*O*ne of the images that often comes to mind when you think about gardening is of a wise gardener with a pair of snips in her hand carefully clipping and snipping in a knowing way. What are gardeners doing when they snip and clip? Well, they're probably doing one of two things: pruning or propagating.

You use both pruning and propagating to promote plant growth, but you use them for different purposes. *Pruning* refers to cutting plants to redirect the plant's growth to where you want it. *Propagating* (or taking cuttings) refers to cutting off a part of a plant and using the cutting to start a new plant.

In this chapter, you find out how to make the cut as a pruner and propagator. Okay, you won't leave this chapter as Edward Scissorhands, but we do give you the fundamentals that will have you happily snipping and cutting in no time.

Practical Pruning

Pruning is one of the most misunderstood, and therefore neglected, gardening techniques. Pruning may be a big job, like removing a heavy, damaged limb, or it may involve the simple removal of a spent flower. Pruning is part maintenance, part preventative medicine, and part landscaping. Because plants grow, they change all the time: A branch that was just right last year, is now too long. Or perhaps the plant is overgrown and needs rejuvenation. Pruning is nothing more than snipping or cutting or pinching away some part of a plant for some good reason.

Here are some common reasons for pruning plants:

- **Sculpting for decorative reasons.** This is your chance to be fanciful. There are no rules, but be aware that once you embark on pruning a plant to a specific shape, it's hard to go back.

- **Shaping a tree or shrub for strength and resistance to wind, snow, and ice damage (or to bear a bountiful crop).** Some fruit trees need annual or semiannual pruning in order to continue bearing crops.

- **Keeping the plant healthy.** By removing dead branches, you make it easier for the tree to seal the remaining wound.

As a general rule, don't prune unless you must. Always consider whether the plant really needs to be pruned. Many native or naturalized trees grow perfectly well without pruning. But roses and fruit trees, among others, need thoughtful pruning for maximum production of flowers and fruit. Table 15-1 describes when to prune schrubs and trees.

Table 15-1	When to Prune
Type of Plant	*When*
Shrubs that bloom in spring	Just after flowers fade
Shrubs that bloom in summer or fall	Early spring
Rhododendrons and azaleas	Just after flowers fade
Pine trees	Late spring
Formal hedges	Late spring and, if necessary, fall
Most trees, shrubs, and vines	Late winter or early spring

How pruning affects plant growth

To understand how and when to prune, you need to know a bit about a plant's biology (and its inner struggles). As with a fast-growing teenager, a tree's growth is controlled by a mixture of hormones and food. Its food consists of carbohydrates generated in the leaves by photosynthesis. Some of the tree's important hormones — growth stimulators or regulators — come from the bud at the tip of each leafy shoot or branch. Biologists refer to this bud as the *apical, leading,* or *tip* bud. The tip bud stimulates new, lengthy, vertical growth and stifles the growth of lower potential shoots — called *dormant buds.*

When you clip out any tip bud, you take away the stifling tip hormones and their dominance. The dormant buds below the cut burst into growth and begin to produce the tip hormones themselves.

When a branch is positioned at a 45 to 60 degree angle, the flow of carbohydrates, hormones, and nutrients naturally favours the formation of flower buds. With many deciduous fruit trees, like apple, almond, and pear trees, the flower buds become long-term fruiting places, called *spurs,* in the following years.

The kindest cuts

All pruning cuts, whether made with a chain saw or finger tips, fall into one of two categories: *thinning* cut or *heading* cut. Both kinds are important, but it helps to know the difference and when to use them.

You prune plants using the following techniques:

- **Thinning cuts.** Thinning cuts remove an entire branch or limb all the way to its origin. You do this with your fingertips when pinching a coleus or tomato seedling; with hand pruners for larger plants or shrubs; or pruning shears (even a saw) for trees. Regardless of scale, the principle is the same. When thinning, you remove a branch or stem completely to create better air circulation or to reduce crowded conditions. Always make thinning cuts to just above a dormant bud. Cut at a slight angle and leave about 7 millimetres (¼ inch) of the shoot above the bud — not a long stub.

- **Heading cuts.** These cuts shorten a branch or stem. As opposed to thinning, this type of pruning cut shortens a branch and doesn't remove it entirely.

- **Pinching.** This action can be either a heading or thinning cut. Usually, you pinch soft growth between your thumb and forefinger. Pinching is handy with soft annuals and perennials, but also good for larger plants, if you do it early enough when their shoots are still young and soft. Any pruning done at this early stage is ideal because the plant suffers minimal harm and recovery is quick.

- **Shearing.** For this cut, use scissorlike pruning shears or hedge clippers to keep hedge lines straight and neat. Boxwood and yews are commonly sheared.

Check out Figure 15-1 to see examples of these pruning cuts.

a) Thinning

b) Heading

c) Pinching

d) Shearing

Figure 15-1: Can you cut it as a gardener?

Pruning trees

When pruning trees, you should usually use thinning cuts, but don't cut absolutely flush to the remaining limb or branch. Leave the *branch collar* intact. The branch collar is slightly wider than the shoot you're removing, is marked with many compact wrinkles, and is usually a slightly different tone or texture than the shoot. Natural chemicals within the branch collar encourage rapid healing and help prevent rot from entering the heart of the tree. Flush cuts allow the rot to slip past the collar and invade the very core of the tree or plant.

Consider these pruning tips before you take out your saw:

- **Sawing a medium-sized limb.** If the limb is small enough to hold so that it doesn't fall while cutting, you can use only one cut with a pruning handsaw. Leave the larger and more noticeable branch collar intact. Don't let the limb drop as you cut through it, or the bark will tear or rip.

- **Sawing a large limb.** You use three cuts to remove large, heavy limbs, as shown in Figure 15-2. First, about 8 centimetres outside of the branch collar, cut halfway through the limb from the underneath side. Then, about 8 centimetres outside of the first cut, make a second cut (from the top), this time going all the way through the limb. If any bark begins to tear, it will stop at the cut underneath. Trim off the remaining stub with a final cut just outside the branch collar.

- **Treating your tree's wounds.** Covering pruning wound with tar or asphalt doesn't really help the tree. The toxins in the tar might even slow wound healing. If you want to cover the wound for appearance sake, use a diluted water-based paint. Some of the newest kinds of lanolin-based wound sealers might actually be beneficial.

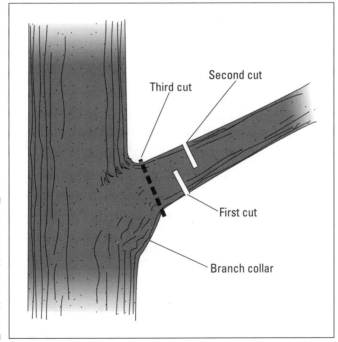

Figure 15-2: Removing a large limb without ripping the bark is a three-cut process.

Pruning in winter

The traditional season for pruning *deciduous* (leaf shedding) plants is while all the buds are dormant — in late winter or very early spring before the sap runs and flowers or leaves open. Such pruning stimulates new vegetative shoots — which are less fruitful with fruit trees. Cutting back a dormant branch causes two or more side shoots to emerge below the cut as a result of lost tip dominance. (See this section "How pruning affects plant growth" in this chapter for more about tip dominance.) Winter pruning is done when you want to force new shoots to fill air space around the trunk with branches, or to shape the tree by cutting off large branches.

When you have many long, vertical shoots — called *suckers* or *watersprouts* — you want to thin out, consider some summer pruning. Commercial fruit growers often prune out suckers after the trees have set their terminal buds and stopped growing for the season, which usually occurs the end of July or early August, to allow light in to develop ripening apples or peaches. You can do the same, for fruit or to thin out an overgrown tree. But don't remove too much— about one-third of the suckers is enough. More and the tree might try to replace the removed branches, in spite of the fact that it's starting the dormant process. If you have a neglected and overgrown tree dense with suckers, it might take five years to remove them.

Pruning in summer

Summer pruning can become the most valuable technique in a gardener's repertoire. Careful summer pruning has the effect of mildly stunting or dwarfing trees. The partial removal of the foliage in summer means fewer leaves to convert sunlight into stored carbohydrates. Because summer pruning is so appropriate for removing unwanted branches, it is the preferred way to begin a program of restoration with neglected and overgrown trees.

Pruning trees and shrubs

A few "rules of limb" apply when pruning all trees and shrubs:

✔ Remove dead or diseased wood as soon as possible. (Be sure not to spread certain diseases, like fireblight, with the pruning tools: Clean the blade with a 10 percent solution of bleach after *every* cut.)

✔ Cut out one or two branches or shoots if they rub against each other.

✔ Prune in the winter to encourage new shoots and leafy growth.

✔ To remove unwanted shoots or limbs without stimulating too many new shoots, prune in the summer.

Summer is also the best time for thinning cuts. The active photosynthesis allows the trees to begin forming a *callus* over the cut. The well-knit callus tissue that forms a ring around the cut resists the sprouting of new shoots the coming spring.

Pruning too early in the season, during spring's burst of vegetative growth, has a stimulating effect more like dormant pruning. Summer-prune after the initial flurry of spring growth, as the weekly growth rate slows down.

Summer-prune by the middle of summer: later pruning sometimes forces new, succulent shoots. These tender shoots don't harden off before freezing weather arrives and can die off.

Pruning tools

Poorly constructed tools can cripple or maim a gardener, so select a set of well-made, sturdy pruning tools. Here's a brief list of the essentials.

- **Hand pruner.** Hand pruners or secateurs are usually reserved for cuts up to 13 millimetres to 2.5 centimetres (½ to 1 inch) in diameter. Our favourite is the Felco brand — in our opinion, the most comfortable and easily used bypass pruner on the market.

- **Lopper.** Loppers can cut limbs up to several inches in diameter. You never need a lopping shear if your trees are well trained from the start. If you're restoring an abandoned tree or shrub, you need a lopper to remove older wood. We suggest choosing a 40- to 60-centimetre (16- to 24-inch) or 75-centimetre (30-inch) lopper. Aluminum- or fiberglass-handled loppers are lighter than wood, and thus easier to handle.

- **Hand saw.** The one hand saw required is probably a folding saw with a 30-centimetre (12-inch) blade. Make sure that you get one with a locking mechanism for the open position.

  If you're working on a disheveled or abandoned tree with large limbs slated for removal, you may want a large, 60- to 90-centimetre (24-to 36-inch) long curved pruning saw with large 2.5- to 5-centimetre (1- to 2-inch) saw teeth. The bigger the saw's teeth and the wider the space between the teeth, the faster the saw cuts.

- **Ladder and pole pruner.** If you're caring for really large shade or fruit trees, you need a pruning ladder and/or a pole pruner.

  First, buy a three-legged, aluminum (not wooden) orchard pruning and picking ladder. These ladders come in heights of 2 to 5 meters (6 to 16 feet) and cost from $75 to more than $225. They're not cheap, but they are the most comfortable way to prune a large tree with hand pruners and a lopper.

If standing on a ladder makes you nervous, an extending pole pruner is your next best option. Buy one with fibreglass poles (which are lightweight and won't conduct electricity if you happen to touch a wire) that telescope from about 2 to 4 metres (6 to 12 feet). The only variety worth buying has a cast-metal head and a chain-and-gear-driven mechanism. A good pole pruner can set you back up to about $150 to $200. Appendix B lists several mail-order companies that sell these tools.

Down-to-Earth Propagating

When people speak of propagating, mostly they mean *taking cuttings* — using pieces of stems, roots, and leaves to start new plants. (See Figure 15-3.) The best technique for most gardeners to know is how to take stem cuttings, which you can use to propagate perennials and shrubs.

Softwood stem cuttings, taken from spring until midsummer, root the quickest. During this time, plants are actively growing, and the stems are succulent and flexible. Here's how to take a softwood stem cutting:

Figure 15-3:
Taking a stem cutting.

1. **Use a sharp knife to cut a 10- to 12-centimetre (4- to 5-inch-long) stem (or side shoot) just below a leaf, and remove all but two or three leaves at the top.**

2. **Dip the cut end into *rooting hormone*.**

   Rooting hormone is a powder or liquid containing growth hormones that stimulate root growth on cuttings. Some also contain a fungicide to control root rot. Check local nurseries or garden centres for the product.

3. **Insert the cutting into a box or container (with drainage holes), filled with about 7.5 centimetres (3 inches) of moistened pure builder's sand, vermiculite, or perlite.**

4. **Slip the container into a self-sealing plastic bag.**

   Prop up the bag with something like toothpicks or short twigs so that the plastic doesn't touch the leaves. Seal the bag to minimize water loss, but open it occasionally to let in fresh air.

5. **Place the covered container in indirect light.**

6. **When the cuttings are well-rooted (starting in four to eight weeks, for most plants) and are putting on new growth, transplant them into individual containers of potting soil. As they continue to grow, gradually expose them to more light.**

7. **When the plants are well established in the pots and continuing to put on top growth, *harden them off* and plant them in their permanent garden location.**

Here are some easy-to-root plants to grow from stem cuttings.

   ✓ **Perennials:** Begonia, candytuft, chrysanthemum, carnations or pinks *(Dianthus)*, geraniums *(Pelargonium)*, penstemon, phlox, sage, sedum

   ✓ **Woody plants:** Heather, forsythia, honeysuckle, ivy, pyracantha, willow

Getting Plants for Free

Sometimes the best source for plant material for propagating is neighbours and friends. If your neighbour has a plant you'd like to grow (maybe a splendid fuchsia or a geranium you can't find at the nursery), ask to take cuttings. (Gardeners love to share.)

Another great way to get new plants is through *division,* the process of pulling apart clumps of plants to create new clumps. (See Figure 15-4.) As plants (like daylilies and peonies) become established in a garden, most develop into larger and larger clumps made up of small plants. Dividing the clumps and replanting the sections is the easiest means of spreading and increasing the plant. Dividing works great with all but "tap-rooted" plants, which have a main root that grows straight down, like carrot and baby's-breath. For a list of plants you can't divide, please check out *Perennials For Dummies* by Marcie Tatroe and the Editors of The National Gardening Association (IDG Books Worldwide, Inc.).

Figure 15-4:
Divide by pulling apart the root ball or by using a spade.

You can divide plants by using the following techniques:

- ✔ Use a spade or digging fork to lift out a mature clump (usually 3 to 5 years old).

- ✔ Divide fine-rooted types such as lamb's-ears by hand, gently teasing apart the clump into separate plants.

- ✔ Divide tough or fleshy-rooted types with a spade by cutting down through the roots, or use two garden forks back-to-back to pry the clumps apart.

Each new section for replanting should include several buds. Discard the older central section and replant the divisions as soon as possible.

Knowing the best season to divide plants is important — and it varies by plant and climate. As a general guideline, divide spring-flowering plants in very late summer or early autumn so that the new divisions can become established before winter. Divide summer- and autumn-flowering plants in early spring, while new top growth is just 5 to 7.5 centimetres (2 or 3 inches) high.

The hybrid tea rose 'Chicago Peace' illustrates why the rose is called the queen of flowers. While roses have a reputation for being finicky, several hundred species grow successfully in North America. Growers have crossed and re-crossed the species to form many different hybrids, and some have been specifically hybridized to grow well in Canada.

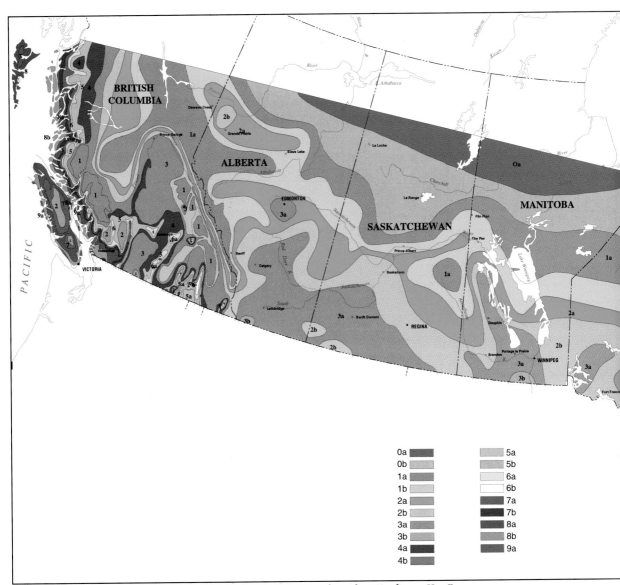

0a ▪	5a ▪
0b ▪	5b ▪
1a ▪	6a ▪
1b ▪	6b ▪
2a ▪	7a ▪
2b ▪	7b ▪
3a ▪	8a ▪
3b ▪	8b ▪
4a ▪	9a ▪
4b ▪	

Hardiness areas are divided into 10 zones in the most populated areas of Canada; 0 is the coldest and 9 the mildest. Most zones are divided into dark ("a") and light ("b") sections to represent colder and milder protions.

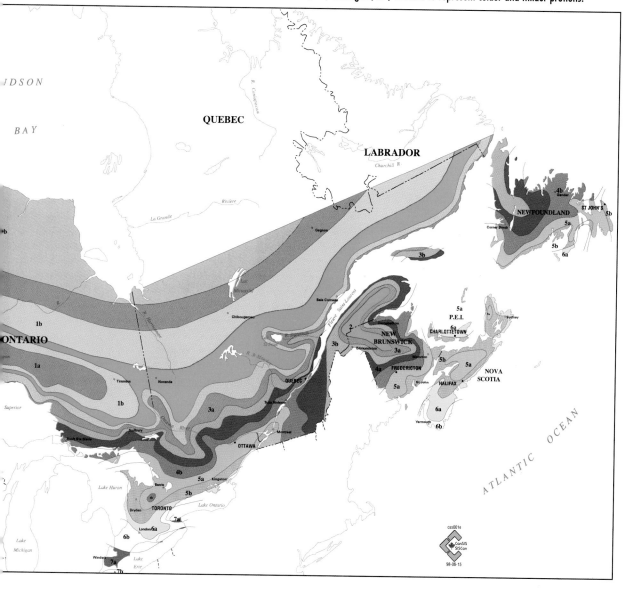

Violas like 'Sorbet Blueberry Cream', a cool weather annual, will often self-seed.

Annual zinnias are the essence of summer and make wonderful cut flowers.

The sweet, spicy stock *Matthiola incana* is indispensable in a fragrant garden.

The common sunflower, *Helianthus annuus,* is a staple of every summer garden.

The delicate larkspur should be seeded in place in early spring and will often self-seed.

Nasturtium 'Alaska', with variegated foliage, makes a good partner to magenta *Verbena.*

Mauve moss phlox, *Phlox sebulata,* and perennial alyssum, *Aurinia saxatilis,* make good spring rock garden plants.

The common lemon daylily, *Hemerocallis lilioasphodelus,* is the earliest daylily to bloom.

Delphiniums and shasta daisies are classic perennials for a sunny border.

Late spring-blooming peony and lady's mantle, *Alchemilla mollis.*

A home gardener can copy nature with mauve asters, goldenrod, and Canada rye grass.

The perennial—McKana giant columbine grows in Zone 3.

A trio of complementary colours: lady's mantle, deep blue salvia 'May Night', and Artemisia 'Silver King'.

A spring-blooming crocus, *Tomasinianus*, is a good naturalizer.

The 'Anaconda' trumpet lily, hardy to Zones 3-4, is beautiful in July.

A tender tuber, the dahlia comes in many forms and must be stored indoors over the winter.

Allium 'Purple Sensation' and the blue camassia, hardy to Zone 5, both bloom in mid-spring.

Tulips come in many forms, such as the lily-flowered 'Ballade', a cultivar shown here with Japanese sandcherry. Tulips are hardy from Zones 3 to 5, depending on the species.

The vibrant *Iris reticulata* is among the smallest and earliest bulbs to bloom.

A bountiful bed of *Hyacinthus orientalis* and blue forget-me-nots, *Myosotis sylvatica,* is a stunning display of beauty.

Floribunda roses such as 'Lavaglow', hardy to Zone 5, are crosses of cluster-flowered polyantha roses and hybrid teas, and offer blooms in abundance.

'Graham Thomas' is one of the most popular of the English shrub roses bred by David Austin.

'Rosa Mundi', a once-blooming gallica rose, is a favourite of The Canadian Rose Society.

The ginkgo tree, *Ginkgo biloba,* is the oldest tree known to man and has beautiful lemon yellow leaves in fall.

Our native red maple, *Acer rubrum,* glows brilliant scarlet in fall.

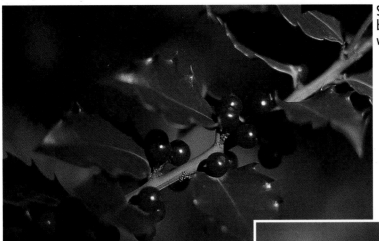

Shrubs are important in a garden for spring blooms, fall colour, and, like the holly here, winter berries.

Blue spirea, *Caryopteris* X *clandonensis,* blooms late in the summer and attracts bees and butterflies.

Spirea and weeping forsythia bloom in spring.

Japanese blood grass, hardy to Zones 5-6, glows in the sunshine.

Zebra grass, *Miscanthus sinensis* 'Zebrinus', is a happy note in any garden.

Grasses add a note of colour and texture to this cottage garden. The tall grass in the center is *Miscanthus sinensis* 'Zebrinus'. Below it are three tufts of blue fescue, *Festuca glauca*, and Japanese blood grass.

Canadians of all ages can get into the act! A bean teepee is an easy project to get a child involved in gardening.

Tiny tomatoes now come in many colours and varieties.

Flowers are replacing grass in many front gardens. An arbour of roses, yellow daylilies, pink dianthus, blue salvia, and yellow loosestrife grace this garden.

A seed mix of annual poppies and blue bachelor's buttons dominate this small front garden.

A birdbath is a focal point in this spring garden which features blue forget-me-nots and white narcissus 'Thalia'.

Healthy gardens teem with insects. In the petals of a yellow flower, this ladybug lies in wait for red aphids.

A swallowtail butterfly sips nectar from *Lillium* 'Elora'.

A bumblebee buzzes the many bright purple blooms of the ultra-hardy rhododendron 'PJM'.

Chapter 16

Fighting Pests, Diseases, and Weeds

· ·

In This Chapter

▶ Adding an ounce of prevention

▶ Dealing with pesky insects

▶ Controlling 31 common garden pests

▶ Keeping beneficial insects happy

▶ Curing 14 plant diseases

▶ Outwitting greedy animals

▶ Keeping weeds from muscling out your plants

· ·

*W*hen you begin creating that little piece of paradise that is your garden, you may envision picture-perfect plants with no weeds at their feet or holes in their leaves or half-eaten flowers. The reality can be startling, prompting some discouraged gardeners to run to the store for the most potent insect-disease-weed killer they can find. As we explain in this chapter, bringing out the big guns early on can be a big mistake, yet completely understandable from an emotional point of view.

The key to a healthy garden may sound a bit strange to some of you, but here it is: Don't sweat the small stuff. The more you try for a perfect, pest-free garden, the more likely you are to invite problems. Accepting a certain amount of damage is not only realistic, it also makes gardening more fun and less frustrating. Don't try to vanquish all enemies, but do try to outsmart them, perhaps losing a battle but winning the war. In addition, when you learn more about insect and animal pests, diseases, and weeds — and the conditions that invite them — you arm yourself with new techniques to reduce damage while promoting a healthier garden. This chapter gives you a start in that direction.

Preventing Bad Things from Happening

Research suggests that plants emit a chemical signal when they are under stress, and insects home in on this chemical signal like a landing pattern from air-traffic control. Diseases are similarly opportunistic, causing the most problems when plants are already weakened. So, what can you do to give your plants the best possible chance at a good life? Here are some suggestions:

- **Choose the proper site and soil.** Azaleas planted in full sun, for example, are apt to be more ravaged by azalea lace bugs than those planted in their natural woodland. Planting blueberries in alkaline soil — instead of the acid soil they require — guarantees poor performance. (See Chapter 11.)

- **Avoid planting the same vegetables or flowers in the same location year after year.** Crop rotation prevents pests and diseases that are specific to certain crops from accumulating in the soil.

- **Plant several small patches of the same type of vegetable rather than one large patch.** This approach makes it more difficult for insects to home in on and decimate their favourite crop.

- **Keep your garden clean and tidy.** During the growing season, remove damaged leaves. At season's end, remove crop residue and add it to the compost pile. Place diseased plants in the trash, not the compost pile to avoid spreading. As you prune, sanitize pruning shears between cuts by spraying with Lysol or a bleach solution. Some insect pests — such as aphids, cucumber beetles, and tarnished plant bugs — can spread diseases. Keep them under control, and you'll help prevent disease.

- **Choose resistant plants when possible.** Many plants (or varieties of plants) are less attractive to plant pests and less susceptible to certain diseases. To reduce corn earworm damage, for example, choose varieties that form a tight husk that extends over the tip of the ear, where the worm normally finds its entry. Look for this information in plant and seed catalogues.

- **Take steps to attract beneficial insects to your garden.** (See this chapter's section, "Encouraging 'good' insects.")

- **Cultivate the vegetable garden soil in the fall and early spring**. Loosening the soil exposes insect eggs, larvae, and pupae that will provide a tasty treat for birds.

- **Mulch to reduce insects, weeds, and disease.** Keep mulch several inches away from trunks and stems to discourage collar rot. Lightly rake the mulch once or twice a season to expose and kill pests' eggs. Though mulch may provide a haven for slugs, you can use baits and traps to reduce their numbers.

✔ **Provide for good soil drainage to discourage root rot.**

✔ **Space plants to provide good air circulation.** Leaves dry quickly, preventing spores of some fungus diseases from growing.

✔ **Water the soil, not the plants.** Early morning watering is best because the sun will evaporate any water on the leaves. Avoid evening watering.

✔ **Don't walk amid plants when the foliage is wet because you can spread disease spores from plant to plant.** Avoid handling cucumbers or tomatoes after handling tobacco, including flowering tobacco *(Nicotiana)* to reduce spread of tobacco mosaic virus.

An insect or disease problem is often a symptom that something else is out of whack. Table 16-1 lists conditions and the pests they promote. Treating the causes, not just the symptoms, helps to prevent problems.

Table 16-1	Conditions That Promote Pests and Problems	
Condition	*Pest/Problem*	*Preventative Measure*
High or excessive organic matter	Cutworms	Reduce additions of organic matter, rototill to speed soil decomposition
Partially decomposed debris	Damping-off disease, cutworms	Clean and cultivate garden crop in fall after harvest
Poorly decomposed manure	Root maggots, weeds	Use only composted manure
Dry and dusty weather	Spider mites	Wash leaves of plants with water
Sandy soils	Root-knot nematode	Plant resistant plants
Acid soils	Clubroot of cabbage, broccoli, and related plants	Raise pH by using ground dolomitic limestone crops
Too much water	Damping-off and other root rots	Reduce irrigation or improve drainage
Too much nitrogen	Weeds, aphids	Reduce fertilizer applications

Identifying Damage

When a problem does occur, correctly identifying the cause is essential. Finding out what's wrong can require some sleuthing unless you happen to witness the damage in the making. You can make more-reliable guesses about what's going on in your garden if you visit it often. Taking a stroll just before sunset or in the early morning can reveal insects that hide during the heat of the day. Slugs, for example, feed at night, so an investigative tour with a flashlight (and gloves) after dark can yield a containerful that the birds will appreciate the next day. Japanese beetles are sluggish in the cool hours of the evening and early morning, so you can easily knock them into a can of water.

One of the most frustrating experiences is to care for seeds and seedlings and then have them die or fail to appear at all. Table 16-2 offers a listing of common problems and causes.

Table 16-2	Common Pests of Vegetable Seedlings
What the Problem Looks Like	*Probable Cause*
Seeds fail to germinate or seedlings fail to appear	Seed corn maggots, damping-off, birds
Seedling collapses	Damping-off, heat, planted too early, planted in soil that is too cold or wet
Stems eaten at soil line	Cutworms
Leaves and stems chewed, torn	Snails, slugs, caterpillars, rabbits
Severely wilted plant (roots eaten)	Wireworms, root maggots, gophers
Small, round pits in leaves	Flea beetles
Threadlike, twisting lines in leaves	Leaf miners
Clusters of small, pear-shaped insects	Aphids
Plants completely removed	Animal pests such as birds or gophers

Homemade compost tea

Compost tea is a genetic cocktail teeming with microorganisms that appear to boost a plant's natural defenses and suppress the growth of some fungi. It can help reduce the spread of botrytis molds, tomato early and late blights, downy mildew, and powdery mildew by 50 to 90 percent. Make the tea by mixing one part mature compost that contains some manure with five parts water in a bucket. Let the mixture sit in the shade for about 10 days. Then filter the solution through cheesecloth, dilute the tea to half strength if you wish, and spray it or dribble it on the leaves. Try to coat both sides. Reapply after two to three weeks. You can also spread the leftover residue on the ground around your plants. Avoid spraying any products containing manures directly on leafy vegetables such as lettuce and spinach that you'll soon be harvesting.

Warning: When you use any disease-control remedies on food crops, be sure to wash your harvest well before eating it.

Insect Pests You're Most Likely to Encounter

Do borers drive you buggy? Don't know the difference between a cutworm and a caterpillar? In this section, we describe common North American pests and give you some tips on how to deal with them.

- ✔ **Aphids.** These tiny, soft-bodied, pear-shaped pests (shown in Figure 16-1) suck plant sap with their needlelike noses. Colours vary: They may be black, green, red, or even translucent. Aphids leave behind sticky sap droppings that may turn black if covered with sooty mould. Aphids can proliferate quickly on weakened plants. Blast them off with a hose, control with beneficial insects or sticky yellow traps, or spray with insecticidal soap. The beneficial insects green lacewings and ladybird beetles are also excellent controls.

- ✔ **Apple maggot.** Slightly smaller than houseflies, these pests overwinter in soil, then appear in June or July to begin laying eggs in apples, crabapples, plums, and other fruits. Always dispose of infested fruit before maggots emerge and establish themselves in the soil. Trap adult flies by hanging red, apple-shaped spheres coated with sticky goo. Begin trapping by early July and continue through August, cleaning and refreshing the sticky stuff every two weeks. Bait traps with butyl hexanoate pheromone.

Instead of coating the red trap itself with the sticky stuff, enclose the trap in a small, clear plastic bag and cover the bag with the trapping material. To renew the trap, dispose of the old plastic bag and replace with a new one.

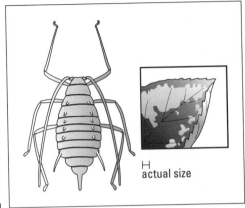

Figure 16-1:
Aphids
proliferate
quickly on
weakened
plants.

actual size

✔ **Bean leaf beetle.** These small, orange-red beetles have a black head and black spots and are about the size of a ladybird beetle. The beetles feed on leaves, creating a lacy pattern. Cover seedlings with lightweight row covers to exclude exploring beetles. To reduce damage caused by an existing infestation, spray with neem or insecticidal soap.

✔ **Black vine weevil.** This dark, crawling, 2.5- to 5-centimetre long (1- to 2-inch) beetle chews on the foliage of grapes, strawberries, evergreen trees and shrubs such as rhododendrons and yews, while the larvae attack from the other end, eating the roots. Black vine weevils also attack potted plants. Control adults and larvae with beneficial nematodes. Use Tanglefoot or another sticky substance to trap adults on trees, and don't let branches or leaves touch the ground.

✔ **Borers.** Several kinds of beetle and caterpillar larvae (they look like small worms and are usually less than 2.5 centimetres or 1 inch long) tunnel into the wood or stems of fruit trees, white birches, dogwoods, shade trees, rhododendrons, German irises, and squash vines. The boring weakens the plant and makes it more susceptible to diseases. The holes can also cut off nutrient flow to the affected limb or vine. Choose species that are less susceptible to borers. For example, try Siberian irises instead of German bearded irises. Keep susceptible plants growing vigorously and watch for signs of borer damage — dead bark, sawdust piles, and poor performance. When you find borers, cut off and destroy severely infested limbs. Inject parasitic nematodes into the remaining borer holes.

✔ **Carpenter ants.** Ants are scavengers who clean up the environment, and ants become a problem when there are things around they like to eat. Aphids, for instance: They secrete honeydew, which ants collect to feed their families. To protect their food source, ants will even protect aphids from attack by ladybird beetles and lacewings. Carpenter ants like wood — usually the soft, rotting kind, but sometimes new wood — in which they burrow to build nests. (It's not dinner). Sawdust may be a clue that they're nesting in your old stumps, or even the 4 x 4s in your house, as may be the presence of large, dark brown or black winged ants, nearly 2 centimetres (¾ inch) long. Remove dead stumps and raise stored firewood above ground level, then call pest control.

✔ **Caterpillars.** Moth and butterfly larvae are avid eaters that can cause damage to a variety of plants. However, you may decide to overlook the activities of some butterfly caterpillars so that you can enjoy the handsome butterflies later. (See Chapter 20 for more about gardening for butterflies.) Eliminate caterpillars such as the cabbage looper, tomato hornworm, and corn earworm before they do too much damage. If beneficial insects don't keep them in check, spray with Bt.

✔ **Chinch bug.** These 6-millimetre-long (¼-inch), brown or black insects suck grass sap, releasing toxins that make grass discolour and wilt. Generally a problem in eastern Canada, where they can turn entire patches of lawn brown, especially in dry and hot areas. Dethatch the lawn and let it grow a little longer than usual to discourage chinch bugs. For control, treat with a neem insecticide. Or mix an ounce of dish detergent in an 8-litre (2-gallon) watering can of water and drench soil. Cover with a white sheet and after 20 minutes remove and dump bugs into hot soapy water.

✔ **Codling moth.** This 2.5-centimetre-long (1-inch), pinkish-white caterpillar emerges from eggs laid on apples, peaches, pears, and other fruits. The adult moth is about 13 millimetres long (½ inch) and brown. The caterpillars tunnel inside the fruit, usually ruining it. In early spring while the tree is still dormant and leafless, spray dormant oil to kill overwintering eggs. Right after flowering, use pheromone traps to trap egg-laying females. Spray with Bt when apples are about 13 millimetres (½ inch) in diameter, or spray with neem as needed to prevent egg-laying through the growing season. Eliminate wild or unsprayed trees nearby that shelter codling moth populations.

Pheromones are the perfumes of the insect world. Undetectable to us, female butterflies and moths release tiny amounts of these chemicals, which are a siren song to a wandering male of the right type. Professionals use synthetic pheromones to monitor pest populations; you can use them to trap and disorient codling moth. (You can buy pheromone lures from several of the companies listed in Appendix B.)

Hang traps at eye level and spray Bt or neem oil three or four times beginning a week to 10 days after beginning of petal fall, or after the first codling moth is trapped.

✔ **Colorado potato beetle.** This yellow-and-black-striped beetle — 0.8 centimetre (⅓ inch) long, and nearly round — is notorious for obliterating potato plantings, but it also eats tomatoes, eggplant, petunias, and flowering tobacco. Discourage Colorado potato beetles by rotating planting sites. Cover potato plants with floating row covers to keep the beetles off. Spray with Bt formulated for Colorado potato beetles, or use neem. Beneficial nematodes also destroy larvae in soil.

✔ **Corn earworm.** This annoying caterpillar feeds right at the tips of ears of corn. They'll chew right through silk to get to kernels, and sometimes eat leaves. A daub of mineral oil on the developing silk prevents most damage. You can also spray Bt and rely on the help of beneficial trichogramma wasps that parasitize the worms. See this chapter's section, "Encouraging 'good' insects" for more about trichogramma wasps.

✔ **Cucumber beetle.** These 8-millimetre-long (⅓-inch) beetles with yellow and black stripes (or spots) swarm on cucumber, squash, and melon plants. You're likely to spot them first crawling around inside flowers. The main threat they pose is a bacterial wilt disease they carry that will kill your plants. That disease is reason enough to keep the beetles away entirely. Cover young vines with floating row covers. Uncover when several flowers open, and spray as needed with pyrethrin or dust with diatomaceous earth. (See the later section "Safe and effective pest chemicals.") Till the soil in autumn to eliminate overwintering hideouts.

✔ **Curculio.** These 6-millimetre-long (¼-inch) beetles are easy to identify by the crescent-shaped, egg-laying cut they make in fruit. Unfortunately, after the beetles lay the eggs, the fruit may be ruined. Spread out a tarp or old sheet underneath the tree, shake apple and pear tree branches to knock the beetles off and then step on them. Also destroy prematurely fallen fruit, which may contain larvae. If the problem is severe, consider spraying the insecticide imidan. Experts recommend the insecticide as the safest and most effective of available sprays.

✔ **Cutworms.** These 13-millimetre-long (½-inch), grayish caterpillars emerge on spring and early summer nights to eat the base of young seedling stems, cutting the tops off from the roots, as shown in Figure 16-2. To control, surround seedlings with a barrier that prevents the cutworms from crawling close and feeding. These devices can be as simple as an empty cardboard toilet paper roll, a bottomless paper cup or a collar made from aluminum foil — just make sure that the collar encircles the stem completely and set 2.5 centimetres (1 inch) deep in the soil.

✔ **Earwigs**. They look a little like a long beetle (about 2 centimetres, ¾ of an inch), with a nasty looking pair of forcep-like pincers at the rear end. (They can bite.) They feed at night on young vegetable and plant leaves (they love basil), and attack whatever takes their fancy. Dark, quiet places are their retreats. Set out rolls of cardboard or lengths of old garden hose in the evening, and in the morning, when the bugs are settling in for the day, dump the critters into a bucket of water with a little oil in it. Or check your garden with a flashlight at midnight and spray munching earwigs with insecticidal soap.

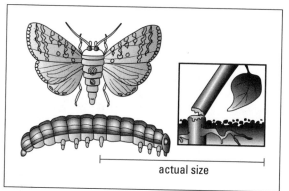

Figure 16-2:
Cutworms can do a great deal of damage before sprouting wings and flying off.

actual size

✔ **Flea beetles.** These tiny black beetles feed on vegetable plants such as egg-plant, radish, and broccoli, sometimes riddling the entire leafy area of seedlings with tiny holes. Cover susceptible plants with floating row covers as soon as you plant them. Keep them covered until the plants get fairly large and can withstand a few beetle bites. You also can spray with neem.

✔ **Grasshoppers.** These pests like dry warm areas, and generally avoid coastal British Columbia and the Maritimes. They dine on all plants, but especially like corn and they feed from August to heavy frost. Lush, green gardens close to fields and woodlots that dry out in summer are their favourite abodes. Frequent watering may discourage them, other-wise there's not much you can do.

✔ **Gypsy moths.** These 5-centimetre-long (2-inch), grey (with brown hairs), foliage-eating caterpillars or their egg clusters hitchhike across the country on cars, campers, and trains. They can be a real problem in eastern Canada and British Columbia, eating the foliage of a number of shade trees, including oaks and apples, and can defoliate trees when their population gets large enough. (They don't like junipers). Monitor population sizes with pheromone traps. Catch caterpillars as they attempt to crawl up tree trunks by using duct tape treated with a sticky barrier. Spray with Bt or neem. Coat egg masses with dish detergent, scrape off and burn or immerse in hot water with ammonia.

Sticky pest barriers are just that — bands of goop that a crawling insect cannot navigate. Buy this stuff at garden centres or from one of the mail-order suppliers listed in Appendix B.

✔ **Japanese beetles.** These beetles (pictured in Figure 16-3) are 13 millime-tres (½ inch) long, and are metallic blue-green with coppery wing covers. They eat almost any plant with gusto. Their fat, white, C-shaped, 2-centimetre-long (¾-inch) larvae consume turf roots. To control, treat your lawn with spores of milky disease, which takes several years to spread through the lawn, or with parasitic nematodes, a quicker-acting helper. Inspect your garden in the evening or after dark for the beetles, knocking them off plants into a can or bucket of soapy water. You can also spray with neem (See the section on neem coming up).

Avoid using hanging Japanese beetle traps. The pheromones in these traps attract beetles not only from your yard, but from your neighbours' yards as well. You'll end up with more beetles than you would have had without the traps.

✔ **Leaf miners.** The larval form of tiny flies, these maggots tunnel randomly through the leaves of plants such as columbine, peppers, beans, and lilacs. They disfigure plants and are hard to eliminate because they are protected inside the leaf. Prevent infestation by covering predisposed seedlings with floating row covers and removing and destroying infested leaves. Spray with neem in spring when adults begin to lay eggs.

✔ **Mealybugs.** These small sucking insects cover their bodies with a white, cottony substance that makes them easy to identify. Plus, they usually feed in groups. Mealybugs are common on houseplants. You can wash off small numbers with cotton dipped in rubbing alcohol. Spray indoor plants with an oil-based "leaf shine" product, and use horticultural oil for landscape plants. Insecticidal soap and neem are also effective remedies.

✔ **Mexican bean beetles.** These 6-millimetre (¼-inch), round beetles are yellowish with black spots. They resemble ladybugs but are avid plant eaters. They can destroy an entire bean planting, enjoying snap beans most but also lima beans, soybeans, and other legumes. The spiny, yellow larvae that appear on the bean plants soon after the adults arrive are just as bad as the adults. Pull up and destroy infested plants, beetles and all, immediately after harvesting. Till the ground to kill beetles hiding there. If necessary, spray with soap, pyrethrin, horticultural oil, or neem.

✔ **Oriental fruit moths.** These small moths produce 13-millimetre-long (½-inch), white-to- pink larvae that tunnel into the young wood or fruit of fruit and ornamental trees. In spring, work the soil shallowly around infested trees to kill overwintering larvae. Catch adult males in pheromone traps or use pheromones to confuse males and prevent breeding. You can kill moth eggs with horticultural oil.

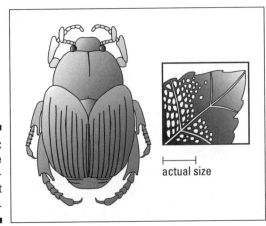

Figure 16-3: Japanese beetles consume almost any plant.

actual size

Aliens invade!

The speed and convenience of modern travel and mail has been a boon to insects and diseases, too. That's how pests — such as the Asian longhorn beetle, gypsy moth, Japanese beetle, Mediterranean fruit fly, and silverleaf whitefly — got to North America. Historically, the spread of pests has been blocked by geography. Not any more. Do farmers and fellow gardeners a favour and don't mail fruits home from foreign locations. Observe customs regulations when traveling overseas. If you intend to bring plants home, get information about the need for a phytosanitary certificate, which verifies plants are free of pests and disease, from agricultural officials or the nursery in the country you're visiting. Some plants require import permits as well as phytosanitary certificates, and it's good to know what you're in for before you make your purchases. For information, contact: Permit Office, Plant Protection Division, Food Production and Inspection Branch, 59 Camelot Dr., Nepean, ON. K1A0Y9

✔ **Root maggots.** A variety of fly larvae — most are white and less than 6 millimetres long (¼ inch) — that attack the roots of carrots, the cabbage family, and onions. They can disfigure or destroy these plants. Look for resistant plants. Cover new plantings of susceptible types of cabbage, turnips, rutabagas, radishes, kohlrabi, carrots, parsnips, and onions with floating row covers.

✔ **Scale.** Looking like bumps on plant stems and leaves, these tiny sucking insects cling to plant branches, hiding under an outer shell that serves as a shield. These pests suck plant sap and can kill plants if present in large numbers. Look for sticky, honeylike sap droppings, one clue that scale may be present. Remove and destroy badly infested stems. Indoors or on small plants, clean off light infestations with a cotton ball soaked in rubbing alcohol. Spray larger plants with horticultural oil in early spring or summer.

✔ **Snails and slugs.** These soft-bodied mollusks (see Figure 16-4) feed on tender leaves during the cool of night or in rainy weather. Sometimes they're hard to spot: All you see is the slime trail they leave behind. They proliferate in damp areas, hiding and breeding under rocks, mulch, and other garden debris. Clean up dark, damp hiding spots to relocate slugs elsewhere. Catch the ones that remain by setting out a saucer, with the rim at ground level. Fill the saucer with beer. Slugs crawl in and can't get out. Refill regularly. Or surround plants with copper barriers — metal strips that seem to shock slugs if they attempt to crawl across. Set out traps, commercial or homemade. Look for new, nontoxic baits that contain iron phosphate.

Make your own slug trap by placing a few boards or rolled-up newspaper in the garden. In the early morning, lift the board and destroy the slugs. Toss out the newspaper if it has slugs.

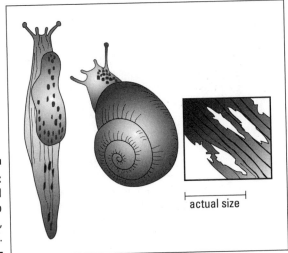

Figure 16-4:
Slugs and snails like to live in cool, damp areas.

actual size

✔ **Spider mites.** These tiny arachnoids (shown greatly enlarged in Figure 16-5) are almost microscopic, but when they appear in large numbers, you can begin to see the fine webs that they weave. They suck plant sap, causing leaves to discolour and plants to lose vigour. They are especially active in arid conditions. You find spider mites on fruit trees, miniature roses, potted begonias, and many houseplants. Indoors, wash houseplants often and spray with insecticidal soap. Outdoors, wash plants with a strong blast of water, or use dormant oil in early spring or light horticultural oil in summer.

✔ **Tarnished plant bugs (lygus bugs).** These 6-millimetre-long (¼-inch), yellow-to-brown plant eaters attack many kinds of plants — more than 400, including some of our most important economic crops — leaving behind dark, sunken leaf spots and wilting or dead shoots. They especially like the growing points of apples and strawberries. Catch them with white sticky traps. Prevent problems by covering susceptible plants with a floating row cover.

✔ **Tent caterpillars.** These caterpillars form tentlike webs full of teeming caterpillars on trees and shrubs. In large numbers, they can defoliate an entire tree. Knock caterpillars off severely infested branches with a broom or pole, or burn the nests by igniting them with a flaming cloth on a long broom handle.

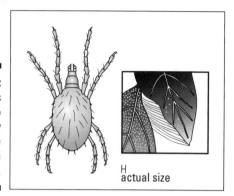

Figure 16-5:
Spider mites
are easier to
identify by
the damage
they do than
by sight.

H
actual size

- **Tomato hornworm.** This large, 7.5- to 12.5-centimetre (3- to 5-inch) long, green caterpillar is notable particularly for its white stripes and the threatening "horn" protruding from its rear. As dangerous as it appears, the horn can do no harm (although the mouth of the caterpillar will reduce tomato leaves to bare veins in no time at all), which is why hand-picking is one of the preferred controls. If you have lots of tomatoes (or peppers or potatoes), you may want to spray or dust with Bt in late spring or early summer. Bt is effective as long as worms remain small. Several tiny wasps also parasitize this caterpillar.

- **Whiteflies.** Whiteflies look like small, white gnats, but they suck plant sap and can proliferate in warm climates or greenhouses. They can also spread diseases with their sucking mouth parts. Trap whiteflies with yellow sticky traps. Cure infestations with regular sprays of hot (66°C, 150°F) water (directly from your water heater to your infested plants), insecticidal soap, light horticultural oil, or pyrethrin. Be sure to treat leaf undersides where whiteflies and their larvae reside.

Managing Pests

Think of pest management as a staircase. On the first step you can find the least disruptive, innocuous actions, and on the top step are the most toxic and the most potentially harmful measures. The best way to control pests is to start at the bottom and move up the stairs only when absolutely necessary. This strategy is called integrated pest management, or IPM. This approach takes advantage of the complex interrelationships between insects and plants to find the least toxic ways to reduce damage to crops.

The following list outlines the actions you can take in your garden to keep a pest from getting the upper hand. The measures move from the least aggressive and potentially harmful to the most aggressive.

- **A strong blast from a hose** knocks small pests such as aphids and spider mites off your plants. Spraying daily can provide good control.

- **Barriers** such as floating row covers (translucent, lightweight fabrics that cover plants) keep flying insects from reaching plants; cutworm collars and copper strips encircle plants and give crawlers like slugs an electric shock. Make cutworm collars 10 centimetres (4 inches) high out of rolled newspaper, or use toilet tissue rolls. Push 5 centimetres (2 inches) into the soil.

- **Insect traps** use chemical attractants and colours, such as sticky red balls for apple maggots, to lure insect pests to their deaths.

- **Bacterial insecticides**, such as Bacillus thuringiensis (Bt) for caterpillars, and milky spore disease for soil-dwelling grubs, destroy a multitude of insects.

- **Insecticidal soaps and horticultural oils and rotenone insecticides** kill pests but cause minimal impact on the environment.

- **Botanical insecticides**, such as neem (described in an upcoming section).

Encouraging "good" insects

The average square yard of garden contains more than a thousand insects. Some are plant pollinators, some help break down organic matter, and some prey on other more damaging ones. Only a small proportion of the insects cause much damage to your plants.

Beneficial insects prey upon or parasitize garden pests. In nature, beneficial insects keep plant-eating pests under control.

Here are some beneficial bugs and insects you'll want to keep around your yard:

- **Lady beetles.** You're probably aware of the ladybug's voracious appetite for aphids. Both larva and adult stages prey on pests. One ladybug can dine on 40 to 50 aphids a day. Ladybugs also prey on mites and other soft-bodied insects.

- **Green lacewing.** Larval stage lacewings feed on aphids, thrips, mites, and various other insect eggs; overall, the most useful insect in home gardens. Both larval and adult stages are beneficial, but the larval much more so.

- **Trichogramma wasps.** These tiny wasps parasitize many kinds of caterpillars by laying eggs in them. The wasps are effective against corn earworm, loopers, and tomato hornworm. They cannot attack people in any way.

✔**Parasitic nematodes**. The tiny worms parasitize many soil-dwelling and burrowing insects, such as grubs, cutworms, and weevils. These are different from the pest nematodes that feed on plant roots.

✔**Chinese praying mantis.** This general predator is interesting to watch but doesn't provide reliable control of pests.

All these beneficial insects are available from mail-order gardening companies. (You can find several listed in Appendix B.) They each have special requirements about the best time to release them into the garden. Whether you choose to buy beneficials or rely on the ones already present in your yard, you can take steps to encourage them to stick around:

✔ Avoid indiscriminate pesticide spraying, which kills beneficial insects as well as the pests. If you must spray, choose a product that specifically targets the pests you want to eliminate, and use it when it will be least harmful. For example, sprays that are harmful to bees can be used in the evening after bees have returned to the hive.

✔ Make sure that the beneficials have plenty to eat by allowing small numbers of pests to reside in your garden. If you release ladybugs before you've even spotted aphids, they may move elsewhere to find food.

✔ Provide beneficials with shelter. Grow a variety of plants — tall, short, spreading, and upright — to give the insects many potential homes.

✔ Many beneficials also feed on nectar and pollen, so grow flowers such as Queen Anne's lace and evening primrose. Lacewings love fennel, caraway, and dill. Goldenrod has been found to attract more than 75 different species of beneficial insects.

Safe and effective pest chemicals

Gardeners today have at their disposal a handful of effective and safe pesticides. All the following are approved for use by certified organic farmers.

Bacillus thuringiensis (Bt)

Bt exists naturally in most soils. Different strains of Bt occur that produce protein crystals that are toxic to certain insects. The strain for most caterpillars is *Bt. kurstaki.* Commercially prepared Bt spray or powder has no effect on adult butterflies or moths. Remember, however, that not all caterpillars are pests. Strains of Bt have been developed for a few other pests. Some leaf-feeding beetles (including Colorado potato beetle) are susceptible to *Bt. tenebrionis,* for example.

Advantages: One advantage is safety — Bt is essentially nontoxic to humans, other mammals, and birds. The label specifies no waiting period between application and harvest. Bt is also highly selective and easily incorporated with existing natural controls.

Disadvantages: A limitation of Bt is its slow action. After pests consume it, their feeding slows down. But their deaths may not occur for two to five days. Bt also breaks down quickly — if the caterpillars don't eat some while it's fresh, it probably won't work.

Because Bt is a near-perfect insecticide, there is danger of overuse. Any overused insecticide gradually becomes less effective as insects evolve defenses to it. Some insect pests, such as the diamondback moth and Indian meal moth, were once susceptible and are now at least partially immune to Bt.

How to use: Use Bt against cabbageworms, cutworms, and other caterpillars. Use *Bt. tenebrionis* against Colorado potato beetles. The bacterial toxin causes caterpillar death two to five days after it is eaten; the toxin dissipates in two days or less. It is available as liquid spray or dust. Bt must be ingested by the bug to cause damage, so apply at feeding time. Apply in late afternoon and reapply after rain. Repeat applications as needed. Mix with insecticidal soap for greater effectiveness.

Diatomaceous earth (DE)

Diatomaceous earth, or DE, is a powderlike dust made of the silicate skeletons of tiny water creatures called diatoms. Millions of years ago, as the diatoms died, their skeletons gradually accumulated into deep layers that are mined today from deposits where oceans or large lakes once covered the land. DE acts like ground glass, cutting into the waxy coat of many kinds of insects and causing them to dry out and die. DE is often combined with the botanical insecticide, pyrethrin (described in this section). The addition of pyrethrin makes DE more lethal for many insects.

Advantages: Easy to handle and apply. DE is not toxic and leaves no residue.

Disadvantages: DE is not selective and kills spiders and beneficial insects as well as pests. DE is available in two forms. One, which is used primarily in swimming pool filters, is not an effective insecticide and is dangerous to inhale (can cause a lung disease called silicosis). In your garden, use only the natural grade of DE. Always wear goggles and a dust mask during application.

How to use: Dust DE onto leaves and stems to control pests such as aphids, immature Colorado potato beetles, immature forms of squash bug, immature Mexican bean beetles, and whiteflies. Sometimes a band of DE makes an effective slug and snail barrier. It works best in dry situations; reapply after rain.

Horticultural oils

Horticultural oils are most often highly refined extracts of crude oil. (Some vegetable oils, such as cottonseed and soybean oil, are also sometimes used.) They kill insects by plugging the pores through which the insects breathe.

Advantages: These oils are increasingly recommended for vegetable garden pest control because they present few risks to either gardeners or desirable species and integrate well with natural biological controls. Also, oils dissipate quickly through evaporation, leaving little residue.

Disadvantages: Oils can damage plants if applied at excessive rates or on particularly hot (above 38°C, or 100°F) or cold (below 5°C, or 40°F) days.

How to use: Spray oils in vegetable gardens to kill aphids, leafhoppers, spider mites, and whiteflies. A few drops of oil in the ear tips of corn control corn earworm.

Use highly refined horticultural oils and dilute according to label directions. Do not apply oils to drought-stressed plants, or on hot, cold, or very humid days. Don't apply horticultural oils to green plants at rates recommended for leafless, dormant plants.

Insecticidal soaps

Insecticidal soaps are specific fatty acids that have been found by experiment to be toxic to pests, primarily soft-bodied insects like aphids, mealybugs, spider mites, and whiteflies. Surprisingly, adult Japanese beetles are also susceptible.

Advantages: Insecticidal soap is one of the safest insecticides. Most nontarget insects are unaffected, and the soaps are not toxic to animals. Soap insecticides act fast and leave no residue. You can use them on vegetables up to the moment of harvest.

Disadvantages: Soaps readily burn some plants such as peas, and the effectiveness of the soap diminishes greatly when mixed with hard water (water high in dissolved minerals). Soaps kill pests only when they make direct contact.

How to use: Use against aphids, earwigs, grasshoppers, Japanese beetles (adults), leafhoppers, spider mites, and whiteflies. Apply diluted concentrate or ready-to-use liquid when the air is still. To improve effectiveness, mix with warm, soft water and be sure to cover both sides of leaves. Reapply after rain. Can burn leaves of certain plants during hot weather.

Neem

Neem is an extract derived from the crushed seeds of the tropical neem tree *(Azadirachta indica)*. Though intensely studied for many years now, it is still a new botanical insecticide. The primary active ingredient is the compound azadirachtin. Two forms are commonly available. One is a 3 percent solution of azadirachtin, the most insecticidal component, and the other is "clarified hydrophobic extracts of neem seeds," essentially a syrupy oil (make sure the oil is warm before mixing with water).

Both forms of neem work as both an insecticide and as an agent that prevents insects from feeding. They also kill insects in the juvenile stage by thwarting their development and are most effective against aphids, thrips, and whiteflies. Neem oil is also fungicidal and can control black spot of roses, powdery mildew, and rust diseases.

Advantages: Neem has no measurable toxicity to mammals. (In some countries, neem extract is considered healthful to people and is added to various food and personal products.) The U.S. Environmental Protection Agency stipulated that neem was exempt from food crop tolerances because it is considered nontoxic.

Disadvantages: Neem doesn't have a quick "knock-down" effect, but a week or so after application, you'll notice a steady decline in the number of pests. It is not effective against adult insects (though it may interfere with egg production) and has little impact on beneficial insects. Once beetle numbers build up on the plant, neem no longer discourages them.

How to use: Neem sprays degrade very quickly in water. Mix only the amount you need and apply all of it immediately. Reapply after rainfall. On the plant, neem retains its activity against juvenile insect pests for about one week. Use neem to kill juvenile aphids, Colorado potato beetles, and thrips and to repel whiteflies, Japanese beetles, and adult Colorado potato beetles. Apply liquid spray morning or evening when humidity is highest. Repeat weekly; spray lasts on plants about one week. As a toxin, apply when pests are young. As an antifeedant, neem is effective against Japanese beetles; apply before the pests appear.

To mix neem oil with water, the oil needs to be a least room temperature. But neem mixes still better if you warm it first in water on the stove, or even in the microwave for about 30 seconds. If you try the latter, be sure to remove the aluminum seal under the cap first.

Pyrethrins

Derived from the painted daisy, *Tanacetum cinerariifolium,* pyrethrins are considered one of the most important natural insecticides. When you must either use a broad-spectrum insecticide in the vegetable garden or lose the crop, pyrethrins are among your best choices.

Broad-spectrum insecticides are products that kill a diversity of insects, pest and beneficial alike. If you need to use an insecticide to control a particular pest, use a product that targets that particular kind of pest without harming beneficial insects. The terminology can be confusing, however. Pyrethrum is the ground-up flowers of the daisy. *Pyrethrins* (most always plural) are the insecticidal components of the flowers. *Pyrethroids,* such as cypermethrin, permethrin, and resmethrin, are synthetic compounds that resemble *pyrethrins* but are more toxic and persistent.

Advantages: Pyrethrins are of low toxicity to mammals and kill insects quickly. In sunlight, they break down and are nontoxic within a day or less.

Disadvantages: Often, pure pyrethrins only stun insects, which is why they often get combined with a synergist (a chemical that enhances the effectiveness of the active ingredients) such as piperonyl butoxide or with another botanical insecticide, such as rotenone. Also, pyrethrin is toxic to honeybees — apply it in the evening after bees are in their hives. Don't use with a soap spray or lime treatment; the products are incompatible.

How to use: Use against most vegetable garden pests, such as flea, potato, and bean beetles, including the hard-to-kill pests, such as beetles, squash bugs, and tarnished plant bugs. For best results, apply in the late afternoon or evening. Pyrethrins degrade within one day.

Rotenone

Rotenone is often recommended for organic gardeners because of its botanical origin (derived from the roots of tropical legumes).

Advantages: It is approved for use in organic gardens and breaks down quickly in sunlight.

Disadvantages: Rotenone is toxic to pests and beneficials alike. Also extremely toxic to pigs and fish, and in large quantities can affect humans.

How to use: Use this broad-spectrum insecticide as a last resort against cabbageworms, Colorado potato beetles, flea beetles, fruit worms, Japanese beetles, loopers, Mexican bean beetles, thrips, and weevils. Apply in early evening when bees are inactive, and never use near waterways. It remains toxic up to one week.

Several other types of pesticides are available at nurseries and home centres, but we regard some of them with suspicion and a few with scorn. Our advice: If a pest problem is so resistant to any of these materials and so bothersome, call a professional. Check with your local Agriculture and Agri-food Canada office first. Consider hiring a professional pest control applicator to spray.

Preventing Plant Diseases

Many plant diseases are difficult — in some cases impossible — to cure. If you suspect a certain disease is going to show up on your prized plant, such as black spot on roses, you can take steps to prevent infection. Find out when the disease is most likely to strike. Then identify the best product to use and apply it according to recommendations on the label.

Scab-free apples and crab apples

The best way to beat scab, the most common apple disease, is to plant only varieties of apples that are resistant to it. Here are the best scab-free apples and crab apples. These apples have been bred using a parent with good fruit and another with high-quality fruit. They're demonstrably hardy to Zone 5, and many to Zone 4.

Variety	Fruit colour	Edible/Ornamental
'BriteGold'	Yellow, sweet	Ornamental
'Dayton'	Deep red, hardy tree	Edible
'Dolgo'	Dark red, white flowers	Edible and ornamental
'Donald Wyman'	Red	Ornamental
'Enterprise'	Yellow with deep red, needs a long season	Edible
'Freedom'	Red	Edible
'Gold Rush'	Yellow, long season	Edible
'Jonafree'	Red	Edible
'Liberty'	Dark red	Edible
'Macfree'	Red over green	Edible
'Makamik'	Red, pink flower	Ornamental
M. sargentii	Dark red	Ornamental
'McShay'	Red over green	Edible
'Nova Easygro'	Green-yellow, washed with red	Edible
'Novamac'	Red over green	Edible
'NovaSpy'	Yellow striped with red, like a Spy	Edible
'Prima'	Yellow green	Edible
'Priscilla'	Green-yellow and striped with red	Edible
'Pristine'	Yellow with slight blush, sweet fruit	Edible
'Redfree'	Bright red over pale yellow	Edible
'Sir Prize'	Yellow with red blush	Edible
'William's Pride'	Bright red, extra-large early fruit	Edible

When you spot a disease on your plants, try to identify it with the help of reference books or personnel at a local nursery, garden centre, botanical garden, or agricultural office. Sometimes you can buy products that will eradicate or prevent further spread of the disease. At the very least, adapt the following cultural techniques to make your garden less susceptible to disease damage.

Solarization

You can cook the disease right out of your soil by a process called solarization. To do this, first cultivate the soil and get it ready for planting. Then moisten the soil to a depth of 60 centimetres (2 feet). Cover the area with a sheet of 2- to 4-mils-thick, clear, UV-stabilized plastic and secure the edges so air can't leak. The heat of the sun will raise the temperature underneath high enough to kill many disease organisms (and weeds) that are contained in the upper several inches of soil. Leave the plastic on for one or two months, then remove it and plant. Don't cultivate again before planting or you run the risk of bringing pathogens up to the surface again.

Solarization is most effective if done during the hottest part of the year. Increase the heat by using double layers of plastic or by spreading chicken manure or another hot manure on the soil before laying down the plastic.

Fourteen dirty diseases: What to do

Here are some tips on how to prevent, identify, and — if possible — treat some common plant diseases:

- **Anthracnose.** This fungus can attack many trees, including dogwoods and fruit trees, as well as tomatoes and melons. It begins by producing small, discoloured leaf spots or dead twigs, which can spread to become serious. Avoid by choosing resistant plants. Destroy fallen diseased leaves and dead branches and twigs. Hire an arbourist to spray trees that have had the disease three consecutive years. Consider removing susceptible trees and replanting with resistant varieties.

- **Apple scab.** This fungus attacks apple and crab apple trees, producing discoloured leaf spots and woody-brown fruit lesions. Avoid by planting scab-resistant varieties. (See the sidebar, "Scab-free apples and crab apples.") Rake up and destroy leaves in fall to reduce the number of overwintering spores. Prune to improve air circulation. Susceptible varieties need a preventive spray program during wet spring weather to prevent reinfection.

Spray sulfur, copper, or *Bordeaux mixture* (a mixture of copper sulfate, lime, and water), as a protective spray at the beginning of scab season (before flower buds open in spring), then two or three more times at approximately weekly intervals.

✔ **Blackspot.** This rose disease causes black spots on foliage and can spread, causing complete defoliation. Avoid problems by growing disease-resistant roses and cleaning up and destroying any diseased leaves that fall to the ground. To prevent black spot on susceptible roses, use a preventive fungicide spray during damp weather. Sprays of captan, copper, or lime-sulfur are most effective. Also try potassium bicarbonate (or baking soda — sodium bicarbonate) at the rate of 1 tablespoon each per gallon of water, weekly or after rain. Apply in morning and not during periods of hottest weather. Neem oil is also effective.

✔ **Botrytis blight.** This fungus attacks a wide variety of plants, including peonies, tulips, geraniums, and strawberries. It causes discoloured patches on foliage, browning and droopy stalks on flowers, and premature rotting of fruits. Discourage botrytis by allowing air to circulate freely around susceptible plants. Remove and destroy any infected plant parts. Spray emerging peony shoots in early spring with copper sulfate.

✔ **Brown rot.** This fungus disease is common on peaches, nectarines, and other stone fruits. Brown rot can attack flowers and fruit, ultimately coating the infected parts with brown spores. The fruit rots and shrivels. To avoid, select disease-resistant plants or at least less-susceptible types. Remove and destroy infected plant parts. You'll probably also need a preventive spray program.

✔ **Cytospora canker.** This bacterial disease attacks woody stems on susceptible plants, such as fruit trees, spruces and maples, forming cankers that can kill infected branches. To avoid, plant resistant or less-susceptible plants. If possible, remove and destroy infected branches.

✔ **Damping-off.** This fungus disease attacks the base of seedling stems, cutting the stem off from the roots. Avoid damping-off by sowing seeds in sterile seed-sowing mix and spacing the seeds so that they don't come up in a crowded mass. Cover the seeds thinly with finely shredded sphagnum moss, which has natural antibiotic action that helps prevent disease. Keep the soil moist but not soggy.

✔ **Dutch elm disease.** This fungus disease is spread by the bark beetle, which makes holes in the bark through with the fungus spore enter and travel up the tree. As it cuts off nutrients and water to the tree, the leaves yellow, and branches and limbs gradually die. Diagnose early by looking for tiny holes in the bark, and dark streaks in the wood under the bark. Immediately cut off and destroy affected parts, sterilizing tools after each cut in a solution of 1 part bleach to 4 water. Improve growing conditions with deep watering, and consult an arbourist. Serious tree surgery may help.

✔ **Mildew** (downy and powdery). These two fungi produce similar symptoms: white, powdery coating on leaves. A variety of plants are susceptible, including roses, grapes, bee balms, zinnias, and lilacs, but a different kind of mildew attacks each kind of plant. A mildew that attacks lilacs won't harm roses. The fungi disfigure plants but may not kill them outright. Instead, they weaken plants, making them unattractive and susceptible to other problems. Downy mildew attacks during cool, wet weather; powdery mildew (shown in Figure 16-6) comes later in the season during warm, humid weather and cool nights. Avoid downy mildew by planting resistant plants and by not getting the leaves wet. Use drip irrigation. Avoid powdery mildew by planting resistant plants.

✔ **Peach leaf curl.** This fungal disease overwinters on peach tree twigs and migrates to the emerging leaves in humid, wet weather when temperatures are between 50°F and 60°F (10°C and 16°C). The leaves curl, turn red, and eventually die. Typically, the disease develops early the first year, and the tree may grow through it and appear fine. But when the disease becomes established, the leaf curl returns and gets progressively worse each year. Eventually, the tree becomes debilitated. When you see the symptoms, it's too late to stop the organism that season.

You can control peach leaf curl with one or, at most, two applications. First, spray a fungicide such as lime-sulfur or Bordeaux mix in fall when the trees are dormant (leafless). For extra insurance, spray again in early spring before leaves emerge.

Figure 16-6:
Powdery mildew thrives during warm, humid days and cool nights.

✔ **Phytophthora blight**. This bacterial disease attacks a variety of plants, including rhododendrons. It causes leaves to discolour and stems to die, often killing the entire plant. Another form can cause root rot and rapid plant death. Start with healthy plants and provide them with well-drained soil. Work bark into the soil; it seems to discourage the fungus. Try not to wet the foliage in the afternoon or evening.

✔ **Rust.** This fungus disease is easy to identify: It forms a rusty coating on the foliage of susceptible plants, like roses, snapdragons, hollyhocks, blackberry, apples and junipers. (See Figure 16-7.) Avoid susceptible plants or look for disease-resistant varieties. Provide good air circulation and avoid overhead watering late in the day. Remove and destroy infected parts. Use lime-sulfur on fruit trees and woody ornamentals before buds open.

✔ **Sooty mould.** Insect pests that release sticky drops of honeydew, such as aphids, scale, whiteflies and mealybugs, encourage this harmless but unattractive fungus disease. The black-coloured mould grows on the honeydew, a sure sign that sucking insects are at work. Rinse off the mold and sap with soapy water and then control the insect pests.

✔ **Wilt** — *fusarium* and *verticillium*. These soil-borne fungus diseases cause susceptible plants such as tomatoes, peppers, melons, cabbages, and strawberries to suffer leaf yellowing, wilting, and often death. The fungus survives many years in the soil without a host. Grow wilt-resistant or wilt-tolerant varieties. Resistant tomato varieties have the letters VF as part of their name.

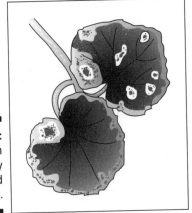

Figure 16-7:
Rust is an easily identified fungus.

Least-toxic disease remedies

Use the following fungicides to make a protective coating on susceptible plants. Most are certified by organic gardening groups and are widely available at nurseries and garden centres.

- ✔ **Sulfur.** This naturally occurring mineral is nontoxic but is a potential skin and eye irritant. You can buy sulfur in powder or liquid form. Powders can be applied with a dust applicator, or mixed with water according to label directions.

- ✔ **Lime-sulfur.** Powerful and caustic but highly effective for some problems, lime-sulfur can burn the leaves of some plants.

- ✔ **Copper**. This strong, broad-spectrum spray can be toxic to some plants, especially when overused. Use only as a last resort.

- ✔ **Bordeaux mixture.** A mix of copper and sulfur, this old-time fungicide is less toxic than pure copper but has the same limitations.

- ✔ **Remedy fungicide.** Harmless as baking soda, the key ingredient, this spray controls a range of fungal diseases on ornamental plants and fruit trees.

Controlling Weeds

The challenge of combating insects, disease and animal pests is fraught with unknowns: What works today might not work tomorrow. As soon as you let down your guard, your plants get chewed to nubs. Weeds, however, are much more predictable: They don't change their minds. You can always count on weeds to behave in a certain way, and there is one strategy that always works: pulling.

Of course, we're not talking here about fields full of wild brambles that you're trying to eliminate. We're talking about common weeds that you're likely to find in your lawn and garden. Some general techniques can make your yard less attractive to weeds.

Weed-control basics

The principle is pretty simple: Stop the weeds before they start. Okay, prevention isn't so simple in many situations. But if you take some minor steps before the weeds take hold, you can avoid the really big jobs once they do.

Outwitting animals

When trying to coexist with wild animals, the first priority is to keep your sense of humour. Beyond that, you can use a few techniques to protect some of that garden produce for you to enjoy. If you don't succeed with one method, try another:

✔ **Deer**. Deer are creatures of habit. They often travel along the same routes day after day, moving between two locations. Build a deer-excluding fence about 2.4 metres (8 feet) high (deer have been known to jump 3-metre, or 10-foot, fences). Before you invest in a fence, you may want to try surrounding your garden with a heavy fishing line attached to posts at about 1 metre (3 feet) high. This can startle deer because they don't see the fishing line, and they may retreat. This wouldn't be a method to try with young children around who could injure themselves on the line.

Deer avoid some plants, although they are notorious for changing their minds about what they want for dinner. In general, pungent or fuzzy-leafed plants are safe.

✔ **Gophers**. These are burrowing, antisocial rodents that can carve out 585 square metres (700 square yards) of elaborate underground tunnels. While they tunnel, they work up quite an appetite and any plant roots that happen to be in the way turn into lunch.

Underground barriers made of hardware cloth are effective. Install barriers at least 60 centimetres (2 feet) deep to block their borrowing.

Various traps are available to catch gophers dead or alive, and traps are the only method used by orchardists and others who are serious about limiting gopher damage. Traps work best when set inside the tunnels.

✔ **Groundhogs (woodchucks)**. The easiest way to eliminate groundhogs is a fence, one that extends 1 to 1.2 metres (3 to 4 feet) above ground and 45 centimetres (18 inches) below ground. Traps are next best. Groundhogs are one of the easier garden raiders to trap alive. Check with local and provincial ordinances about any restrictions on live trapping, and take care when releasing any wild animal so that it doesn't turn on you.

If you're at wit's end, dealing with marauding deer, gophers or woodchucks, consult your local animal control officer.

✔ **Racoons**. These cute, nocturnal, smart masked bandits will probably outsmart you whatever you try. They can open garbage cans and even remove outdoor light bulbs from their fixtures. They'll eat almost anything and relish fresh fish from your pond, as well as the plants. Animal repellants made of fox urine and the like work some of the time because they rely on the smell of the racoon's natural enemies. Try baby powder, or used pantyhose filled with hair clippings from your local barber shop placed where raccons visit. Use moving or flashing lights, or leave a radio playing in the garden at night. And good luck.

✔ **Squirrels**. These bright-eyed, bushy-tailed chattering and convivial little creatures are fun to watch but can be the bane of the garden. Try animal repellant sprays right on the flowers — like tulips — the squirrels love to behead. Cover corn ears, after the tassels have browned, with paper bags. Place chicken wire over newly planted bulb beds.

✔ **Mulch.** No matter what kind of mulch you use, it cuts down on weed growth. A thick mulch for garden pathways and between beds can be made quite easily from layers of newspapers topped with straw or hay. At season's end, till the mulch into the garden to provide organic matter.

✔ **Cultivation.** Prior to planting, cultivate (loosen the soil) to expose weed seeds to sunlight and start them growing. After a couple of weeks, you can pull the weeds or till them under and thus eliminate some major competition for your plants.

✔ **Cover crops.** Being patient when preparing a garden bed can pay off big time later on. You can dramatically reduce weeds in your newly dug garden by sowing a cover crop such as buckwheat in the spring. The buckwheat grows so densely that it outcompetes the weeds. When you till the buckwheat under, it also enriches the soil with organic matter. Then you can plant another cover crop such as annual rye in the fall, which you can till under the following spring. Your garden will then be practically weed-free and ready to plant. Alternatively, you can plant a late garden after you till under the buckwheat.

✔ **Landscape fabrics.** Place these barriers on the soil after planting trees and shrubs, and then top with mulch. Annual weeds are successfully impeded, woody perennials less so.

✔ **Hand hoeing and pulling.** Not glamorous but still one of the most effective means for most small home gardens, the key is to yank the weeds while they're young.

✔ **Solarization.** Follow the directions given in the section "Solarization" earlier in this chapter.

The most critical time to control weeds is during the first few weeks after transplanting or sowing seed. As long as you help your plants get off to a good start, they will have a fighting chance of producing a crop of food or flowers in spite of future competing weeds.

Thirteen common weeds

If you remember nothing else about controlling weeds, keep this strategy in mind at all times: Remove perennial weeds as soon as you spot them, and pull annual weeds before they flower. Treat biennials as perennials.

✔ **Bindweed.** *Convolvulus arvensis.* Spreading from underground roots, this vining perennial can snake around your garden and wrap itself around your plants. The leaves are shaped like an arrowhead and the flowers resemble morning glories, a more appreciated cousin. Beware, however, that if you allow bindweed to flower, you greatly compound your problem. The seeds have been found to be viable after 50 years. Use a digging fork to remove the plants rather than a spade, which can divide the roots into pieces that will each grow new plants.

Repeated *flaming* is an effective control strategy for bindweed. Cook your weeds to death. With a propane torch in hand, you can kill weeds in ¹⁄₁₀ of a second by boiling the water in the plant's cells until they burst. Flaming is most effective in spring and early summer against annual weeds. Perennial weeds may require several treatments. Follow all safety precautions, of course, if you use this method.

✔ **Bermuda grass.** *Cynodon dactylon.* This wiry perennial grass (see Figure 16-8) has thin blades with creases down the center. Its creeping stems travel quickly, rooting at the nodes. Any piece of stem or root left behind after you weed can establish a new plant. Bermuda grass has a secret weapon to reduce competition from nearby plants: It releases a chemical to impede their growth. Flaming provides good control.

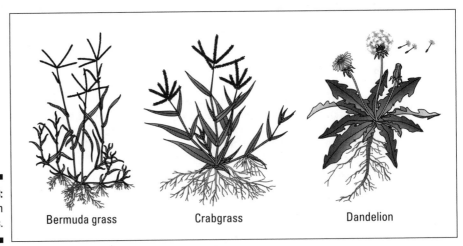

Figure 16-8:
Common
weeds.

Bermuda grass   Crabgrass   Dandelion

Chickweed. *Stellaria media.* You can easily spot this densely matting annual weed in late winter and early spring, when the stems of 13-millimetre (½-inch), oval leaves reach toward the sun. The tiny white flowers open fully on sunny days. Broken stems can root if dropped on the ground.

Crabgrass. *Digitaria.* Most common in dry, sandy soil, this annual has leaves with a bluish cast and spreading stems that root at the nodes. (Refer to Figure 16-8.) It's easy to grab hold of the clump and pull it up. Mulch effectively smothers crabgrass. Control by maintaining a vigorous lawn.

Creeping Charlie. Also called *creeping ivy, field balm,* and *gill over the ground. Glechoma (or Nepeta) hederacea.* A pretty perennial weed with almost round leaves and small deep-blue flowers. Mostly seen in eastern Canada. Likes shady, moist areas. Hoe or hand pull, removing all runners and roots. Creeping Charlie can poison horses if they eat too much.

Curly dock. *Rumex crispus.* Perennial curly dock often arrives in gardens courtesy of manure. Left alone, it grows to 1.2 metres (4 feet) tall with clusters of heart-shaped, reddish brown seed pods. The taproot can extend 60 centimetres (2 feet) underground, but if you can remove just the top 13 centimetres (5 inches), the root dies.

Dandelion. *Taraxacum officinale.* The first leaves of this perennial, which emerge in early spring, are low and oval. Later leaves are arrow-shaped with deep lopes. The unmistakable yellow flowers quickly go to seed, so cut them down early. The edible flowers are reported to be tasty when battered and fried, and the young leaves are good steamed or in salads. Long-handled weeders seem made to remove this common weed from lawns and gardens. Remove as much of the taproot as possible because the plant regrows from any portion that's left.

Lamb's-quarters. *Chenopodium album.* This upright-growing annual is distinctive for the white sparkles on the surfaces of young leaves. Leaf undersides are dusty white. Adding to the rather attractive display, the stems are often red or lighter green, and it's often used in spring salad mixes. Frequent hand-pulling and hoeing can keep the rapidly growing weed under control.

Oxalis. Also called wood sorrel and sourgrass. A perennial weed with clover-like leaves and bright yellow flowers. Control by repeated cultivations or flaming. Don't let it go to seed.

Redroot pigweed. *Amaranthus retroflexus.* The reddish stems of this annual can grow up to 3 metres (10 feet) tall, with oblong, pointy leaves. Green, upright flowers resemble a bottle brush. These plants are quite easy to pull, but they also reroot easily so uprooting them and leaving them in the garden won't help much. As for all annuals, slice them off at the surface with a sharp scuffle hoe. Or use Safer's SuperFast herbicide.

- **Purslane**. *Portulaca oleracea*. Think of the popular bedding plant called portulaca and you'll be able to identify annual purslane. The succulent leaves are prostrate and branching, forming dense mats. Pulling and cultivation help, but plants reroot readily. Or use Safer's SuperFast soap herbicide to spray.

- **Shepherd's purse**. *Capsella bursa-pastoris*. Seed pods of this annual are thought to resemble the purses carried by early shepherds. These tiny green triangles perch on thin stalks all along upright stems that emerge from the base of the plant, which resembles a dandelion. Remove seed pods before they drop seeds or you'll never get rid of them.

- **Spotted (or prostrate) spurge**. *Euphorbia maculata*. This very low growing and spreading annual weed loves hot weather and compacted soil. Eliminate by cultivating, flaming, or with a soap herbicide.

Chapter 17

Tools of the Trade

. . . .

In This Chapter

▶ Looking at the seven most essential and the five handiest hand tools

▶ Finding the right lawn mower

▶ Using string trimmers

▶ Getting to know tillers and chipper-shredders

▶ Knowing where — and how — to shop for garden tools

. . . .

*G*ardening really doesn't require a shed full of tools. In fact, we recommend starting with just a few essentials and building your collection as specific jobs call for more-specialized tools. But having the right tool for the job often makes the difference between a pleasurable experience and a frustrating chore, or between a job well done or not. That's what this chapter is all about: choosing the right tool for the job.

Hand Tools

To save money over the long haul, buy high-quality, durable tools. Generally, forged-steel tools hold up better than welded types. Relatively new on the market are tools with fibreglass handles, which are stronger than wood. Hardware stores and garden centres offer what you need to get started. Mail-order garden supply catalogues, such as Lee Valley Tools Ltd., offer more-specialized tools. (See Appendix B.)

The magnificent seven tools

Following is a list of the tools that you absolutely must have:

- **Garden hose.** Buy a top-quality hose with a lifetime guarantee. A good hose coils easily, resists kinking, and remains flexible even in cold weather. Choose one long enough to reach all corners of your garden. Or choose two, if that's what it takes.

- **Hand trowel.** A hand trowel is important for transplanting seedlings, scooping soil into containers, and doing close-up weeding jobs. Buy one that fits your hand and is light enough to be comfortable.

- **Hoe.** Forgo the conventional garden hoe designed to chop at the soil; buy a *scuffle hoe* instead. This type of hoe is easier to use — instead of chopping, you push the hoe along the soil's surface. A scuffle hoe is indispensable for weeding on packed, level surfaces such as garden paths. Although scuffle hoes vary in design, all work with a push-pull motion. Some cut and scrape the tops off weeds on both strokes. Our favorite, the *oscillating* or *action* hoe, has a hinged blade that moves back and forth as it cuts.

- **Lawn rake.** Nothing works better than a bamboo, polypropylene, or metal rake with long, flexible tines for gathering up lawn clippings, leaves, and even small rocks on both paved and natural surfaces. (See Figure 17-1.)

- **Pruners or secateurs** Once you own a pair of pruning shears or secateurs that you can hold comfortably and that produces a clean cut with little effort, you'll find it hard to imagine gardening without them. Most gardeners favor *by-pass pruners,* which cut like scissors. *Anvil pruners* that cut by pressing a blade into a soft metal anvil are less expensive. Use either type to cut soft and woody stems up to about 13 millimetres (½ inch) thick. Use this tool to clip flowers, harvest vegetables, groom shrubs, and prune trees.

- **Shovel.** A regular round-nose shovel, as shown in Figure 17-1, is the single most versatile tool you can own. You need it for digging, turning, and scooping. When used in a chopping motion, the shovel effectively breaks up clods of earth. Choose a length and weight that's comfortable.

- **Stiff-tined rake.** The first rake you should buy is a *stiff-tined* or *steel bow* rake, as shown in Figure 17-1. This rake is an important tool for spreading and leveling soil and for gathering organic materials. The rake also is a good tool for breaking up small clods of earth. Use both the *tines* (the thin, pointed prongs) and the back edge of the rake for building and smoothing raised garden beds: Keep the tines facing downward when breaking up lumps of soil or collecting stones, and keep the flat edge of the head downward when leveling.

Hand-tool maintenance

Take care of your hand tools — they'll last longer and work better. Try to clean and dry your tools each time you finish your gardening chores, but also know that primary maintenance consists of keeping

Figure 17-1:
The lawn rake is effective for gathering leaves and lawn clippings. The round-nose shovel can dig, scoop, turn and chop. A stiff-tined rake is useful for spreading and leveling soil.

- ✔ Wood handles smooth and sound
- ✔ Metal tool heads rust free
- ✔ Blades sharp

When wooden tool handles show wear, sand off the factory varnish and apply boiled linseed oil. Apply several coats, allowing the oil to soak in each time. Clean metal tool heads with a wire brush and sharpen edges with a file. Protect the metal by coating with rust-proof primer followed by a coat of rust-proof paint. Many by-pass pruners have replacement cutting blades that are easy to install. You can also sharpen pruners (the beveled side of the curved blade only) with a fine-grit diamond file.

Replace worn hand tool grips with a liquid plastic, sold in most hardware stores. The best tool lubricants are synthetic oils that lubricate, repel dust, protect against rust, and leave only a light film.

Five more tools to buy

After you invest in the seven essential tools — and if you still have space in your shed or garage — here's what to buy next. Though not as critical as the seven essential tools, these all-purpose tools are very useful to most gardeners. Which tools you need to own depends entirely upon the jobs that you're trying to accomplish. If, for example, you've just moved into a home with a garden that includes massive, overgrown shrubs, buy loppers before a trowel.

- ✔ **Garden cart.** A lightweight, well-balanced cart that manoeuvres easily makes daunting tasks a cinch. With a cart, a gardener can haul big, heavy loads of soil, compost, plants, containers, or wood with little effort.

- ✔ **Gardening gloves.** Sooner or later, you'll wish you had a good pair of gloves. Gloves should fit well and be thick enough to protect your hands, yet not so clunky that you can't handle small objects. Cloth gloves with leather reinforcement hold up well to general garden tasks. Gloves with extra-long cuffs help protect your wrists from branches and thorns.

  Glove materials and their best uses are: cotton/polyester and leather — general garden chores; synthetics — working with saws and knives; latex or PVC — working with and around water; chemical-resistant nitrile or neoprene — working with chemicals.

- ✔ **Lopping shears.** When you get serious about pruning trees and shrubs, loppers are a must. These tools cut easily through branches an inch or more in diameter. Figure 17-2 shows a pole lopper, which allows you to prune branches that are well above your head.

- ✔ **Tape measure.** A metal tape measure is essential for laying out garden beds and helpful in spacing plants. When staking out an entire landscape, a 30-metre (100-foot) length helps you measure precisely.

- ✔ **Water wand.** This hose-end attachment is great for watering containers, garden seedlings, and seedbeds. Choose one with a shut-off valve. The wand should provide a full but gentle flow that doesn't wash away soil and seeds.

Powering Up Your Tools

Which is it for you: "That cursed internal combustion contraption!" or "Praise be the internal combustion!" Does anyone really *need* power equipment? In our experience, most gardeners use at least one of these tools from time to time.

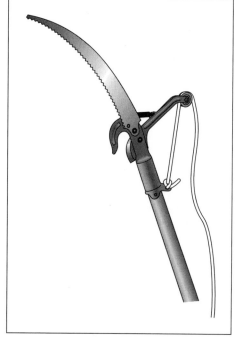

Figure 17-2:
A pole
lopper
allows you
to prune
branches
above your
head.

Lawn mowers

Lawns may not be the most politically correct corner of the garden, but most of us have one — or wish we did. (For more about lawn care, see Chapter 6.)

One of the reasons people get fed up with lawns is because lawns require regular, monotonous maintenance called *cutting the grass,* which, for some of you, may conjure up memories of noisy, dirty, hard-to-start engines. We're here to tell you that times have changed! You have so many more choices now that you're more likely to find the mower that's right for you. New lawn mowers are quieter, better working, less polluting, and safer to use.

Choose a lawn mower according to the size of your lawn, the type of grass, your tolerance (or lack thereof) of noise, and your desire for exercise. Allow about an hour to mow 232 square metres (2,500 square feet) of grass, using a 50-centimetre (20-inch-wide) rotary mower. The wider the mower or the faster it moves, the more quickly you can get the job done.

Push-reel mowers

The original teenager's nightmare, push-reel mowers have been rediscovered, reinvented, and improved. Guess what? These mowers are good for the environment and for your body, too. Push-reel mowers are quiet and completely nonpolluting, they give your body a workout that equals a session (at the least) with a treadmill. If your lawn is 93 square metres (1,000 square feet) or less and composed mostly of soft grasses such as fescue, Kentucky bluegrass, or ryegrass, this type of mower is a serious option. Basic push-reel mowers cost around $100, but fancy ones can be twice that.

Power-reel mowers

The power-reel mower is the type professional gardeners and greenskeepers use. In all cases, the engine drives both the cutting blades and the wheels, but some types throw clippings to the front, and others throw to the rear. These mowers are much more expensive than rotary mowers ($350 and up), but they are unsurpassed at providing a close, even cut, even of dense, thick southern grasses.

Push rotary power mowers

The push rotary power mower is the type most used. You provide the push power, but the engine and the spinning blade do the grass cutting. This type is relatively inexpensive ($250–$500, depending on features) and easy to operate. One decision you need to make is choosing between *side* or *rear bagging*. Side-baggers are cheaper; they are slightly less convenient (because you can cut close on one side of the mower only) but work just as well.

Don't buy a push rotary power mower that doesn't include a blade brake system, colourfully termed a *deadman switch*. This device makes the spinning blade stop within 3 seconds after the operator releases a lever on the handle. This makes the mowers more expensive, but reduces mower-caused injuries.

Self-propelled and mulching rotary mowers

Self-propelled and mulching rotary mowers are basically the same as push rotary power mowers but with added features. Naturally, the price is steeper: $500–$700, usually. The *self-propelled* feature is plain enough: Pulleys and gears link the engine to the front wheels. The mulching concept is a bit more involved: The mower is basically the same, but the cutting blade and deck are redesigned to cut and recut the grass and leaves, resulting in smaller pieces. These mowers also have no exit chute on the side or rear (or it's optional).

Mulching mowers chop grass blades small enough that the grass filters back down into the lawn. As the cut blades decompose, they release nutrients to the growing lawn, and you don't have to bag and put clippings out for recycling (presuming yor municipality is eco-aware enough to be composting biodegradable garbage).

Electric rotary mowers

Electric rotary mowers are great, especially if you live next to a hospital or absolutely refuse to deal with anything gasoline-powered. The machines are virtually silent — all you hear is the low hum of the spinning blade. And these mowers are easy to start — you turn a switch, and the blade spins. Electric rotary mowers do have a downside, though. A long cord, usually of a maximum length, restricts your movements (and how much lawn you can cut), and you have to be careful not to mow over the cord. The umbilical-free, battery-powered kinds are a bit heavy and pricey. A variety of solar-powered mowers are available now, but these are expensive and not practical in many situations.

Lawn mowers you can sit on

This category is broad. The simplest are correctly called *riding mowers,* which do nothing but cut grass. Typically, the engine is in the rear, the mowing deck out in front, and you sit somewhere in between. The mowing deck is 75 to 106 centimetres (30 to 42 inches) wide, and engines are 8 to 13 horsepower. Prices range from $800 to about $2,000.

Lawn-and-garden tractors

Lawn-and-garden tractors are somewhat larger than sit-down lawn mowers and look a bit more like real farm tractors. You sit and look out over a hood that covers the engine, and the mowing deck is right below your chair. Most have a channel steel frame and front axle, and most have 12 to 18 horsepower. These mowers cut 96 to 120 centimetres (38 to 48 inches) of grass in one swipe. Some models take attachments such as tillers and snow throwers. Some even offer cruise control! The lawn-and-garden tractor is the type for a homeowner with a large property. Cost? Expect to pay anywhere from $1,500 to $5,000.

Don't buy more horsepower than you need. Lawn-and-garden tractors with 14 horsepower are enough to cut several acres of grass and occasionally till the soil.

Garden tractors

Garden tractors are actual, scaled-down versions of farm tractors. Equally heavy-duty as their full-size brethren, their frames are heavy, 10-gauge steel, and both front and rear axles are cast iron. These machines use anywhere from 12 to 20 horsepower and cut 96 to 150 centimetres (38 to 60 inches) of grass at once. The benefit of a garden tractor over a lawn tractor is that the garden tractor can accept a variety of attachments, such as rototillers, chippers, and snowblowers. A garden tractor is a good tool for a weekend farmer who needs to do lots of chores. Expect to pay at least $3,500 and as much as $12,000.

Trimmers

The string trimmer is (after lawn mowers) the most widely used power tool. Some are electric (power cord or battery), and some are gas powered. Most of the gas-powered kinds use two-stroke engines. This type of engine requires that you mix special oil into the gasoline. A few manufacturers now offer quieter and less polluting four-stroke engines on their trimmers. Gas-powered trimmers are louder than electric versions.

Most trimmers cut soft grass and weeds with a spinning nylon cord. Some use a solid nylon disk, and some can accept other, heavy-duty cutting blades. For a basic string trimmer, look for one with an automatic or semiautomatic "feed" system for the nylon whip. Some trimmers force you to stop the engine and lengthen the string or whip by hand every time the string wears down.

Electric trimmers

Electric trimmers with power cords are the least expensive kind. These trimmers enable you to work 15 to 30 metres (50 to 100 feet) from an outlet, they're lightweight, and they're quiet. Prices start at about $50. Models powered by batteries allow you to roam more freely but limit you to about 45 minutes of continuous trimming. They cost more, about $150.

Gasoline-powered trimmers

Trimmers with gas power work roughly the same as the electric models, but they give you more power, need more maintenance, make more noise, and let you do more work in less time.

Even though the spinning whip of cord is safer than a whirling blade, it can damage the bark of young trees and shrubs (not to mention hands and feet). If you use this type of trimmer around trees, protect the lower trunk with a heavy plastic collar (available at garden centres). Or better yet, add a ring of mulch around the tree and eliminate the need for close trimming!

Tillers and chipper-shredders

Most tillers and chipper-shredders (sometimes called grinders) are hefty machines. Weight begins at about 32 kilograms (70 pounds) and goes up to a few hundred pounds. Engine horsepower begins at 3, but some have 8 or more. The cost begins at around $800 and ranges upward to $3,000. As big and heavy as they are, both are big time-savers. If you regularly garden a quarter acre or more, both may be smart investments.

A tiller consists of an engine that provides the power to a transmission that channels the power to the wheels and the tiller. Tillers with the tines in front don't have powered wheels, so the transmission has only to drive the tiller.

If you need a tiller or chipper just once or twice a year, buying your own may not make good economic sense (and where would you store it?). Renting one for a day or two is a sensible option.

All rotary tillers are categorized as either *front tine* or *rear tine*. Front-tine rotary tillers are lighter in weight and cheaper; consider them medium-duty machines. If the soil you're tilling is relatively loose, these are very effective. These tillers, however, are not as efficient if the soil is compacted or rocky. The tines pull the tiller forward; so if the tines connect with a big stone or root, the machine lurches forward. The other downside of front-tine tillers is that you must walk directly behind them, through the freshly fluffed soil.

Heavy-duty tillers have the engine in front and the tines in the rear. Expert gardeners prefer rear-tine tillers because they're much easier and less jarring to operate (even though heavier). The tines dig down into the soil rather than force the machine to lurch forward, and the operator doesn't need to walk through freshly tilled soil.

As the tines turn

Most tines rotate in the direction of travel. The resistance of the soil on the blades causes the tiller to drive itself forward. You need to restrain this driving force to ensure even tilling of the soil.

Tillers offer several kinds of tines, with many different functions. By far, the most common is the *bolo* tine, which is shaped like an *L* and is sharpened on the cutting edge. The bottom of the *L* is twisted slightly so that the soil lifts up and away as the tine turns. Some tines are further bent so that they can enter the soil more easily.

The higher the tine speed, the more easily and finely you can prepare the seedbed. A higher tine speed is also necessary to adequately chop up crop residues or compost and incorporate them into the soil. The common tine speed for front-tine tillers is 100 to175 rotations per minute. Commercial tillers often allow you to vary the tine speed for different uses. The throttle setting also affects tine speed.

Mini-tillers

Also referred to as *lightweight tiller/cultivators, hand-held tiller/cultivators,* and *power cultivators,* mini-tillers are 9- to 13-kilogram (20- to 30-pound), gasoline-powered (usually two-cycle) machines. In most designs, the horizontally mounted engine (1 to 11/2 horsepower) sits directly above the tines. Connected to this engine and tine unit are handlebars with a lever for throttle control and an on/off switch. The cost of mini-tillers varies with the number of attachments you buy, but expect to pay about $350.

Mini-tiller tines are made of sharper-edged spring steel and spin faster than the heavier tines of large tillers. The patented Mantis tines are star-shaped, so they tend to slice into the soil. The others have conventional, L-shaped tines that dig like a hoe.

On small patches of ground that are in good condition, hand tools are probably just as quick and efficient. Additionally, hand tools are not as damaging to soil structure as tillers, which tend to pulverize particles more than plants need for good root growth. Tillers of any kind may create a layer of packed and hardened soil at the bottom of their cultivating depth — the so-called *plough sole*. But on larger stretches of relatively stone-free ground, mini-tillers can be worthwhile. They dig about twice as fast as a person skillful with a fork and spade and require much less bending than working the soil with hand tools does.

An automatic clutch activates the tines, which control forward motion. A lever on either the right or left handlebar controls engine speed. At idle, the tines don't move. As you squeeze the lever, the engine speeds up, and the tines engage.

Tines work soil to a depth of 7.5 to 25 centimetres (3 to 10 inches). An average working depth after two passes through an average soil is probably about 15 centimetres (6 inches), but by working the machine back and forth, you make it dig deeper. Some gardeners use mini-tillers for digging trenches and planting holes for trees.

Here's what you should use a mini-tiller for:

- Tilling loamy, stone-free soil
- Tilling soil in small or raised beds
- Cultivating compacted, weedy soil between rows of vegetables
- Cultivating soil in narrow, tight locations
- Weeding in compacted walkways
- Mixing compost and amendments into planting beds
- Digging planting holes for trees, shrubs, and perennials

Chipper-shredders

The chipper part of the machine consists of a 7.5- to 10-centimetre (3- to 4-inch) hardened steel blade inserted into the main flywheel of the machine. You feed material — branches or corn stalks for instance — to it via a narrow tube. The shredder part is a larger opening designed to accept armloads of preferably dry leaves. The opening leads to a chamber in which a number of 5-centimetre (2-inch) long flails spin and "shred" the material. One manufacturer, Troy Bilt, currently produces a chipper that is essentially a scaled-down version of commercial chippers. Instead of a blade spinning in a flywheel, it has larger blades mounted in a drum. This version has no flails or shredding chamber.

Chipper-shredders are powered by electric motors, gasoline engines, or power-take-off (PTO) connections of garden tractors. Electric machines are suitable for chipping small prunings up to an inch or so in diameter. Gasoline-powered ones have 3- to 12-horsepower engines and a manual or automatic clutch.

Chipper-shredders are among the most dangerous tools gardeners regularly use. Wear goggles or protective glasses at all times and avoid loose-fitting clothing. Follow all the safety precautions carefully, and always turn the engine off and wait for it to stop completely before reaching in to unclog the machine, which happens more frequently than you'd probably like.

Where to Shop for Garden Tools

All plants are not created equal, nor are tools, potting mixes, and most gardening implements. So to get what you want for your garden — the best quality, a true bargain, or something really strange (like an electric bulb-planting drill) — you need to know where to shop.

By the way, you can order an electric drill and a variety of bulb and plant augers from Echo Power Equipment Canada. Check out their Web site `www.echo.ca/dealers.htm` or e-mail `info@echo.ca`.

Nurseries

In addition to plants and information, large nurseries offer seeds, bulbs, soil amendments, bark mulches, containers, fertilizers, pesticides, tools, irrigation supplies, and even garden ornaments.

Other sources for tools and garden supplies

Shop at hardware stores and home-building centres for garden tools. Also look to these places for materials to build garden structures, such as lumber, nails, and twine for trellises.

If you live in rural areas, turn to farm and feed stores. These stores are a great source for seeds, tools, soil amendments, fertilizers, pesticides, fencing, and irrigation supplies.

If you know a quality product by brand name or know how to judge the quality of a product, then you are well-positioned to find a true bargain at a discount store. But just because something is inexpensive doesn't mean it's a bargain. Heed this warning: Know what you're paying for.

Shopping by mail greatly broadens your choice of seeds, plants, tools, and supplies. However, as well as having to wait for delivery, the downside of shopping by mail is not being able to see what you're buying. That's why it's especially important to know that your sources, especially nurseries, are reliable. Appendix B lists some reliable mail-order catalogues. Also look for the Source icon throughout this book.

Part VI
Special Gardens

The 5th Wave   By Rich Tennant

"That should do it."

In this part . . .

A garden may be in a teacup or a barrel, or it may cover an acre or more. What makes a garden is the interest and intent of the gardener, not grandeur or super plantsmanship.

Inevitably, many gardeners adopt specialties. Some like to grow their own food; others cultivate only flowers. For some, a garden must be neat and orderly; for others, the more casual the better.

Here are a few of our favourite gardens: in containers and food gardens. But remember — countless other types of gardens also exist.

Chapter 18

Food Gardens

In This Chapter

▶ Making a vegetable garden

▶ Choosing your favourite vegetables

▶ Squeezing in herbs

▶ Getting started with fruits

▶ Looking at favourite fruits and berries

*I*f you have a bit of farmer in you — or even if you don't — you can get a lot of satisfaction out of growing good things to eat. Vegetables, herbs, fruits, and berries can make your yard productive as well as good looking.

Surprisingly, most edible plants (especially vegetables) are easy to grow. You don't need a lot of space, either. Gardening has no rule that says you must lay out vegetables in long rows — many of them grow better in beds. You can even mix vegetables, herbs, fruits, and flowers together and end up with a garden that pleases all your senses.

Planning a Vegetable Garden

Vegetable gardening can be downright simple if you follow a few guidelines. Planting at the right time is key, and to do that you need to know a little about both the vegetables you want to grow and your climate.

Pay especially close attention to the seasons. (Why do you think farmers are always talking about the weather?) Most vegetables are annuals. Their lives begin and end within the scope of one season. Exactly when that season begins and ends is the rub.

Seasonal preferences

Regarding season, vegetables are broadly categorized as either "warm season" or "cool season." Warm-season vegetables like warmth and they don't like cold. Their season is pretty much bracketed by frosts: the last one in spring and the first one in fall. The days or months between those two markers are the season for warmth-loving vegetables such as corn, peppers, and tomatoes. (See Figure 18-1.)

Figure 18-1: Plant warm-season vegetables after all danger of frost has passed.

Now you can guess about cool-season vegetables (see Figure 18-2) such as peas, lettuce, and radishes: They like cool weather; many also can withstand a little bit (sometimes a lot) of frost.

Figure 18-2: Cool-season vegetables stand up to colder weather, but avoid frost!

Vegetable garden calendar

Suppose you live in an area like Baie Comeau, Quebec, and your last spring frost comes about May 28. (See Chapter 2 for details on frost dates.) A few weeks before that, you kick off the planting season with seeds of three cool-season vegetables: lettuce (because there's nothing like a home-grown salad after a long winter), radishes (because they grow so fast), and peas (because they love cool weather).

Then you cruise through the garden centre and pick up some tomato and pepper plants. As soon as you get the feeling in your bones that the last frost is a done deal, and the soil is feeling a little more like summer, into the ground they go.

Now it's a beautiful weekend in mid June. You sow seeds of bush beans, sweet corn, and cucumbers. Stash a few basil plants where you see gaps, and sow some dill seeds where the lettuce didn't come up. Now you have a diversified garden going. Keep it more or less weeded and mulched, and the garden will behave while you're on vacation.

Summer's midpoint has passed, so you start some crops like spinach and more lettuce from the cool-season list and get them going. By the time frost comes in fall, you've had your fill of zucchini and tomatoes anyway, and the spinach will taste a bit better after being touched by frost.

The last piece of information you need — before actually planting — is the pattern of cool and warm temperatures where you live and how that pattern relates to vegetables. Chapter 2 gives lots of details about how this pattern works, but this section offers some examples specifically for vegetables.

For most Canadian gardeners, the timing is pretty simple: The last frost in spring usually occurs sometime between the end of March and early June. Plant cool-season crops a couple weeks before that date in your area; warm-season crops one or two weeks after. The first frost in fall occurs from early September to mid or late October, depending where you live. Warm-season crops die as soon as frost hits them, but cool-season crops live on, sometimes well into November, again depending where you live.

Choose the right location

Most vegetables need six to eight hours of direct sun daily for best results. Leafy greens, like spinach and lettuce, can thrive with a bit less. Fruit-producing vegetables like tomatoes, peppers, pumpkins, and squash need more. Be mindful of nearby trees. Deciduous trees allow much light to pass through in winter and early spring, and cast increasingly dense shade as the season progresses.

If possible, locate the garden so that access to and from the kitchen is easy and convenient — you'll be more apt to notice what needs to be tended and to take full advantage of the harvest.

In many areas, the foundations of houses are drenched with pesticides to keep termites from eating the footings. Instead of growing edible plants right next to your exterior walls where their roots can contact death-wish chemicals, use those places for inedible flowers and shrubs.

Make the garden the right size

Start small. A 6-x-9-metre (20-x-30-foot) garden may be average, but a 3-x-6-metre (10-x-20-foot) plot is sufficient for a garden sampler that will yield a variety of greens, some herbs, a few tomatoes and peppers, beans, cucumbers, and even edible flowers such as nasturtiums for garnishes.

A 6-x-9-metre (20-x-30-foot) garden gives you room to grow a wide range of crops, including some tasty space hogs like corn and winter squash. By growing plants in succession and using 90-centimetre (3-foot-wide) beds with 45-centimetre (18-inch) paths, you should have plenty of luscious vegetables for fresh eating — even extras for friends.

Designing the garden

The process of designing a vegetable garden is both practical and creative. You need to give plants enough room to grow and arrange them so that taller vegetables don't shade lower-growing types. You also need to be aware of the appropriate planting techniques that fit the growth habits of different kinds of vegetables. How you will water your garden is also a strong influence on the garden design. And you should also think about access — how will you get to your plants to harvest, weed, or water? How will you keep out deer and other creatures?

Following are three basic planting arrangements for vegetables:

- ✔ **Rows.** You can plant any vegetable in rows, but this approach works best with plants that need quite a bit of room, such as tomatoes, cabbage, corn, potatoes, melons, and squash.

- ✔ **Beds.** Beds are wide, flat-topped rows of soil, usually at least 60 centimetres (2 feet) wide and at least 15 centimetres (6 inches) high. You can install permanent borders of wood or other material, which makes maintaining edges easy. You can also concentrate all your amendments and fertilizers in the bed more easily and without waste. Beds are ideal for smaller vegetables that don't mind living in close quarters — such as let-tuce, carrots, radishes, and turnips — but any vegetable can thrive. Plant the vegetables in a random pattern in the bed or in closely spaced rows. If you're feeling especially ambitious, you might even arrange your beds in a four-square pattern, like an old-fashioned potager, and plant in decorative patterns.

✔ **Containers**. Of course you can grow vegetables in containers. In fact, containers are ideal for apartment dwellers who may have only a patio or balcony to use for outdoor living. You can find more about container gardening in Chapter 19.

✔ **Hills.** Hills are best for vining crops like cucumbers, melons, and squash. You create a 30 centimetre (1-foot) wide, flat-topped mound for heavy soil, or just a circle at ground level for sandy soil, surrounded by a moat-like ring for watering. Plant two or three evenly spaced plants on each hill. Space the hills at the recommended distance for between rows.

Proper plant spacing is a compromise of sometimes competing needs. Gardeners want to squeeze as many plants into the available space to maxi-mize harvest or appearance. Plants need enough physical room (in soil for roots, too) to grow and spread. Also, leave enough space between plants for you to get in to inspect, water, and harvest. Check the catalogue or seed packet for mature plant size and planting distance recommendations.

Sketching out your plan on paper can help you purchase the right amount of seeds or transplants and use space more efficiently.

Drawing out the design is a good way to see the possibilities for *succession planting* (following one crop with another) and *interplanting* (planting a crop that matures quickly next to a slower-maturing one and harvesting the two before they compete for space). For example, you may see that you can follow your late peas with a crop of broccoli, and you'll be ready with transplants in July. Or you may see that the garden still has space for you to tuck in a few let-tuce plants among your tomatoes while the vines are still small.

Improving the soil

The ideal garden location has loose soil that drains well. If you haven't had your soil tested to determine the pH, do so now. Most vegetables require a pH between 6.0 and 6.8. (See Chapter 11 for more on soil testing and adjust-ing the pH.)

In most gardens, soil that's going to be used to grow vegetables can stand some improvement. Apply several inches of compost or natural fertilizers like decomposed chicken manure over the surface and work it with a rake.

If your soil is hopeless or if you like convenience, consider growing vegetables in *raised beds* — actually just any planting area that rises above the surrounding ground level. The bed simply can be a normal bed with the soil piled 13 or 15 centimetres (5 or 6 inches) high, or it can be a large containerlike structure with wood, stone, or masonry sides. Wooden raised beds should be made of rot-resistant redwood or cedar or recycled plastic timbers. If you put in several raised beds, leave at least 90 to 120 centimetres (3 to 4 feet) for access paths between them.

Don't use pressure-treated lumber or railway ties treated with creosote as borders for raised beds in the vegetable garden. There are questions about their safe use with food crops.

What to start with

Many vegetables are best started from seeds sown directly in the ground (*direct-sown*); others go in as young plants called *seedlings.* You can grow your own seedlings or buy them. (See Chapter 13 for specifics on raising your own seedlings and transplanting.)

Two of your best sources of information about seeds and seedlings are free: seed packets and seed catalogues. To acquire several seed catalogues free, subscribe to a garden magazine; you will begin receiving a selection of catalogues almost immediately. *Canadian Gardening* magazine publishes a list of more than 200 catalogues in its December/January issue every year.

Other sources you can use, which may be a little bit faster than snail mail, are the computer and phone. *Canadian Gardening's* catalogue list also contains fax and e-mail addresses, as well as toll-free phone numbers where they apply. Or see Appendixes A and B.

It's all in the timing

The key date in vegetable planting timing is the average date of the last spring *frost* (when all danger of frost has likely passed). Though frost may not always kill your young plants, it's damaging to most vegetables. If you don't know the date for your region and it's not listed in the chart in Chapter 2, check with your local Agriculture office or a large nursery.

Table 18-1 lists "tough" crops that you can plant two to four weeks before the last frost date.

Table 18-1	Frost-Resistant Crops
Direct-sow	*Transplant*
Beets	Broccoli *
Carrots	Brussels sprouts * ***
Dill	Cabbage * ***
Onions *	Parsley *
Peas *	
Radishes *	
Salad greens *	
Spinach *	

* You can sow these crops in midsummer for a second autumn harvest.
***These plants benefit from a touch of fall frost.

Table 18-2 shows examples of "tender" crops to go into the garden after danger of frost is past and the soil has warmed up.

Table 18-2	Frost-Tender Crops
Direct-sow	*Transplant*
Beans	Basil
Cucumbers	Eggplant
Squash	Peppers
Corn	Tomatoes
	Melons

Successfully planting seeds in the ground hinges on two factors: depth and moisture. The general rule: Plant the seeds twice as deep as they are wide. So you plant really big seeds like beans and squash 2.5 to 5 centimetres (1 to 2 inches) deep, medium-sized seeds like corn 2.5 centimetres (1 inch) deep, small seeds like beets and spinach 13 millimetres (½ inch) deep, and itty-bitty lettuce, carrot, and turnip seeds no more than 6 millimetres (¼ inch) below the surface. You can also buy strips of paper with small seeds glued on at exactly the right spacing. You plant these strips, called *seed tapes,* and eliminate thinning. Most seed catalogues offer seed tapes.

Keep the seeds moist. Water helps soften the seed's coat or shell so that the sprout can break through more easily. Either set up a sprinkler to help keep newly seeded beds moist or cover the bed with an old sheet in between daily watering. As long as the soil isn't clammy (cold and wet), the seeds should sprout within a week.

Whether you set out plants or sow seeds, weeds will appear all over your garden about three weeks after you plant. This is a natural occurrence, but you do have to stifle those wild invaders. Get a comfortable pad to sit on and hand-weed right around your plants. Then use a hoe to clear weeds from large areas of bare soil.

After you finish weeding, mulch over the weeded space to keep more weeds from taking the places of the ones you killed. You can use rolls of fabric mulch or plastic, chopped leaves, grass clippings, hay, newspapers covered with enough leaves or grass clippings to keep them from blowing away, and even old carpeting. (See Chapter 11 for more on mulching.)

Have a happy harvest

If you plant what you like to eat, you'll have to hold yourself back to keep from picking your vegetables too early. Fortunately, most veggies are best when picked on the young side, especially leafy greens, snap beans, peas, cucumbers, and squash. With some other vegetables, especially root vegetables, the old-timers taste better. Wait for carrots to reach full size — that's when they're full of flavour; and tomatoes and peppers are best when allowed to hang on the plants until they're very ripe.

When in question, take a bite! If you don't like what you taste, spit it out, wait a few days, and try again. You'll probably be enthralled with the superior taste of really fresh, ripe vegetables from your own garden.

You Can't Go Wrong with These

Following is a top 10 list of easy-to-grow vegetables, along with a few tips on planting them and recommended varieties. For much more detail about vegetable gardening and especially good home garden varieties, see _Vegetable Gardening For Dummies_ by Charlie Nardozzi and the Editors of The National Gardening Association (IDG Books Worldwide, Inc.).

✔ **Carrot.** Plant seeds several times throughout the growing season, early spring into fall, for a continuous harvest. Soil should be loose and deep. to allow carrots to develop. Varieties: 'Nantes', 'Chantenay', 'Ingot', 'A-Plus', 'Short-and-Sweet'.

✔ **Cucumber.** Wait until warm weather to plant seeds, or start indoors. Keep well watered. Varieties: 'Sweet Slice', 'Marketmore 80'.

✔ **Green beans.** Plant seeds after frost danger. To inhibit fungal disease, plant far enough apart to allow air circulation. Bush types are easier to manage, but pole types are more productive in an equal space (because they're taller!). Varieties: 'Green Crop', 'Derby', 'Blue Lake'.

✔ **Lettuce.** Plant seeds as soon as soil can be worked — hot weather ruins the plants. Varieties: 'Black Seeded Simpson', 'Buttercrunch', 'Lollo Rossa', 'Oakleaf', 'Canasta'.

✔ **Onion.** Timing the planting of seeds or the miniature onion bulbs called *sets* can be tricky. Also consider mail-order onion seedlings. Check locally for availability.

✔ **Peas.** Sow seeds of shelling, snap or snow peas early in spring as soon as you can work the soil. Varieties: 'Alderman', 'Sugar Snap', 'Green Arrow', 'Super Sugar Mel'.

✔ **Radish.** Sow seeds during the short, cool days of spring and fall. During these times, radishes are perhaps the easiest and fastest vegetable to grow. Varieties: 'Cherry Belle', 'White Icicle', 'French Breakfast'. You might also try Oriental radishes (the round lo bok is sweeter than super-long daikon); 'China rose' or Black Spanish' mature in less than 2 months from a midsummer planting.

✔ **Summer squash.** Sow seeds after weather warms up. Deliciously tender when harvested soon after pollination, while still small. Grow bush types. to save space. Varieties: 'Sunburst', 'Yellow Crookneck', 'Scallopini'.

✔ **Sweet pepper.** Plant seedlings in warm weather along with tomatoes, or grow them in a protected glass frame as described in Chapter 2. Varieties: 'Stokes Early Hybrid', 'Gypsy'.

✔ **Tomato.** Set out seedlings after the air and soil have warmed up. Tomatoes come in countless varieties; among the best: 'Early Girl', 'Big Boy', 'Brandywine', and the tiny varieties 'Yellow Pear', 'Red Pear' and 'Sweet Million'.

Tomatoes are one of those rare plants that actually benefit if seedlings are planted deeper than they grew in the nursery pot. Plants will be more anchored and sturdier, and roots will develop along the buried portion of the stem. Pinch off lower leaves, and plant as shown in Figure 18-3.

Figure 18-3:
Planting tomatoes deeply provides stability and forces roots to develop along the buried stem.

What about Hybrids and Heirlooms?

As you look through seed catalogues or read seed packets, you may notice the words *hybrid* and *heirloom*. *Hybrid vegetables* are the result of a cross (where pollen from one flower fertilizes another, resulting in seed) of selected groups of plants of the same kind. Hybrid plants may show what's called *hybrid vigour* — a significant increase in qualities such as early and uniform maturity and increased disease resistance. The increased vigour and predictably good performance make hybrids worth the extra cost to many gardeners.

If you choose hybrid seeds, you need to buy a new batch every season rather than save your own. When hybrid plants cross with themselves and form seeds, the seeds lose the specific combination of genetic information that gave the hybrid its predictable qualities. If you plant seed saved from hybrids, you end up with a very mixed bag of plants.

At the other end from hybrid varieties are *open-pollinated varieties*. These plants are basically inbred lines that are allowed to pollinate each other in open fields. The resulting seeds are pretty predictable, but you won't have the consistency of hybrids.

Heirloom vegetables, like the varieties your grandparents grew, have been open-pollinated for years. Heirlooms are enjoying quite a revival because of the variety of fruit colours, tastes and forms, and because many gardeners consider it important to maintain a strong and varied gene pool among all plants. Many heirlooms are selected for and perform best in specific regions. If you live where these varieties were grown and selected over many years, the plants should thrive. Remember that many growers don't start heirloom varieties to sell as transplants; often you have to buy the seed for these varieties and start them yourself. Try all kinds of vegetables, especially ones that sound promising to you. Then see what works best, what you like most, and plant more of them.

Squeezing in Herbs

You can always use fresh herbs in the kitchen, so try to squeeze a few into a vegetable garden — or into pots or even a flower garden.

Many herbs are annuals (like basil) that require full sun and a long warm season. Some, like chives and parsley, are biennials; and several, such as oregano and thyme, are perennials. Most all herbs grow best in soil that is not too rich and drains water quickly.

The following are among the easiest and most useful herbs to grow:

✔ **Basil.** This annual is easy to start from seed or transplants. Sow seeds indoors six to eight weeks before the last frost; plant outdoors, in full sun after all danger of frost has passed. Plants grow 30 to 46 centimetres (12 to 18 inches) high. Pinch out centre leaves of seedlings to encourage branching. Pick off flowers as soon as they start to form to prolong leafing. Six plants are plenty for most gardeners.

✔ **Chives.** Start plants from seeds or clumps. Plant in early spring as soon as the soil is workable, in full sun or partial shade. Plants grow about 30 centimetres (12 inches) high and produce round, pinkish flowers in early summer. Use scissors to snip leaf tips as needed. Divide slowly expanding clumps every three years or so.

✔ **Garlic.** Start with bulbs from the market, nursery, or mail-order supplier (the latter can provide a more extensive variety selection). Plant in fall. Separate bulbs into individual cloves; leaving the papery membrane in place. Set cloves pointed end up, 5 centimetres (2 inches) deep and 7.5 centimetres (3 inches) apart. Harvest all types in midsummer before plants go to seed.

✔ **Mints.** These tremendously varied plants all have leaves that are rich with aromatic oils, and all share a love of moist soil. Peppermint *(Mentha piperita)* is a favourite. You can snip the tip of a branch, pour hot water over it, and have instant peppermint tea. Plants grow about 30 centimetres (12 inches) high.

✔ **Oregano and marjoram.** We place these two plants together here because they are so closely related and so often confused. Oregano *(Origanum vulgare)* is a 90 centimetre (3-foot) tall hardy perennial, and marjoram *(O. majorana)* is a 60 centimetre (2-foot) tall tender annual. Both are strongly aromatic and flavourful, but marjoram is a little sweeter and milder. Grow the true Greek oregano, *O. vulgare hirtum,* for best flavour. The best way to start either plant in your garden is to buy plants from your nursery or by mail.

✔ **Parsley.** This herb is so familiar as a restaurant garnish it's possible to overlook how attractive and useful it is in the garden. The rich green leaves are a perfect foil for colourful annuals. Snip or pinch a few leaves whenever you need it for a recipe. Grow the flat-leaf Italian kind or curly parsley and start from seeds or plants. We recommend plants because gardeners often have trouble starting the seeds.

✔ **Rosemary.** Gardeners anywhere can grow this resinous, aromatic shrub as an annual or in large pots brought indoors for winter. But if you live on the west coast or the most southern parts of Ontario, you may be able to grow it as a landscape plant. Many named varieties are available, and all have flavourful leaves and stems. They differ primarily in growth habit: Some trail and some are upright. All have blue flowers and need full sun and well-drained soil. Buy rosemary plants at your local nursery or from mail-order suppliers.

✔ **Sage.** This plant is a hardy perennial *(Salvia officinalis)* that gardeners anywhere can have in their gardens for years. They are ornamental: Several kinds have variously coloured leaves, but all have the same distinctive flavor that cooks desire. Sage grows 60 to 75 centimetres (24 to 30 inches) high and produces violet flowers in early summer. Plant in full sun and well-drained soil. Start with plants from your local or mail-order nursery.

✔ **Thyme.** These hardy perennials are mostly low growing (a few very low growing). Some are ornamental only, with faint flavour. Most, however, have leaves and stems that are rich with fragrant oils. Common thyme *(Thymus vulgaris)* grows 15 to 20 centimetres (6 to 8 inches) high and is the form that cooks prefer. But lemon thyme *(T. citriodorus),* with its citrus scent, runs a close second. Mother-of-thyme *(T. praecox arcticus)* grows only about 5 centimetres (2 inches) high and is excellent growing between stepping-stones where an occasional step releases the wonderful scent.

Is There Fruit in Your Future?

If you have just ¼ acre (30 x 30 metres, or 100 x 100 feet) in your backyard or side yard, you can grow the full range of temperate tree fruits (apples, pears, cherries, peaches, and plums), plus berries and brambles. Of course your climate will impose a few restrictions. Some varieties of apples aren't hardy colder than zones 4 or 5, but there are plenty of delicious varieties that have been bred for cold conditions, such as 'Norland' and 'Goodland', both dwarfs, and the regular-size 'Parkland'. And even though southern Ontario and the Okanagan Valley are the preserve of peaches and apricots, you can grow varieties like 'Sub-Zero' apricot and' Reliance' peach in your backyard in Winnipeg or Moosomin, Saskatchewan. Actually, we're lucky in Canada: many tree fruits need a minimum period of cold weather to bear fruit. You can't grow apples, for instance, in the southern parts of the U.S. But in case you didn't know, we can grow kiwi and passion fruit here: the hardy kiwi, *Actinidia arguta* 'Issai', bears smooth, sweet green fruits a year after planting in Zone 2; the decorative passion fruit, which has lime, lavender and white flowers, bears yellow fruits ideal for juices to Zone 4.

But think in terms of a fruit garden rather than an orchard. A handful of trees will give you more than enough fruit. One full-grown peach tree, for example, produces three or more bushels. Apples are available as true dwarf varieties, so you can plant several varieties without outpacing your ability to use the fruit. With careful pruning, you can keep the trees as small as 1.8 metres (6 feet) tall. Spaced 60 centimetres (2 feet) apart, each tree can yield between 4.5 and 6.8 kilograms (10 and 15 pounds) of fruit.

Also check with your local Master Gardeners — and perhaps become one yourself. You can learn about the program — which isn't in every province, by the way — through your local agricultural office or horticultural society. For more information about Master Gardeners, see Appendix A, or check Canadian Gardening's Web site horticultural hotlines at www.canadiangardening.com.

Six steps to a fruit tree harvest

You don't need to don a tin-pot hat, à la Johnny Appleseed, to grow fruit trees. Just take a look at the following general tips:

- ✔ **Be patient.** Most fruit trees require at least five to eight years from planting to the first harvest. But if you're in a hurry, plant dwarf trees. They bear fruit much quicker.

- ✔ **Plant varieties adapted to your climate.** Most gardening comes down to matching the plant with your climate and fruit gardening is no different. If you live where winters are –4°C (25°F) or colder, guess what? You can't grow mangoes. Likewise, if you live where winters never drop below 4°C (40°F) — we should be so lucky!— you can't grow apples.

- ✔ **Provide pollinizers.** Many fruit trees need the pollen from a different but compatible variety — called *cross-pollination* — to produce a crop of fruit. Apples, pears, sweet cherries, and Japanese plums are in this category. Exceptions include most peaches, figs, and sour cherries. Apples need cross-pollination, but ornamental crab apples can serve too, so you can get by with only one apple tree if you live where apples (and crab apples) are abundant.

✔ **Plant in the right place.** A good site means full sun and fertile, well-drained soil. If you live in an area with strong winds, plant trees in protected locations. If spring frosts threaten developing buds and flowers, plant on a gentle slope so that cold air travels downhill and away from the trees.

✔ **Keep trees well watered and fertilized.** Water trees deeply every two weeks. The soil should be moist down to at least 60 centimetres (2 feet) for dwarf trees and 90 to 120 centimetres (3 to 4 feet) for full-sized trees. Use mulch, such as compost or straw, to help maintain even soil moisture. Apply an organic fertilizer, like compost or aged manure, or a complete commercial fertilizer, like 10-4-4, if growth is poor. But be aware that too much fertilizer can cause bland, soft fruit that is susceptible to brown rot.

✔ **Prune and thin.** The primary objectives of pruning fruit trees are to create a strong tree form and maximize the harvest. Check with local experts or your agriculture office for specifics on pruning various types of fruit trees.

Thin the number of fruits that the tree sets after flowering to get larger, higher-quality fruit and to encourage steady, year-to-year production. The best time to thin most fruit trees is when fruits reach 13 millimetres to 2.5 centimetres (½ to1 inch) in diameter. In most cases, thin to allow 15 to 20 centimetres (6 to 8 inches) between fruits. For apples and Japanese plums, thin to one fruit per cluster.

SOURCE

Get help

Provincial governments are gold mines of helpful information for farmers and home gardeners. Some provinces offer free factsheets — you just have to pick them up at your local agricultural office. Other provinces charge a fee, and still others offer both kinds. Ontario, for instance, stocks dozens of free fact sheets but also charges $10 for a booklet called Gardener's Handbook, about insects and diseases found in Ontario.

Unfortunately, because of the ever-present government cutbacks, many printed fact sheets are being phased out. However, for anyone with access to the Internet there's great news — every province has its own Web site featuring online fact sheets chock-full of growing information. Some offer more information than others, but one of the benefits of the Net is that you can browse through the sites of any province, choosing the facts pertinent to your situation. For more about where to click your mouse, see Appendix A.

Planning a fruit garden

Your fruit garden needs lots of sun, at least six hours at midday in summer. Orient the rows north to south, if you can. That way, shade in the morning and evening falls on adjacent walkways rather than on adjacent trees. Plan to maintain walkways that are at least 1.2 metres (4 feet) wide between rows of trees. As for aesthetics, put lush, free-growing plants like peaches and apricots up front. Plan for as long a harvest season as you can by planting different kinds of fruit. And if you want fruit plantings nearer the house and among the vegetables, stick to berries. They rarely need spraying and give you the earliest fruit.

Fruits for the home garden

The following sections describe some good choices for your mini fruit orchard.

Apples

Apples are easiest to grow and harvest when you buy dwarf varieties, which grow 1.8 to 2.4 metres (6 to 8 feet). (See Figure 18-4.) Plant several varieties to provide a range of flavours and ripening times. Because apples need spraying more than other fruits, isolate them from vegetable gardens, patios, and pools. The average yield of an apple tree is 35 to105 litres (1 to 3 bushels) and they fruit from late summer through autumn. Some apples are hardy to Zone 3, 'Rescue' to Zone 2.

Scab is the most common disease problem of apples, especially in regions that get plenty of rainfall in summer. See the chart in Chapter 16 for a list of scab-free and scab-resistant varieties.

Peaches

Peaches can be tricky but are worth the effort. Peach trees get big, so put them where you'll enjoy their profile and glossy green foliage. Mulch to thwart grass and nourish trees. Choose hardy varieties like the freestone 'Reliance' (Zone 5, worth a try in 4) in colder parts of Canada. Apricots are also a good crop, and there are several cold-climate varieties to choose from, such as the above-mentioned 'Sub-zero'. The yield is 105 to 175 litres (3 to 5 bushels) of peaches per tree (mid- to late summer).

Pears

Pears are a bit easier to grow than apples. On dwarfing rootstock, pears reach 2.4 to 3 metres (8 to 10 feet) tall. Train them as small pyramidal trees (pyramidal varieties are available). You need two or more compatible varieties for pollination. The yield is 105 to 140 litres (3 to 4 bushels) per tree (late summer through autumn). Full-size pears produce reliably through zone 4; dwarf pear trees are hardy through Zone 6, some to Zone 5 with protection.

Cherries

Sweet cherries become medium to large trees. Tart cherries on a dwarf root-stock are scarcely larger than a bush, and because they're self-fertile, one is enough. The yield for sweet cherries is 31 litres (30 quarts), and for tart, 15.2 litres (15 quarts) (early summer). Cherries produce reliably through Zone 5; tart or sour cherries through Zone 5, 'NorthStar' to Zone 4.

Plums

Plums make nice small- to medium-size trees for a yard. Japanese and Japanese-American hybrids need cross-pollination by another variety from either group. Most European plums need another European pollinator; a few are self-fertile. The yield is 70 to 105 litres (2 to 3 bushels) (mid- to late summer). Plums regularly produce through Zone 5. 'Pembina' and 'Manchurian' are both hardy to Zone 3, 'Patterson's Pride' to Zone 2.

Figure 18-4:
Comparing the size of full-size and dwarf apple trees.

Strawberries

Strawberries are the first fruits of the season, which may be why people treasure them so. An early and a late variety provide strawberries for two to three weeks. Grow them in 90- to 120- centimetre (3- to 4-foot) wide beds and be ready to lay netting over the plants to keep out the birds. You need to renovate strawberry beds every two or three years. The yield is 1 litre (1 quart) per plant (late spring to early summer). Strawberries are hardy to all zones.

Grapes

Grapes on a trellis are good for masking a fence or for making a windbreak for vegetables or other tender plants. Traditionally, gardeners train the vines over arbours or trellises, but putting the vines so far overhead makes pruning and picking tough to do. The most-productive types of grapes yield up to 7 kilograms (15 pounds) per plant (late summer to early autumn). Grapes are productive through Zone 4, 'Riverbank' to Zone 3.

Blueberries

Blueberries are a good candidate for a hedge because they grow in bushes. You need two varieties for cross-pollination — three or more are better and can extend the blueberry harvest to two months. Some blueberries can grow nearly anywhere in North America if you can provide acid soil rich in organic matter. The yield is 4 litres (4 quarts) per plant (mid- to late summer). Blueberries are productive through Zone 4. Low-bush blueberries to Zone 2 — they grow wild in many areas, including Labrador.

Bramble fruits

Bramble fruits — red and black raspberries and blackberries — are best grown as rambling hedges on large properties or trained to a wall or trellis on small properties. Raspberries are generally hardy to Zone 2, blackberries to Zone 3. 'Double Delight' and 'Red River' are low-maintenance raspberries that can be mowed to the ground in spring to clean up old canes. The thornless blackberry has glossy fruit and needs three or four years of growth before fruiting. 'Himalayan Giant', developed in Holland, produces fruit 3 centimetres (1¼ inches) in diameter. The bramble harvest can stretch from early summer into autumn. To get the most from red raspberries, plant at least two kinds: A main-crop variety for heavy, early summer harvests and an autumn (or everbearing) type to close out the berry harvest. Bramble fruits are productive throughout all zones. The yield is 2 litres (2 quarts) per plant.

Gooseberries

Red or yellow gooseberries make terrific pies and jam. Easy to grow. Plant 60 to 120 centimetres (2 to 4 feet) apart in spring before plants leaf out, or in fall after the leaves drop. If white pines are near, plant varieties like 'Consort' and 'Ben Sarek', which are resistant to white pineblister rust. Some giant self-fertile varieties, such as the yellow 'Invicta' and the red 'Hinnonmaki', produce huge fruit the size of a quarter. Zone 2b.

Elderberries

They grow wild in many parts of Canada, and although they're not especially tasty eaten fresh, they make wonderful pies, jams and jellies. And didn't Aunt Kate used to make elderberry wine? The fast-growing shrubs produce dense clusters of purple-black fruit in July and August. Birds like the fruit, too, so you may have to protect it. Zone 3.

Saskatoons

What self-respecting Canadian can refuse to plant Saskatoons in the fruit garden? The shrubs are dead simple to grow, they're hardy almost everywhere, and their spring blooms and colourful fall foliage make them decorative, too. Feed the birds or make pies and jam. 'Honeywood' and 'Martin' are good varieties. Zone 2.

Chapter 19

Container Gardens

In This Chapter
▶ Choosing pots to plant in
▶ Designing with container plants
▶ Matching up pots and plants
▶ Offering just the right soil mix
▶ Providing special care

Some people grow plants in containers (or pots or planters) because that's the only suitable place they can find — maybe they have infertile garden soil or their space is too limited. Others who have abundant garden space are just as motivated to grow plants in pots — container plants can add height, charm, and surprise to a garden.

Whatever your reason, you can't find a better way to observe plants up close and get to know them. Growing plants in pots can bring out different sides of your personality: The artist (Should I put the yellow pansy with the red tulips?) and the scientist (How do I lower the pH of this soil mix?).

Welcome to the fun and challenge of container plants. If you enjoy what you see in this chapter or want to learn more about planting in pots, take a look at *Container Gardening for Dummies,* by Bill Marken and the Editors of The National Gardening Association (IDG Books Worldwide, Inc.).

Choosing the Right Pots

Containers come in a huge variety of materials — especially if you start making your own or finding them. As you look, be sure you consider at least two key factors: porosity and drainage.

- **Porosity.** Some materials used to create containers are more porous than others and allow moisture and air to penetrate more readily. For example, unglazed terra cotta, wood, and paper pulp dry out faster than nonporous material, but also allow soil to cool by evaporation and to *breathe* (roots need oxygen). Porosity has the effect of drawing away excess water, thereby preventing waterlogged soil. Nonporous materials such as glazed terra cotta, plastic, and cans hold soil moisture better, which helps to reduce watering frequency. That characteristic, however, may make the plants vulnerable to waterlogged soil.

- **Drainage.** For healthy root development, soil must drain water properly and have enough space for air. Soil that's too heavy or dense can slow drainage — so can lack of a drain hole or a blocked drain hole. If drainage is slow or nonexistent, water may collect at the bottom (where it can stagnate and smell bad); roots can rot, and the plant can die. Look for drain holes when selecting containers. If you have a container you love but it has no drainage hole, you can *double-pot* (place a container within a larger container) so that the inner pot can drain into the larger one; or you can drill drain holes in the pot you love using a carbide-tipped drill.

The following list contains the materials used most often for making containers these days. Each has its strengths and weaknesses.

- **Terra cotta (or unglazed clay).** Unglazed clay, or terra cotta (which means *baked earth* in Italian), is usually reddish orange but comes in other colours as well — tan, cream, black, and chocolate brown. These pots come in many shapes and sizes, as shown in Figure 19-1. Higher-quality pots — those with thick walls and fired in high heat — last longer. Pots fired at low heat have a more grainy texture and weather away more quickly.

  Unglazed clay pots generally offer good value for the money. Their earthy colours and natural surface make the pots look comfortable in almost any garden situation, from rustic to formal. The porosity in unglazed clay enables plant roots to breathe and excess moisture to evaporate — all desirable for many plants. Porosity also means soil dries out quickly so plants in such pots are likely to need more frequent watering.

  A downside of terra cotta: It can crack when moist soil freezes and expands inside the pot. Empty the container and store it in a garage or basement until spring.

- **Glazed clay.** Usually inexpensive, these pots come in many more colours than unglazed ones — bright to dark, and some with patterns. Many are made in Asia and fit nicely in Japanese-style gardens. Glazed clay containers are great in formal situations and can liven up a grouping of plain clay pots. Although glazed pots are less porous than unglazed and hold moisture better, they are also breakable. They also hold moisture because water doesn't evaporate through the walls of the pot.

✔ **Wood.** Square and rectangular boxes and round tubs come in many styles and usually made of rot-resistant redwood and cedar. Wood containers are heavy, durable, and stand up well to cold weather. Appearance is usually rustic, at home on decks and other informal situations. Wood provides good soil insulation, keeping roots cooler than terra cotta. Evaporation is also slower than with clay pots. Thicker lumber is better — at least 23 millimetres (⅞ inch). Bottoms may rot if they stay too moist; raise containers at least an inch off the ground with stands or saucers.

To make wood last longer, treat the insides with wood preservative such as a copper-based product. Or build your planter with wood that has been pressure-injected with CCA or ACQ preservatives (the latter is less toxic because it contains no chromium or arsenic, and is often used to make play structures for children, but is harder to find). Avoid pressure-treated wood of any kind for containers that will hold food crops. For more details about landscaping lumber, check out *Decks & Patios For Dummies,* by Robert Beckstrom and the Editors of the National Gardening Association (IDG Books Worldwide, Inc.).

✔ **Plastic.** Many plastic pots imitate the look of standard terra cotta pots. The newest — and most costly — ones on the market are nearly indistinguishable from high-quality clay pots. Plastic is less expensive, easier to clean, and weighs less than terra cotta. This material is nonporous, so

soil doesn't dry out as quickly as with terra cotta — be careful that you don't overwater. Watch for poor quality plastic pots, which can fade in the sun and become brittle.

✔ **Other materials.** *Cast concrete* is durable, heavy, and cold-resistant. *Paper pulp* is compressed recycled paper that degrades in several years. Although all growers don't recommend it, you can plant pot and all directly in the ground, and the roots will grow through the sides as the paper decomposes. Inexpensive and lightweight but not particularly handsome, paper pulp pots also are candidates for slipping into larger, more attractive containers. Use pulp pots where looks don't matter. *Metal* is a favourite choice for antique and Asian planters. Look for iron, aluminum, and other metal containers at boutiques and antique shops. Make sure that a metal pot provides drainage.

✔ **Improvised containers.** Turning mundane items — wheelbarrows, wagons, old boots, even old plumbing fixtures and engineless convertibles — into plant containers is fun. The only thing a plant container absolutely *must* have is a drainage hole in the bottom — no problem with the plumbing fixtures.

Designing with Container Plants

Does *designing* sound pretentious for determining what plants to put in which pots, how to combine different plants in the same pots, and how to combine different types of pots? Whatever designs you come up with, they should make sense in terms of maintenance. Whatever designs you create, be sure to combine plants or pots that have similar maintenance requirements. For example, you wouldn't plant a water-loving plant with a cactus, nor a shade-lover with one that needs eight hours of sun.

One plant in a container standing alone can be stunning — it had better be if that is all you have space for. However, combining several or many container plants creates a fuller, lusher effect, almost like a garden growing in the ground. Containers can do all the things that a whole garden can: Announce the seasons, flash bright colour, and create miniature slices of nature.

Style points

Talking about style and taste is never easy — there are seldom any definite answers. We give you a few reminders about style, anyway, to keep in mind when creating container plantings:

✔ **Work with what you already have.** Use container plants to complement your home or garden. In an informal setting, for example, you may want to use tubs of mixed summer annuals. Cacti in shallow bowls lend a dramatic note to a contemporary setting.

✔ **Think about colour.** Using mostly green or white creates a cooling effect. Bright, hot colours (zinnias, for instance) heat things up.

✔ **Consider the different shapes of the plants you're using** — whether they're in individual containers, mixed plantings, or multiple containers. Think about the shapes of the plants and use shape to complement and contrast them. Plant shapes fall into several categories. For example:

- **Tall, spiky plants:** Snapdragons, astilbe

- **Round, mounded shapes:** Impatiens, dusty miller

- **Trailers:** Lobelia, ivy

✔ **Think about formality.** Topiary is formal. So are symmetrical plantings — two boxwoods in classical urns flanking the front door or tree roses lining a walk, for instance. Containers with flowers all in the same colour are formal. A more casual look would be mixed-colour annuals, or groups of containers of different sizes, materials, and shapes.

✔ **Decide on something old or something new.** A sleek, contemporary atmosphere in your garden calls for uncluttered, geometric lines in the shapes of your containers and plants. A few boldly shaped containers can be effective filled with bromeliads, cacti, or echeveria, or several tall lily of the Nile.

If you prefer an always-been-there look, choose used containers that show a bit of wear and tear. One speedy way to "age" a new concrete or terra cotta pot is to paint a combination of buttermilk or yogourt and a little live moss onto the outsides. The buttermilk (or yogourt) helps promote moss growth, quickly creating a nice "old" patina. You can also paint plastic imitations of terra cotta with a thin coat of whitewash or white paint.

✔ **Remember the value of repetition.** Repeat the same colours or plants. For example, use yellow marigolds in a cluster of pots near the beginning of a front walk and again on the front porch. Of course, moderation is important. Going overboard on repetition — for instance, a long border of alternating red and white impatiens that looks like a giant candy cane — can spoil the intent.

✔ **Scale is a big subject.** Big spaces demand large containers — at least 50 to 60 centimetres (20 to 24 inches) across the top. If you cluster pots, make sure to include at least one good-sized container with a taller plant in it. It's also a good idea to vary the heights of pots by setting some on low tables or overturned empty pots.

One special plant

Hundreds of plants — annuals, cacti, fruit trees, even eggplant — can make special showings in individual pots. This approach is *elemental container gardening:* one plant in one pot, or several plants of the same type (ten pansies, for example) in one pot.

As a rule for good looks, the plant should be at least as tall as the container. This rule applies most consistently to annuals. Put 30-centimetre (12-inch) tall snapdragons in a pot that is no more than 30 centimetres (12 inches) tall. Don't put 15-centimetre (6-inch) pansies in a 30-centimetre pot — it won't look good, you have our word.

That rule of height also applies to succulents or bonsai; these low-growing, mound-shaped plants look best in low or shallow containers. Don't follow the rule with big shrubs and trees, which can be much taller in proportion to the container, or with bulbs, which are often planted in relatively shallow containers known as *bulb, azalea, or fern* pots.

Combining plants in containers

Mixed annuals, annuals with perennials, perennials with bulbs — depending on your climate, you can combine different types of plants in the same container. Keep this basic strategy in mind:

If you live where it's safe to leave containers outside all year (Zone 8), you can have a garden in pots. Start with one dominant plant (Japanese maple, snapdragons, delphiniums, whatever), and then place compatible mounding or trailing plants (lobelia, impatiens, and many others) around it.

How to arrange containers

Arranging groups of container plants is like hanging pictures or moving furniture. Don't be afraid to experiment, to move around your plant-filled containers again and again. Remember the most important thing: The results should look good to you.

The most visually effective groupings use a minimum of three plants and up to dozens. (As a rule of composition, an uneven number of items usually looks better than an even number.)

A few basic rules apply for grouping container plants:

✔ Start by using matching types of containers (for example, terra cotta) in different sizes. Make one or two pots a lot larger than the others. If you want, throw in a maverick, like a glazed pot.

✔ For a big deck or expanse of paving, use lots of pots and mix sizes, styles, and shapes.

✔ Mix plants of different textures, colours, and heights in a pot, as shown in Figure 19-2. Think about the basic categories of shapes described in "Style points" in this chapter.

✔ Group identical pots with identical plants. Nothing looks more smashing in spring than three 35-centimetre (14-inch) terra cotta pots stuffed to the gills with red tulips.

✔ Raise some containers higher than others; provide a lift with a couple of bricks underneath, use plant stands or overturned empty pots. Height adds emphasis and puts the plants at a better viewing level.

✔ Be careful when placing small plants by themselves. People can overlook or trip over them. Small containers should accompany bigger ones.

✔ Try to place containers where people gather — a seating area, for instance — and can view plants up close and appreciate their beauty and fragrance.

Figure 19-2:
Vary the height, colour, and texture in a container planting.

 ✔ In large gardens, place containers near the house where you can easily notice them often. Selectively scatter container plants along garden paths. Another good spot is in the transition zone between a patio and lawn or between lawn and wild garden.

 ✔ Hang your containers. There's no easier and quicker way to get favourite plants up to eye level. Use wood, plastic, or moss-lined wire frames. Make sure supports are strong because a plant gains weight as it grows, not to mention the weight after watering. See Figure 19-3.

Putting It All Together

As you think about the possibilities of designing with containers, consider the following suggestions for growing and displaying them effectively in your garden — making use of the principles we discuss in the section titled "Designing for Container Plants" in this chapter.

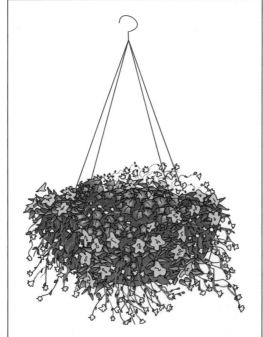

Figure 19-3:
A hanging basket can add colour and height to an empty spot.

✔ Put a single cactus in a low, 30-centimetre (12-inch) diametre bowl. Make a drainage hole if necessary. The cactus will grow slowly. Let it fill the pot. Bring it in to a sunny windowsill for winter.

✔ Circle a small tree, where roots don't allow anything to grow, with eight or so terra cotta containers overflowing with white impatiens. Plant eight impatiens seedlings in each 30-centimetre (12-inch) container.

✔ On a balcony create a privacy screen with containers of annual cucumber vine or moonflower.

✔ By your front door, where shade can make growing conditions tough, use a pair of ivy topiary balls in matching containers to greet visitors in a formal way.

✔ Announce spring with a window box full of sun-loving, early blooming pansies and species narcissus.

✔ For the holiday season, buy 4-litre (gallon-size) cans of spruce, pine, or other conifer trees available in your area, transplant them to terra cotta or glazed pots, and decorate them with tiny glass balls for tabletop decorations. Keep them indoors for a minimum time over Christmas, then transfer them to an unheated sunroom or greenhouse to harden off again before setting them outside in early spring. Be warned that some won't survive the inside-outside trauma.

✔ Lead the way up front steps by flanking steps with big pots of white marguerites — one plant per each 35-centimetre (14-inch) pot.

✔ At the edge of a sunny patio overhead, hang baskets of bougainvillea — normally a vine, but a vivid-blooming trailer when grown in a hanging basket.

✔ On a blank, shady wall, attach wire half-baskets — at least three, staggered at different heights — filled with blooming begonias and impatiens, plus ferns for greenery.

Favourite Container Combos

Wondering what to plant in containers? Because summer annuals and bulbs are downright easy to grow in pots, why not start with one or both of them? We throw in some edible ideas as well.

Perennial accents

In most of Canada — southern, coastal regions of British Columbia being the exception — perennials and bulbs can't survive through the winter in a container outdoors. If you want to try this type of gardening in cold regions, move the pots into an attached garage or basement that stays cool but protects the plants from frigid outdoor temperatures and winds. Or insulate the whole pot with leaves or straw held in place with chicken wire or burlap. You can also enjoy perennials all summer in pots and move them to the garden bed a few weeks before you expect frost, to allow them to get established in their new home.

You can also grow tender plants outdoors in containers during warm weather and then winter them indoors near a bright window. Hibiscus, oleander and lemon trees commonly grow like this in regions far colder than their native ones.

All plants brought indoors after a summer in the garden must be acclimatized first. Since they tend to bring unwanted guests in with them, they should also be debugged. First, move the plants to a shady part of the garden that's isolated from other plants. Give them a good spray with the hose to wash off adult pests and lurking larvae. Leave them for a few days and them spray the tops and undersides of leaves, as well as the stems, with horticultural oil or insecticidal soap. Start bringing plants indoors for longer periods each day, starting with a couple of hours in the evening. Within a week, spray plants with insecticidal soap again. Plants should be relatively bug free and ready to spend all day and night in the warmer, drier confines of your home within two to three weeks. A fresh outbreak of spider mites or whitefly might occur later, but a quick spray should eradicate them. Just remember to spray again after a week to get any eggs that may have hatched.

Delectable edibles

Your adventures in containers don't need to stop with flowers and evergreens. Try some tastier side trips: carrots, red- and green-leaf lettuces, dwarf or cherry tomatoes, peppers and radishes are some suggestions. Herbs — chives, marjoram, parsley, and thyme — are also good choices.

Growing just about any vegetable in a container is possible, but a giant pumpkin or something similarly huge may not be worth the effort (although it is possible!). Look for container-friendly vegetable varieties. These are the ones described as compact, or bush type.

Container gardening with vegetables makes good sense for many gardeners. With containers, you can have a vegetable garden on a balcony, patio, or a rooftop. Also, maintaining a few vegetables in some pots is much easier than a traditional garden, and you can move the containers around to follow the sun.

For more about growing vegetables in containers, see *Container Gardening For Dummies,* by Bill Marken and the Editors of The National Gardening Association (IDG Books Worldwide, Inc.).

A Container for Four Seasons

With a little thought and a strong dose of imagination, you can have a variety of looks in a container planting from spring to fall, and even into winter. One of the most effective approaches we've seen was an installation of two huge urns sitting on each side of a sidewalk leading to a formal, Georgian style home in Toronto. In early spring they were filled with plastic pots of forced purple and pink tulips; grey Spanish moss was liberally tucked in around the pots to hide the rims, and it spilled over the sides in a casual way. When those tulips faded, they were replaced with white and red ones. For the summer, the urns were filled to the point of being stuffed with grey *helichrysum* (or licorice plant), pink trailing verbena, pink diascia, purple/blue heliotrope, white marguerites and trailing white bacopa. Once fall was approaching, the gardener replaced the summer planting with pots of ornamental cabbage combined with hardy pink chrysanthemums. When the mums stopped blooming, branches of red osier dogwood took their place, and when the cabbages finally gave up the ghost in December, grasses, branches of pine and berried firethorn took over.

If you want to try this, plan ahead. Think of what you want to fill your urns or other containers as the season advances, buy the plants and grow them on in larger plastic pots while they're waiting for their turn on stage. Be sure you have trailing plants like ivies or helichrysum to soften the container's edges.

A Primer on Soil for Pots

Plants in containers are especially dependent on the soil or growing mix in which they grow because the roots have so much less soil area to explore in the confines of the pots. So to keep your plants happy and healthy, you need to first take care of the roots — and that means growing them in the right stuff.

Finding the ideal soil mix for container gardening isn't difficult. Fortunately for the rest of us, a whole lot of people have studied just what plants in containers need. You can go into just about any nursery or garden centre and find an aisle with packages marked with something like "growing mix." (To get a better understanding of what all plants need from soil, dip into Chapter 11.)

You can find a whole slew of soil mixes for containers on the market under a variety of brand names and companies. Some mixes consist of special formulas for starting seedlings, potting up transplants, or growing nursery stock. However, if you take a look at the ingredients, one of the first things you may notice is that the mixture has very little real soil, if any, listed.

Why not use ordinary garden soil to grow your prize plants in containers? After all, many of the plants that you grow in containers on your patios and decks also grow successfully in the open ground. Why can't you just take a shovelful of soil and dump it in a pot?

Although you may think that a good garden soil would make a good pot or planter, it just isn't so. When you lift the soil from the garden, it loses its structure. Also, as garden soil settles in a shallow container (which is much different from the natural depth of the soil in a field), it forms a dense mass that roots can't penetrate. The soil drains poorly, saturating the roots. As a result, not enough oxygen reaches the root zone, and the roots suffocate. Plus, garden soil harbours disease-causing organisms that can devastate container plantings; and it could have weed seeds and insect eggs, as well.

Plants in containers have different soil and water requirements than plants in the ground, and they need a special soil mix that meets those needs. The following list provides a rundown of the particular needs of container plants:

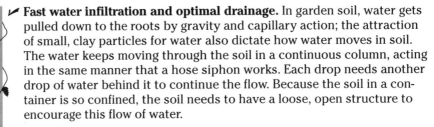

✓ **Fast water infiltration and optimal drainage.** In garden soil, water gets pulled down to the roots by gravity and capillary action; the attraction of small, clay particles for water also dictate how water moves in soil. The water keeps moving through the soil in a continuous column, acting in the same manner that a hose siphon works. Each drop needs another drop of water behind it to continue the flow. Because the soil in a container is so confined, the soil needs to have a loose, open structure to encourage this flow of water.

✓ **Plenty of air spaces in soil.** This goes hand in hand with good drainage. Air space is actually the most important requirement for a good container mix. Container plantings must have plenty of air in the soil after drainage because they require air for growth and to keep roots healthy. (Disease organisms abound in the absence of oxygen.) For more about the importance of good air circulation in soil, see Chapter 11.

✓ **Water retention.** You're probably thinking, "Hey, hold it now. You just said that container plants need plenty of air and good drainage. Doesn't that go against holding on to moisture?" This point is where mixtures get tricky. This last requirement is a trade-off, because the soil mix that holds on to the most water and drains slowest also has less room for air.

Although you may hear that you can improve drainage in pots by putting a layer of pea gravel or other potting shards in the bottom of your container to improve drainage, don't do it! A drainage layer may sound logical, but using pea gravel in the bottom of a pot actually results in *less* air for the plant's roots and *more* water in the bottom of the pot. Instead, cover the drainage hole at the bottom with one or two pieces of shard, or a bit of hardware cloth or screen as shown in Figure 19-4. Next, fill the entire container with soil mix. You can also put the smaller, soil-filled pot in a larger decorative pot that has gravel in the bottom.

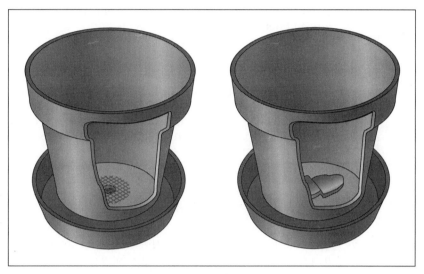

Most people who grow plants in containers use bagged potting soils or *soilless* mixtures made up of *peat moss* plus *perlite* or *vermiculite*. These products are (or should be) free of microorganisms that cause plant diseases; their pH has been corrected with the appropriate addition of lime; and they hold just the right amount of moisture. The downside is that soilless mixtures contain few plant nutrients, so you must feed your plants regularly with some kind of fertilizer.

Would you rather make your own potting soil? Sooner or later, you may delve into creating special mixtures for ferns, cacti, or some other plants that have strange tastes in soil. The following list describes your basic ingredients and the flavour that each one brings to the stew:

✔ **Peat moss.** Basically rotted moss, peat moss is soft-textured and almost never hosts diseases — and it's like a feather bed to delicate plant roots. The final content of peat in a potting mixture can run as high as 80 percent (for ferns), or 40 to 75 percent for other plants. Peat has an acidic pH and contains negligible plant nutrients. Be sure to moisten it first to make it easier to work with.

✔ **Sand.** Sand drains quickly and doesn't hold water worth a flip, which makes it a good addition to pots planted with cacti, herbs, and bulbs. The sand content of the mixture rarely, if ever, exceeds 20 percent.

✔ **Vermiculite or perlite.** These popcornlike mineral particles lighten up a mixture and help keep it porous yet damp. For potted plants, 20 percent of one or the other of the 'lites is right, or maybe use a little of each material.

✔ **Lime.** Ground-up *dolomitic limestone* corrects the acidic pH of peat; and plants that prefer neutral-to-alkaline conditions (such as wallflowers and clematis) need an extra dose. Always add lime with restraint. Use too much and you make the soil too alkaline, the flip side of a soil that is too acid. Five millilitres (1 teaspoon) of dolomitic limestone per gallon of potting mix is the max.

How to Plant Containers

Ready to get your fingers dirty? Follow these steps to plant a pot, one step at a time. The procedure is the same whether you're planting bedding plants (annuals and perennials sold as small seedlings), vegetables, or herbs:

1. **Cover the drainage holes in your container.**

   If you cover the holes with a small section of window screen, water can't puddle up in the bottom of the pot, and the soil won't gush out through the holes. Note the difference between *covering* holes and plugging them up. Avoid the outdated practice of putting a layer of gravel in the bottom of the container.

2. **Fill the container about ⅔ full with soil.**

3. **Remove the plant you're putting in from its container.**

   If you're working with lightweight plastic containers, simply push on the bottom until the seedling pops out. Or use one hand to turn the container upside down while supporting the plant with the other hand. Gently pull out the plant. Whatever method you use to remove a plant from its container, try to keep the root ball intact. A moist root ball doesn't fall apart as easily as a dry one, so water the plant at least an hour before you plant.

4. **Plant plants at the same depth they grew in their previous pots, adding more soil almost to the top of the pot.**

   Don't add soil up to the brim of the pot. Leave some space at the top of the pot to hold water. Put plants in tightly, so that the root balls are almost touching. This could mean 10 plants in a 25-centimetre (10-inch) pot. You want a good show.

5. **Place the whole container in a small tub (or your kid's wagon) and water the plant thoroughly. Next, add water 13 mm (½ inch) deep to the tub (or wagon).**

   Letting the pot soak ensures that all the soil, top to bottom, is wetted.

6. **Wait 15 minutes and then water your plants again.**

7. **Finally, set the container on the ground and let it drip dry.**

Is Everybody Happy?

Plants growing in containers can't let their roots wander about in search of food and water, so you must take care of these needs.

You can make watering as scientific as you want (including the use of a drip irrigation system designed for container plants), but we'll leave our advice at this for now:

In mild spring weather, you probably don't need to water your plants more than once a week, but as temperatures rise and the plants get bigger, you need to water almost every day— even twice a day in dry periods. Big plants need more water than little ones do (but big containers hold more water, too).

A fertilizing plan

Plants growing in containers need more water than those growing in the ground. The more you water, the more you flush nutrients from the soil, and the more often you have to fertilize.

You can offset some of the constant loss of nutrients by mixing slow-release granular fertilizers into the soil mix before planting. But we also like to take the approach of less food, more often — the best looking container plants we've seen are on a constant-feed program. In other words, you give plants a little liquid fertilizer every time, or every other time, you water. Of course this means using less, sometimes a lot less, fertilizer with each water. Some fertilizer products will include directions for *constant* (same as *every time*) feeding, which you need to follow. Wait until you see the results!

If that method is too much hassle for you, use a liquid or water-soluble fertilizer once every week. Follow the rates recommended on the label. Your container plants will still do great.

You can use granular fertilizers on container plants. Just beware, it's not a very precise technique, and you may burn plants if you put on too much.

Part VII
The Part of Tens

In this part . . .

List, list, O, list! — The ghost to Hamlet (Hamlet I, V)

Throughout this book, we give you lots of lists: lists of
can't miss annuals; lists of our favourite perennials; and
lists of our favourite trees, shrubs, and more. Well, here
we are in a part dedicated to lists.

In this part, you can find two more lists, though we
weren't necessarily constrained by the number ten. You
can find a list of Canada's provincial flowers (an even ten,
and of course the territories — but we said we weren't
held back by a simple number, didn't we?). Plus, in the
second part, lists of flowers for perfumed gardens —
maybe ten, maybe more, maybe less. Does it really
matter?

Then don't miss the appendixes, which are substantial
lists in themselves far exceeding the number ten. These
helpful references point you to other gardening resources
(like books, magazines and the Web) and to mail-order
gardening suppliers. We think you'll find this section
invaluable, and you'll thank us for being flexible about
sticking to the part of tens in this chapter.

Chapter 20

Ten Provinces, Three Territories, Twelve Official Flowers

In This Chapter

▶ The official flowers of ten provinces and two territories

*P*rovincial and territorial flowers turn up in many official places — government stationery, publications, documents and seals, highway signs, provincial parks, maybe your driver's licence, and even on the Internet. You probably recognize yours in an instant. Emblems are important because they symbolize official business. They also preserve traditions and inspire love for your province or territory.

All but one Canadian province and territory has an official floral emblem. Nunavut is odd one out, and not because much of the territory lies north of the Arctic Circle (plenty of beautiful possibilities bloom enthusiastically there every summer), but because Nunavut has only been a territory since April, 1999. Give it time. It took most of the provinces and territories years to reach their decisions. For example, Nova Scotia — first off the mark among the original nine provinces in 1901 — took 34 years; Ontario took 70 years, and Prince Edward Island 80. The shortest on record? Newfoundland. It adopted its floral emblem a short five years after joining Canada in 1949. Obviously, selecting a floral emblem is not always easy, perhaps because there are so many wonderful plants to choose from.

In spite of the variety, however, some flowers have been favoured by more than one province. Manitoba considered the wild rose and prairie lily before finally deciding on the prairie crocus. The wild rose was later chosen by Alberta and the prairie lily by Saskatchewan. And if the prairie crocus hadn't already been taken by Manitoba, the Yukon would have snapped it up. Other provinces have been totally original. British Columbia, for one, chose the Pacific dogwood, which can survive nowhere else in Canada.

However, many of the flowers selected grow just about everywhere across the country. In fact, one grows wild in every province and territory. Read on to find out which one.

British Columbia

Pacific dogwood. *Cornus nuttalli.* The showy white petals in mid-spring are not flowers at all, but stunning bracts that attract bees and other insects to the plant's real flowers — the tiny green clusters growing in the centre. Because the bracts don't fall off until all the flowers are pollinated, the Pacific dogwood "blooms" for a long time. What's more, by August the flowers overcome their insignificance by developing into attractive bright red, ovoid fruit, providing food for birds. The changing display continues as the leaves turn reddish in fall. Interestingly, although it's the province's floral emblem, it's hardy only to Zone 8, which means southwestern British Columbia, plus western Washington and Oregon. The tree grows to 20 metres (70 feet), preferring moist but well-drained soil, usually near streams or in shaded coniferous forests. Problems include anthracnose and borers.

Alberta

Wild rose or prickly rose. *Rosa acicularis.* There's little wonder why this fragrant shrub rose was chosen by schoolchildren in 1930 to be Alberta's provincial flower. From June to August, large pink blooms dot the Prairies, brightening aspen bluffs, hillsides, clearings, riverbanks and roadsides. As if its floral display were not enough, scarlet pear-shaped hips 2.5 centimetres (1 inch) across ripen from mid-August through late September and remain on the bushes all winter.

The wild rose ranges from British Columbia to Quebec, northward to just below the Arctic Circle, and southward to the Dakotas and Great Lake states. It grows to 75 centimetres (2½ feet) and succeeds almost anywhere as long as it can bask in at least 5 hours of full sun (preferably in the morning so the leaves dry off early in the day). It likes well-drained, rich, slightly acidic soil, and is easily grown from seed, by transplanting suckers or by rooting cuttings. Just make sure you give it about a foot more space all around than you think it will need, to improve air circulation and discourages foliar diseases.

Saskatchewan

Prairie lily or orange-red lily. *Lilium philadelphicum.* This star of the tall-grass prairie has been appreciated for centuries, but not always for its good looks. Native Americans — from Quebec to British Columbia and southward to New Mexico — boiled the bulbs and ate them like potatoes. In today's Saskatchewan, the prairie lily still flourishes in moist, low-lying prairie that's not heavily grazed or regularly mowed for hay.

A favourite of hummingbirds, the plant's orange-red flower faces upward atop a 60-centimetre (24-inch) stem. Black spots decorate the base of each petal and sepal. It blooms in late June or early July and often measures 7.5 to 10 centimetres (3 to 4 inches) in diameter. Once fertilized, a 2.5-centimetre-long (1-inch), three-sided seedpod appears. The prairie lily also reproduces vegetatively: Scales uneaten by wildlife and dropped at favourable sites often become new plants.

Prairie lilies are also easily grown from seed planted in spring or fall, but the plants take 4 to 5 years to flower. For a quicker show, plant bulbs in fall or spring while still dormant, 10 to 13 centimetres (4 to 5 inches) deep and 20 to 30 centimetres (8 to 12 inches) apart in full sun or light shade.

Manitoba

Prairie crocus, pasque flower or prairie anemone. *Pulsatilla ludoviciana.* It's a sure sign of spring when the prairie crocus blooms, fuzzy buds opening into pretty 4-centimetre (1¾-inch) pale blue or purple flowers. As if to keep itself warm in the frigid air, its grey-green buds, leaves, and stems are completely covered in woolly hairs, and the plant huddles close to the ground. But as the season warms, the plant grows to 30 centimetres (12 inches). Sometimes it blooms as early as Easter, giving rise to another common name, *pasque flower.* And, although the plant is called a crocus, it's actually an anemone, which explains another of its common names. Like all anemones, the flowers don't have petals — the bluish parts are really modified sepals. Later, the flowers transform into attractive feathery seed heads, a yummy treat goldfinches find irresistible in summer.

The wild prairie crocus thrives in hot, dry areas in sandy soils and in full sun from Manitoba to British Columbia, northward to the Yukon and the Northwest Territories, and southward to Texas. It also grows in Siberia. It's sometimes hard to cultivate because it requires special fungi that grow in the plant's native soil. Gather seeds in June. To break dormancy, place the seeds in a plastic bag with damp sand and refrigerate 1 to 3 weeks. Don't transplant plants from the wild — the plant has deep roots that don't like to be disturbed.

Ontario

White trillium. *Trillium grandiflorum.* Three petals, three sepals, and three leaves explains the 'tri' in trillium. In mid-spring, when the almost bare-branches of deciduous trees are only a haze of green, colonies of pristine trilliums bloom white and then fade to deep pink beneath them — a lovely contrast to the weedless dark soil. It's a beautiful scene most gardeners, horticulturists, and even politicians find hard to ignore. The long-lived perennial, which boasts the largest flowers of all the trilliums, are native to rich woods in southern Ontario, western New England, and farther south.

In fall, plant rhizomes 5 to 10 centimetres (2 to 4 inches) deep and 13 to 20 centimetres (5 to 8 inches) apart in humus-rich, slightly acidic to neutral soil, making sure the eyes point up. A southeast location is best. To enrich the soil — and to protect the rhizomes over winter — cover with 2.5 or 5 centimetres (an inch or two) of leaf mould or compost in late fall. You can also plant trillium from seed, but it takes at least two years for the seeds to germinate and another two years for the plants to flower. And no matter how tempting, don't pick the flowers. The leaves attached to them nourish the plant's rhizomes for the next year's crop.

Quebec

Madonna lily or white garden lily. *Lilium candidum.* Its fragrance is absolutely delicious; and the blossoms (10 to 20 per plant blooming in June or July on 1-metre or 40-inch stems) are dazzling. The plant has been cultivated for centuries: It was grown in cloister gardens during the Middle Ages and used to decorate churches. In fact, this lovely white lily may be the world's first cut flower. Although it's Quebec's official floral emblem, the wild iris (fleur-de-lis) remains the unofficial provincial flower.

Madonna lilies are hardy and easy to grow. They flower best in rich, moist, alkaline soil, but also thrive in almost any sunny spot as long as the soil is well drained, and especially if left undisturbed for years. They resent being transplanted, so don't move unless they show signs of deteriorating. Transplant bulbs (or plant new ones) in August, soon after the stalks decay. Plant 7.5 to 10 centimetres (3 to 4 inches) deep and 15 to 20 centimetres (6 to 8 inches) apart. Top dress with wood ashes, decayed manure, and a dusting of bone meal. Watch for *botrytis cinerea,* a mould that attacks foliage and sometimes bulbs.

New Brunswick

Marsh blue violet or purple violet. *Viola cucullata.* What child, on finding a sea of wild purple violets, hasn't delighted in making a pretty spring bouquet? Perhaps that's why schoolchildren in 1936 chose the marsh blue violet for their province's floral emblem. This variety distinguishes itself from the other 14 violets indigenous to New Brunswick by flourishing in wet meadows, springs, and bogs. Wild marsh blue violets range from Nova Scotia to Ontario and southward to Florida.

Each flower has five purple petals with darker colour toward the throat and grows from 13 to 25 centimetres (5 to 10 inches) tall, slightly higher than its green foliage. The plant is somewhat shade tolerant, and makes a lovely groundcover when blooming under flowering fruit trees. But be forewarned: Once you have a patch, you'll probably always have one. Don't blame the pretty purple flowers for spreading the seeds; at fault are the tiny insignificant ones near the roots. Cultivars 'Freckles' (white to eggshell blue dotted with deeper blue) and 'Alba' (white) tolerate drier soil than the wild variety.

Nova Scotia

Trailing arbutus, mayflower, or ground laurel. *Epigaea repens.* It was no surprise to most Nova Scotians when the trailing arbutus was declared the official provincial flower in 1901. Often blossoming among the last remnants of winter snow, it was already the native symbol of high achievement in spite of adversity, and in the 19th century had decorated provincial stamps, coins and even the buttons of the Nova Scotia militia.

Just take a whiff of the plants waxy, delicate blossoms, and you'll know another reason the trailing arbutus is a favourite shrub. The odour is wonderfully strong and spicy. The blooms begin as shell pink or white tubes and then open into delicate five-petal flowers amid leathery evergreen leaves. Hairy, rust-coloured limbs, growing only 7.5 to 15 centimetres (3 to 6 inches) high, stretch up to 150 centimetres (6 feet) horizontally from the roots. It grows wild from Newfoundland to Manitoba and southward to Kentucky and Florida, in sandy, acidic soil in woods, usually where moss likes to grow. Trailing arbutus is difficult to transplant because it needs highly acidic soil in which healthy colonies of fungi live. Better to experiment with soft root cuttings in August, planting them in a mixture of sand and peat moss. Keep them watered until roots are established.

Prince Edward Island

Pink lady's slipper or pink moccasin-flower. *Cypripedium acaule.* This member of the orchid family is a treasure, and clever in the way it tricks a bumblebee into fertilizing it. Lured by the flower's sweet scent and pink colour — ranging from purplish to whitish, but rarely pure white, the unsuspecting bumblebee slips through a slit in the orchid's pouch only to find itself trapped inside with one way out — under the stigma, where the pollen it's collected from another pink lady's slipper brushes off. Unfortunately, a bee can be fooled by this ruse only a few times, which may be the reason many of these native orchids go unpollinated each year.

In Prince Edward Island the pink lady's slipper blooms in forests beneath beechwood, spruce and pine trees in late May or June. It also grows from Newfoundland to Alberta and southward to Alabama, in moist, acidic soil (pH 4 to 5) in woods, or sometimes in sphagnum bogs. The flower — consisting of a pink cleft pouch and purplish-brown to brown (often striped with green) sepals and petals — sometimes measures 7.5 centimetres (3 inches) across. Each one blooms singly atop a 25- to 40-centimetre (10- to 16-inch) stalk. This is one of the most difficult native orchids to cultivate. In the wild, roots and rhizomes grow in an intermediate area between constantly moist but well-drained soil below and leaf litter or sphagnum moss above. Some gardeners have tried growing them in a mixture of coarse sand, chopped sphagnum moss and pine needles, with mixed success. In most cases, the pink lady's slipper should not be taken from the wild because it depends on certain soil fungi for nutrients. Without these fungi, it will eventually die.

Newfoundland/Labrador

Pitcher-plant, Indian dipper or the huntsman's cup. *Sarracenia purpurea.* The pitcher-plant is an *insectivore,* which means it captures insects in its red or green heavily veined, tube-shaped leaves, then digests them to supplement the few nutrients it gets from the wet, acidic soils in which it lives — swamps, sphagnum bogs, wet meadows and lakeshores — from Newfoundland westward to eastern Manitoba, southward to just below the Great Lakes, and southward along the Atlantic coast to Florida.

Blooming in spring, dull red, nodding flowers grow on leafless stalks 20 to 60 centimetres (8 to 24 inches) high. The pitcher-plant prefers full sun. Sow seeds or divide plants in spring after they flower. No need to fertilize, they feed themselves quite well. Don't take plants from the wild — in many localities, they're threatened by land development for farms and recreation.

Northwest Territories

Mountain avens, arctic dryad or white dryad. *Dryas integrifolia.* A plant needs to be tough to survive the Far North from the Yukon to Ellesmere Island and Labrador, and the mountain aven has the right stuff. The plant's hardy semi-evergreen leaves — leathery on top and woolly on the undersides — have a tendency to curl to conserve moisture. Its saucer-shaped flowers turn to follow the sun like solar collectors, gathering heat towards the centre and attracting flies to pollinate the ovaries. Its low-growing habit withstands abrasive, drying winds and slowly collects dirt and leaves to create a thick layer of humus beneath it.

But just being hardy was not enough for it to be adopted as the Northwest Territories' floral emblem in 1957. Mountain avens is pretty, too. In June and July the plant sports abundant, long-lasting creamy white flowers with 7 to 10 daisy-like petals. And soon after, attractive, feathery seed heads appear.

To enjoy a bit of Arctic summer elsewhere in Canada, plant mountain avens in a rock garden. Begin by refrigerating the seeds for two or more months. In spring plant seeds in moist, well-drained sandy soil where you want them to grow. Even seedlings have long taproots that resent being moved. Once plants are established, they multiply by growing shoots that root to create a slow-growing mat.

Yukon Territory

Fireweed, rosebay, or blooming Sally. *Epilobium angustifolium.* Hardy, bold, beautiful, and loved by hummingbirds — a natural choice for Yukon's official flower, chosen in 1957. Magenta fireweed spreads brilliant colour over disturbed areas beside riverbeds, on mountains and along roadsides from June through August. Its name refers to its habit of being one of the first plants to appear after a fire. Not just another pretty face, fireweed is also versatile: First Peoples twisted the fibrous outer parts of the stem to make fishnets, ate the inside parts raw, and steeped the leaves to make tea. This hummingbird favourite grows in every Canadian province and territory, as well as throughout the United States, except for the southeast states and Texas.

Showy four-petal magenta flowers form terminal clusters on 150-centimetre (5-foot) stems. Long, narrow seed capsules split when ripe to expel seeds, which parachute into the wind, sometimes flying long distances. Plant seeds in full sun or part shade in any well-drained soil. Fireweeed also propagates by spreading rhizomes. To create floriferous masses, slice the rhizomes in fall with a spade. Each slice will eventually flower. But beware, this plant can become an aggressive weed.

Chapter 21

Perfumed Garden Flowers

· ·

In This Chapter

▶ Planning your perfumery

▶ Discovering the most fragrant annuals and perennials

▶ Finding surprises after dark

▶ Deciding which trees, vines, and shrubs to grow for fragrance

▶ Exploring sweet-scented bulbs

▶ Enjoying the essence of roses

· ·

Growing fragrant plants is a sure way to lift our spirits and stir good memories.

Sweet scents come with all types of plants — from annuals to shrubs to vines and trees. We tend to focus on flowers when we think of scent, yet many garden plants have luscious-smelling leaves — certainly the fragrant foliage of lemon verbena or a mint-scented geranium rivals that of many a rose. Although flower fragrances waft on high, you often need to seek out leaf fragrance. Only when you rub or crush the leaves of such fragrant delights as Corsican mint or rosemary do they release their aromas.

Think of your favourite flower and foliage fragrances when you plan and plant your garden. Including them is easy.

Getting the Most for Your Whiff

Much current garden literature encourages readers to cluster fragrant plants together in a collection. But the most sensual gardens of all are infused with perfumed plants through and through. Cultivate sweet-scented plants in prime locations so you are certain to catch their drift. Target the following areas:

✔ **Locate potted plants under windows or on your balcony** so that you can enjoy the aromas indoors and out. Perfumed annuals (such as sweet alyssum, carnations, and stocks, which release their fragrance at night) or bulbs (such as freesias and lilies) are excellent choices.

✔ **Frame your front door or garden entrance** with a sweet-smelling vine such as goldflame honeysuckle. Or plant the strongly perfumed thornless climbing rose 'Zephirine Drouhin'.

✔ **Cover a sturdy arbour or patio** with a robust climber like the old-fashioned wisteria; its fragrant blooms in 30-to 60-centimetre (1- to 2-foot) pendulous clusters are legendary.

✔ **Edge pathways** with fragrant herbs (like lavender and thyme), annuals (mignonette, for example), and perennials (such as chocolate cosmos and lemon daylily).

Flowers Most Possessed with Scent

In a single gardening season, you can work perfume magic simply by planting fast-growing annuals and perennials. Enjoy their instant fragrance gratification while your slower-growing perfumed trees and shrubs become established.

✔ **Sweet sultan.** *Centaurea moschata* (annual, all zones). This plant has erect branching stems to 60 centimetres (2 feet) with thistlelike, 5-centimetre (2-inch), musk-scented flower heads. Common colours include lilac, rose, yellow, and white.

✔ **Chocolate cosmos.** *Cosmos atrosanguineus* (annual, all zones). Deep brownish-red fragrant flowers adorn this perennial. The flowers, nearly 5 centimetres (2 inches) wide, appear on top of stems that grow up to 75 centimetres (2½ feet). Some say the fragrance is chocolate — others say vanilla.

✔ **Pinks.** *Dianthus* (perennial, Zone 4). Several kinds of strongly fragrant perennial pinks, or border carnations, are available. Tops for fragrance are cheddar pink *(D. gratianopolitanus)*, cottage pink *(D. plumarius),* and maiden pink *(D. deltoides)*.

✔ **Carnations.** *Dianthus caryophyllus* (annual, all zones). Choose spicy-sweet border carnations, which are bushier and more compact than the florist type.

✔ **Common heliotrope.** *Heliotropium arborescens* (annual, all zones). This plant's sweet fragrance comes from clusters of rich purple flowers on 90- to 120-centimetre (1- to 4-foot) stems.

- **Sweet pea.** *Lathyrus odoratus* (annual, all zones). The old-fashioned varieties are the most fragrant by far. Look for 'Old Spice' and 'Painted Lady'. Other truly fragrant sweet peas are 'Mammoth Mix' and the 'Old Royal' series.

- **Stock.** *Matthiola incana* (annual, all zones). Spicy-sweet flowers cluster along erect stems 30 to 90 centimetres (1 to 3 feet) tall, depending on variety. Stock is good for cutting.

- **Mignonette.** *Reseda odorata* (annual, all zones). Old-fashioned and considered one of the most fragrant of all flowers, mignonette has been described as possessing a sweet pea-raspberry-tangerine scent. The plant reaches from 30 to 45 centimetres (1 to 1½ feet) with inconspicuous flowers in dense, spikelike clusters. Compact forms are the most fragrant.

- **Sweet violet.** *Viola odorata* (perennial, Zone 5). This plant has been long cherished for its sweet oils, which were extracted for perfumes. It has dark green, heart-shaped leaves and, depending on the variety, grows from 5 to 30 centimetres (2 to 12 inches). Sweet violet spreads by runners near the soil surface, and it can become a pest.

Some types of flowers are not usually sought after for fragrance, yet particular species or varieties among them are quite nicely scented. So if you're planting peonies, for example, look for the pink 'Monsieur Jules Elie'; white 'Festiva Maxima'; or 'Cheddar Charm', a Japanese variety with a brilliant yellow centre set off with white guard petals. Daylilies noted for fragrance include the lemon daylily *(Hemerocallis lilioasphodelus)* and hybrids such as 'Fragrant Light', 'Hyperion', 'Ida Jane', and 'Citrina'. Among tulips, some single early types have a sweet scent. Examples are butter-yellow 'Bellona' and golden-orange 'General de Wet'. Also, the multiflowered *Tulipa sylvestris* has a pleasant, sweet fragrance.

Fragrance after Dark

Certain plants release their heady scents only near or after dark. Plant them near the spots where you hang out on summer nights — close to porches and bedroom windows and next to your most comfy garden bench.

- **Dame's rocket.** *Hesperis matronalis* (annual, all zones). This plant is excellent for the wild garden, where it often self-sows. Its branching plants reach 60 to 120 centimetres (2 to 4 feet) high with rounded clusters of richly fragrant phloxlike blooms in lavender or purple.

- **Moonflower.** *Ipomoea alba* (annual, all zones). A perennial vine grown as a summer annual, moonflower's fragrant white trumpet blooms open to 15 centimetres (6 inches) wide at sunset.

✔ **Evening stock.** *Mathiola longipetala bicornis* (annual, all zones). Only 7.5 to 30 centimetres (3 to 12 inches) tall, this inconspicuous annual with small purplish flowers has a blockbuster fragrance at night.

✔ **Flowering tobacco.** *Nicotiana alata* (annual, all zones). This wild species has large white flowers that open toward evening on 60- to 90-centimetre (2- to 3-foot) stems. 'Grandiflora' is exceptionally fragrant.

✔ **Fragrant evening primrose.** *Oenothera caespitosa* (perennial, Zone 5). Low-growing with grey-green fuzzy leaves, this primrose has white, 10-centimetre (4-inch) blooms.

✔ **Night phlox.** *Zaluzianskya capensis* (annual, all zones). Fragrant, 5-centimetre (2-inch) flowers are dark red with white interiors.

The Most Aromatic Herbs

Following is a sampling of some of the best herbs for fragrant foliage. In addition to smelling great, thyme and lavender are extremely useful and rugged landscape plants. Rosemary can be grown in pots brought indoors for winter.

✔ **Lemon verbena.** *Aloysia triphylla.* Zone 8b.

✔ **Chamomile.** *Chamaemelum nobile.* Zone 3.

✔ **Lavender.** *Lavandula.* Zone 5.

✔ **Corsican mint.** *Mentha requienii.* Zone 7.

✔ **Scented geraniums.** *Pelargonium* species, including *P. citrosum, P. graveolens, P. nervosum, P. odoratissimum, P. quercifolium,* and *P. tomentosum.* All zones.

✔ **Rosemary.** *Rosmarinus officinalis.* Zone 9.

✔ **Thyme.** *Thymus.* Zones 4 to 5.

Heavenly Scented Trees, Shrubs, and Vines

Here's a handful of readily available, pleasantly fragrant trees, shrubs, and vines.

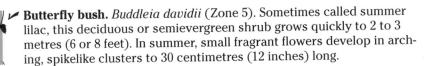

✔ **Butterfly bush.** *Buddleia davidii* (Zone 5). Sometimes called summer lilac, this deciduous or semievergreen shrub grows quickly to 2 to 3 metres (6 or 8 feet). In summer, small fragrant flowers develop in arching, spikelike clusters to 30 centimetres (12 inches) long.

✔ **Daphne.** *Daphne* species (Zones 5 to 9, varies by species) These shrubs can be a bit temperamental, but the flowers' seductive scent encourages serious fragrance fanciers to persist. You can choose from several species, including *D. burkwoodii* (white flowers fading to pink, Zone 5), *D. cneorum* (rosy-pink flowers, Zone 7), *D. mantensiana* (purple flowers, Zone7), and *D. odora* (flowers pink to deep red with creamy pink throats, Zone 9). All parts of the daphne are safe to handle but poisonous if ingested.

✔ **Goldflame honeysuckle.** *Lonicera heckrottii* (Zone 4) A sweet-smelling vine that grows up to 3.7 metres (12 feet) and displays rose-pink and pale yellow flowers.

✔ **Mock orange.** *Philadelphus* spp (Zones 3 to 5, depending on variety.) A great display of creamy white flowers in early summer with a scent like orange blossoms, they tolerate some shade and they're not particular about soil. What more could you ask? They grow 3 to 3.7 metres (10 to 12 feet).

✔ **Lilac.** *Syringa vulgaris* (Zone 2b). Common lilac includes many named varieties. But there are also the French hybrids and miniature ones to choose from.

✔ **Summersweet.** *Clethra* spp. (Several varieties, from the dwarf 'Hummingbird' (Zone 4), which grows 75 centimetres (30 inches) tall to the upright *C. alnifolia* (Zone 5) at nearly 150 centimetres (5 feet). They have fragrant white flowers in summer and yellow fall colour.

✔ **Viburnum**. *Viburnum* spp. (Zones 2b to 6, depending on variety). Many varieties of mostly compact and bushy shrubs with small, glossy green leaves and sweetly scented flowers followed by fruits. Korean spice viburnum *V. carlesi* (Zone 4) is one to look for.

Best Bulbs for Fragrance

You can find some of the most highly scented flowers among bulbs. For more information about bulbs, see Chapter 6.

✔ **Amaryllis, or belladonna lily.** *Amaryllis belladonna* (all zones in containers). Evocatively named because 90-centimetre-high (3 feet) flowering stalks emerge in late summer, but not leaves. Its pink, trumpet-shaped flowers are about 7.5 centimetres (3 inches) in diameter.

✔ **Lily-of-the-valley.** *Convallaria majalis* (Zone 3). Starting this hardy and resilient bulb in your own garden is easy. The tiny, hanging, bell-shaped flowers that appear in early spring are wonderfully scented.

✔ **Freesia.** *Freesia* (all zones in containers). Not all are fragrant, but the white and yellow varieties can usually be depended on for a strong, spicy sweet scent.

✔ **Hyacinth.** *Hyacinthus orientalis* (Zone 5 or all zones in containers). You can easily force these large bulbs indoors (see Chapter 6 for details on forcing bulbs), and you can get special vases to fit the bulbs. Several colours are available, and all are equally fragrant. One flowering hyacinth is enough to perfume an entire house. Or plant outdoors in clumps or in containers.

✔ **Lily.** *Lilium* (Zones 4 to 9, depending on variety). Lily species include gold-banded lily (*L. auratum*, Zone 7), Madonna lily (*L. candidum*, Zone 5) and trumpet lily (*L. longiflorum*, Zone 6), as well as Oriental lilies, such as 'Casa Blanca' (Zone 4), 'Pink Pearl' (Zone 6), 'Olympic Star' (Zone 5) and 'Journey's End' (Zone 8).

✔ **Grape hyacinth.** *Muscari azureum* (Zone 3). Put your nose down to the blue flower spikes and smell a glass of fresh grape juice.

✔ **Narcissus.** *Narcissus jonquilla* (Zone 3) and *N. tazetta* (in containers indoors). Jonquils are the shorter narcissus that produce two to four flowers per flowering stalk. The tazettas include the pure white paper-whites and the golden 'Soleil d'Or'. As is often the case with these highly scented flowers, a single paperwhite can perfume a whole room or more, but it's not a universally loved scent. Try it for yourself.

✔ **Tuberose.** *Polianthes tuberosa* (all zones in containers). Flowers of this tender summer-to-fall tuber are heavy and waxy — almost unreal looking. The scent is equally unbelievable. Plant in spring, after frost danger is past.

✔ **Tulip 'Bellona'.** (Zone 4). This bright-yellow, single early tulip hybrid grows about 30 centimetres (12 inches) tall and has a heavenly scent.

Redolent Roses

Nothing is quite like sniffing an old rose (meaning an antique type) for the most intense floral-fragrance experience. Fragrance aficionados can even identify the class of old rose — Tea, China, Damask, and Bourbon, for example — by its characteristic perfume. Entire books are devoted to old roses, and we recommend in particular *Roses For Dummies* by Lance Walheim and the Editors of the National Gardening Association (IDG Books Worldwide Inc.).

Modern roses are another story. In their quest for improved flower colour and growth habits in modern roses, breeders have sacrificed the fragrance of the older varieties. Some dedicated rose lovers, however, have managed to develop garden rose varieties with the attributes of a modern rose *and* a delicious fragrance. The following modern roses (all hardy in Zones 6 to 10 without protection) are known for their intense fragrance. (See Chapter 7 for more about hardiness and the definition of these rose types):

- ✔ **'Chrysler Imperial'**. Hybrid tea; rich crimson with darker shadings.
- ✔ **'Crimson Glory'**. Hybrid tea; deep crimson aging to purplish.
- ✔ **'Double Delight'**. Hybrid tea; cherry-red surrounding creamy centre.
- ✔ **'Fragrant Cloud'**. Hybrid tea; orange-red.
- ✔ **'Papa Meilland'**. Hybrid tea; bright, dark crimson.
- ✔ **'Sundowner'**. Grandiflora; orange and salmon-pink.
- ✔ **'Sunsprite'**. Floribunda; yellow.
- ✔ **'Tiffany'**. Hybrid tea; soft pink with yellow at the petal base.
- ✔ **'Gertrude Jekyll'**. Austin rose; large, warm pink flowers.
- ✔ **'Madame Isaac Pereire'**. Bourbon; deep rose pink with purple overtones
- ✔ **'Abraham Darby'**. Austin rose; apricot/yellow cupped flowers.
- ✔ **'Sweet Juliet'**. Austin rose; pure apricot blooms with cupped shape.
- ✔ **'Royal Blush'**. Alba; pale to flesh pink quartered blooms.
- ✔ **'Golden Celebration'**. Austin rose; giant golden yellow flowers.

One last note here on experiencing your favourite floral fragrance: A flower's perfume is usually strongest on warm and humid days and weakest when the weather is hot and dry. For an intense rush of flower fragrance, bring the blossom to your face and lightly breathe into it before inhaling. The warmth of your breath releases the flower's volatile oils.

Appendix A

Gardening Resources

● ●

*L*earning about gardening is an endless pursuit. Anyone can spend a life-time learning (and many have) and never know everything about gardening. But if you're just getting started and want to learn more, this appendix is for you. Here we tell you about gardening books, magazines, software, and the Internet.

If you want to learn more even after exploring all the resources here, consider taking classes at a local college, or — if you live in British Columbia, Alberta, Saskatchewan or Ontario — you can become a certified Master Gardener. For more information, call:

British Columbia: Master Gardener Program at VanDusen Botanical Garden, 604-257-8672

Saskatchewan: The Saskatchewan Master Gardener Program, Division of Extension at the University of Saskatchewan, 306-966-5551

Alberta: Master Gardener Program at Devonian Botanic Garden, 403-987-2064

Ontario: Master Gardeners of Ontario Inc., 800-298-4809

Books and Magazines about Gardening

Sooner or later, most gardeners get hooked on books and magazines. You can find publications for all types of gardeners, from novices to specialists. Those specialists can focus on a particular type of plant, such as rhododendrons, orchids, or wildflowers; or a particular type of gardening, such as edible land-scaping, rock gardening, or indoor gardening. Because the natures of books and magazines differ, each type of publication tends to treat the various gardening topics in different but complementary ways. Books are ideal for treating broad subjects in depth and for bringing together in one place information that otherwise would be scattered. Magazines are ideal for reporting new trends and seasonal topics and for approaching specific topics from interesting and unusual angles. Using books and magazines together, you easily can form an impressive knowledge base.

The resources included in this appendix are predominantly North American, the territory we know best. On every continent — not to mention in every region — you can find gardening information that directly targets plants and conditions there. Also, international trade rules are still complex enough to discourage easy exchange: All the prices noted here are in Canadian dollars and assume Canadian delivery. We encourage you to seek out the resources where you live, beginning perhaps at local botanical gardens.

Books

Gardening books fall into two basic categories: practical and inspirational. Inspirational books are those that stimulate and invite you to stretch your thinking. These books feed your dreams. Inspiration can be visual, with books of exciting full-colour photographs, or literary, with works that capture the imagination through the excellence of the writing.

Practical books include how-to books that show you how to do the basic tasks of gardening and reference books that you can refer to over and over. Essential reference books include encyclopedias of plants, dictionaries of gardening terms and practices, and directories of sources. Sources include nurseries and mail-order companies for obtaining seeds and plants, lists of organizations that provide information, and descriptions and addresses of gardens to visit and events to attend.

Gardens are very personal, and your favourite books will be a very personal selection also. Nevertheless, you should watch for the following points when considering the practical type of book:

- ✔ **Plant requirements.** Make sure that any book of plants you buy includes the light, moisture, soil type, and temperature requirements for growing them successfully. You can be frustrated if you discover belatedly that the "perfect" plant in terms of size, shape, colour, and seemingly every other aspect is not cold-hardy in your area.

- ✔ **Plant names.** Beginning gardeners are intimidated by botanical names of plants and find it much easier to use common names. However, common names of plants are so ambiguous that planning gardens or buying plants based on common names alone isn't wise. Don't buy a book of plants that doesn't also give the Latin name, or you'll never be sure of getting the plant that you saw in the book.

- ✔ **Conditions in your geographical region.** Climate, soil, and temperature vary; thus, the plants that grow well and the cultivation methods gardeners use to make them flourish will also vary. A book that tells you how and particularly when to do tasks such as planting and mulching must address your particular region.

✔ **Qualifications of the author.** Look for authors who have experience in the type of gardening that you want to do or the style of garden that you want to create. But ultimately, what's important is an author's ability to communicate and provide useful information to you.

✔ **Quality and number of illustrations.** Are gardening steps illustrated and clearly labeled? Are photographs in focus and true to colour? Do photos illustrate the subject, or are they merely big, beautiful pictures? Do captions accompany illustrations? If the book is on garden design, does the book include design plans? Do the plans have labels? Do they show plant names? Is the scale clear?

✔ **Size and type of index.** Good books have indexes, usually at the back of the book. The best indexes include names of gardens, organizations, nurseries, people, and plants, as well as the topics mentioned in the book. Dictionaries and encyclopedias preclude the need for an index by arranging entries in alphabetical order.

We recommend that beginning gardeners start with one or two general how-to books and a few reference books. As your skill level progresses and your tastes develop, you can branch out and read in-depth treatments of your specific subjects. We selected the practical books in this list because they are both easy for beginners to understand and have content substantial enough to be useful as your gardening skill grows.

Where-to-find-it books

Take a look at the following reference guides.

✔ *Gardening by Mail: A Source Book, 5th Edition.* Written by Barbara J. Barton and Ginny Hunt. Houghton Mifflin, 1997. $35 (paperback).This is an Amercian book, but it has a lot of Canadian information. On its pages, you can find enough information to support any kind of gardening: Plant and seed sources, garden suppliers and services, professional societies, trade associations, conservation and umbrella groups, horticultural and plant societies, magazines and newsletters, libraries, and books.

✔ *The Canadian Plant Source Book.* Written by Anne and Peter Ashley, 1996-97. Where to find what plants in Canada. Order from the Garden Possabilities Bookstore, 1065 Davis Dr., Newmarket, Ont., L3Y 2R9; 800-723-2666; fax 905-830-0996. $17.95 plus $4 shipping and handling.

Basic gardening primers: ...For Dummies!

Of course we're convinced that the best gardening primers on the planet are *...For Dummies* gardening books written by the NGA. The titles include the following:

✔ *Perennials For Dummies,* 1997, with Denver-based garden guru Marcia Tatroe

✔ *Roses For Dummies,* 1997, with central California's most famous gardener, Lance Walheim

✔ *Lawn Care For Dummies,* 1997, again with Lance Walheim

✔ *Annuals For Dummies,* 1997, with San Francisco-based gardener and editor Bill Marken

✔ *Container Gardening For Dummies,* 1997, also with Bill Marken

✔ *Decks & Patios For Dummies,* 1998, with Napa Valley contractor and editor Robert Beckstrom

✔ *Flowering Bulbs For Dummies,* 1998, with New York Botanical Garden's horticulture instructor and international bulb expert, Judy Glattstein

✔ *Houseplants For Dummies,* 1998, with Quebec City's own one-person horticultural tour de force, Larry Hodgson

✔ *Landscaping For Dummies,* 1999, with Venice, California-based landscape contractor Philip Giroux

✔ *Vegetable Gardening For Dummies,* 1999, with National Gardening Association senior horticulturist, vegetable gardening expert, and TV personality, Charlie Nardozzi

A word about British books

British gardens and British gardeners have a definite cachet. Great Britain, with good reason, has been called the garden capital of the world. Gardens around the world emulate British gardens, and some of the best gardeners and garden writers are British.

Gardening in Great Britain, however, is not like gardening in Canada, the United States, Australia, South Africa, or anywhere else, for that matter. Some differences include climate, soil, pests, diseases, light, and availability of plants, and how and when to perform garden tasks. Indoor conditions are different, too. For example, in winter, Canadians tend to keep their houses hotter and drier. We also use different terminology.

Beginning gardeners find some of the how-to advice in British books confusing and the results disappointing. Novices who seek how-to books should buy books by authors familiar with the conditions where they garden. Experienced gardeners are better able to filter out advice not appropriate to their situations, and thus to benefit from exposure to new ideas and different ways of doing things. As you gain gardening skills, we recommend you explore the full and wonderful world of garden books, but be cautious at first.

The British excel in matters of taste, plant collecting, and plant breeding. British books on gardens, garden history, garden design, garden ornamentation, floral arrangement, plant exploration, plant breeding and propagation, biography, and essays can be used with far fewer caveats than books whose main intent is to show you how to do something, like plant a vegetable garden, yourself.

Magazines

Magazines — good value for the money — are important sources of information and inspiration, covering a wide variety of topics and situations. Articles usually include practical information, such as sources for obtaining plants or seeds, and generally have illustrations such as full-colour photographs, plot plans, diagrams, and botanical drawings. Many magazines offer reviews of garden books, a very useful service in helping you decide which books are right for you. Other features can include regular columns for presenting news, discussing trends, or answering readers' questions. Magazines are published frequently, so articles are often more up-to-date than books

Hundreds of periodicals publish articles about plants and gardens. Like books, a magazine exists for every skill level and type and style of garden imaginable. Start with a few of the most popular national magazines and then add subscriptions to specialty periodicals as you find appropriate. You can write or call any of the following magazines directly.

Some of the gardening magazines in Canada are

- ✔ *Canadian Gardening.* Published seven times a year. Canadian Gardening, Box 717, Stn. Main, Markham, ON, L3P 7V3; phone 905-946-0893; Web site http://canadiangardening.com/. Subscriptions $22.95 plus GST.

- ✔ *Coastal Grower.* Published nine times a year. 322 John St., Victoria, BC., V8T 1T3; phone 800-816-0747; fax 604-360-1709; e-mail mag@coastalgrower.com. Written by and for West Coast home gardeners. Subscriptions $22 plus GST.

- ✔ *East Coast Gardener.* Published eight times a year. East Coast Gardner, 5 Wrights Cove Rd., Dartmouth, NS, B3B 1M8; phone 800-717-4442; e-mail ecg@klis.com. Subscriptions $13.99 including GST.

- ✔ *The Gardener for the Prairies* (Formerly *The Saskatchewan Gardener*). Published 4 times a year. The Gardener for the Prairies, Box 379, RPO University, Saskatoon, SK, S7N 4J8. Phone: 306-966-5593; fax: 306-966-5567; e-mail The.Gardener@usask.ca. Subscription $15.

- ✔ *Gardening Life.* Published six times a year. Canadian Home Publishers, 120-511 King St. West, Toronto, Ontario M5V 2Z4. Phone 905/ 946-0410; fax 905/ 946-1021; www.canadianhouseandhome.com. HYPERLINK mailto:exec@canhomepub.com. Subscription $19.95 ($21.44 for NS, NF, NB, LB including GST).

- ✔ *Gardens West.* Published nine times a year. Gardens West, Box 2680, Vancouver, BC, V6B 3W8. Phone 800-263-1088; fax 604-879-5110; e-mail: grow@gardenswest.com. Subscription $23.50 including GST.

- ✔ *The Gilded Herb.* Published five times a year. The Gilded Herb, 15 Clifford Drive, Dunsford, Ontario, K0M 1L0; phone 877-843-4372 (toll free) or 705-793-3868; fax 705-793-3260, Web site: www.gildedherb.com. Subscription $17.99 including GST.

✔ *Harrowsmith Country Life.* Published 6 times a year. 11450 Blvd. Albert-Hudon, Montreal N., Que., H1G 3J9. Phone 800-387-0581. The focus is on country life, which includes gardening. Subscription $21.38 including GST.

✔ *The Manitoba Gardener.* Published 5 times a year. 130A Cree Cresent, Winnipeg, Man., R3J 3W1. Phone 204-940-2700; fax 204-940-2727; e-mail mbgarden@escape.ca. Subscription $24.95 plus tax.

✔ *Plant & Garden.* Published 6 times a year. 1200 Markham Rd., Suite 300, Scarborough, ON, M1H 3C3. Phone 905/ 856-4178; e-mail p&gmag@nzen.net. Subscription $14.93 including GST.

✔ *New Prairie Garden Annual.* Published once a year. (1999 Prairie Garden-Featuring Perennials comes out in November.) The Prairie Garden, Box 517, Winnipeg, MB, R3C 2J3; phone 204-489-3466; e-mail fransays@mb.sympatico.ca. Subscription $8 including GST.

✔ *Seeds of Diversity.* Published three times a year. Seeds of Diversity Canada, Box 36, Station Q, Toronto, ON, M4T 2L7. Phone 905/ 623-0353; e-mail mail@seeds.ca. Seed exchange for heirloom, rare and non-hybrid vegetables, fruits, flowers, grains and herbs. Subscription, membership and annual seed listing $25.

✔ *Water Gardening: The Magazine for Pondkeepers.* Published 10 times a year. 519-842-6049; fax 519-688-5459; e-mail lilypad@oxford.net. Subscription $30 U.S.

✔ *Wildflower.* Published four times a year. North American Plant Society, Box 336, Station "F", Toronto, Ontario, M4Y 2L7. Phone 416-924-6807; e-mail ann.melvin@sympatico.ca. Subscription $35.

Gardening Online

Ask gardeners, "What's your favourite gardening tool?" and they'll tell you about an old pair of oft-sharpened pruners or a nicely balanced watering can or how they finally splurged and bought a really good spade. Not one of them will say, "My computer." But a computer is probably one of the most versatile tools a gardener can own.

With a computer and access to the Internet, you can select the right plants for your particular climate and site, design and lay out a new garden, learn more about plants and their care, find authoritative answers to gardening questions, join in discussions or live chats with other gardeners, read magazine articles, find information on garden catalogues or browse through online catalogues, do your shopping online, and just plain have fun browsing.

The World Wide Web

Way back in 1996, when the first edition of Gardening For Dummies was written, it was possible to offer a comprehensive listing of all gardening-related sites on the World Wide Web. Such sites numbered in the dozens. Now they number in the many thousands, and keeping track of them all is no longer possible.

In selecting Web sites for this section, we looked for well-designed, well-maintained sites with substantial content and demonstrated staying power on the ever-growing Web.

For help getting started, check out *The Internet For Canadians For Dummies,* by Andrew Dagys, John Levine, Carol Baroudi, and Margaret Levine Young; or *Netscape and the World Wide Web For Dummies,* 2nd Edition, by Paul Hoffman (both published by IDG Books Worldwide, Inc.).

Most (but not all) Internet addresses begin with the characters `http://`. But you can save a few keystrokes simply by beginning the address with "www" and letting your browser automatically add the `http://`. That's why in most of the addresses that follow we dropped the `http://`.

Where to look for answers

The secret to finding what you're looking for among the many millions of Web pages is knowing where to start. Are you looking for an authoritative answer to a specific gardening question? Illustrated plant information? Web sites on a particular topic? Regional information? Tips and tricks from fellow gardeners? It's all out there if you know how and where to look.

When should I divide my irises? Is fresh horse manure safe for my plants? How do I dry and store my herbs? Every week, Canadian farmers and home gardeners phone their local agricultural offices to ask hundreds of questions, And for good reason — provincial agricultural departments are treasure troves of growing information. Some offer free publications covering a wide variety of topics; others charge a modest fee. And all have made their mark on the World Wide Web. True, some provinces have posted more information on the Net than others, but nothing stops you from surfing the online fact-sheets of any province and selecting the facts you need. Check it out for yourself. Here's where to look:

- ✔ **Alberta Agriculture, Food and Rural Development:** `www.agric.gov.ab.ca/navigation/crops/horticulture/specialties/col_index.html`. A gold mine of online factsheets, including diseases, insects, weeds, turf grasses, trees, fruits, vegetables and even houseplants.

- ✔ **British Columbia Ministry of Agriculture and Food:** www.agf.gov.bc.ca/publicat/publications.htm. Most online information is for commercial growers, but some information of interest to home gardeners, such as late blight disease on tomatoes and potatoes, fruit tree diseases, and a few factsheets on insects and weeds.

- ✔ **Manitoba Agriculture:** www.gov.mb.ca/agriculture/crops/index.html. Wide variety of online factsheets covering soil, weather, climate, vegetables and diseases.

- ✔ **New Brunswick Department Agriculture and Rural Development:** www.gov.nb.ca/agricult/index.htm. Weather and climate information, and online factsheets covering diseases, insects and weeds.

- ✔ **Newfoundland and Labrador Agricultural Services:** www.gov.nf.ca/agric/. Online lawn and garden factsheets covering topics such as lawn and garden nutrition, insect pests, and pesticide safety.

- ✔ **Nova Scotia Department of Agriculture and Marketing:** http://agri.gov.ns.ca/pt/hort/hortfact.htm. A variety of factsheets of interest to home gardeners, including information on fruit trees, berries and organic gardening.

- ✔ **Ontario Ministry of Agriculture and Food:** www.gov.on.ca/OMAFRA/english/sitemap.html. A good choice of online factsheets, including information on lawns, most vegetables, and fruits and berries.

- ✔ **Prince Edward Island Agriculture and Forestry:** www.gov.pe.ca/af/agr-info/index.asp. Factsheets include information on soil fertility, growing potatoes and fertilizing fruit trees.

- ✔ **Saskatchewan Agriculture and Food:** www.agr.gov.sk.ca/level3.asp?firstPick=Crops&pick=Horticulture. Online fact sheets include Dutch elm disease, woolly elm aphids, and browning of evergreens.

- ✔ **Yukon Department of Renewable Resources:** http://renres.gov.yk.ca/agric. A short description of the Yukon's climate and soil. The following site featuring Yukon government publications was under construction when *Gardening For Canadians For Dummies* went to press. Try it, you might like it: http://renres.gov.yk.ca/pubs/

Many cooperative extension services in the U.S. are also on the Web. Following is a sampling of extension service Web sites:

- ✔ **Factsheet Database (Ohio State University).** Check out the Web site at www.hcs.ohio-state.edu/factsheet.html. If every gardener could have only one bookmark, this would be it. OSU's specialized search engine searches only through the fact-filled publications of university and Cooperative Extension Web sites around the country.

- ✔ **Horticulture Solutions (Illinois Cooperative Extension Service).** Web site www.ag.uiuc.edu/~robsond/solutions/hort.html. Quick answers to common gardening questions; organized by topic. Includes a glossary.

Soil testing

If you suspect you soil needs help, but you're not sure what to do, you can take or send samples to a private or provincial soil testing lab. For a modest fee, one of the following can tell you what amendments you need to increase your crop or improve your flower garden.

- ✔ **Alberta.** Alberta Soils and Animal Nutrition Laboratory, 905 O.S. Longman Building, 6909-116 Alberts Street, Edmonton, AB T6H 4P2; 403-427 2727.

- ✔ **British Columbia.** Griffin Labs Corp., 1875 Spall Rd., Kelowna, B.C. V1Y 4R2; 604-861-3234. Or try Pacific Soil Analysis, Unit #5, 11720 Voyageur Way, Richmond, B.C. V6X 3G9; 604-273-8226.

- ✔ **Manitoba.** Manitoba Provincial Soil Testing Lab, Department of Soil Sciences, Room 262, Ellis Building, University of Manitoba, Winnipeg R3T 2N2; 204-474-9257. May give organic results on request.

- ✔ **New Brunswick.** NB Agricultural Lab, NB Dept. Of Agriculture and Rural Development, Box 6000, Fredericton, NB E3B 5H1; www.nbfarm.com/genfaqs.htm.

- ✔ **Newfoundland and Labrador.** Soil Plant and Feed Laboratory, Department of Forest Resources and Agrifoods, Provincial Agriculture Building, Box 8700, Brookfield Road, St. John's, NF A1B 4J6; 709-729-6638; www.gov.nf.ca/agric/_vti_bin/search.htm0.idq.

- ✔ **Nova Scotia.** Soils and Crops Branch, Nova Scotia Department of Agriculture and Marketing, Box 550, Truro, NS B2N 5E3; 902-895-4469; agri.gov.ns.ca/pt/hort/garden95/gg95-95.htm.

- ✔ **Ontario.** Laboratory Services a division of the University of Guelph, 95 Stone Road West, Guelph, ON N1H 8J7; 519-767-6242, fax 519-767-6240; www.uoguelph.ca/labserv/. Or try Nutrite, Box 160, Elmira, ON N3B 2Z6; 519-669-5401(toll-free in southern Ontario, 800-265-8865). Will give organic results. Or you could also try the Royal Botanical Gardens, Box 399, Hamilton, ON L8N 3H8; (905) 527-1158.

- ✔ **Prince Edward Island.** P.E.I. Soil and Feed Testing Lab, P.O. Box 1600, Research Station, Charlottetown, PEI C1A 7N3, 902-368-5631; www.gov.pe.ca/af/soilfeed/index.asp. Will give organic results, if requested. Samples may also be left at your nearest District Agricultural Office.

✔ **Quebec.** Nutrite, Box 1000, Brossard, PQ J4Z 3N2; 514-462-2555. Will give organic results.

✔ **Saskatchewan.** Saskatchewan Soil Testing Lab, Department of Soil Science, General Purpose Building, University of Saskatchewan, Saskatoon, SK S7N 0W0; 306-966-6890; `www.ag.usask.ca/cofa/departments/hort/hortinfo/misc/soil2.html` **May give organic results on request.**

Getting the Bugs Out

If garden pests are bugging you, a pest identification centre near you can help identify those irritating little beasties for a reasonable fee. Then you can choose the best treatment for controlling them.

✔ **Alberta.** Alberta Environmental Centre, Plant Services Division, Bag 4000, Vegreville, AB T0B 4L0; 403-632-6767. Will also refer to labs in other areas.

✔ **British Columbia.** Syd Cannings, Department of Zoology, University of British Columbia, Vancouver, BC V6T 2A9; 604-228-3379.

✔ **Manitoba.** Manitoba Agriculture Entomology, Section 911-401 York Ave., Winnipeg, MA R3C 0P8 204-945-3857.

✔ **New Brunswick.** NB Agricultural Lab, NB Dept. Of Agriculture and Rural Development, P.O. Box 6000, Fredericton, NB E3B 5H1; Plant Industry Branch, Department of Agriculture, Box 6000, Fredericton, NB E3B 5H1; 506-453-2108 .

✔ **Newfoundland and Labrador.** Soil Plant and Feed Laboratory, Department of Forest Resources and Agrifoods, Provincial Agriculture Building, P.O. Box 8700, Brookfield Road, St. John's, NF A1B 4J6; 709-729-6638; . Research Station, Agriculture Canada, Box 7098, St. John's, NF A1E 3Y3; 709-772-4619.

✔ **Nova Scotia.** Soils and Crops Branch, Nova Scotia Department of Agriculture and Marketing, Box 550, Truro, NS B2N 5E3; 902-895-4469; Horticulture and Biology Branch, Nova Scotia Department of Agriculture and Marketing, Box 550, Truro, NS B2N 5E3; 902-895-1570 .

✔ **Ontario.** Pest Diagnostic Advisory Clinic, Rm. B14 Graham Hall, University of Guelph, Guelph, ON N1G 2W1; 519-824-4120.

✔ **Prince Edward Island.** P.E.I Dept. of Agriculture, Master Gardener Program, Box 1600, Research Station, Charlottetown PEI C1A 7N3; 902-368-5619.

✔ **Quebec.** National Identification Service, Room 3119, K.W. Neatby Building, Ottawa, ON KIA 0C6; 613-995-5222.

✔ **Saskatchewan.** Meewasin Garden Line, Department of Horticulture, University of Saskatchewan, Saskatoon, SK S7N 0W0; 306-966-5855.

Weather and Climate Online

Another source of useful information is Environment Canada. Check out these Web sites for weather and climate information (moving across the country from east to west):

- **Atlantic Province:** www.ns.ec.gc.ca/weather/index_e.html
- **Quebec Region:** www.qc.ec.gc.ca/envcan/indexe.html
- **Ontario Region:** www.cciw.ca/green-lane/or-home.html
- **Prairies and Northern Region:** www.mb.ec.gc.ca/ENGLISH/
- **Pacific and Yukon Region:** www.cciw.ca/green-lane/or-home.html

And if you're concerned about the environment — as most gardeners are — take a look at another great Environment Canada Web site:

Environment Canada's Green Lane: www.ec.gc.ca/

What if you've done some homework but still haven't found an answer? Try one of the many garden information hotlines posted on Canadian Gardening magazine's Web site: http://canadiangardening.com/HTML/cg_info-lines.html. You'll find horticulturists, Master Gardeners and other avid gardeners who are ready to answer your gardening questions. Some hot lines are staffed, others are connected to an answering machine — leave a message and someone will get back to you.

Online articles on particular topics are numerous, and one of the best ways to find them is to go to a Web site with oodles of links. Here are some of the best:

- _Canadian Gardening Online's_ GARDENet, http://canadiangardening. com/GARDENet/gardenet.html. Quick, easy access to a variety of Web sites selected specifically for Canadian gardeners.
- AgriWeb Canada, http://aceis.agr.ca/agriweb/ho.htm A huge list of Web sites that includes plant societies, botanical gardens, nurseries. . . lots of information for Canadian gardeners.
- Dig the Net (Virtual Garden Toolshed), www.digthenet.com. The considerable resources of Time-Life are behind this well-organized site. Individual sites are briefly reviewed.
- Gardening (Miningco), http://gardening.miningco.com/. Unlike most sites that use frames to keep you on their site, Miningco has made it possible to bookmark other Web sites you visit.
- GardenNet, www.gardennet.com/. It's one of the oldest garden Web sites and contains book reviews, gardener roundtables, links to other garden sites, and links to many companies. visit.

- IcanGarden, `www.icangarden.com`. Three lists of links: Gardening with Kids, Gardening — Canadian Sites, and Other Gardening Sites Around the World.

- Internet Directory for Botany: Gardening, `www.helsinki.fi/kmus/bothort.html`. All gardening Web sites are simply lumped under "Gardening," but this listing is still worth a visit. The collection is searchable.

- The Garden Gate, `www.prairienet.org/garden-gate`. One of the few remaining noncommercial directories, The Garden Gate offers gardeners and nature lovers a carefully selected and well-organized collection of links to informative and interesting horticulture sites around the world.

Global search engines like AltaVista, Infoseek, Hotbot, and Lycos can indeed find a needle in a haystack. The problem is that they will find all the needles in all the haystacks in the world. Then, it's up to you to find a needle in a needlestack. In other words, the more general your topic or search term, the more widely occurring it is and the harder it is going to be to zero in on the right information. Try searching for gardening and then for air-layering to see the difference.

Web search engines number in the hundreds, but the following are the largest and most extensive:

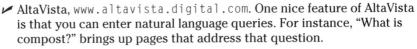

- AltaVista, `www.altavista.digital.com`. One nice feature of AltaVista is that you can enter natural language queries. For instance, "What is compost?" brings up pages that address that question.

- Excite! `www.excite.com`. The results of your search are ranked by relevance, with the most likely page presented first.

- Hotbot, `www.hotbot.com`. A dropdown menu of choices makes it easy to specify whether you are searching for an exact phrase, all, or any of the words you've entered.

- Infoseek, `www.infoseek.com`. An excellent Advanced Search page makes it easy for you to zero in on the information you're seeking.

- Lycos, `www.lycos.com`. In addition to offering a powerful search engine, Lycos also provides a selection of reviewed and rated Web sites covering a number of gardening topics. Look for Gardening under "Home/Family."

- Yahoo! `www.yahoo.ca`. Yahoo!'s searchable directory is organized hierarchically by topic.

Each search engine uses its own unique search syntax. For example, a search for horticulture therapy at AltaVista returns a few hundred sites that discuss this topic, whereas Infoseek returns a list of over one million pages that contain either the word horticulture or the word therapy. Pick two or three search engines and take a little time to read through their online help and learn the syntax for each one. Your searches will be far more efficient if you speak the search language.

Plant information

Even experienced gardeners unwittingly kill plants by choosing the wrong plant and planting it the wrong place. Plant databases offer you something even the best plant book can't: the ability to select the right plants for a particular site based on a variety of criteria. Most databases let you search by a combination of criteria, such as USDA zone, soil type, light and water requirements, and soil pH, as well as flower and foliage colour, blooming period, and special uses such as butterfly gardens or rock gardens. Databases generally provide colour photos or botanical illustrations of plants along with information on their planting and care.

For information on CD-ROM databases that you can use on your own computer, see the section "Gardening Software" in this appendix., All of the following databases are American — unfortunately there are no Canadian — so be aware that where you find hardiness zone information it's based on the USDA system. See Chapter 2 to find out how the Canadian and American zone maps are different.

✔ Garden Encyclopedia, www.sierra.com/sierrahome/gardening/encyc/. An online sampler of the Sierra Garden Encyclopedia. (See later under Gardening Software.)

✔ Houseplant Pavilion (Time-Life), www.pathfinder.com/vg/timelife/houseplants. For help with selection and care of houseplants.

✔ Interactive Plant List (Ohio State University), www.hcs.ohio-state.edu/hort/plantlist.html. Search both the Plant Dictionary and the Factsheet Database for comprehensive information about a particular plant. Includes: annuals, bulbs, grasses, ground covers, perennials, shrubs, trees, and vines.

✔ Plant Dictionary (Ohio State University), www.hcs.ohio-state.edu/hcs/TMI/TR2/pmTOC.html. A searchable database of almost 3,000 high-quality images depicting ornamental plants and accompanying pests and diseases.

✔ Plant Encyclopedia (Time-Life), www.pathfinder.com/cgi-bin/VG/vg. This searchable plant database features the lovely botanical illustrations by Allianora Rosse that have graced the pages of *The Time-Life Encyclopedia of Gardening* through many editions. (When the Time-Life site was first being developed, the Web masters tracked down the original watercolours and saved them in the nick of time from an Indiana warehouse where they were about to be discarded.)

✔ Plant Information Online (University of Minnesota), plantinfo@jaws.umn.edu. This site lists mail-order sources of 60,000 plants, a detailed source information on 1,000 North American nursery and seed catalogs, and an index of 75,000 plant images. Access is to members only, $40 U.S. per individual.

For a more detailed look at finding answers, see The Garden Gate's Gardener's Guide to Finding Answers on the Internet, at `www.prairienet.org/garden-gate/answers.htm` online

Shopping

The true harbinger of spring isn't the robin. The true harbinger of spring is that first mail-order gardening catalogue that always seems to arrive right around the winter solstice, just as the days are beginning to get longer again. The winter solstice may mark the first day of winter, but with the help of that catalogue, the gardener is already thinking spring.

- *Cyndi's Catalog of Catalogs,* `www.cog.brown.edu/gardening/cat.html`. Cyndi's catalogue is organized by topic and comprises a collection of almost 2,000 mail-order sources for just about any gardening interest you can imagine.

- *Garden Escape,* `www.garden.com`. Although this site is very much aimed at selling you things, and it claims to be "the ultimate source for everything gardening". It is worth a visit. If your Web browser is Java-capable, you can try your hand at online garden design.

Many people naturally are concerned about the security of online credit card transactions. Electronic mail offers little security, so it is inadvisable to send credit card information via e-mail. Unless you are on a Web site with a secure server and feel confident that you are dealing with an established, reputable company, do not provide your credit card number or other personal information online. A secure server encrypts transmissions over the Internet, making it safer to send sensitive information. Most new Web browsers can detect when you are on a secure server. Watch for a blue border and a closed lock in the lower left-hand corner. When in doubt, however, do your mail-order shopping the old-fashioned way: via phone or postal mail.

Some Canadian online catalogues you might enjoy browsing include the following:

- Brentwood Bay Nurseries, Victoria, BC `http://www.coastnet.com/ ~plants/`.
- Buds, Toronto, ON `www.budsgarden.com`.
- Devonian Botanic Garden, Edmonton, AB `www.discoveredmonton.com/ Devonian/greenzon.html`.
- Holt Geraniums, Abbotsford, BC `www.holtgeraniums.com`.
- Hortico Nurseries Inc., Wartedown, ON `http://hortico.bigwave.ca/ default.htm`.

- Island Specialty Nursery, Chemainus, BC. www.island.net/~isn/.
- JDS Gardens, Harrow, ON www.jdsgardens.com.
- Living Prairie Museum, Winnipeg, MA www.city.winnipeg.mb.ca/city/parks/envserv/interp/living.html.
- NATS Nursery Ltd., Surrey, BC http://www.nats-nursery.com.
- Richters, Goodwood, ON www.richters.com.
- Salt Spring Seeds, Salt Spring Island, BC www.saltspring.com/ssseeds.
- Siloam Orchards, Uxbridge, ON www.uxbridge.com/siloam.
- South Cove Nursery Ltd., Box 615, Yarmouth, NS www.klis.com/scove.
- Vesey's Seeds Ltd., York, PEI http://itas02.itas.net/veseys.
- V. Kraus Nurseries Ltd., Carlisle, ON http://www.krausnurseries.com.
- West Coast Seeds Ltd., Vancouver, BC www.westcoastseeds.com.

Just browsing

The Web also can be just plain fun, a pleasant entertainment on a chilly winter's afternoon. The following sites offer lots of useful information as well as some enjoyable bells and whistles.

- Gardening at Miningco.com, http://gardening.miningco.com. An informative mix of articles and well-organized collections of links on a wide range of gardening topics.
- Canadian Gardening Online, http://canadiangardening.com. This site — from the publishers of Canada's top gardening magazine — includes a comprehensive list of Canadian gardening catalogues (updated every year in December), seasonal tips, Internet gardening links, and Garden Talk (four online garden forums).
- ICanGarden. http://icangarden.com. A fun Canadian site with lots of pages to visit, including articles by gardening experts, book reviews, plant profiles, gardening news and events, and a Canadian Hardiness Zones Map that you can click on to zoom into your area of Canada
- The Garden Web, www.gardenweb.com. Garden forums, articles, directories of resources, calendar of gardening events.
- Virtual Garden (Time Life), www.pathfinder.com/vg. This site has a lot to offer and it's easy to get lost as you navigate. For an overview, check out the Virtual Garden At a Glance: www.pathfinder.com/vg/ataglance.

Discussion groups

The Internet offers many ways to communicate with your fellow gardeners. Newsgroups are like electronic bulletin boards. Anyone can post a message and anyone can read it.

Newsgroups

The following minitable lists newsgroups that are available to gardeners around the world:

rec.gardens	Gardening, methods, and results
rec.gardens.ecosystems	Ecosystems and organic gardening
rec.gardens.edible	Edible gardening topics
rec.gardens.orchids	Growing, hybridizing, and general care of orchids
rec.gardens.roses	Gardening information related to roses

In the past year or two, many new regional newsgroups have been springing up. You can check for newsgroups for your region at liszt.bluemarble.net/news, Liszt's Usenet Newsgroups Directory.

If you are unfamiliar with newsgroups and how they work, the easiest way to start is to use the newsreader that is part of your Web browser. (Newer versions of Netscape and Microsoft Internet Explorer have a newsreader built in.) Check with your Internet Service Provider (ISP), because you need to enter the name of their news server in your Web browser's setup before you start.

If checking out the discussion on a newsgroup or finding discussions on a given topic interests you, visit the searchable news archives at Deja News, www.dejanews.com. If you have some time on your hands, you can also browse the newsgroups: www.dejanews.com/home_bg.shtml.

Most ISPs carry only a subset of all the newsgroups that are available. If you find a newsgroup that interests you, most ISPs will add an existing newsgroup upon request. Be sure to give the full name of the newsgroup in your request.

Mailing lists

Electronic mailing lists are growing steadily in popularity as a way for groups of like-minded people to discuss topics of mutual interest. Mailing lists come in many flavours: open forums; moderated lists where a moderator approves each post before being distributed to the subscribers; and one-way lists used for announcements and newsletters. A good mailing list can develop into a friendly community with people sharing information on a favorite topic.

Programs called mailing lists managers (MLMs) run electronic mailing lists, which run on the list host. You may encounter different brand names such as listserv, listproc, majordomo, or smartlist. The MLM automatically handles tasks such as distributing messages to subscriber lists and adding and deleting subscribers upon request. Each list has a human list owner. The list owner is responsible for managing the list and providing assistance to list subscribers. The list owner often is the person who has the last word on list policy.

If you aren't already in the habit of checking your e-mail regularly, you may be better off with newsgroups and other online discussion forums. A busy mailing list can pile up unwanted messages in your mailbox pretty quickly.

When you first subscribe to a mailing list, you will receive a welcome message. Save this message for future reference. It will usually give the list's purpose and scope, posting guidelines, and the list owner's address, as well as information on unsubscribing or changing your list setting.

If you prefer to receive list mail as a single larger post, check your welcome file for instructions on how to set your setting to "digest."

Be aware that some lists, especially general-interest ones, can generate very high volume, delivering over a hundred messages a day.

If you are new to mailing lists, check out the Introduction to Mailing Lists (Liszt.com), `www.liszt.com/intro.html`. You'll find lists of mailing lists at the following sites:

- Mailing Lists for Gardeners (The Garden Gate), `www.prairienet.org/garden-gate/maillist.htm`. Choose from a selection of established mailing lists from A for Alpine to W for Woody Plants.
- Publicly Accessible Mailing Lists, `www.neosoft.com/internet/paml/`. Lists are organized alphabetically and by topic. Look for lists under gardening, botany, and horticulture:

  `www.neosoft.com/internet/paml/bysubj-gardening.html`

  `www.neosoft.com/internet/paml/bysubj-botany.html`

  `www.neosoft.com/internet/paml/bysubj-horticulture.html`.
- Liszt, the mailing list directory, `www.liszt.com`.

  New mailing lists come online every day. Liszt offers a searchable database of tens of thousands of lists.

Web forums and live chat

Some live chat sites are open around the clock. Some are open only for specially scheduled chats by gardening experts.

- ✔ GardenWeb Forums, `www.gardenweb.com/forums`. GardenWeb offers dozens of Web-based discussion forums on a wide variety of garden topics.

- ✔ Canadian Gardening Online Garden Talk, `http://canadiangarden-ing.com/forum/forums.shtml`. Four forums to chose from: Garden Design and Techniques, Garden Pests and Diseases, Garden Plants, and Gardening Gear.

- ✔ Compuserve and AOL. If you are a member of AOL or Compuserve, you can take advantage of members-only forums offered by these services. Forums also host chats with gardening experts and celebrities.

- ✔ Live Chat at Miningco.com, `http://gardening.miningco.com/mpchat.htm`.

- ✔ Virtual Garden Chat, `www.pathfinder.com/vg/Info/Chats/`.

New forums and chats are popping up every month. Forum One keeps track of them in a searchable database: `www.forumone.com`.

Gardening Software

The last few years have seen a proliferation of gardening software programs, which fall into three categories:

- ✔ Garden design
- ✔ Plant selection and care
- ✔ Troubleshooting

Be familiar with your computer's configuration, its processor type and speed, hard-disk size, amount of memory, sound and video capability, and CD-ROM drive speed. Always check its configuration against the requirements of a particular software program before you buy to be sure you can run the program you're buying.

Gardening software programs probably number in the hundreds by now. We selected a few programs in each category that are suitable for beginning gardeners.

Garden design software

Design programs naturally are going to be graphical, allowing you to lay out your garden plan. Additional information is available for each of the programs from the company Web sites.

Plant graphics can be the abstract symbols used by landscape architects, more colourful symbols that look more like the plant they represent, or even photographic representations of plants. Both of these are American because — much to our dismay — we couldn't find any great Canadian ones.

✔ **Flowerscape** (Windows, Macintosh), Voudette Software, `www.fscape. com`. Flowerscape is an attractive and easy-to-use program that uses photo-real images of plants. The layout interface is clear and straightforward. You can easily master the program without referring to the documentation. Some satisfied users report that their small children play with it, calling it "the flower game."

The searchable plant database is relatively limited but contains a good selection of plants that you would expect to find at your neighbourhood garden centre. A seasonal feature lets you see how the garden will look through the year, so you can plant a garden with year-round interest! If you have a newer computer, Flowerscape does have a drawback in that it requires you to step down your colour display to 256 colours.

✔ **Complete LandDesigner 5.0** (Windows 95/ 98. Sorry, not for Mac.) from Sierra Online. Phone 800-757-7707 or try `www.sierra.com` on the Internet. You can also write to Havas Interactive, Box 62900, El Dorado Hills, California, 95762. This full-featured program includes 3D Landscape 2.0, Garden Encyclopedia 3.0, Photo LandDesigner 4.5 and 3D Deck. The package costs about $50 U.S., plus $5 shipping and handling. Keep in mind that these programs use the USDA plant hardiness zone numbers. Canadian zone numbers are not the same. See Chapter 2, devoted to Canada's zone system

Plant selection and care

Both of these programs offer searchable plant databases with colour photos of plants and information on their care:

✔ **Garden Companion** (Windows 3.1, Windows 95), Lifestyle Software Group, `www.lifeware.com/catalog`.

✔ **Garden Encyclopedia** (Windows 95), Sierra Online, `www.sierra.com`.

Troubleshooting

One of the keys to good gardening is learning how to nip problems in the bud, so to speak. An excellent resource is Ortho's Home Gardening Problem Solver (Windows 95, with book). The CD-ROM comes with the book but also is sold separately. It's available from www.ortho.com/content/books.

Gardening software is available from a number of sources, as well as direct from the companies via their Web pages. A few reliable mail-order and Internet sources for gardening software include:

- ✔ **PC Connection,** www.pcconnection.com, 800-800-0009.
- ✔ **Computer Discount Warehouse,** www.cdw.com, 800-840-4239.
- ✔ **Amazon.com,** www.amazon.com.
- ✔ **Chapters.ca,** www.chapters.ca.

Appendix B

Mail-Order Resources

• •

*M*ore than any other type of garden literature, seed and nursery catalogues inspire, cajole, inform, enthuse, sell, and, in general overflow with the sometimes singular plant passions of their owners.

Of course those of us lucky enough to live near a home centre or a great garden centre can find just about everything we need to make and keep a garden. And buying locally has one significant virtue: Plants are more likely to be better adapted to your climate. Another plus is that you can return the plant to the nursery if you have problems with it. Even the biggest home store in the biggest city, however, cannot match the variety of plants and products available through the resources below.

Catalogue and online shopping are essential for gardeners who live in remote areas or for those who seek a plant or product that isn't mainstream — and those products include most of the nifty stuff that makes gardens and gardening fun. If you're looking for something special, you'll love the companies in this appendix.

Even though we think most catalogues make great reading, we assembled this descriptive listing so that you can quickly find what you're looking for. First we created categories, such as "Seeds" and "Daylilies and Iris," to narrow choices. We also provide brief descriptions of the company and products, enough hopefully to steer you right toward what you need. Want to make sure to have vegetable varieties adapted to your area? Try Vesey's Seeds Ltd. (Atlantic provinces), Prairie Habitats (Prairie provinces) or Island Specialty Nursery (southwestern B.C.). Or what about organic seeds? Antique varieties of apples? Check out Seeds of Diversity Canada and West Coast Seeds Ltd., or go straight to Les Jardins De La Pèpiniëre Fruitiëre.

Beyond the hundreds of mail-order gardening suppliers that appear in this appendix, still more exist. You can find sources for gardening products (including seeds, bulbs, plants, tools, supplies, and accessories) by visiting Canadian Gardening Online at www.canadiangardening.com.

Note: In the lists that follow, we indicate which suppliers charge a fee to send a catalogue. Most refund the catalogue cost with your first order. If we don't list a fee, then the catalogue is free.

Daylilies & Iris

Ambrosia Gardens, Box 1135, Vernon, BC, V1T 6N4; 250-766-1394; fax same; Web site: http://www.icangarden.com/catalogue/ambrosia.htm. Catalogue $2. Daylilies grown for northern gardens.

Arcadian Daylilies, 72 Hendrick Ave., Toronto, ON, M6G 3S5; 416-657-1444. Catalogue $2, refundable. Modern introductions, older cultivars and species.

Beachwood Daylily and Perennial, 7075-264th St., Aldergrove, BC, V4W 1M6; 604-856-8806; fax 604-856-8747. Catalogue $2. Five hundred varieties of daylilies, including miniatures, doubles, spiders, antiques and exotics.

Borealiris, Box 592, Deschenes Rd., Chelsea, PQ, J0X 1N0; 819-827-2592. Catalogue free. Beardless irises, Siberians 175 varieties (and species versicolours and pseudacorus).

Bramley Gardens, RR 4, Waterford, ON, N0E 1Y0; 519-443-5569. Catalogue $1. Wide variety of tetraploid, miniature, and spider daylilies.

Chuck Chapman Iris, RR 1, 8790 Hwy. 24, Guelph, ON, N1H 6H7; 519-856-4424; fax same. Catalogue $2, refundable. More than 2,000 varieties of bearded iris: miniature, miniature dwarf, standard dwarf, intermediate, border, and tall. Also reblooming spring and fall-and iris with variegated foliage. New introductions each year.

Dunrobin Daylilies, 3098 Ridgetop Rd., RR 2, Dunrobin, ON, K0A 1T0; e-mail: esellers@cyberus.ca. Catalogue $2. New daylily cultivars.

Erikson's Daylily Gardens, 24642 51st Ave., Langley, BC, V2Z 1H9; 604-856-5758; e-mail: pamelal@istar.ca. Catalogue $2. More than 1,300 varieties.

Hemerocallis Montfort, 349 Des Montfortains, Montfort, PQ, J0T 1Y0; 450-227-7684; fax same; e-mail: lagroixl@sympatico.ca. Catalogue $2, refundable. Classics and new varieties, to Zone 4; organically grown.

Iris & Plus, 595 River St., Cowansville, PQ, J2K 3G6; 450-266-0181; fax same. Catalogue $2, refundable. More than 400 bearded iris; also daylilies, hostas, astilbes, peonies and unusual perennials.

Kilmalu Farms Daylily Nursery, 624 Kilmalu Rd., RR 2, Mill Bay, BC, V0R 2P0; 250-743-5446; fax same; e-mail: kilmalu@coastnet.com. Catalogue $2 or four 46¢ stamps. Classics and new introductions, field-grown on Vancouver Island.

McMillen's Iris Garden, RR 1, Norwich, ON, N0J 1P0; 519-468-6508; fax 519-468-3214; e-mail: iris@execulink.com. Catalogue $2, refundable. Iris, including miniature and dwarf bearded, tall bearded and Siberian; hostas and daylilies.

The Potting Shed Garden Emporium, Box 804, Cayuga, ON, N0A 1E0. Catalogue $2, refundable. Daylilies and hostas.

Red Lane Gardens, RR 3, Belfast, PEI, C0A 1A0; 902-659-2478; fax same; Web site: www.peisland.com/day/lilies.htm. Catalogue $2, refundable or download catalogue from Web site. More than 400 daylily cultivars.

Strong's Daylilies, Box 11041, Stoney Creek, ON, L8E 5P9; 905-643-3271; e-mail: mstrong@cgocable.net. Catalogue $2. More than 1,400 varieties of hardy daylilies suitable for northern gardens, including traditional favourites and recent introductions.

Vivaces Nordiques, 2400 Ch. Principal, St-Mathieu du Parc, PQ, G0X 1N0; 819-532-3275; fax 819-532-2727. Catalogue $3. Daylily specialists.

We're in the Hayfield Now Daylily Gardens, 4704 Pollard Rd., RR 1, Orono, ON, L0B 1M0; 905-983-5097; Web site: www.distinctly.on.ca. Catalogue $2. Large-flower tetraploids, miniatures, small-flower diploids and own daylily introductions bred for cold Canadian climates.

Herbs

Belbecks, Box 356, Campbellville, ON, L0P 1B0; 519-822-8419; fax 519-822-1795. Catalogue free. Herb plants and seeds, and dried herbs; topiary, bonsai and wire forms.

Country Lane Herbs and Dried Flowers, RR 3, Puslinch, ON, N0B 2J0; 905-659-7327; e-mail: paul.michaud@sympatico.ca. Free list with business-size SASE. Herb plants, dried herbs, potpourri supplies, dried flowers.

Durand's Nursery, 9 Johnson Rd., Christina Lake, BC, V0H 1E2; 250-447-6299. Catalogue $2, refundable. Organically grown culinary, medicinal and aromatic herbs.

The Herb Farm, RR 4, Norton, NB, E0G 2N0; 506-839-2140. List $2 with SASE. More than 80 herbs, scented geraniums, roses and other plants.

The Herbal Touch, Box 300, 30 Dover St., Otterville, ON, N0J 1R0; 519-879-6812; fax same; Web site: www.theherbaltouch.com. Online catalogue only. Herb seeds, books and gifts for gardeners.

Herbs for All Seasons, 3383 8th Line Rd., RR 3, Metcalfe, ON, K0A 2P0; 888-267-2536; fax 613-821-1168; e-mail: herb4all@magma.ca. Catalogue free. Herb teas, books, supplies, essential oils.

Kettleby Herb Farms, 15495 Weston Rd., RR 2, Kettleby, ON, L0G 1J0; 905-727-8344; fax same; Web site: www.webx.ca/kettleby. Catalogue free. Herb seeds, herbal products and related supplies.

Richters, 357 Hwy. 47, Goodwood, ON, L0C 1A0; 905-640-6677; fax 905-640-6641; Web site: www.richters.com. Catalogue free. More than 800 kinds of herb seeds and plants, including Chinese medicinal herbs, alpine flowers, vegetables, wildflowers; beneficial insects.

River View Herbs, Box 92, Hwy. 215. Maitland, Hants Co., NS, B0N 1T0; 902-261-2274; fax 902-261-2427. Catalogue free. More than 350 kinds of herb plants and seeds; scented geraniums.

Houseplants

The Banana Tree Inc., 715 Northampton St., Easton, Pennsylvania, 18042, U.S.A.; 610-253-9589; fax 610-253-4864; Web site: www.banana-tree.com. Catalogue $3. Seeds for tropical plants, including teas, gingers, bananas, coffees, heliconia, neem, champaca, miracle fruit and chocolate; books.

Clargreen Gardens, 814 Southdown Rd., Mississauga, ON, L5J 2Y4; 905-822-0992; fax 905-822-7282. Catalogue $2, refundable. Exotics, orchids and supplies.

Dusty's Hybrid African Violets, Dept. CG, Box 56538, Woodbridge, ON, L4L 8V3; 905-851-0681. Catalogue two 46¢ stamps. Minis, semi-minis and trailers; some with variegated foliage.

Huronview Nurseries, 6429 Brigden Rd., RR 1, Bright's Grove, ON, N0N 1C0; 519-869-8518; e-mail: jonathonc@wwdc.com. Free list. Orchids, growing supplies.

Marie K. Lowen, 31527 Oakridge Cres., Abbotsford, BC, V2T 6A6; 604-850-9588; fdax same; e-mail: marie_lowen@bc.sympatico.ca. Catalogue $2, refundable. Epiphyllums.

Microclimes, 1054 Centre St., Suite 323, Thornhill, ON, L4J 8E5. Catalogue $2 or four 46¢ stamps with business-size SASE. Exotic seeds for light gardens or windowsills. Alpines, temperate exotics, bonsai, carnivorous plants, cacti and succulents, pelargoniums, and rhododendrons.

Orchid Haven, 900 Rossland Rd. E., Whitby, ON, L1N 5R5; 905-668-8534; fax same; Web site: web.idirect.com/~orchaven. Send 71¢ stamp for list. Orchids.

Orchids In Our Tropics, Box 394, Gormley, ON, L0H 1G0; 905-727-3319; e-mail: ourtropics@ica.net. Free list. Onoidiuminter generics, lycastes, mini cats, and miltonias.

Sally & Co., Box 24121, 300 Eagleson Rd., Kanata, ON, K2M 2C3; 613-836-6216. List with SASE. Seeds of more than 40 varieties of tropical plants, including Japanese pine, pink orchid tree, and orange jessamine.

Violets in Vogue, 9249 Mainwaring Rd., Sidney, BC, V8L 1J9; 250-656-5170; fax 250-656-8190. Catalogue $2. More than 300 varieties of African violets including miniatures, standards, trailers and rare striped chimeras. Also sinningias, streptocarpus, episcias, and other gesneriads.

Lilies

Gratrix Garden Lilies, Box 186, Coldwater, ON, L0K 1E0; 705-835-6032. List with SASE. More than 500 varities of lilies and daylilies.

Greystone Bulb Farm; 676 Regional Rd. 30, RR2; Tillsonberg, ON, N4G 4G7; 519-842-8134; fax 519-842-7579. Free list. More than 200 varieties of lilies: Asiatics, trumpets, Orientals, species, and interdivisional hybrids.

Honeywood Lilies, Box 68, Parkside, SK, S0J 2A0; 306-747-3296. Catalogue $2, refundable. Prairie-hardy lilies, perennials, and peonies.

Horner Lilies, 23505 Valleyview Rd., Thorndale, ON, N0M 2P0; 519-461-0492. Catalogue free. Hybrid lilies and hemerocallis

The Lily Nook, Box 846, Neepawa, MB, R0J 1H0; 204-476-3225. Catalogue $2. Asiatics, tetraploids, martagons, Orientals, and species.

Riverside Gardens, 18 Pony Trail, Riverside Estates, SK, S7T 1A2. Free list. More than 70 varieties of Asiatic lilies; Fred Fellner and Johan Mak hybrids.

Roses

Classic Miniature Roses, Box 2206, Sardis, BC, V2R 1A6; 604-823-4884; fax 604-823-4046. Free list with business-size SASE. More than 130 varieties of miniature roses, including micro-minis, mini-climbers and mini-moss.

The Fragrant Rose Co., RR 1, Site 19-C8, Fanny Bay, BC, V0R 1W0; 888-606-7673; fax 250-335-1135. Catalogue $2, refundable. Importers and distributors of fragrant English-grown roses from R. Harkness & Co. Ltd. of the U.K. Bareroot roses shipped November through March.

Greenbelt Farm, RR 5, Mitchell, ON, N0K 1N0; 519-347-2725; fax same. Catalogue $5. Ninety varieties of roses, woodlot regeneration stock, perennials.

Martin & Kraus, Box 12, 1191 Centre Rd., Carlisle, ON, L0R 1H0; 905-689-0230; fax 905-689-1358; Web site: www.gardenrose.com. Catalogue $1. Hardy roses grown on own roots or on Rosa multiflora understock. Hybrid tea, grandiflora, floribunda, miniature, climbing, David Austin, antique, shrub, Explorer, Parkland, Meidiland, and Pavement roses.

McConnell Nurseries Inc., Box 248, Strathroy, ON, N7G 3J2; 800-363-0901, French 800-461-9445; fax 800-561-1914. Free catalogue. Roses; also bulbs, trees, shrubs, perennials.

Mori Miniatures, Box 772, Virgil, ON, L0S 1T0; 905-468-0315; fax 905-468-7271. Free catalogue. Miniature roses.

Old Rose Nursery, 1020 Central Rd., Hornby Island, BC, V0R 1Z0; 250-335-2603; fax 250-335-2602. Catalogue $2 plus SASE. Own-root, old-fashioned garden roses; also English, ramblers, climbers, rugosas, and Canadian Explorers. Ships to western Canada.

Carl Pallek & Son Nurseries, Box 137, Virgil, ON, L0S 1T0; 905-468-7262; fax 905-468-5246. Free catalogue. Hybrid tea, floribunda, grandiflora, climber, miniature, and old garden roses.

Pickering Nurseries Inc., 670 Kingston Rd., Pickering, ON, L1V 1A6; 905-839-2111. Catalogue $5. More than 900 varieties of antique, rugosa, shrub, climbing, rambler, David Austin, and modern hybrid roses.

Sylvan Roses, 848 Stonybrook Rd., Kelowna, BC, V1W 4P3; 250-764-4517; fax 250-764-0166; e-mail: SylvanRoses@bc.sympatico.ca. Catalogue $3. English and Agriculture Canada roses, all on own roots.

Seeds

Abundant Life Seed Foundation, Box 772, Port Townsend, Washington, 98368 U.S.A.; 360-385-5660; fax 360 385-7455; e-mail: abundant@olypen.com. Catalogue $2 U.S. Non-profit organization. Specializing in open-pollinated, heirloom seeds.

Alberta Nurseries & Seeds Ltd., Box 20, Bowden, AB, T0M 0K0; 403-224-3545; fax 403 224-2455; e-mail: dectool@telusplanet.net. Free catalogue. Flower and vegetable seeds, shrubs, trees, books, garden supplies.

Ken Allan, 61 South Bartlett St., Kingston, ON, K7K 1X3. Catalogue free with SASE. Sweet potato seed-roots; seeds for tall peas, tomatoes, black popcorn, tetraploid watermelons.

Aurora Farm, 3492 Phillips Rd., Creston, BC, V0B 1G2; 250-428-4404; fax same. Web site: www.syberspace.com/aurora. Catalogue $3. Open-pollinated and heirloom herb, flower and vegetable seeds.

Becker's Seed Potatoes, RR 1, Trout Creek, ON, P0H 2L0; 705-724-2305. Catalogue free. Seed potatoes including brown, purple or blue skin, and yellow, blue or white flesh.

Blue Heron Specialty Nursery, 2881 Church Way, RR 2, Mill Bay, BC, V0R 2P0; 250-743-3876; fax same. Catalogue $3. Cultivars of herbaceous perennials, including meconopsis, alpines, and rare plants.

Blueberry Hill, RR 1, Box D, Maynooth, ON, K0L 2S0; 613-338-2535. Free catalogue. Winter-hardy native, half-high and highbush blueberry plants; government-certified strawberry and raspberry plants. All Zone 3 or 4, some Zone 2.

Bluestem Ornamental Grasses, 1949 Fife Rd., Christina Lake, BC, V0H 1E3; 250-447-6363; fax same. Catalogue $2. Ornamental grasses, willows and native-plant seed.

Borealis Wildflowers, RR 2, Heatherton, NS, B0H 1R0; 902-386-2952. Catalogue $1, refundable. Northeastern native wildflowers and ferns.

Boughen Nurseries Valley River Ltd., Box 12, Valley River, MB, R0L 2B0; 204-638-7618; fax 204 638-7172. Free catalogue. Hardy plants for Zones 1, 2, and 3, including roses, perennials, shrubs, trees and fruit trees. Nursery stock field-grown in Zones 2b and 3.

Brentwood Bay Nurseries Ltd., 1395 Benvenuto Ave., Brentwood Bay, BC, V8M 1J5; 250-652-1507; fax 250-652-2761; e-mail: plants@coastnet.com. Each list $2, refundable. Perennials, shrubs, vines, grasses, and roses.

Buds, 107 Hocken Ave., Toronto, ON, M6G 2K1; 416-658-9429; fax 416-658-5104; Web site: www.budsgarden.com. Catalogue $2, refundable. Rare and unusual perennials and bulbs.

The Butchart Gardens Ltd., Box 4010, Victoria, BC, V8X 3X4; 250-652-4422; fax 250-652-1475; e-mail: email@butchartgardens.bc.ca. Free catalogue. Seeds for annuals and perennials, including collections for window boxes, and children's, cottage, and rock gardens.

Leonard W. Butt, Box 109, Huttonville, ON, L0J 1B0; 905-455-8344. Catalogue $1. More than 200 kinds of show-quality gladioli corms; star-of-Bethlehem; gloriosa lilies.

Campbell Craig Delphiniums, 14219 Middlebench Rd., Oyama, BC, V4V 2B9; 250-548-9271. Catalogue free with SASE. Hardy delphinium plants: Clansman series Scottish and New Zealand hand-pollinated crosses.

Campberry Farm, R. D. Campbell, RR 1, Niagara-on-the-Lake, ON, L0S 1J0; 905-262-4927. Catalogue $2 payable to R. D. Campbell. Hardy nut, fruit and Carolinian trees; rare ornamentals.

Canadian Wildflower Society, Box 336, Station F, Toronto, ON, M4Y 2L7. Free brochure; sample of quarterly magazine, $10. Membership includes seed exchange, plant sources, garden tours.

Cardinal Gardens Nursery, 13050 Cardinal St., Mission, BC, V2V 5X4; 604-820-0845. Catalogue $2 refundable. More than 800 varieties of hardy perennials, many to attract bees, butterflies, and hummingbirds.

Chiltern Seeds, Bortree Stile, Ulverston., Cumbria, LA127PB, England; 011-44-229/581137; fax 011-44-229/584549; e-mail: `chilternseeds@com-puserve.com`. Catalogue $4 Cdn. More than 4,000 seeds for unusual perennials, annuals and trees.

Companion Plants, 7247 N. Coolville Ridge, Athens, Ohio, 45701, U.S.A.; 740-592-4643; fax 740 593-3092; Web site: `www.frognet.net/companion_plants/`. Catalogue $3 U.S. Seeds for more than 200 varieties of common and exotic herbs; mushroom kits, including shiitake and oyster.

The Conservancy, 51563 Range Rd. 212A, Sherwood Park, AB, T8G 1B1. Catalogue $2. Seeds for wildflowers, ornamental grasses, trees, shrubs, perennials and annuals.

Copperbush Seeds, Box 61, Port Alberni, BC, V9Y 7M6; 250-724-6241; fax same. Catalogue $1 or two 46¢ stamps. Pacific northwest native plant seeds, trees, shrubs, wildflowers, sedges, rushes.

Corn Hill Nursery Ltd., RR 5, Route 890, Petitcodiac, NB, E0A 2H0; 506-756-3635; fax 506-756-1087. Catalogue $2. Hardy roses, flowering shrubs, fruit trees, vines.

Cottage Trail Gardens, 2507-36th Ave., Vernon, BC, V1T 2V6; 250-558-7791. Catalogue $2. Hardy perennials, geraniums and erodiums.

Country Lane Nursery; 346 Cooper Crt., Oshawa, ON, L1J 6V4; 905-571-0329; fax same. Catalogue free. Bare-root shrubs and evergreens, including spireas, lilacs, cedars, boxwoods and sandcherries.

Crescent Nursery; RR 4, Rockwood, ON, N0B 2K0; 519-856-1000; fax 519-856-2712. Plant list, free; catalogue for Daylily Discounters, $3; Swan Island dahlias, $4; B&D lilies, $3. Perennials, including hostas, hardy geraniums, astilbes, and bearded, Siberian and Japanese iris.

Cruickshank's Inc., 780 Birchmount Rd., Unit 16, Scarborough, ON, M1K 5H4; 800-665-5605; fax 416-750-8522. 3 catalogues yearly; $3/year. Bulbs, irises, poppies, peonies, lilies, gladioli, tuberous begonias and dahlias. Gardening tools and accessories.

Cut & Dried Flower Farm, Box 9, Glencairn, ON, L0M 1K0; 705-424-9319; fax same. Catalogue free. Annuals, perennials and hanging baskets; dried flowers.

Dahlias Galore, RR 1, Legion Site, C-22, Sechelt, BC, V0N 3A0; 604-885-9820; fax 604-885-4841. Free list with business-size SASE. Dahlias and Japanese iris.

William Dam Seeds, Box 8400, Dundas, ON, L9H 6M1; 905-628-6641; fax 905-627-1729; e-mail: willdam@sympatico.ca. Catalogue free. Untreated seeds; more than 800 varieties of vegetables, flowers and herbs.

Devonian Botanic Garden, University of Alberta, Edmonton, AB, T6G 2E1; 403-987-3054; fax 403 987-4141; Web site: www.discoveredmonton.com/Devonian/. Catalogue $3. Open-pollinated seeds collected in the garden from annuals, and herbaceous and woody perennials, herbs, alpines, and native plants.

Howard Dill, RR 1, Windsor, NS, B0N 2T0; 902-798-2728. Catalogue free. Pumpkin seeds, including 'Dill's Atlantic Giant', which produced two pumpkins in 1996 weighing more than 1,000 pounds (454 kilograms) each.

Dominion Seed House, Box 2500, Georgetown, ON, L7G 5L6; orders, 800-784-3037; fax 800-282-5746. Catalogue free. Seeds for new and hard-to-find flowers and vegetable seeds; unusual plants and bulbs; gardening accessories.

Early's Farm and Garden Centre Inc., 2615 Lorne Ave., Saskatoon, SK, S7J 0S5; 306-931-1982; fax 306-931-7110. Catalogue free. Flower and vegetable seeds, garden supplies.

Eco-Source, RR 7, Pembroke, ON, K8A 6W8; 613-735-3002; fax 613-735-7374; e-mail: hmarkussen@msn.com. Catalogue free with SASE. Seeds for conifers and hardwoods; also seed kits.

Far North Gardens, Box 126, New Hudson, Michigan, 48165-0126, U.S.A.; 248-486-4203. Catalogue $2 U.S. Rare seeds and wildflowers.

Farm Gate Seed Potatoes, Box 123, Summerside, PEI, C1N 4P6; 902-436-0407; fax 902-436-6588; Web site: www.peiseedpotato.com. Catalogue free. New and traditional varieties of PEI seed potatoes.

Ferncliff Gardens, 8394 McTaggart St., Mission, BC, V2V 6S6; 604-826-2447; fax 604-826-4316. Catalogue $3, refundable. More than 200 dahlias; also irises, peonies, daylilies.

Fish Lake Garlic Man, RR 2, Demorestville, ON, K0K 1W0; 613-476-8030. Catalogue $3 with SASE. Organically grown garlic seeds and bulbs.

Florabunda Seeds, Box 3, Indian River, ON, K0L 2B0. Catalogue $2, refundable. Untreated seeds for heirloom and unusual flowers, wildflowers, ancient medicinal herbs; gothic black flower collection, and fragrant and white flowers. Some organically grown.

Forest View Gardens, 32414 Feeder Rd. N., Wainfleet, ON, L0S 1V0; 905-899-0293. Catalogue $3, refundable. Ferns, perennials, grasses, groundcovers, herbs, vines and wildflowers.

Fragrant Flora, 3741 Sunshine Coast Hwy., RR 5, Site 21, C-11, Gibsons, BC, V0N 1V0; 604-885-6142; fax same; e-mail: fragrant_flora@sunshine.net. Catalogue $3. Fragrant, butterfly and hummingbird plants including lilacs, magnolias, lavenders, buddleias, honeysuckles, grapes, dianthus, meconopsis, nepetas, penstemons, salvias, and violets.

Fraser's Thimble Farms, 175 Arbutus Rd., Salt Spring Island, BC, V8K 1A3; 250-537-5788; fax same. Catalogue $3; fall bulb list $2. Pacific northwest natives, ferns, hardy orchids, erythronums, trilliums, hostas, corydalis, and rare plants and bulbs.

Gardenimport Inc., Box 760, Thornhill, ON, L3T 4A5; 905-731-1950; fax 905-881-3499. Catalogue $5/2 years 4 issues, refundable. Unusual perennials, flowering shrubs, David Austin roses, Evison clematis, hostas, summer flowering bulbs, Sutton seeds.

Garden of Eden Tree Farm, Box 20, Eden, ON, N0J 1H0; 519-866-5269. Catalogue free. Native and Carolinian trees.

The Garden Path Nursery, RR 4, Renfrew, ON, K7V 3Z7; fax 613-433-9889; Web site: www.seedcatalog.com. Catalogue $2, refundable. Seeds for unusual shade perennials and annuals.

Gardens North, 5984 Third Line Rd. N., North Gower, ON, K0A 2T0; 613-489-0065; fax 613-489-1208; e-mail: garnorth@istar.ca. Catalogue $4. More than 1,300 species of rare perennial and woody seed for northern gardens; including natives, exotics, alpines, climbers, ornamental grasses, trees and shrubs.

Gaze Seed Co. 1987-Ltd., 9 Buchanan St., Box 640, St. John's, NF, A1C 5K8; 709-722-4590; fax 709-722-9945. Catalogue $2. Seeds, trees, garden and pet supplies.

Golden Bough Tree Farm, Box 99, Marlbank, ON, K0K 2L0. Catalogue $2/2 years. Shade, flowering, fruit and nut trees; winter-hardy, exotic evergreens.

Gottard Nursery, RR 2, Dalkeith, ON, K0B 1E0; 613-874-2662. Catalogue, send two 46¢ stamps. Coniferous and deciduous trees and shrubs hardy to Zone 5, including nuts, fruit, and unusual plants.

The Gourmet Gardener, 8650 College Blvd., Suite 205CG, Overland Park, Kansas, 66210, U.S.A.; 913-345-0490; fax 913-451-2443; Web site: www.gourmet-gardener.com. Catalogue free. Seeds for more than 200 varieties of hard-to-find herbs, vegetables and edible flowers.

Grimo Nut Nursery, 979 Lakeshore Rd., RR 3, Niagara-on-the-Lake, ON, L0S 1J0; 905-934-6887; fax 905-934-9463; Web site: www.grimonut.com. Catalogue, send two 46¢ stamps or $1. Fifteen kinds of grafted, hardy edible nut trees, seedlings, minor fruits.

Groen's Nursery Ltd., 1512 Brock Rd., Dundas, ON, L9H 5E4; 905-659-7072; fax 905-659-3294; Web site: www.groens-nursery.on.ca. Catalogue free. Growers of ornamental and native trees and shrubs; available in containers, plugs and as bare roots.

Halifax Seed Co. Inc., Box 8026, 5860 Kane St., Halifax, NS, B3K 5L8; 902-454-7456; also Box 2021, 664 Rothesay Ave., Saint John, NB, E2L 3T5, 506-633-2032; e-mail: hfxseed@ns.sympatico.ca. Catalogue free. Flower, herb and vegetable seeds; bulbs, roses, perennials; seed-starter kits, fertilizers, tools and pest-control products.

The Heather Farm, Box 2206, Sardis, BC, V2R 1A6; 604-823-4884. Catalogue free with business-size SASE. More than 200 varieties of heaths and heathers.

Heirloom Seeds, Box 245, W. Elizabeth, Pennsylvania, 15088-0245, U.S.A.; Web site: www.heirloomseeds.com. Catalogue $1 U.S, refundable. Old-fashioned, open-pollinated, untreated vegetable and flower seeds.

Heronswood Nursery Ltd., 7530 NE 288th St., Kingston, Washington, 98346-9502, U.S.A.; 360-297-4172; fax 360-297-3321; Catalogue $5 U.S. New and hard-to-find conifers, shrubs, trees, vines, perennials and grasses.

Hole's Greenhouses and Gardens Ltd., 101 Bellerose Dr., St. Albert, AB, T8N 8N8; 888-884-6537; fax 403-459-6042. Catalogue free. Perennials, annuals, roses, seeds, fruit and shade trees, garden accessories.

Holt Geraniums, 34465 Hallert Rd., Abbotsford, BC, V3G 1R3; Web site: www.holtgeraniums.com. Catalogue $2. More than 700 varieties of pelargoniums: stellars, angels, regals, tri-colour zonals, gold leaf, silver leaf, dwarf, miniature, ivy leaf, scented leaf, frutetorum hybrids, uniques.

Hortico Inc., 723 Robson Rd., RR 1, Waterdown, ON, L0R 2H1; 905-689-9323; fax 905-689-6566. Each catalogue, $3. Perennials, roses and shrubs.

J. L. Hudson, Seedsman, Box 1058, Redwood City, California, 94064, U.S.A. Catalogue $1 U.S. Rare seeds.

Humber Nurseries Ltd. & Butterfly Conservatory, RR 8, Brampton, ON, L6T 3Y7; 416-798-8733; fax 905-794-1311; Web site: www.gardencentre.com. Catalogue $5, refundable with orders over $20. Rare plants, including 3,200 varieties of perennials, ornamental grasses, hostas, bamboos, aquatics and ferns.

Ed Hume Seeds, Inc., Box 1450, Kent, Washington, 98035, U.S.A.; fax 253-859-0694; Web site: www.HumeSeeds.com. Catalogue $2 US. Vegetable, herb and flower seeds for short-season climates.

Inner Coast Nursery, Box 115, Mansons Landing, Cortes Island, BC, V0P 1K0; 250-935-6384; fax same. Catalogue $5. More than 300 varieties of organically grown heritage or unusual fruit trees on rootstock suitable for West Coast.

Island Specialty Nursery, 8797 Chemainus Rd., RR 1, Chemainus, BC, V0R 1K0; 250-246-9355; fax 250-246-4528; Web site: www.island.net/~isn/index.html. e-mail: isn@island.net. Catalogue $2.25 in stamps. Unusual trees, shrubs and perennials.

Jardin Marisol, Marisol St., Bromont, PQ, J2L 2K7; 450-534-4515; fax same. Catalogue $2. 60 varieties of wildflower seeds; seed mixes.

Les Jardins De La Pèpinière Fruitière, 680 10 rang N., St-Pierre-Baptiste, PQ, G0P 1K0; 418-453-2998. Catalogue $2. Organically grown hardy fruit trees (apple scab-free and heritage varieties), pears, plums, cherries; berry plants.

JDS Gardens, RR 4, 2277 County Rd. 20, Harrow, ON, N0R 1G0; 519-738-9513; fax 519-738-3539; Web site: www.jdsgardens.com. Catalogue $2, refundable. More than 750 perennials.

Johnny's Selected Seeds, Foss Hill Rd. RR 1, Box 2580, Albion, Maine, 04910, U.S.A.; orders 207-437-4301; fax 207-437-2165; Web site: www.johnnyseeds.com. Catalogue free. More than 900 varieties of seeds for vegetables, flowers and herbs; gardening accessories.

Limestone Creek, RR 1, Campbellville, ON, L0P 1B0; 905-854-2914; fax 905-854-3363. Catalogue $2. Seeds, seed mixes and plants for woodland, prairie, meadow and wetland habitats. Ship only to Ontario.

Lindenberg Seeds Ltd., 803 Princess Ave. Brandon, MB, R7A 0P5; 204-727-0575; fax 204-727-2832. Catalogue free. Flower and vegetable seeds, and perennials and bulbs for the prairies.

Little Otter Tree Farm, RR 6, Tillsonburg, ON, N4G 4G9; 519-842-2419; fax same. Catalogue free. Woodlot regeneration and Carolinian species.

Living Prairie Museum, 2795 Ness Ave., Winnipeg, MB, R3J 3S4; 204-832-0167; fax 204-986-4172; Web site: www.city.winnipeg.mb.ca/city/parks/ envserv/interp/living.html. Catalogue $1. Native wildflower and grass seeds.

Loon Designs, RR 1, Uxbridge, ON, L9P 1R1; 905-852-5455; fax same; e-mail: expressod@interhop.net. Catalogue $4, refundable. Old and new perennials, some rare.

Lost Horizons Perennials, RR 1, Acton, ON, L7J 2L7; 519-853-3085; fax 519-853-2279; Web site: www.eridani.com/losthorizons. Catalogue $3, refundable. Alpine and rock garden plants, species iris, hostas and shade plants.

La Maison Des Fleurs Vivaces, 807 Boul. Sauvè C.P. 268, St. Eustache, PQ, J7R 4K6; 450-472-8400; fax 450-472-7207. Catalogue $15, refundable. Perennials.

Mapple Farm, RR 1, Hillsborough, NB, E0A 1X0; 506-734-3361; e-mail: wingate@nbnet.nb.ca. Catalogue free with SASE. Certified organic sweet potato slips, French shallots, Egyptian and potato onions, Chinese and Jerusalem artichokes, chufa nuts, early tomato, Indian tomatillo, and horseradish. Plus IRT mulching film.

McFayden Seed Co. Ltd., 30 9th St., Suite 200, Brandon, MB, R7A 6N4; 800-205-7111; fax 204-725-1888. Catalogue free. Seeds, hardy perennials, bulbs, roses, trees, shrubs and garden products.

Marc Meloche Native Plants, 2567 rang St-Jacques, St-Jacques, PQ, J0K 2R0; 450-839-3527; fax 450-839-2291. Catalogue $2. Seeds and plants of North American natives; wild species from Europe and Asia.

Mason Hogue Gardens, 3520 Durham Rd. 1 Brock Rd.), RR 4, Uxbridge, ON, L9P 1R4. Catalogue $2. Perennials including hardy geraniums, drought-tolerant plants, unusual container plants.

Nature's Garden Seed Co., Box 32105, 3749 Shelbourne St., Victoria, BC, V8P 5S2; 250-595-2062; fax same; e-mail: naturesgarden@bc.sympatico.ca. Catalogue free. Native plant and tree seeds; seeds for herb/salsa gardens; children's vegetable gardening book.

Nettlecreek Nursery, 1759 Hollow Rd., Fonthill, ON, L0S 1E6; 905-892-6893; fax 905-892-8529. Catalogue free. Kalmia, rhododendrons, azaleas.

New Meadows Wildflower Seeds, 38 Katherine Cr., Kitchener, ON, N2M 2K1; 519-576-5956. Catalogue $3, refundable. Native prairie, wildflowers for wetlands and woodlands, and grass and sedge seed to attract birds and butterflies.

Northcott Gardens, 154 Centennial Park Rd., Argyle, ON, K0M 2T0; 705-439-2588; fax 705-439-1416. Catalogue $2. Exotic bulbs, plants and seeds including allium, eremurus, fritillaria, species lilies, peonies, hostas, and seeds for cut flowers.

Northern Oasis Tropical Seeds and Plants, 445 Selsey Dr., Mississauga, ON, L5A 1B7; 905-897-6816; e-mail: jrichter@worldchat.com. Catalogue $1. Tropical, subtropical and native flowering/fruiting trees and shrubs; propagating and irrigation supplies.

Oh Deer *@$#! Perennials, Herbs and Ground Covers, Box 1815C, Grand Forks, BC, V0H 1H0; e-mail: pulpfictions@bc.sympatico.ca. Catalogue $2 refundable. Deer-resistant perennials; dye plants.

Old English Perennials, RR 3, Saltsprings, NS, B0K 1P0. Catalogue $2/2 years. Rare perennial plants and seeds.

Ontario Seed Co. Ltd., Box 7, 330 Phillip St., Waterloo, ON, N2J 3Z6; 519-886-0557; fax 519-886-0605. Catalogue free. Flower and vegetable seeds; most untreated.

P. & J. Greenhouse, 20265-82 Ave., Langley, BC, V2Y 2A9; 604-888-3274; fax same. Catalogue $2, refundable. More than 1,000 varieties of geraniums, new and old, and other plants.

Park Seed Company, 1 Parkton Ave., Greenwood, South Carolina, 29647-0001, U.S.A.; 800-845-3369; Web site: www.parkseed.com. Catalogue free. More than 2,000 varieties of flower and vegetable seeds.

Peek's Perennials, Box 6443, Edson, AB, T7E 1T8; 403-723-5701; fax 403-723-5781. Catalogue $2, refundable. Hardy perennials including unusual varieties for Zones 1 to 4.

The Pepper Gal, Box 23006, Ft. Lauderdale, Florida, 33307-3006, U.S.A.; 954-537-5540; fax 954-566-2208. Catalogue $1 U.S. More than 250 varieties of seeds for hot, sweet and ornamental peppers.

P.K. Growers, 22646 48th Ave., Langley, BC, V2Z 2T6; 604-530-2035; fax 604-530-2022; e-mail: pfitness@uniserve.com. Catalogue $2 refundable. Fuchsias including trailers, uprights, species and hardies; pelargoniums including regals, angels, stellars and scenteds.

The Plant Farm, 177 Vesuvius Bay Rd., Salt Spring Island, BC, V8K 1K3; 250-537-5995; fax same. Catalogue $3/2 years. Bamboos, hostas, roses, rhododendrons (including hardy Finnish), heathers, ornamental grasses, beardless iris, deciduous azaleas, daylilies and other exotica; water plants and liners also available.

Prairie Habitats, Box 1, Argyle, MB, R0C 0B0; 204-467-9371; Web site: www.prairiehabitats.com. Catalogue $2. Native Manitoba grasses and wildflower seeds; books on edible and medicinal wild plants, wildflower identification, folklore, conservation, and native plant landscaping.

The Pure Seed Company, Mail Bag 6227, Fort St. John, BC, V1J 4H7; 250-774-1029; fax same; e-mail: john-austin@ima.connections.com. Catalogue free. Vigorous disease-free seed potatoes; 18 varieties, certified organic.

Rainbow Tropicals, 377 Burnhamthorpe Rd. E., Unit 39, Box 29572, Mississauga, ON, L5A 3Y0. List $1. Australian native plant seeds, eucalyptus trees, bottlebrush.

Rainforest Gardens, 13139-224th St., Maple Ridge, BC, V4R 2P6; 604-467-4218; fax 604-467-3181. Catalogue $4/2 years. Spring catalogue: hostas, geraniums, primulas, ferns, ornamental grasses, astilbe and unusual perennials. Fall catalogue: daylilies, iris, bulbs and other perennials.

Rainforest Mushroom Spawn, Box 1793, Gibsons, BC, V0N 1V0; 604-886-7799. Catalogue $2, refundable. Morels, enokitake, shaggy mane and shiitake; books.

Rawlinson Garden Seed, 269 College Rd., Truro, NS, B2N 2P6; 902-893-3051; fax 902-897-7303. Catalogue free. Untreated vegetable, herb, flower and cover-crop seeds.

The Redwood City Seed Company, Box 361, Redwood City, California, 94064, U.S.A.; Web site: www.ecoseeds.com. Catalogue free. Ancient varieties of vegetables, and culinary and medicinal herbs.

Rhora's Nut Farm & Nursery, RR 1, 32983 Wills Rd., Wainsfleet, ON, L0S 1V0; 905-899-3508; fax same. Catalogue $2 refundable. Hardy edible-nut trees, including pines; minor fruits, such as paw paw and persimmon; rare ornamental trees.

Rockwood Forest Nurseries, RR 1, Cameron, ON, K0M 1G0; 705-374-4700; fax same. Catalogue free. Shade trees, evergreens including broadleaf; flowering shrubs; perennials. Ship only to Ontario and Newfoundland.

Rothwell Seeds International, Box 511, Lindsay, ON, K9V 4S5; 888-768-4935; fax 705-324-0882; Web site: www.rothwellseeds.com. Catalogue free. Lawn seed, wildflower mixture, reclamation grasses, crown vetch, certified Kentucky bluegrass and perennial rye grass varieties.

Salt Spring Seeds, Box 444, Ganges P.O., Salt Spring Island, BC, V8K 2W1; 250-537-5269; Web site: www.saltspring.com/ssseeds. Catalogue $2. Beans, grains, tomatoes, lettuce, garlic, amaranth, quinoa; all certified organic.

Saskaberia Nursery, Box 26, Prairie River, SK, S0E 1J0; 306-889-4227. Catalogue 46¢ stamps. Hardy clematis, featuring own introductions; tomato seeds, some heirloom and short-season varieties.

The Saskatoon Farm, RR 1, Dewinton, AB, T0L 0X0; 403-938-6245; fax same; Web site: www.saskatoonfarm.com. Catalogue free. Saskatoon seedlings, native prairie trees.

Scents of Time Gardens Co. Ltd., 204-11948 207th St., Maple Ridge, BC, V2X 1X7. Catalogue $10. Seeds for herbs, vegetables and flowers, including old-fashioned sweet peas; from ancient to Victorian times.

Seed Dreams, Box 1476, Santa Cruz, California, 95061-1476, U.S.A.; 408-458-9252. Catalogue free. Open-pollinated, organic, untreated heirloom vegetable and grain seeds; many native American.

Seeds of Diversity Canada, Box 36, Station Q, Toronto, ON, M4T 2L7. Magazine three times per year and annual seed listing with $25 membership. Seed exchange for heirloom, rare and non-hybrid vegetables, fruits, flowers, grains and herbs.

Select Plus International Nursery, 1510 Pine Rd., Mascouche, PQ, J7L 2M4; 450-477-3797; fax same; e-mail: lilacs@axess.com. Catalogue $2, refundable. Three hundred varieties of lilacs, hardy roses and rare plants.

Select Seedling Nursery, Box 1A, RR 3, Saskatoon, SK, S7K 3J6; 800-806-7577; fax 306-384-1747; Web site: www.interspin.com/berry. Catalogue $1. Saskatoon berry seedlings; small fruits and plants for shelterbelts.

Select Seeds - Antique Flowers; 180 Stickney Hill Rd.; Union, Connecticut, 06076, U.S.A.; 860-684-9310; fax 860-684-9224; Web site: www.selectseeds.com. Catalogue $2 U.S. money order. Seeds for more than 225 fragrant old-fashioned annuals and perennials, including vines, heirloom sweet peas, everlastings.

Sherry's Perennials, Box 39-Z, Cedar Springs, ON, N0P 1E0; 519-676-4541; fax 519-676-7412. Catalogue $4/2 years. Perennials, including many shade-tolerant and long-blooming varieties.

Silk Purse Farm Perennials, RR 4 Peabody, Chesley, ON, N0G 1L0; 519-363-3055; Web site: silkpursefarm.on.ca. Catalogue $1. Hardy, drought-tolerant, shade-loving and low-maintenance perennials, including hostas, geraniums and campanulas; woodland and alpine plants.

Siloam Orchards, RR 1, 7300 3rd Concession, Uxbridge, ON, L9P 1R1; 905-852-9418; fax 905-852-3182; Web site: www.uxbridge.com/siloam. Catalogue $2, refundable. Heritage, disease-resistant fruit trees, including hardy apple, plum, pear, peach and cherry; small fruits including gooseberries, cherry plums, blueberries, and red, white and black currant; asparagus and horseradish.

Skinner's Nursery, Box 220, Roblin, MB, R0L 1P0; 204-564-2336; fax 204-564-2324. Catalogue $2, refundable. Hardy trees and shrubs from an 80-year-old testing and development program in Zone 2.

South Cove Nursery Ltd., Box 615, Yarmouth, NS, B5A 4B6; 902-742-3406; fax 902-742-8260; Web site: www.klis.com/scove/. Catalogue $2. Perennials including groundcovers and herbs.

Spillner's Seedhouse, Box 22035, Halifax, NS, B3L 4T7; 902-477-3017; fax 902-477-3003; e-mail: dieter.spillner@ns.sympatico.ca. Catalogue free. Seeds for perennials, shrubs and trees, including maple, birch, dogwood, flowering quince, smokebush, cotoneaster, hawthorn, white ash, spruce, pine, balsam fir, eastern cedar, elm and snowball.

Spruce Croft Native Plants, 4181 McKee Rd., RR 1, Blackstock, ON, L0B 1B0; 905-986-0276; fax same. Catalogue $3 refundable. Native plants, wildflowers and others that attract, feed and shelter wildlife; shrubs, trees, seeds, perennials for woodlands, prairies and wetlands.

Stirling Perennials, RR 1, Dept. CG, Morpeth, ON, N0P 1X0; 519-674-0571; fax same. Catalogue free. Hardy perennials and rock garden plants including geraniums, hostas, daylilies, low-growing phlox and veronicas.

Stokes Seeds Ltd., 39 James St., Box 10, St. Catharines, ON, L2R 6R6; 905-688-4300; fax 888-834-3334; Web site: www.stokeseeds.com. Catalogue free. Flower, herb and vegetable seeds.

Sunstar Nurseries Ltd., RR 6, Site 6, Box 17, 810-167 Ave. NE, Edmonton, AB, T5B 4K3; 403-472-6103; fax 403-472-9218; e-mail: sunstar@netcom.ca. Catalogue free. Prairie-hardy trees, shrubs, evergreens, perennials, fruits, climbers and shelter-belt plants.

Suttell's Dahlias, 5543 Blezard Dr., Beamsville, ON, L0R 1B3. List with 46¢ stamp. Exhibition dahlias — giants to pompoms and own introductions.

Terra Edibles, Box 164, Foxboro, ON, K0K 2B0; 613-968-8238; fax 613-968-6369; e-mail: kdwright@intranet.ca. Catalogue free. Organically grown vegetable, herb and flower seeds, specializing in rare and heirloom varieties.

Thompson & Morgan Inc., Dept. PR99, Box 1308, Jackson, NJ, 08527, U.S.A.; 800-274-7333; fax 888-466-4769. Catalogue free. Seeds for hundreds of common and hard-to-find annuals and perennials.

Tregunno Seeds, 126 Catharine St. N., Hamilton, ON, L8R 1J4; 905-528-5984; fax 905-528-1635. Catalogue free. Herb, flower and vegetable seeds; bulbs, lawn and bird seed; books.

Tropic To Tropic Plants, 1170 53A St. S., Delta, BC, V4M 3E3; 604-943-6562; fax 604-948-1996. Catalogue $3, refundable. More than 100 exotic varieties for Zone 8; also bamboos, eucalyptus, flowering ginger, bananas, cannas, passionfruit, vines and silk trees.

Van Dongens Landscaping & Nurseries Ltd., 6750 Trafalgar Rd., Hornby, ON, L0P 1E0; 905-821-1281; fax 905-875-2060. List $2, refundable. More than 1,500 varieties of nursery stock including large sizes for instant shade and privacy.

Vesey's Seeds Ltd., York, Box 9000, Charlottetown, PEI, C1A 8K6; 800-363-7333; fax 902-566-1620; Web site: www.veseys.com. Catalogue free. Vegetable, herb and flower seeds for short seasons.

West Coast Seeds Ltd., 206-8475 Ontario St., Vancouver, BC, V5X 3E8; 604-482-8800; fax 604-482-8822; Web site: www.westcoastseeds.com. Catalogue free. Vegetable, herb and flower seeds, including European, Oriental and heritage varieties.

Western Biologicals Ltd., Box 283, Aldergrove, BC, V4W 2T8; 800-363-7333; Web site: www.catscan.com/western/western.html. Catalogue $3. Mushroom spawn and rare or medicinal herbs, including stevia.

Whitegate Farm Nursery, 3700 Kingburn Rd., RR 1, Cobble Hill, BC, V0R 1L0; 250-743-7106; fax same (call first). Catalogue SASE with 92¢ postage. Perennials, shrubs and bulbs noted for fragrance, architectural value and garden performance.

Whitehouse Perennials, RR 2, Almonte, ON, K0A 1A0; 613-256-3406; fax 613-256-6827; e-mail: jpatry@igs.net. Catalogue $3, refundable. More than 200 varieties of daylilies, 100 varieties of Siberian iris, peonies, astilbe, and 160 varieties of hostas; Ladbrooke soil blockers.

Wildflower Farm, RR 3, Schomberg, ON, L0G 1T0; 888-476-7303; Web site: www.wildflowerfarm.com. Catalogue free. More than 100 species of native North American wildflowers and grasses, some for butterfly gardens.

Windover Nurseries Inc., 3662 Petrolia Line, RR 4, Petrolia, ON, N0N 1R0; 519-882-0120; fax 519-882-3886. Catalogue $2, refundable. Roses, perennials, shrubs, vines and trees, especially native and Carolinian species.

Woodwinds Nursery, Box 21-13, Bluevale, ON, N0G 1G0; 519-335-3749. Catalogue $2. Custom-grafted apple and pear trees; rare, old-fashioned, hard cider and hardy varieties.

Wrightman Alpines, RR 3, Kerwood, ON, N0M 2B0; 519-247-3751. Catalogue $2. Alpine and rock garden plants as well as tufa plantings.

Tools, Books, and So On

Abbey Garden, Indian Hill Rd., RR 1, Pakenham, ON, K0A 2X0; 613-256-3973. Catalogue $1, refundable. Solid bronze, hand-cast sundials designed in Britain.

Amaranth Stoneware Ltd., Box 266, Kingston, ON, K7L 4V8; 800-465-5444. Free catalogue with SASE. Natural stoneware garden markers hand-crafted in Kingston; more than 100 herb, perennial and theme names. Also plaques, pot markers, vinegar labels, herb-drying hangers, garden angels, saints, aromatherapy diffusers and foot scrubbers.

Arbour Recycled Products, 800 Bank St., Ottawa, ON, K1S 3V8; 613-567-3168; fax 613-567-3568; Web site: www.arbour.on.ca. Online catalogue only. Rain barrels, red worms, vermicomposting kits, books, solar lights.

Atlantic Hydroponics & Greenhouses Inc., Box 807, Moncton, NB, E1C 8N6; 506-858-0158; fax 506-855-0164; e-mail: ALPHYDRO@nbnet.nb.ca. Catalogue $2. Greenhouse supplies and organic hydroponic products.

Berry Hill Ltd., 75 Burwell Rd., Box A, St. Thomas, ON, N5P 3R5; 800-668-3072; fax 519-631-8935; Web site: www.berryhill.on.ca. Free catalogue. Garden equipment, country-kitchen equipment, decorations and hobby-farm supplies.

Bowker & Scudds for Gardeners, 46 McRae St., Okotoks, AB, T0L 1T0; 888-938-1161; fax 403-938-0068. Free catalogue. Garden gifts.

Brite Lite, 1991 Francis Hughes, Laval, PQ, H7S 2G2; 800-489-2215; fax 514-669-9772; Web site: www.brite-lite-hydroponix.com. Free catalogue. Indoor gardening equipment: lights, hydroponics, nutrients; books.

Cambridge Metalsmiths, 347 Lynden Rd., Lynden, ON, L0R 1T0; 519-647-3326; fax same. Catalogue $3, refundable. Personalized cast-aluminum signs, brackets and poles for home, cottage and business.

Courtyard Creations, 7-841 Sydney St., Ste. 167, Cornwall, ON, K6H 3J7; 888-327-1130; fax 613-933-1987. Catalogue $3, refundable. Garden signs made of handcast stone; decorative garden stones. Products made in Canada.

Ferme et Centre de Preservation, Bruno Messier, 15 rue Chenier, Lac aux Oiseau, Gore, PQ, J0V 1K0. Free catalogue with SASE. Ducks, geese, swans shipped for weeding, pond clean-ups, and slug, snail and insect control in the garden.

Frank's Magic Crops Inc., 480 Guelph Line, Burlington, ON, L7R 3M1; 800-668-0980; fax 905-639-9190; Web site: www.lara.on.ca/~fmci. Free catalogue. Hydroponic growing and lighting systems made in Canada for vegetables and flowers.

Garden Possabilities Bookstore, 1065 Davis Dr., Newmarket, ON, L3Y 2R9; 905-830-9693; fax 905-830-0996. Free catalogue. Books for gardeners, amateur to professional. Seasonal catalogue/newsletter.

Garden Room Books, 2097 Yonge St., Toronto, ON, M4S 2A4; 416-932-8318; fax 416-489-7933. Free list of 150 to 200 books; $3, list of used and rare books. New, used and rare books on horticulture.

Gardenscape Ltd., 2255b Queen St. E., Box 358, Toronto, ON, M4E 1G3; 888-472-3266; fax 416-698-9068; Web site: www.gardenscape.on.ca. Free catalogue. Garden tools and accessories by Haws, Felcos, Fiskars, Dramm and others.

Gardens Past, 22 King St. E., Cobourg, ON, K9A 1K7; 905-372-5847; fax same. Catalogue with SASE. Gear for gardeners, includes gloves, tools, books and zinc plant markers.

International Irrigation Systems, Box 1133, St. Catharines, ON, L2R 7A3; 905-688-4090; fax 905-688-4093; Web site: www.irrigro.com. Free catalogue. Drip irrigation systems for home gardeners and commercial growers; growth accelerator/protector tubes for saplings and grapevines.

Iron Age Originals, 9 Grenville Cres., Kingston, ON, K7M 3A9; 613-549-6608; fax same; e-mail: ironage@kos.net. Catalogue $2. Designer garden structures, obelisks and sculptures.

Jacobs Greenhouse Mfg. Ltd., 371 Talbot Rd., Delhi, ON, N4B 2A1; 519-582-2880; fax 519-582-4117; Web site: www.jacobsgreenhouse.com. Free catalogue. Free-standing and lean-to greenhouses and atriums.

Lee Valley Tools Ltd., 1090 Morrison Dr., Ottawa, ON, K2H 1C2; 800-267-8767; fax 800-668-1807; Web site: www.leevalley.com/; e-mail: customerservice@leevalley.com. Free catalogue. Hundreds of unusual tools and work-saving products imported from around the world.

Limestone Trail Company Ltd., 4290 Bartlett Rd., Beamsville, ON, L0R 1B1; 905-563-8133; fax 905-563-7526; Web site: www.limestonetrail.com. Free catalogue. Manufacturer of gazebos, garden sheds and cabanas.

Linden House Gardening Books, 148 Sylvan Ave., Scarborough, ON, M1M 1K4; 416-269-0699; fax 416-269-0615; Web site: www.icangarden.com/linden.htm. Free catalogue. Books on gardening, landscaping and horticulture.

Martin House Garden Pottery, 299 Penetanguishene Rd., Barrie, ON, L4M 4Y8; 705-722-6535; fax same. Catalogue $3, refundable. Metal obelisks, topiary forms, sculptural furniture and terra cotta planters.

Natural Insect Control, RR 2, Stevensville, ON, L0S 1S0; 905-382-2904; fax 905-382-4418; Web site: www.natural-insect-control.com. Free catalogue. Non-toxic insect controls, including ladybugs; drinking-water systems.

The Kentish Man, 66 Peach Willoway, Willowdale, ON, M2J 2B6; 416-499-4725; fax 416-502-1265. Free catalogue. Sussex trug baskets made of willow and sweet chestnut.

Randall Prue, Box 545, N.D.G., Montreal, PQ, H4A 3P8; 514-984-4385; Web site: www.jacinet.com/~randall. Catalogue two 46¢ stamps. Mineral products for plants, pets and people, derived from seaweed, sea plasma and volcanic rock.

Schindler Crafts, Box 1383, Cardston, AB, T0K 0K0. Catalogue $1. Garden ornaments, including bunnies, skunks, frogs, geese and ducks.

Sitting Pretty, RR 4, Lanark, ON, K0G 1K0; 613-259-3033; fax 613-259-5568. Free catalogue. Hammocks and stands, rope chairs, garden and porch swings, and portable canvas chairs.

Sundials of Distinction, 148 Hillview Dr., Richmond Hill, ON, L4C 1T2; 905-737-4922; fax same. Catalogue $2, refundable. Sundials, weather vanes and wall fountains.

The St. George Company Ltd., 20 Consolidated Dr., Paris, ON, N3L 3T5; 800-461-4299; fax 519-442-7191; e-mail: stgeorgeco@sympatico.ca. Free catalogue. Tom Chambers hanging baskets, stainless-steel garden tools, cutting tools and garden furniture.

Thomas Wildbird Feeders, 30 Furbacher Lane, #4, Aurora, ON, L4G 6W1; 905-727-3110; fax 905-727-3565. Free catalogue. Hand-crafted pine bird feeders, 28 models.

William Wallace Garden Furniture Ltd., Box 159, Fordwich, ON, N0G 1V0; 519-335-3759; fax 519-335-3096; e-mail: wwallace@wcl.on.ca. Free catalogue. Teak and iroko garden benches, chairs, tables and planters made in Canada.

West Coast Creations Ltd., Unit 6C, 13136 Thomas Rd., RR 1,, Ladysmith, BC, V0R 2E0; 800-939-9933; fax 250-245-0530; Web site: www.island.net/~wstc-stcr. Free catalogue. Cedar planters, birdhouses, feeders, birdbaths, pottery, and objects made of ceramic and glass.

The Worm Factory, RR 3 G, Perth, ON, K7H 3C5; 613-267-5540; fax 613-267-4346. Free catalogue. Vermiculture kits, bulk redworms, books on earthworms, replacement bedding and worm castings. Year-round delivery across Canada.

Water-Garden Supplies

A Fleur D'eau Inc., 140 Route 202, Stanbridge E., PQ, J0J 2H0; 514-248-7008; fax 514-248-4623; e-mail: fleurdo@acces-cible.net. Catalogue $2. Aquatic plants, fish, liners, pumps.

Aquatics & Co., Box 455, Pickering, ON, L1V 2R7; 905-668-5326; fax 905-668-4518; e-mail: aquaticsco@aol.com. Free catalogue. Pond and wetland regeneration plants.

Burns Water Gardens, RR 2, 2419 Van Luven Rd., Baltimore, ON, K0K 1C0; 905-372-2737; fax 905-372-8625; Web site: www.eagle.ca/~wtrgdn. Online catalogue only; photos, botanical names. Pond plants, including waterlilies grown on site; aquatics, pumps, liners, accessories, books and fountains.

Dubè Botanical Gardens, 1919 West Branch Rd., River John, NS, B0K 1N0; 902-351-3273; fax same; toll free in Atlantic Canada 877-426-5459; Web site: members.tripod.com/~Dube_Watergardens. Free catalogue. Maritime waterlilies and other aquatic plants.

The Lily Pool, 3324 Pollock Rd., RR 2, Keswick, ON, L4P 3E9; 905-476-7574. Catalogue $2, refundable. Pools, plants and equipment.

Moore Water Gardens, Box 70, Dept. CG, Port Stanley, ON, N5L 1J4; 519-782-4052; e-mail: moorewg@execulink.com. Free catalogue. Hardy and tropical waterlilies, bog plants, liners, pumps and fountains.

Parkside Gardens, 251 Demetri Way, Salt Spring Island, BC, V8K 1X3; 250-653-4917; fax 250-653-4918. Catalogue $2, refundable. Bog, aquatic and marginal plants, hardy waterlilies and damp-land irises.

Picov's Water Garden & Fisheries Centre, 380 Kingston Rd. E., Ajax, ON, L1S 4S7; 800-663-0300; fax 905-686-2183; Web site: www.picovs.com. Free catalogue. Native and tropical aquatic plants, liners, pumps, ornamental fish and accessories.

Pond Liners, Box 55, Nestleton, ON, L0B 1L0; 905-986-4305; fax 905-986-5865. Free list. Multi-layer polyethylene, UV-stabilized liners; sizes up to an acre.

Reimer Waterscapes, Box 34, Tillsonburg, ON, N4G 4H3; 519-842-6049; fax 519-688-5459; e-mail: lilypad@oxford.net. Catalogue $2. Ornamental grasses, water plants, fertilizers, fish, fish-care products, CrystalClear natural bacteria, filters, pumps, liners, fountain kits, and floating and submersible lights.

Water Arts Inc., 4158 Dundas St. W., Etobicoke, ON, M8X 1X3; 416-239-5345; fax 416-237-1098. Free catalogue. Pond and fountain supplies, including pumps, pools, liners, filters and underwater lights.

Index

• *Numbers* •

3D Deck, 43
3D Landscape 2.0, 43

• *A* •

A. novae-anglia, 69
A. sphaerocephalon, 86
A. X frikartii, 69
acidity, 176
action hoe, 276
activators, 231
activities and site analysis, 32
aerating tool, 231
A. filipendulina 'Moonshine,' 68
agapanthus, 76–78
aggregate, 39
Agriculture Canada, 19
air pollution, 21
Alba, 118
alba roses, 98
Alba Semiplena, 98
Alberta official floral emblem, 326
alkalinity, 176
all-brick walkway, 39
allium (*Allium* spp.), 76, 86
almond trees, 237
Alpine cider gum *(E. archeri),* 121
alpine currant, 21
alpines and mulch, 27
alstroemeria, 76
alyssum, 51, 55
amaryllis, 337
American Rose Society Consulting Rosarians Online, 100
anaerobic containers, 230
anemones, 77

animals
  bulbs, 82–83
  damage, 28
annual grasses, 53
annual rye, 271
annuals, 10, 35
  beautiful effects with, 51
  bicolour flower, 49
  caring for, 56
  colour combinations, 52–53
  containers, 55–56
  cool-season, 49, 57
  deadheading, 56
  definition of, 47
  double flower, 49
  dwarfs, 49
  experimenting with, 51–56
  favourite, 57
  fertilizer, 56, 225
  flower types, 49
  fragrance, 53–54
  fully double flower, 49
  height, 53
  life cycle of, 48
  lower-growing compact, 56
  low-growing, 55
  mixing different types, 55
  planting en masse, 55
  reseeding themselves, 51
  as seedlings or transplants, 201
  seeds, 191–194
  shade, 50
  shape, 53
  single flower, 49
  sowing seeds, 50–51
  spreading, 55
  star flower, 49
  starting seeds indoors, 50, 198–200
  structure, 53
  sunlight, 50
  trailers, 49
  transplants, 50–51

  versatility, 51
  volunteers, 51
  warm-season, 50, 59–60
  watering requirements, 56
Annuals For Dummies, 344
annual vinca, 59
annual vines, 164–165
annual wildflowers, 51
anthracnose, 265
anvil pruners, 276
aphids, 247, 249, 259, 260–262, 268
apical bud, 237
Apothecary Rose, 99
apple maggot, 249
apples, 256, 268, 300–301, 303
  preventing drying, 28
  scab, 265–266, 303
  scab-free, 264
apple trees, 253, 265
  spurs, 237
apricots, 301
aralia, 21
arborvitae, 28
arbours, 162
architectural salvage, 40
arctic dryad, 331
Aristocrat, 120
artemisia (*Artemisia* species), 68, 100
art pavers, 39
Asian longhorn beetle, 255
Aster (*Aster* species), 69
astilbe, 41
Austin, David, 95
automated irrigation system, 35
automated watering systems, 219
autumn, gardening into, 25–26
azalea food, 224
azalea pots, 312
azaleas, 123, 130, 246

• *B* •

baby gladiolus *(G. colvillei),* 87

bachelor's buttons *(Centaurea cyanus),* 57

backyard, designing landscape, 37

bacterial insecticides, 258

balanced fertilizer, 180

balled-and-burlapped plants, 211–212

bamboo stakes, 67

bamboo teepees, 159

bare-root plants, 209–210

bark beetle, 266

basil, 252, 299

basket-of-gold *(Aurinia saxatilis),* 69

bean beetles, 263

bean leaf beetle, 250

beans, 159, 254

beardtongue *(Penstemon* species), 73

bedding begonia *(Begonia semperflorens),* 59

beds, 292–293

bee balm *(Monarda* species), 70, 267

bees, 259

beetles, 263

beets, 23

begonias *(Begonia tuberhybrida),* 77–78, 86

belladonna lily *(Amaryllis belladonna),* 337

bellflower *(Campanula* species), 70

beneficial insects, 246

bergamot, 70

bermuda grass *(Cynodon dactylon),* 272–274

bicolour flower, 49

big blue stem *(Andropogon gerardii),* 72

bindweed *(Convolvulus arvensis),* 272–274

bins for static pile, 230

bittersweet, 156

blackberries, 268, 305

black dragon, 80

black-eyed Susan *(Rudbeckia fulgida* 'Goldsturm'), 16, 65, 74

black-eyed Susan vine, 160

black plastic, 171

black raspberries, 305

black spot, 263, 266
  roses, 106, 262

black vine weevil, 250

bloody cranesbill *(Geranium sanguineum),* 71

blooming Sally *(Epilobium angustifolium),* 331

blueberries, 246, 305

'Blue Clips,' 70

blue fescue *(Festuca glauca),* 72

blue salvias, 100

blue star, 16

bone meal, 82

books, 342–344
  mail-order resources, 379–382

Bordeaux mixture, 266, 269

borders, 63

borers, 250

boron, 222

Boston ivy, 155

botanical insecticides, 258

botanical names, 15

botrytis blight, 266

botrytis molds, 249

Bourbon roses, 98

boxwood, 28

Brachychome iberdifolia, 55

Bradford, 120

bramble fruits, 305

branch collar, 238

Brassica species, 57

brick, 40

British books, 344

British Columbia official floral emblem, 326

broccoli, 253

brown rot, 266

Bt. kurstaki, 259

Bt. tenebrionis, 259–260

Bt (Bacillus thuringienis), 258–260

buckwheat, 271

bugs, 34

built-in grill, 34

bulb bark, 85

bulb fertilizer, 82

bulb pans, 85

bulb pots, 312

bulbs, 76
  animals, 82–83
  bone meal, 82
  bulb fertilizer, 82
  caring for, 83
  containers, 84–85
  daffodils and narcissus *(Narcissus* spp.), 88
  defining, 75
  digging and storing, 83
  dividing and propagating, 83–84
  favourite, 86–88
  fertilizer, 83, 225
  forcing, 84
  fragrant plants, 337–338
  fritillaria *(Fritillaria* spp.), 87
  gladiolus *(Gladiolus* spp.), 87
  growing period, 75
  healthy, 79
  how to buy, 77–79
  hyacinth *(Hyacinthus orientalis),* 87
  iris *(Iris* spp.), 87
  mail-order catalogue, 79
  naturalizing, 82
  offsets, 84
  perennializing, 82
  pinching off faded blooms, 83
  planing, 81–83
  ranunculus *(R. asiaticus),* 88
  resting time, 75
  shopping tips, 79
  shriveled, 79
  size, 79
  snowdrops *(Galanthus* spp.), 87
  spring-blooming, 77–78

summer-blooming, 78
superphosphate, 82
tulips (*Tulipa* spp.), 88
well-drained soil, 82
when to buy, 77–79
burlap screen, 28
burlap-wrapped root balls,
    211–212
Burnet rose, 96
butterflies, 259
butterfly bush *(Buddleia
    davidii)*, 336
butterfly larvae, 251
butterfly weed, 12
buying
    roses, 101–102
    seedlings, 202
    sod, 143
by-pass pruners, 276

• C •

C. alnifolia, 337
C. verticillata 'Moonbeam,' 71
cabbage family, 255
cabbage looper, 251
cabbages, 255, 268
cabbage worms, 260, 263
caladiums, 78
calcium, 222
calendula, 49, 51
caliche, 175
California poppy
    *(Eschscholzia
    californica),* 58
callus, 241
camassia, 12
Canadian Gardening, 294, 345
Canadian Gardening Web
    site, 301
Canadian hardiness zones, 19
Canadian originals, 97
*Canadian Plant Source Book,
    The,* 343
Canadian Rose Society,
    The, 100
candytuft *(Iberis
    sempervirens),* 62, 72

canna *(Canna* spp.), 77–78,
    83, 86
caragana, 21
caraway, 259
cardboard, 234
carnations *(Dianthus
    caryophyllus),* 334
carpenter ants, 250–251
carrots, 184, 255, 297
'Casa Blanca,' 80
cast concrete containers, 310
caterpillars, 251, 258–260
catmint *(Nepeta fassenii),* 73
catnip, 73
celosia, 50
centifolias, 98
chain-link fences, 159
chamomile *(Chamaemelum
    nobile),* 336
'Chapeau de Napoleon,' 99
cheddar pinks *(D. caesius),*
    71
cheddar pinks *(D.
    gratianopolitanus),* 334
chelated micronutrients, 223
cherries, 304
chicken manure, 179
chickweed *(Stellaria media),*
    273
children, 13
China asters, 53
'China Girl,' 118
China roses, 98
chinch bug, 251
Chinese forget-me-not
    (Cynoglossum amabile),
    58
chinese praying mantis, 259
Chinese wisteria, 163
Chionodoxa, 77
chipper-shredders, 282–285
chives, 299
chlorine, 222
chocolate cosmos *(Cosmos
    atrosanguineus),* 334
chrysanthemum, 70–71
'Clara Curtis,' 71
clarkia, 58
clay, 172–173
clearing garden, 169–172

clematis, 160, 162
climate, 10
    defining area's, 17
    watering, 216
climatic zone, 10
climbing nasturtiums, 159
climbing roses, 93, 155, 159,
    161
clinging vines, 155
clubroot, 247
clustered bellflower *(C.
    Glomerata),* 70
Coastal Grower, 345
codling moth, 251
colchicum *(Colchicum* spp.),
    76, 86
cold frame, 23–24
coleus *(Coleus hybridus),* 52,
    59, 202
collar rot, 246
Colorado potato beetle, 251,
    259–263
colours
    annuals, 52–53
    cool, 53
    hot, 53
    plants, 41
columbine *(Aquilegia
    species),* 61, 69, 254
columnar arborvitae, 41
columnar Siberia crab apple,
    120
common heliotrope
    *(Heliotropium
    arborescens),* 334
common mignonette *(Reseda
    odorata),* 54
common names, 16
common thyme *(Thymus
    vulgaris),* 300
complete fertilizers, 180, 223
Complete LandDesigner 5.0,
    43
compost, 227–232
compost bins, 228–231
composted manure, 179
compost pile, 227–228
compost tea, 249
computer and designing
    landscape, 43

concrete, 39
conditions promoting pests
    and problems, 247
conifers, 120–122
'Constellation,' 118
Container Gardening For
    Dummies, 316, 344
container gardens
    arranging, 312–314
    changing for seasons, 317
    combining plants, 312
    designing, 310–315
    one plant, 312
    perennials, 315–316
    pots, 307–310
    style points, 310–311
    vegetables, 316
container-grown roses, 104
container-grown trees and
    shrubs, 203, 206–209
containers
    annuals, 55–56
    breathe, 308
    bulbs, 84–85
    cast concrete, 310
    drainage, 308
    drainage layer, 318
    fertilizing, 321
    garden soil, 318
    glazed clay, 308
    for hot compost, 229
    improvised, 310
    lime, 320
    metal, 310
    paper pulp, 310
    peat moss, 319
    perlite, 320
    planting, 320–321
    plant needs, 318
    plastic, 309
    porosity, 308
    sand, 320
    soil, 317–320
    soilless mixtures, 319
    terra cotta, 308
    vegetable gardens, 293
    vermiculite, 320
    wood, 309
cool colours, 53

cool-season
    annuals, 49, 57–59
    grasses, 135
    vegetables, 290
copper, 222, 269
coral bells *(Heuchera*
    sanguinea), 65–72
coreopsis *(Coreopsis*
    species), 67, 71
corms, 75–76
corn, 253
corn earworms, 251–252, 258,
    261
Corsican mint *(Mentha*
    requienii), 336
cosmos *(Cosmos bipinnatus),*
    51, 59
cotoneaster, 124, 130
cottage pinks *(D. plumarius),*
    71, 334
cottonseed oil, 260
cover crops and weeds, 271
covered patio, 34
crab apples, 113, 264
crabgrass *(Digitaria),* 273
crab apple trees, 265
creeping bellflower *(C.*
    rapunculoides), 70
creeping Charlie, 273
creeping ivy, 273
creeping junipers, 41
Crimson King, 118
crocuses, 76–77, 83
crop rotation, 246
cross-pollination, 301
cucumber beetle, 252
cucumbers, 161, 247, 252, 297
cultivar, 15
cultivation and weeds, 271
curculio, 252
curly dock *(Rumex crispus),*
    273
current condition of
    property, 30–33
cutworms, 247, 252, 259–260
cyclamens, 77
cypermethrin, 262
cytospora canker, 266

• *D* •

D. allwoodii, 71
D. burkwoodii, 337
D. cneorum, 337
D. mantensiana, 337
D. odora, 337
daffodils, 75–77, 82–84
dahlia *(Dahlia* spp.), 76, 78,
    83, 86–87
damage, identifying, 248
damask roses, 99
dame's rocket *(Hesperis*
    matronalis), 335
damping-off disease, 247, 266
dandelion *(Taraxacum*
    officinale), 13, 273
daphne *(Daphne species),*
    337
'Darwins,' 88
David Austin roses, 95
daylilies *(Hemerocallis*
    species), 61, 72, 77, 80,
    243
    mail-order resources,
        362–363
deadheading, 66
    annuals, 56
deciduous
    trees, 112, 116–120
deciduous plants
    perennials, 62
    pruning, 240
Decks & Patios For Dummies,
    309, 344
deer, 270
delphiniums, 67
designing landscape
    backyard, 37
    computer, 43
    defining areas, 37–39
    form and shape, 41
    front yard, 37
    hardscape, 39–40
    plants, 40–42
    repetition, 40
    side yards, 37
    size of plants, 41

unity, 40
using space effectively, 37
ways to move through
    areas, 37–39
Devonian Botanic Garden,
    341
diamondback moth, 260
dianthus (*Dianthus* species),
    62, 71
diatoms, 260
digging and storing bulbs, 83
dill, 259
dirt. *See* soil
dividing
    perennials, 67
    and propagating, 83–84
division, 243
dogwoods, 41, 250, 265
'Dolgo,' 119
dolomitic limestone, 320
double digging, 183
double flower, 49
double-nosed daffodil, 79
downy mildew, 267
'Dr. Huey,' 90
drainage, 31
drip emitters, 218
drip irrigation, 218–219
drought-resistant plants, 10
'Duchess of Portland,' 99
dusty miller (*Centaurea
    cineraria*), 16, 57
Dutch elm disease, 266
Dutchman's breeches, 12
dwarf daylilies, 100
dwarf lady's mantle
    (*Alchimella mollis*), 100
dwarfs (plants), 49

• *E* •

E. pallida, 71
Earlisweet cantaloupe, 26
Earlyred, 120
earwigs, 252, 261
East Coast Gardener, 345
Easter lily, 80
'East Freisland,' 74
easy-to-grow vegetables,
    296–297

Echinacea purpurea, 16
Echo Power Equipment
    Canada Web site, 285
effective
    pest chemicals, 259–263
    use of space, 37
eggplant, 23, 26, 251, 253
elderberries, 306
electric rotary mowers,
    281, 282
electric trimmers, 282
encouraging good insects,
    258–259
English ivy, 150, 155
English primrose (*P.
    polyantha*), 58
English roses, 95
entertaining, 13
Environment Canada Web
    site, 21, 351
euonymus, 21, 28, 130
Euphorbia polychroma, 73
evapotranspiration, 220
evening primrose, 259
evening stock (*Mathiola
    longipetala bicornis*),
    336
evening watering, 247
evergreen azalea, 28
evergreen holly, 130
evergreens, 27–28, 116
evergreen trees, 250
evergreen winter creeper
    (*Euonyumus fortunei*),
    159
existing plants, 30
Explorer Parkland roses, 97
Explorer roses, 90

• *F* •

F. meleagris, 87
fairy primrose (*P
    malacoides*), 58
fall, 18
fan flower, 62
fan trellises, 160
farm and feed stores, 285
farm animal manures, 228

fast-growing plants, 35
fast-growing trees, 116
fennel, 259
fern pots, 312
fertilizers, 221–222
    amounts of nutrients in,
        223
    annuals, 56, 225
    bulbs, 83, 225
    chelated micronutrients,
        223
    choosing, 223
    complete, 223
    containers, 321
    elements of, 222
    foliar, 223
    fruit trees, 225, 302
    granular, 224
    hanging baskets, 225
    house plants, 225
    lawns, 225
    liquid, 224
    natural, 226
    organic, 224–226
    perennials, 66, 225
    roses, 104–105, 225
    shrubs, 226
    slow-release, 225
    soil, 180
    terminology, 223–225
    trees, 226
    vegetables, 226
field balm, 273
figs, 301
F. imperialis, 87
'Finale,' 171
final landscape plan, 42–44
firethorn, 130
fireweed, 331
'Flamingo,' 118
flax, 41
flea beetles, 253, 263
floating row covers, 24–25,
    258
floribunda roses, 63, 92
flower beds, 62–63
Flowering Bulbs For Dummies,
    76, 344
flowering cabbage, 57
flowering crab apple, 28

flowering fruit, 130
flowering kale, 57
flowering shrubs, 35, 63
flowering tobacco
   (Nicotiana), 247
flowering tobacco (Nicotiana
   alata), 336
flowering tobacco (Nicotiana
   alata and sylvestris), 54,
   60
flowering trees, 112
flowers
   perennials, 62
   seeds, 188
forcing bulbs, 84
Forest Pansy, 118
forget-me-nots, 51
foxglove, 53
fragrant evening primrose
   (Oenothera caespitosa),
   336
fragrant plants, 333
   after dark, 335–336
   annuals, 53–54
   bulbs, 337–338
   flowers, 334–335
   herbs, 336
   locations, 334
   modern hybrids, 54
   old-fashioned varieties of
      flowers, 54
   roses, 338–339
   shrubs, 336–337
   trees, 336–337
   vines, 336–337
freesia (Freesia), 337
fresh manure, 226
fritillaria, 76
front tine tillers, 283
front yard, 37
frost
   cool-season annual, 49
   number of days between,
      17
   perennials, 67
   vegetable gardens,
      294–296
frost-free days, 19, 21–22
fruit gardens, 303

fruits, 14, 21, 251–252,
   303–306
fruit trees, 112, 250, 254, 256,
   265–266
   cross-pollination, 301
   fertilizers, 225
   fertilizing, 302
   general tips, 301–302
   pruning, 302
   watering, 302
fruit worms, 263
fuchsia, 62
fully double flower, 49
fun, 34
fungicide, 108
furrow irrigation, 217
fusarium, 268

• G •

G. sanguineum striatum, 71
gaillardia, 67
garden cart, 278
Garden Companion, 359
garden design software,
   358, 359
Garden Encyclopedia, 43, 359
The Gardener for the Prairies,
   345
Gardener's Handbook, 302
garden gloves, 278
gardening books, 342
Gardening by Mail: A Source
   Book, 5th Edition, 343
gardening into autumn,
   25–26
Gardening Life, 345
gardening software, 358–360
garden mums (Dendranthema
   grandiflora), 70
gardens
   arranging, 190–191
   beneficial insects, 246
   children, 13
   clean and tidy, 246
   clearing, 169–172
   condition of, 10–12
   cultivating soil in, 246
   defining boundaries, 37
   entertaining, 13

fruit, 14
herbs, 14
language of, 14–16
localized climates, 11
pets, 13
practical work area, 14
private getaway, 13
relaxation, 14
soil type, 12
stripping sod, 170–171
terminology, 14–16
uses for, 13–14
vegetables, 14
watering, 216–219
Gardens West, 345
garden tools
   chipper-shredders,
      282–285
   farm and feed stores, 285
   garden cart, 278
   garden gloves, 278
   hand tools, 275–278
   hand trowel, 276
   hardware stores, 285
   hoe, 276
   home-building centers, 285
   hose, 276
   lawn mowers, 279–281
   lawn rake, 276
   lopping shears, 278
   mail-order resources,
      379–382
   nurseries, 285
   power, 278–285
   pruners, 276
   secateurs, 276
   shopping of, 285–286
   shovel, 276
   stiff-tined rake, 276
   tape measure, 278
   tillers, 282–285
   trimmers, 282
   water wand, 278
garden tractors, 281
garlic, 299
gasoline-powered trimmers,
   282
genus, 15
geraniums, 48, 100, 266
German bearded irises, 250

giant snowdrop (*G. elwesii*), 87
The Gilded Herb, 345
gill over the ground, 273
gladioli, 76, 84
Glechoma (or Nepeta) hederacea, 273
Global Releaf, 115
Globemaster, 86
gloxinias, 77
Godetia (*Godetia grandiflora*), 58
gold-banded lily (*L. auratum*), 338
golden marguerite (*Argyranthemum frutescens*), 65
goldenrod (*Solidago*), 65, 259
goldflame honeysuckle (*Lonicera heckrottii*), 337
good insects, 258–260
gooseberries, 305
goose eggs, 31
gophers, 270
Grandiflora roses, 93
grape hyacinth (*Muscari azureum*), 338
grape hyacinth (*Muscari* spp.), 77, 87
grapes, 156–157, 250, 267, 305
grasshoppers, 253, 261
Great Maiden's Blush, 98
Greek oregano (*O. vulgare hirtum*), 300
green beans, 297
green lacewing, 249, 258
green manure crops, 181
Grey birch, *B populifolia,* 118
ground cover, 35, 133
    Aaron's-beard, 152
    Arcostaphylos uva-ursi Massachusetts,' 151
    Arctostaphylos Vancouver Jade, 151
    bearberry, 151
    big blue stem, 154
    blazing star, 154

blue fescue (*Festuca glauca*), 152
blue grama grass, 154
carpet bugle (*Ajuga reptans*), 151
chamomile (*Chamaemelum nobile*), 151
'Colorata,' 152
cotoneaster (*Cotoneaster* species), 152
creeping lily turf (*Liriope spicata*), 153
creeping thyme (*Thymus praecox arcticus*), 153
culver's root, 154
deciduous rock cotoneaster (*C horizontalis*), 152
dwarf periwinkle (*Vinca minor*), 154
'Ebony Night,' 153
English ivy (*Hedera helix*), 152
evergreen bearberry cotoneaster (*C. dammeri*), 152
evergreen rockspray cotoneaster (*C. microphyllus*), 152
foamflower (*Tiarella cordifolia*), 154
heather (*Calluna vulgaris*), 151
'Ivory Jade,' 152
J. horizontalis Bar Harbor, 153
J. sabina Broadmoor, 153
Japanese spurge (*Pachysandra terminalis*), 153
junipers (*Juniperus*), 153
'Kewensis,' 152
kinnikinnick, 151
L. muscari, 153
little bluestem, 154
long-grass prairies varieties, 154
mixed-grass prairies varieties, 154

mondo grass of lily turf (*Liriope* or *Ophiopogon*), 153
native grasses, 154
nigrescens black mondo grasses, 153
northern sea oats, 154
Ophiopogon japonicus, 153
Otter Valley Native Plants, 154
P. tabernaemontanii, 153
P. verna, 153
planting, 149–150
'Prairie Habitats,' 154
'Prairie Originals,' 154
rose daphne (*Daphne cneorum*), 152
shearing, 150
sheep fescue, 154
side oats grama, 154
spring cinquefoil (*Potentilla neumanniana*), 153
spring heath (*Erica carnea*), 151
St. John's wort (*Hypericum calycinum*), 152
weeds, 147–150
wild asters, 154
wild ginger (*Asarum canadense*), 151
winter creeper (*Euonymus fortunei*), 152
woolly yarrow (*Achillea tomentosa*), 151
ground-cover roses, 95–96
groundhogs, 270
ground laurel (*Epigaea repens*), 329
growing season, 21–22
    gardening into autumn, 25–26
    length, 17, 21
    planting earlier in year, 23–25
    replanting, 26
    row covers, 25
    spray on frost protection, 25–26
    stretching, 23–26
    warming soil, 25

grubs, 259
Guelph Turfgrass Institute
    Web site, 137
gypsy moths, 253, 255

• H •

H. sieboldiana 'Francis
    Williams,' 72
hand-held tiller/cultivators,
    283
hand hoeing weeds, 271
hand pruner, 241
hand saw, 241
hand tools, 275–278
hand trowel, 276
hanging baskets and
    fertilizers, 225
hardening off seedlings, 199
hard green tomatoes, 26
hardiness zones, 17, 19–20
Hardiness Zones Map, 17
hardpan layer, 176, 183
hardscape, 39–40
hardware stores, 285
hardy kiwi (*Actinidia arguta*
    'Issai'), 301
'Harmony,' 87
Harrowsmith Country Life, 346
hawthorns, 28, 113
heading cuts, 237
heating soil, 25
heat traps, 21
heaving, 27
heavy clay soil, 81, 216
heavy-duty tillers, 283
height and annuals, 53
heirloom vegetables,
    298–299
heliotrope, 54
hellebores, 62
Hemerocallis, 61
herbaceous perennials, 19,
    62
herbicides, 171
herbs, 14, 299–300
    aromatic, 336
    mail-order resources,
        363–364

high-powered rose fertilizer,
    105
hills, 293
hoe, 276
holly, 28, 124
hollyhocks, 268
home-building centers, 285
honeybees, 263
honeysuckle, 21, 161
'Hoopsi,' 121
horizontally spreading
    plants, 41
horticultural oils, 258
Horticulture Science
    Department of the
    University of
    Saskatchewan, 26
hose, 276
hosta (*hosta* spp.), 72
Hosta undulata, 15
hot bed, 24
hot caps, 24
hot colours, 53
houseplants, 254, 256
    fertilizers, 225
    mail-order resources,
        364–365
Houseplants For Dummies,
    344
humus, 175
huntsman's cup (*Sarracenia
    purpurea*), 330
hyacinth (*Hyacinthus
    orientalis*), 338
hyacinths, 75–77, 84
hybrid musk roses, 98, 103
hybrid tea roses, 91, 106
hybrid vegetables, 298–299
hydrangea, 123, 130

• I •

I. reticulata, 87
I. siberica, 87
Ichiban Japanese eggplant,
    26
impatiens, 50, 202
improving soil, 177–181
improvised containers, 310
Indian dipper, 330

Indian meal moth, 260
indiscriminate pesticide
    spraying, 259
inoculants, 231
insect eggs, 258
insecticidal soaps, 258
insecticides, 259–263
insect pests
    aphids, 249
    apple maggot, 249
    bean leaf beetle, 250
    black vine weevil, 250
    borers, 250
    carpenter ants, 250–251
    caterpillars, 251
    chinch bug, 251
    codling moth, 251
    Colorado potato beetle,
        251–252
    corn earworms, 252
    cucumber beetle, 252
    curculio, 252
    cutworms, 252
    earwigs, 252
    flea beetles, 253
    grasshoppers, 253
    gypsy moths, 253
    Japanese beetles, 253
    leaf miners, 254
    lygus bugs, 256
    mealybugs, 254
    Mexican bean beetles, 254
    Oriental fruit moths, 254
    root maggots, 255
    scale, 255
    slugs, 255
    snails, 255
    spider mites, 256
    spread of, 255
    sticky pest barriers, 253
    tarnished plant bugs, 256
    tent caterpillars, 256
    tomato hornworm, 257
    traps, 258
    whiteflies, 257
interesting natural features,
    31
*The Internet For Canadians
    For Dummies,* 347

interplanting, 293
IPM (integrated pest management), 257
irises, 77
  mail-order resources, 362–363
iron, 222
IRT mulching film, 25
island bed, 63
ivies, 41, 156

• J •

J. chinensis Paul's Gold, 153
Japanese beetles, 253–255, 261–263
Japanese blood grass (Imperata cylindrica 'Red Baron'), 72
Japanese wisteria, 163
jar method, 173–174
'Jetfire,' 88
jicama, 21
'Johnson's Blue,' 71
jonama snow gum (E. debeuzevillei), 121
junipers, 28, 41, 268

• K •

'King Alfred,' 88
kiwi, 157
kohlrabi, 255
'Konigin von Danemark,' 98
K (potassium), 222

• L •

lacewings, 259
ladder, 241–242
lady beetles, 258
ladybird, 249
ladybugs, 258–259
lady's mantle, 73
'Lambrook Silver,' 68
lamb's ears (Stachys), 64, 74, 100, 244

lamb's-quarters (chenopodium album), 273
landscape
  current condition of property, 30–33
  designing, 36–42
  fenced areas, 39
  field testing, 44
  final plan, 42–44
  fun, 34
  maintenance, 35
  neighbourhood character, 34–35
  pets, 34
  planning, 29
  pleasure routes, 38
  resale value, 35
  restrictive covenants, 37
  roses, 100
  safety, 34
  site analysis, 30–33
  uses of, 34
  wish list, 33–35
landscape architect/designer, 29
landscape fabrics, 271
Landscaping For Dummies, 29, 344
landscaping software programs, 43
larkspur (Consolida ambigua), 57
late blights, 249
lattice trellises, 160
lavender (Lavandula), 336
lawn-and-garden tractors, 281
Lawn Care For Dummies, 135, 146, 344
lawn mowers, 279–281
lawn rake, 276
lawns, 133
  board scraper, 139
  caring for, 146–149
  decisions about, 134–137
  fertilizers, 148, 225
  grass seed, 139
  how much seed to buy, 138–139

lawn roller, 139
lawn spreader, 139
laying sod, 137
mowing, 147
mulching material, 139
overseeding, 148–149
patching, 148–149
planting, 139–141
putting in new, 137
rake, 139
rototiller, 139
selecting grasses, 134–135
shopping for seed, 138
size of, 134
sodding, 142–145
soil amendments, 139
testing soil, 137
types of turfgrasses, 135–137
laying sod, 137, 143–144
leading bud, 237
leafhoppers, 261
leaf miners, 254
leaf piles, 226
leaves, variegated, 52
leggy plants, 11
legumes, 181, 254
lemon daylily (Hemerocallis lilioasphodelus), 335
lemon thyme (T. citriodorus), 300
lemon verbena (Aloysia triphylla), 336
length of growing season, 17
lettuce, 23, 297
light, 11, 31
  evergreens, 28
  seeds, 188
lightweight tiller/cultivators, 283
lilac (Syringa vulgaris), 254, 267, 337
lilies (Lilium), 65, 75–76, 78–80, 84, 338
  mail-order resources, 365
Lilium regale, 80
lily of the Nile, 76
lily-of-the-valley (Convallaria majalis), 337
lima beans, 254

lime, 320
limestone, 180
lime-sulfur, 269
liquid fertilizers, 224
little blue stem (*Andropogon scoparius* 'The Blues'), 72
Little Girl hybrids, 119
live chat, 358
loam, 172, 173
lobelia (*Lobelia erinus*), 55, 60, 202
loopers, 258, 263
loosening soil, 181–184
loppers, 241
lopping shears, 278
love-in-a-mist (*Nigella* spp.), 53, 58
love-lies-bleeding (*Amaranthus*), 53
low and spreading plants, 41
low-care gardens, 102
low growing annuals, 55
low maintenance, 35
lupines, 62
Lychnis coronaria, 15
Lychnis coronaria alba, 15
Lychnis coronaria 'Angel Blush, 15
lygus bugs, 256

• M •

M. *acuminata* Yellow Bird, 119
macronutrients, 222
Madagascar periwinkle (*Cathuranthus roseus*), 59
Madonna lily (*L. candidum*), 328, 338
magazines, 345–346
magnesium, 222
maiden pink (*D. deltoides*), 334
mailing lists, 356–357
mail-order resources, 361–384
  beneficial insects, 259

books, 379–382
bulbs, 79
daylilies, 362–363
herbs, 363–364
houseplants, 364–365
irises, 362–363
lilies, 365
miscellaneous, 379–382
native plants, 12
roses, 365–366
seed companies, 189
seeds, 366–379
tools, 379–382
water-garden supplies, 382–383
maintenance, 35
manganese, 222
The Manitoba Gardener, 346
Manitoba maple (*A. negundo*), 118
Manitoba official floral emblem, 327
maples, 266
marginally hardy plants, 27
marigold (*Tagetes* spp.), 23, 47, 51–52, 60
Marilyn, 88
marjoram (*O. marjorana*), 300
'Marshall's Delight,' 70
marsh blue violet, 329
Master Gardener Program, 341
Master Gardeners, 301
Master Gardeners of Ontario Inc., 341
mayflower, 329
'May Night,' 74
mealybugs, 254, 261, 268
Mediterranean fruit fly, 255
melons, 26, 252, 265, 268
metal containers, 310
metal-rod method, 175
metal trellises, 160
Mexican bean beetles, 254, 260, 263
Michaelmas daisy, 69
microclimates, 11, 20–21
micronutrients, 222–23

mignonette (*Reseda odorata*), 54, 335
mildew, 267
miniature roses, 93–94, 256
minimum winter temperature, 19
mini-tillers, 283–284
mints, 299
miscellaneous mail-order resources, 379–382
mites, 256–258
mock orange (*Philadelphus* spp.), 16, 337
modern hybrids and fragrance, 54
molybdenum, 222
moonflower (*Ipomoea alba*), 335
morning glory, 159
morning watering, 247
moss phlox (*P. subulata*), 73
mother-of-thyme (*T. praecox arcticus*), 300
moth larvae, 251
moths, 259
mountain ash, 28
mountain avens, 331
mowing lawns, 147
mulch, 232–234, 246
  cardboard, 234
  fertile, 233–234
  inorganic, 233
  newspapers, 234
  perennials, 67
  roots, 27
  vegetable gardens, 296
  watering and, 221
  weeds, 271
  winter hardiness, 27
mulching rotary mowers, 280
multicoloured-leaves, 52
Myosotis sylvatica, 58

• N •

narcissus (*Narcissus jonquilla*), 338
nasturtium (*Tropaeolum majus*), 53, 58
nasturtium vine, 164

National Gardening Association, 4
National Gardening Association Web site, 4
native plants, 12–13
native shrubs, 131
native white birch, *B. papyrife,* 118
naturalized plants, 13
nectarines, 266
neem, 261–262
neem tree *(Azadirachta indica),* 261
neighbourhood, character of, 34–35
nematodes, 250
Netscape and the World Wide Web For Dummies, 2nd Edition, 347
New Brunswick official floral emblem, 329
Newfoundland/Labrador official floral emblem, 329
New Prairie Garden Annual, 346
newsgroups, 356
newspapers, 171, 234
nicotiana, 54
night phlox *(Zaluzianskya capensis),* 336
night-scented stock, 54
nitrogen fertilizer, 26
nitrogen-fixing bacteria, 181
N (nitrogen), 222
noise, 31
nonlegumes, 181
nonselective herbicide, 171
Northwest Territories official floral emblem, 331
Nova Scotia official floral emblem, 329
number of days to harvest, 21–22
nurseries, 285

oak leaf hydrangea, 41
oaks, 120, 253

official floral emblems, 325–331
old-fashioned varieties of flowers, 54
old garden roses, 98–99
onions, 255, 297
online gardening
  insects, 350
  live chat, 358
  mailing lists, 356–357
  mail-order Web sites, 354–355
  newsgroups, 356
  plant information, 353
  search engines, 352
  soil testing, 349–350
  useful information, 355
  Web forums, 358
  where to look for answers, 347–350
  World Wide Web, 347
Ontario official floral emblem, 328
oregano *(Origanum vulgare),* 300
organic fertilizers, 224–225
organic matter, 175, 177–178
oriental fruit moths, 254
ornamental grasses, 64, 72–73
ornamental trees, 254
Ortho's Home Gardening Problem, 360
oscillating hoe, 276
Oswego tea, 70
outdoor lighting, 34
outdoor sink, 34
overseeding, 148–149
'Oxalis,' 273
oxeye daisy, 13

P. citrosum, 336
P. digitalis 'Husker Red,' 73
P. divaritaca, 73
P. graveolens, 336
P. nervosum, 336
P. odoratissimum, 336
P. paniculata, 73

P. quercifolium, 336
P. stolonifera, 73
P. tomentosum, 336
Pacific dogwood *(Cornus nuttalli),* 118, 326
painted daisy *(Tanacetum cinerariifolium),* 262
painted daisy *(Tanacetum coccineum),* 70
pansies, 49, 51, 59
paper pulp containers, 310
paperwhites, 84
parasitic nematodes, 259
Parkwood roses, 90
parsley, 300
parsnips, 184, 255
pasque flower, 327
patching lawns, 148–149
pathways, 38–39
patio art pavers, 39
patio roses, 96
peaches, 266, 301, 303
peach leaf curl, 267
peach-leaved bellflower *(C. persicifolia),* 70
peach tree, 267
pears, 303–304
pear trees, 237
peas, 161, 261, 297
peat moss, 179–180, 319
Pelargonium, 71
peonies *(Paeonia),* 61–62, 65, 67, 243, 266
peony rings, 67
peppermint *(Mentha piperita),* 299
peppers, 26, 254, 257, 268
percolation, 175
perennial alyssum, 69
perennial border, 63–65
perennial flowers, 21
perennials, 35, 61
  acting like annuals, 48
  container gardens, 315–316
  as cut flowers, 65
  for cutting, 64–65
  cutting back, 67
  deciduous, 62
  defining, 61

(continued)

perennials *(continued)*
  dividing, 67
  favourite, 68–74
  fertilizers, 66, 225
  flowers, 62
  frost, 67
  herbaceous, 62
  mulch, 27, 67
  pinching and pruning,
    66–67
  planting, 65–67
  in pots, 64
  reblooming, 67
  staking, 67
  stem cuttings, 243
  tender, 62
  watering, 65–66
Perennials For Dummies, 244,
  343
perlite, 320
permethrin, 262
Permit Office, Plant
    Protection Division, 255
personal likes and dislikes,
  30
pest chemicals
  Bt (Bacillus thuringienis),
    259–260
  DE (Diatomaceous earth),
    260
  horticultural oils, 260–261
  indiscriminate spraying,
    259
  insecticidal soaps, 261
  neem, 261–262
  pyrethrins, 262–263
  rotenone, 263
  safe and effective, 259–263
pests, 258–259
pets, 34
petunias, 251
pH, 176
  changing, 180
  vegetables, 293
phlox (*Phlox* spp.), 61, 73
photinia, 130
Photo LandDesigner 4.5, 43
photosynthesis, 222
phytophthora blight, 268
picking tomatoes early, 26

picotee flower, 49
pillars, 161
Pimpinellifolia hybrids, 96
pinching, 237
  bulbs, 83
  perennials, 66–67
pincushion flower
    (*Scabiosa*), 65
pink lady's slipper, 330
pink moccasin-flower
    (*Cypripedium acaule*),
    330
'Pink Perfection,' 80
pinks (*Dianthus*), 62, 334
pitcher-plant, 330
pitchfork, 231
planning
  fruit garden, 303
  landscape, 29
  vegetable garden, 289–296
plant diseases
  anthracnose, 265
  apple scab, 265–266
  blackspot, 266
  Bordeaux mixture, 269
  botrytis blight, 266
  brown rot, 266
  copper, 269
  cytospora canker, 266
  damping-off, 266
  Dutch elm disease, 266
  least-toxic disease
    remedies, 269
  lime-sulfur, 269
  mildew, 267
  peach leaf curl, 267
  phytophthora blight, 268
  preventing, 263–269
  remedy fungicide, 269
  rust, 268
  solarization, 265
  sooty mould, 268
  sulfur, 269
  wilt, 268
Plant & Garden, 346
plant hardiness, 18–19
Plant Hardiness Zones
    Map, 19
planting
  bare-root plants, 209–210

bulbs, 81–83
containers, 320–321
earlier in year, 23–24
ground covers, 149–150
lawn from seed, 138–141
lawns, 139–141
roses, 103
seedlings, 202
trees, 115–116
plant names, 14–16
plants
  acclimatizing, 18
  apical bud, 237
  botanical names, 15
  burning, 226
  colour, 41
  common names, 16
  crop rotation, 246
  designing landscape, 40–42
  drought-resistant, 10
  elements for healthy
    growth, 222
  fast growing, 35
  form and shape, 41, 53
  horizontally spreading, 41
  identifying damage, 248
  leading bud, 237
  leggy, 11
  less attractive to pests, 246
  light, 11
  low and spreading, 41
  macronutrients, 222
  matching to planting site,
    10–11
  micronutrients, 222
  multicoloured-leaves, 52
  native, 12–13
  naturalized, 13
  nitrogen deficiency, 226
  number of days to harvest,
    21
  nutrients, 226
  order, 42
  pH, 176
  photosynthesis, 222
  preventing problems,
    246–247
  primary nutrients, 222
  proper site and soil, 246
  pruning, 235–242

raising from seeds, 187–200
repetition, 40
requirements for good health, 10
root-bound, 206
secondary nutrients, 222
selecting, 10
selection and care software, 359
shade-loving, 11
size, 41
small patches of same type of vegetable, 246
spacing, 247
spiky, 41
sun-worshipping, 11
texture, 41
tip bud, 237
upright, 41
walking among, 247
plastic netting, 161
pleasure routes, 38
plough plan, 183
plough sole, 284
plums, 304
pole beans, 161
pole pruner, 241–242
polyantha roses, 63, 92
popularity of native plants, 12
porcelain vine, 162
potato beetles, 263
potatoes, 251, 257
pot marigold (*Calendula officinalis*), 57
potted begonias, 256
powdery mildew, 73, 262, 267
power cultivators, 283
power-reel mowers, 280
power tools, 278–285
P (phosphorus), 222
practical work area, 14
prairie anemone, 327
prairie crocus, 326
prairie lily, 327
preparing soil, 169
pressure pan, 183
pressure-treated lumber, 35, 294

prevailing winds, 31
preventing
  animal damage, 28
  drying, 28
primary nutrients, 222
primroses (*Primula* spp.), 58
Prince Edward Island official floral emblem, 329
private getaway, 13
problems that need solutions, 30
professional soil test, 177
'Profusion,' 120
propagating, 235, 242–243
property
  natural strengths, 32–33
  personal likes and dislikes, 30
  problems that need solutions, 30
  scale drawing, 38
  strengths and weaknesses, 30
  uses of, 34
pruners, 276
pruning, 235
  cuts, 237
  deciduous plants, 240
  effects on plant growth, 236–237
  fruit trees, 302
  hand pruner, 241
  hand saw, 241
  heading cuts, 237
  keeping plant healthy, 236
  ladder, 241–242
  large limb, 239
  loppers, 241
  medium-sized limb, 239
  pinching, 237
  pole pruner, 241–242
  roses, 106
  sculpting for decorative reasons, 236
  shaping for strength and resistance, 236
  shearing, 237
  shrubs, 240
  suckers, 240
  summer, 240–241

thinning cuts, 237
tools, 241–242
treating tree wounds, 239
trees, 240
vines, 157
watersprouts, 240
when advisable, 236
winter, 240
Pulsatilla ludoviciana, 327
purlane (*Portulaca oleracea*), 274
purple coneflower (*Echinacea purpurea*), 12, 67, 71
purple violet (*Viola cucullata*), 329
pushing the limits, 26
push-reel mowers, 280
push rotary power mowers, 280
pyramidal English oak (*Q. robur Fastigiata*), 120
pyrethrins, 262–263
pyrethroids, 262

Quebec official floral emblem, 328
Queen Anne's lace, 13, 259

R. centifolia, 99
R. chinensis, 98
R. damascena, 99
R. damascena 'Semperflorens', 98–99
R. g. officinalis, 99
R. gallica, 99
raccoons, 270
radishes, 23, 253, 255, 297
railroad ties, 294
rainfall, 10, 19
raised beds, 184, 294
ranunculus, 76
Ratibida genus, 16
rear tine tillers, 283

recycling junk from your house, 24
red 'Henri Martin,' 99
red oak *(Q. rubra)*, 120
red-osier dogwood, 41
red raspberries, 305
redroot pigweed *(Amaranthus retroflexus)*, 273
red spider mites, 73
'Redspire,' 120
regional Environment Canada office, 21
relaxation, 14
remedy fungicide, 269
repeat bloom roses, 92
repeated tilling method, 171
repeating colours and shapes, 40
repellents, 28
repetition, 40
replanting, 26
resale value, 35
resmethrin, 262
Rhizobium, 181
rhizomes, 75, 77
rhododendrons, 28, 123, 250, 268
ribbons-and-bows method, 173
riding mowers, 281
rock garden plants, 27
rodents, 28
root-bound plants, 206
root flare, 212
rooting hormone, 243
root-knot nematode, 247
root maggots, 247, 255
roots, 27
Rosa alba, 98
'Rosa Bianca,' 26
Rosa centifolia, 98
Rosa multiflora, 90, 102
The Rosarian, 100
Rosa rugosa, 99
rosea, 50
rosebay, 331
rose food, 224
rosemary *(Rosmarinus officinalis)*, 100, 300, 336

The Rose Annual, 100
'Rose of Castile,' 99
roses, 89, 130, 161, 184, 267–268, 338
'Abraham Darby,' 339
alba, 98
'Alchymist,' 93
'Arctic Flame,' 91
'Ballerina,' 98
beneficial insects, 107
black spot, 106, 263, 266
'Blanc Double de Coubert,' 100
'Bonica,' 92, 96
bourbon, 98
'Buff Beauty,' 98
buying, 101–102
Canadian originals, 97
'Captain Samuel Holland,' 97
'Carlotte Brownell,' 91
centifolia, 98
'Champlain,' 97
'Chicago Peace,' 91–92
China, 98
'Chrysler Imperial,' 339
climbing, 93
'Climbing Iceberg,' 161
'Crimson Glory,' 339
'Cupcake,' 94
'Curly Pink,' 91
'Cuthbert Grant,' 97
damask, 99
'David Austin,' 95
'David Thompson,' 97
dormant spray, 107
'Dortmund,' 161
'Double Delight,' 91, 339
'Elina,' 92
'Ellamae,' 94
English, 95
'Europeana,' 92
'Explorer Parkland,' 97
fertilizer, 104–105, 105, 225
floribunda, 92
Flower Carpet series, 95
'Folklore,' 92
fragrance, 102
'Fragrant Cloud,' 91, 339
'Frau Dagmar Hastrup,' 100

'Frontenac,' 97
fungicide, 108
'Garden Party,' 91
'Gertrude Jekyll,' 95, 339
'Glamis Castle,' 95
'Glowing Amber,' 94
'Golden Celebration,' 95, 339
'Golden Wings,' 96
'Gourmet Popcorn,' 96
grafted, 90
'Graham Thomas,' 92
grandiflora, 93
ground-cover, 95–96
healthy plants, 107
'Heaven Scent Pink,' 96
'Henry Hudson,' 97
'Heritage,' 95
high-powered fertilizer, 105
hybrid musk, 98, 103
hybrid perpetual, 99
hybrid tea, 91
'Iceberg,' 92
'Ingrid Bergman,' 91
'Jacques Cartier,' 99
'Jeanne Lajoie,' 94
'John Davis,' 97
'John Hudson,' 161
'Just Joey,' 93
kinds of, 90–100
'Lavaglow,' 92
long-flowering, 102
'Love,' 93
low-care gardens, 102
'Madame Isaac Pereire,' 339
mail-order resources, 365–366
miniature, 93–94
'Mister Lincoln,' 92
'Morden Amorette,' 97
'Morden Blush,' 97
'Morden Cardinette,' 96
'Morden Fireglow,' 97
moss, 99
'Mozart,' 98
'Mrs. John McNabb,' 93
'Mt. Hood,' 93
'New Dawn,' 93
old garden, 98–99

'Olympiad,' 91
'Opening Act,' 94
'Papa Meilland,' 339
'Pascali,' 91
patented, 102
patio, 96
Pavement series, 95
'Peaudouce,' 92
'Penelope,' 98
places to use, 102
planting, 103
polyantha, 92
'Portland,' 99
'Prairie Dawn,' 97
'Prairie Maid,' 96
problem-free varieties, 107
pruning, 106
R. centifolia 'Fantin-Latour', 99
R. damask 'Mme Hardy', 99
R. gallica 'Rosa Mundi', 99
'Red Meidiland,' 96
repeat bloom, 92
'Robin Hood,' 98
'Royal Blush,' 339
rugosa, 99–100
rules, 90
'Sea Foam,' 96
'Sea Pearl,' 92
'Sexy Rexy,' 92
'Shining Hour,' 93
shrub, 94–100
'Solitude,' 93
'Sombreuil,' 161
Spinosissima hybrids, 96
'Stanwell Perpetual,' 96
sub-zero, 91
'Sundowner,' 339
'Sunsprite,' 92, 339
'Super Star,' 92
surviving winter, 108
'Sweet Chariot,' 94
'Sweet Juliet,' 339
'Tabris,' 92
'The Fairy,' 92, 96
'The Prince,' 95
'Therese Bugnet,' 100
'Tiffany,' 91–92, 339
top-grade plants, 102
'Tournament of Roses,' 93

'Tradescant,' 95
as trees, 94
'Tropicana,' 92
'Trumpeter,' 92
varieties, 90
watering, 104–105
'Young Cale,' 96
Roses For Dummies, 344
rotenone insecticides, 258
rototillers, 182–183
Roundup, 171
row covers, 24–25
rows, 292
'Rubra,' 118
Rudbeckia genus, 16
Rugosa roses, 99–100
Russian olive, 21
rust diseases, 262, 268
rutabagas, 255

• *S* •

S. farinacea, 60
safe pest chemicals, 259–263
safety, 34
sage *(Salvia officinalis),* 59, 300
'Salmon Beauty,' 68
salvia *(Salvia* spp.), 74
sand, 172
    containers, 320
    watering, 216
Saskatchewan Master Gardener Program, 341
Saskatchewan official floral emblem, 327
Saskatoons, 306
sawdust, 226
scab, 264
    apples, 303
Scaevola aemula, 62
scale, 255, 268
scale drawing, 38
scented geraniums *(Pelargonium* species), 336
scilla, 76, 83
Scilla bifolia, 77
Scotch briar rose, 96
screened-in patio, 34

scuffle hoe, 276
search engines, 352
secateurs, 276
secondary nutrients, 222
sedums, 62
seedlings
    buying, 202
    hardening off, 199
    planting, 202
    steps for planting, 203–205
    vegetable gardens, 294
seeds
    alyssum *(Lobularia maritima),* 191
    annuals, 191–194
    annuals started indoors, 198–200
    bachelor's buttons, 191
    basil *(Ocimum basilicum),* 198
    bells of Ireland *(Moluccella laevis),* 198
    best planting depth, 190
    calendula, 193
    California poppy, 194
    catchfly *(Silene* spp.), 191
    celosia *(Celosia cristata, c. plumosa),* 198
    cherry pie plant, 199
    clary sage, 193
    cleome, 193
    cornflower *(Centaurea* spp.), 191
    corn poppies, 194
    cosmos *(Cosmos sp),* 193
    cup-and-saucer vine *(Cobeaea scandens),* 198
    definite pattern, 190
    depth, 295
    expected germination rate, 189
    flowers, 188
    fragrant heliotrope, 199
    globe amaranth *(Gomphrena globulosa),* 199
    head start, 189
    heliotrope *(Heliotropium aborescens),* 199
        (continued)

seeds *(continued)*
hyacinth bean *(Dolichos lablab)*, 193
light, 188
mail-order resources, 189, 366–379
marigold *(Tagetes patula)*, 193
mature height, 188
Mexican sunflower *(Tithonia rotundifolia)*, 199
moisture, 188, 295
moonflower *(Ipomoea alba)*, 200
morning glory *(Ipomoea* spp.*)*, 193
nasturtium *(Tropaeolum majus)*, 194
nicotiana *(Nicotiana sylvestris)*, 199
packing date, 188
poppies *(Papaver* spp.*)*, 194
pot marigold *(Calendula officinalis)*, 193
preparing planting bed, 189
recognition factor, 189
right season for, 189
saving money, 187
Shirley poppies, 194
shopping for, 188–189
soil temperature, 188
sowing, 189–191
special planting instructions, 188
species and/or variety name, 188
spider plant *(Cleome* spp.*)*, 193
starting indoors, 194–198
sunflower *(Helianthus annuus)*, 194
sweet pea *(Lathyrus odoratus)*, 194
thin out seedlings, 190
tomatoes *(Lycopersicum esculentum)*, 200

tricolour sage *(Salvia viridis, S. horminum)*, 193
variety of choices, 187
watering, 190
weeding, 190
Seeds of Diversity, 346
seed tapes, 295
selecting plants, 10
self-propelled mowers, 280
Semperflorens, 99
Senecio cineraria, 57
shade, 11, 34
annuals, 50
changing, 11
plants, 11
site analysis, 30
tolerance, 11
shade-loving plants, 11
shade trees, 34, 250, 253
shallow-rooted plants, 27
shapes, 53
shasta daisies *(Leucanthemum maximum)*, 41, 70–71
sheared yew, 41
shearing, 237
shearing ground cover, 150
sheep manure, 179
shepherd's purse *(capsella bursa-pastoris)*, 274
shopping for seeds, 188–189
shovel, 276
shrub roses, 94–100
shrubs, 250
as accent, 123–124
Adam's needle *(Y. filamentosa)*, 131
'Afterglow,' 127
'Atropurpurea', 125
azaleas and rhododendrons *(Rhododendron* species*)*, 129
B. darwinii, 125
B. gladynensis, 125
B. julianae, 125
B. mentorensis, 125
B. verruculosa, 125
background, 124

barberries *(Berberis* species*)*, 125
barriers, 124
bigleaf hydrandea *(H. macrophylla)*, 127
bluebeard *(Careoptyris* spp.*)*, 126
blue elderberry *(Sambucus cerulea)*, 131
'Blue Girl,' 127
'Blue Maid,' 127
'Blue Pacific,' 127
'Blue Princess,' 127
Blue Star *(J. squamata)*, 128
bog rosemary *(Andromeda polifolia)*, 131
Boudoir (pink), 129
boxwoods *(Buxus* species*)*, 125
Bridalwreath *(S. vanhouttei)*, 129
buddleias, 125
Buffalo *(J. sabina)*, 128
butterfly bush *(Buddleia davidii)*, 125
C. a. sibirica, 126
C. alba 'Gouchaulti', 126
Canadian-bred Preston hybrids, 130
caragana, 126
Chinese juniper *(J. chinensis)*, 127
'Coloratus,' 126
common lilac *(Syringa vulgaris)*, 130
container-grown, 206–210
cotoneaster *(Cotoneaster* spp.*)*, 126
'Dark Night,' 126
deciduous Japanese *(thunbergerii)*, 125
defining, 122
'Dissecta,' 129
dogwood *(Cornus* spp.*)*, 126
downy serviceberry *(Amelanchier canadensis)*, 131

dwarf flowering almond (*P. glandulosa* 'Sinensis'), 128

dwarf fothergilla (*Forthergilla gardenii*), 131

E. alata, 126

E. japonica, 126

'Elsie Lee,' 129

'Elvira,' 129

'Emerald Gaiety,' 126

'Emerald 'n' Gold,' 126

euonymus (*Euonymus* spp.), 126–127

European snowball (*V. Opulos* 'Roseum'), 130

European spindle tree (*E. europaea*), 126

favourite, 124–131

fertilizers, 226

Finnish hybrids, 129

firethorn (*Pyracantha* spp.), 128

flowering quince (*Chaenomeles*), 126

foundation plantings, 123

fragrant, 336–337

'Garland Gold,' 131

glossy abelia (*Abelia grandifiora*), 125

'Gnome,' 128

'Gold Drop,' 128

'Golden Girl,' 127

'Goldflame,' 130

'Green Mound,' 125

'Green Mountain,' 125

'Green Velvet,' 125

'Gro-Low,' 129

ground covers, 95–96, 124, 149

growing season, 21

H. serrata, 127

hedges, 124

hedge viburnum (*V. opulus* 'Nanum'), 131

'Hellekki,' 129

highbush cranberry (*V. trilobum*), 130

hollies (*Ilex* species), 127

hydrangea (*Hydrangea* species), 127

I. meserveae, 127

'Ivory Tower,' 131

Japanese maples (*Acer palmatum*), 125

junipers (*Juniperus* species), 127

Korean spice (*V. varlesii*), 130

Lepidote hybrids, 129

'Little Rascal,' 127

Manchu cherry (*P. tomentosa*), 128

'Mojave,' 128

mugho pine (*Pinus mugo*), 128

multi-season colour, 130

native, 131

native winterberry (*I. verticillata*), 127

'Northern Highlights,' 129

Northern Lights series, 129

oakleaf hydrangea (*H. quercifolia*), 127

'Orchid Lights,' 129

Oregon grape holly (*Mahonia aquifolium*), 131

organizing by height, 124

ornamental fruit (*Prunus* spp.), 128

panicle hydrangea (*H. paniculata*), 127

'Peter Tigerstedt,' 129

'Pfitzeriana,' 127

photinia (*Photinia fraserii*), 128

'Pleasant White,' 129

'Preciosa,' 127

pruning, 240

purple-leafed sand cherry (*P. cistena*), 128

'Red Pygmy,' 125

repeating small groupings of, 123

rhododendrons, 129

roses (*Rosa* spp.), 129

S. bumalda Anthony Waterer, 130

screens, 124

Siberian pea tree (*Caragana arborescens*), 126

'Skyrocket,' 127

smooth hydrangea (*H. arborescens* 'Annabelle'), 127

'Snowflake,' 127

'Snow Queen,' 127

Spanish bayonet (*Y. glauca*), 131

'Spartan,' 128

'Spicy Lights,' 129

spirea (*Spiraea* spp.), 129

sumac (*Rhus* spp.), 129

summersweet (*Clethra alnifolia*), 131

'Teton,' 128

viburnum (*Viburnum* species), 130

'Waterfall,' 125

what they can do for you, 122–124

'Winter Beauty,' 125

'Winter Red,' 127

witch hazel (*Hamamelis virginiana*), 131

witherod (*V. cassinoides*), 130

'Worcester Gold,' 126

yucca (*Yucca filamentosa, Y. glauca*), 131

'Yukon Belle,' 128

'Siberia,' 128

Siberian irises, 250

side yards, 37

Sierra Online Web site, 43

sifter, 231

silicosis, 260

silt, 172

silverleaf whitefly, 255

silver leaf yarrow (*A. clavenna*), 68

'Silver Mound,' 68

single digging, 181

single flower, 49

site analysis, 30–33

slope, 31

slow-release fertilizers, 225

slugs, 255, 260

slug traps, 255
small-flowered alum root, 12
smells, 31
snails, 255, 260
snap beans, 254
snapdragon (*Antirrhinum majus*), 23, 49, 57, 268
snow, 27
'Snowbird,' 118
snowdrop, 82
sod cutter, 171
sodding lawns, 142–145
softwood stem cuttings, 242–242
soil, 14
    acidity, 176
    adding nutrients, 180
    adding organic matter, 175
    alkalinity, 176
    amending, 169
    amendments, 139
    black plastic, 171
    caliche, 175
    changing pH, 180
    clay, 172–173
    clearing, 169–172
    compost, 178–179
    composted manure, 179
    containers, 317–320
    cover crops, 181
    double digging, 183
    fertilizing, 180
    good drainage, 247
    green manure crops, 181
    hardpan layer, 176, 183
    heating, 25
    humus, 179
    improving, 177–181
    jar method, 173–173
    limestone, 180
    loam, 172–173
    loosening, 181–184
    metal-rod method, 175–176
    moisture, 12
    mulch, 25
    newspapers, 171
    organic matter, 177–178
    peat moss, 179–180
    percolation, 175
    pH, 176

plough pan, 183
plough sole, 284
preparing, 169
pressure pan, 183
professional test, 177
raised beds, 184
repeated tilling method, 171–172
ribbons-and-bows method, 173
sand, 172
silt, 172
single digging, 181
site analysis, 31
solarization, 265
solarizing, 25
stripping sod, 170–171
structure, 174–176
sulfur, 180
temperature and seeds, 188
testing, 173–174
testing structure, 175–176
texture, 172–174
tiller, 182–183
topsoil, 179
type, 12
vegetable gardens, 293–294
warming, 25
water drainage, 175
watering, 216
when to work, 182
solarization, 25, 265, 271
Solomon's seal, 12
sooty mould, 268
sour cherries, 301
sourgrass, 273
'Souvenir de la Malmaison,' 98
soybean oil, 260
soybeans, 254
species name, 15
speedwell (*Veronica*), 65
spider mites, 247, 256, 261
spiders, 260
spinach, 23
Spinosissima hybrids roses, 96
spirea, 41, 130

spotted (or prostrate) spurge (*Euphorbia maculata*), 274
sprawling vines, 155
spreading annuals, 55
spring, 18
spring-blooming bulbs, 77–78
sprinklers, 217
spruces, 266
spurs, 237
squash, 252
squash bugs, 260, 263
squash vines, 250
squirrels, 270
St. John's wort, 150
staking, 67
star flower, 49
'Star Gazer,' 80
starting seeds indoors, 194–198
'State Fair,' 60
steel bow rake, 276
'Stellar Pink,' 118
stem cuttings, 242–243
sticky pest barriers, 253
stiff-tined rake, 276
stock (*Matthiola incana*), 58, 335
Stokes' aster (*Stokesia laevis*), 65
stone wall, 39
strawberries, 27, 250, 256, 266, 268, 305
stretching growing season, 23–26
stripping sod, 171
structure, 53, 174–176
sub-zero roses, 91
succession planting, 293
suckers, 240
sugar maple, 113
sulfur, 180, 222, 269
summer-blooming, 78
summer squash, 297
summersweet (*Clethra* spp.), 337
sunflower (*Helianthus annuus*), 51, 59, 187
sunlight, 11
    annuals, 50
    site analysis, 30

'Sunspot,' 59
sun-worshipping plants, 11
superphosphate, 82
supporting vines, 157
Swan River daisy, 55
sweet alyssum, 54, 202
sweet cherries, 304
sweet pea (Lathyrus odoratus), 54, 58, 159–160, 335
sweet peppers, 23, 297
sweet sultan (Centaurea moschata), 334
sweet violet (Viola odorata), 335
sweet William (D. barbatus), 54, 71

● **T** ●

T. saxatilis, 88
table potato, 76
tape measure, 278
tarnished plant bugs, 256, 263
tart cherries, 304
temperatures, 18
tender perennials, 62
tent caterpillars, 256
'Thalia,' 88
thermometer and compost, 231
thin metal wire loops, 67
thinning cuts, 237
thin out seedlings, 190
thrips, 258, 262–263
'Thumbelina,' 60
thyme (Thymus), 62, 100, 300, 336
tillers, 182–183, 282–285
tip bud, 237
'Toba,' 118
tobacco mosaic virus, 247
tomatoes, 23, 26, 247, 251, 257, 265, 268, 297
  'Beef King,' 21
  early, 26, 249
tomato hornworm, 251, 257–258
topsoil, 179

Trail, Catherine Parr, 58
trailers, 49
trailing arbutus, 329
transplanting
  container-grown trees and shrubs, 207–209
  figuring out spacing for, 202–203
Tree Canada Foundation Web site, 115
trees, 256, 265
  Alpine snow gum (E. niiphophila), 122
  American holly (I. opaca), 122
  arbutus or Pacific madrone (Arbuts menziesii), 121
  ash (Fraxinus species), 119
  attractive bark, 113
  Austrian pine (Pinus nigra), 121
  balsam fir (Abies balsam), 120
  beauty, 112
  branch collar, 238
  bristlecone pine (Pinus aristus), 120
  callus over cut, 241
  choosing healthy, 117–120
  Colorado blue spruce (Picea pungens var. glauca), 121
  colourful fruit, 113
  conifers, 120–122
  container-grown, 206–210
  deciduous, 112, 116–120
  Douglas maple (A. glabrum), 117
  eastern larch or tamarack (Larix laricina), 121
  English holly (I.Aquifolium), 122
  eucalyptus (Eucalyptus species), 121
  European white birch (Betula pendula), 118
  evergreens, 116
  fast-growing, 116
  Fat Albert spruce (Picea pungens glauca 'Fat Albert'), 121

  favourite, 116
  fertilizers, 226
  flowering, 112
  flowering crab apple (Malus species), 119–120
  flowering dogwood (Cornus florida, C. alternifolia, C. Kousa), 118
  fragrant, 336–337
  fruit, 112
  ginkgo (Ginkgo biloba), 119
  goldenchain tree (Laburnum anagyroides), 119
  growing season, 21
  hawthorn (Crataegus species), 118
  holly (Ilex species), 122
  lower heating and cooling expenses, 112
  magnolia (Magnolia species), 119
  maple (Acer species), 117–118
  mountain ash (Sorbus decora, S. americana), 120
  Norway maple (A. platanoides), 117
  Norway spruce (Picea abies), 120
  oaks (Quercus), 120
  ornamental pear (Pyrus calleryana), 120
  pine, 120
  planting, 115–116
  pruning, 238–240
  redbud (Cercis canadensis), 118
  'Red Embers,' 117
  red maple (A. rubrum), 117
  'Red Sunset,' 117
  Russian olive (Elaeagnus angustifolia), 118
  saucer magnolia (M. soulangiana), 119

(continued)

trees *(continued)*
  seasonal colour, 112–113
  selecting right, 113–115
  silver maple *(A. saccharinum dasycarpum)*, 117
  staking, 209
  sugar maple *(A. Saccharum)*, 117
  treating wounds, 239
  tricolour beech *(Fagus sylvatico 'Roseo Marginata')*, 119
  what they can do for you, 111–113
  as windbreaks, 112
trichogramma wasps, 258
trimmers, 282
troubleshooting software, 360
true bulbs, 76
trumpet lily *(L. longiflorum)*, 338
tuber-corms, 75, 77
tuberose *(Polianthes tuberosa)*, 338
tuberous roots, 76
tubers, 75–76
tuber-stems, 77
tulip 'Bellona,' 338
tulips, 15, 75–77, 84, 266
tumblers, 230
turfgrass, 135–138
  types, 135–137
Turfgrass Web site, 137
turnips, 255
twining vines, 156

• U•

understorey trees, 53
United States hardiness zones, 20
unity, 40
University of Saskatchewan, 341
upright or spiky plants, 41
U.S. Department of Agriculture (USDA) map, 20
U.S. Environmental Protection Agency, 262

• V •

VanDusen Botanical Garden, 341
variegated leaves, 52
varieties, 15
Vegetable Gardening For Dummies, 22, 296, 344
vegetable gardens, 34, 294–296
  beds, 292–293
  calendar, 291
  choosing right location for, 291–292
  containers, 293
  designing, 292–293
  direct-sown, 294
  frost, 294–296
  harvesting, 296
  herbs, 299–300
  hills, 293
  horticultural oils, 261
  improving soil, 293–294
  interplanting, 293
  mulch, 296
  planning, 289–296
  pressure-treated lumber, 294
  proper plant spacing, 293
  railroad ties, 294
  raised beds, 294
  rows, 292
  seasons, 290–291
  seedlings, 294
  sizing, 292
  succession planting, 293
  timing planting, 294–296
  weeds, 296
vegetables, 14, 296–297
  container gardens, 316
  cool-season, 290
  fertilizers, 226
  growing season, 21
  heirloom, 298–299
  hybrid, 298–299
  hybrid vigor, 298
  insecticidal soaps, 261
  open-pollinated varieties, 298
  pH, 293
  as seedlings or transplants, 201
  warm-season, 290
Verbena bonariensis, 53
verbena *(verbena hybrida)*, 60
vermiculite, 320
verticillium, 268
viburnum *(Viburnum* spp.), 28, 130, 337
views, 31
vinca, 50–51, 150
vinca rosea, 59
vines
  annual, 164–165
  arbours, 162
  bamboo teepees, 159
  bottle gourds *(Lagenaria siceraria)*, 165
  canary creeper *(Tropaeolum peregrinum)*, 164
  chain-link fences, 159
  choosing support for, 158–162
  clematis *(Clematis* species), 162
  climbing roses *(Rosa* spp.), 163
  clinging, 155
  damaging support, 156
  dropmore honeysuckle *(Lonicera X brownii* 'Dropmore Scarlet')*, 163
  effective use of, 156
  English ivy *(Hedera helix)*, 163
  fan trellises, 160
  favourites, 162–165
  fragrant, 336–337
  grape *(Vitis* spp.), 163
  groups, 155–156
  hyacinth bean *(Dolichos lablab)*, 164
  lattice trellises, 160
  metal trellises, 160
  moonflower *(I. alba)*, 164

morning glory *(Ipomoea imperialis)*, 164
nasturtium *(Tropaeolum majus)*, 165
pillars, 161
plastic netting, 161
providing sturdy support, 156
pruning, 157
sprawling, 155
supporting, 157
sweet peas *(Lathyrus)*, 165
twining, 156
variegated porcelain vine *(Ampelopsis brevipedunculata 'Elegans')*, 162
Virginia creeper *(Parthenocissus quinquefolia)*, 163
wall-mounted supports, 161
wisteria *(Wisteria sinensis and W. floribunda)*, 163
violas, 51, 59
Viola species, 59
Virginia creeper, 156

• *W* •

walkway, 39
wall-mounted supports, 161
warming soil, 25
warm-season
  annuals, 50, 59–60
  vegetables, 290
water drainage, 175
water-filled cloche, 24
Water Gardening: The Magazine for Pondkeepers, 346
water-garden supply mail-order resources, 382–383
waterii 'Vossi', 119
watering
  annuals, 56
  automated watering systems, 219
  basics, 215–221

climate, 216
conserving water, 221
drip emitters, 218
drip irrigation, 218–219
evening, 247
frequency, 220
fruit trees, 302
furrow irrigation, 217
garden, 216–219
genetic disposition, 216
hand, 217
heavy clay soil, 216
location, 216
morning, 247
perennials, 65–66
roses, 104–105
sandy soil, 216
seeds, 188, 190, 295
soil, 12
soil types, 216
sprinklers, 217
weather, 216
waterlilies, 80, 86
watersprouts, 240
water wand, 278
weather, 216
weather and climate online, 351–352
Web forums, 358
weeds, 247
  basics for controlling, 269, 271
  bermuda grass *(Cynodon dactylon)*, 272–274
  bindweed *(Convolvulus arvensis)*, 272–274
  chickweed *(Stellaria media)*, 273
  common, 271–274
  controlling, 269–274
  cover crops, 271
  crabgrass *(Digitaria)*, 273
  creeping Charlie, 273
  cultivation, 271
  curly dock *(Rumex crispus)*, 273
  dandelion *(Taraxacum officinale)*, 273
  flaming, 272–274
  ground covers, 150
  hand hoeing, 271

lamb's-quarters *(chenopodium album)*, 273
landscape fabrics, 271
mulch, 271
Oxalis, 273
pulling, 271
purlane *(Portulaca oleracea)*, 274
redroot pigweeg *(Amaranthus retroflexus)*, 273
seeds, 190
shepherd's purse *(capsella bursa-pastoris)*, 274
solarization, 271
spotted (or prostrate) spurge *(Euphorbia maculata)*, 274
vegetable gardens, 296
weevils, 259, 263
well-drained soil, 82
white alyssum, 54
white birches, 250
'White Clips,' 70
white dryad *(Dryas integrifolia)*, 331
whiteflies, 257, 260–262, 268
white garden lily *(Lilium candidum)*, 328
white petunias, 54
white trillium *(Trillium grandiflorum)*, 328
wild animals, 270
wildflower, 346
wild rose or prickly rose *(Rosa acicularis)*, 326
wilt, 268
winter, 18–19, 26–28, 240
wire bins, 229
wish list, 33–35
wisteria, 157, 162
wood chips, 226
woodchucks, 270
wooden compost bin, 229
wooden landscape elements, 35
woodland tobacco *(Nicotiana sylvestris)*, 53

wood sorrel, 273
woody perennials, 19
woody plants, 243
woolly yarrow (*A.tomentosa*),
    68
wrapping with twine, 28

• Y •

yard, 34
yarrow (*Achillea* species), 65,
    68
yews, 28, 250
Yukon Territory official floral
    emblem, 331

• Z •

zinc, 222
zinnia (*Zinnia elegans*),
    50–51, 60, 267
zones, 17, 19–20, 21–22

SUBSCRIBE TODAY
AND SAVE
UP TO **44%*** **OFF** THE NEWSSTAND PRICE!

CANADIAN
GARDENING

"...the most popular magazine for our Canadian climate and growing conditions!"

Glorious gardens to inspire, instruct, dazzle and delight — yours in *Canadian Gardening* magazine. Seven colourful issues a year whisk you off to gardens — some wild, some formal, some quirky, some quaint — from coast to coast. *Canadian Gardening* offers loads of practical tips, techniques and inspiration to help make your garden the best ever.

Special Offer to readers of **Gardening For Canadians For Dummies**

WE'LL SHOW YOU:
- how to grow healthy, delectable edibles
- what flowers provide the best seasonal colour and fragrance
- how to create a pleasing design to show off your beds and borders

Plus regional experts address conditions, events and issues in your area.

It's all here in *Canadian Gardening*, Canada's most popular gardening magazine.

SUBSCRIBE TODAY!

Come visit us at
www.canadiangardening.com

SUBSCRIBER SAVINGS FORM

☐ **YES!** I want to become a *Canadian Gardening* subscriber and take advantage of the savings I've checked below.

Best Deal!

☐ **I SAVE 44%**
Send me 2 years for only $38.95 + $2.73 GST for a total of $41.68

☐ **I SAVE 37%**
Send me 1 year for only $21.95 + $1.54 GST for a total of $23.49

Name

Street Address   City   Prov.   Postal Code

☐ Payment enclosed; Charge my ☐ Visa ☐ MasterCard; ☐ Bill me

Card #   Expiry Date

Signature   *Based on $4.95 newsstand price

CLIP & MAIL TO:
CANADIAN
GARDENING
P.O. Box 717,
Markham, ON L3P 7V3

CGDU99

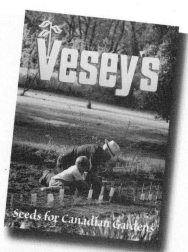

Discover Dummies Online!

The Dummies Web Site is your fun and friendly online resource for the latest information about ...*For Dummies*® books and your favorite topics. The Web site is the place to communicate with us, exchange ideas with other ...*For Dummies* readers, chat with authors, and have fun!

Ten Fun and Useful Things You Can Do at www.dummies.com

1. Win free ...*For Dummies* books and more!
2. Register your book and be entered in a prize drawing.
3. Meet your favorite authors through the IDG Books Author Chat Series.
4. Exchange helpful information with other ...*For Dummies* readers.
5. Discover other great ...*For Dummies* books you must have!
6. Purchase Dummieswear™ exclusively from our Web site.
7. Buy ...*For Dummies* books online.
8. Talk to us. Make comments, ask questions, get answers!
9. Download free software.
10. Find additional useful resources from authors.

Link directly to these ten fun and useful things at
http://www.dummies.com/10useful

For other technology titles from IDG Books Worldwide, go to
www.idgbooks.com

Not on the Web yet? It's easy to get started with *Dummies 101*®: *The Internet For Windows*®*98* or *The Internet For Dummies*®, 6th Edition, at local retailers everywhere.

Find other ...*For Dummies* books on these topics:
Business • Career • Databases • Food & Beverage • Games • Gardening • Graphics • Hardware
Health & Fitness • Internet and the World Wide Web • Networking • Office Suites
Operating Systems • Personal Finance • Pets • Programming • Recreation • Sports
Spreadsheets • Teacher Resources • Test Prep • Word Processing

IDG BOOKS WORLDWIDE BOOK REGISTRATION

We want to hear from you!

Visit **http://my2cents.dummies.com** to register this book and tell us how you liked it!

- ✔ Get entered in our monthly prize giveaway.

- ✔ Give us feedback about this book — tell us what you like best, what you like least, or maybe what you'd like to ask the author and us to change!

- ✔ Let us know any other *...For Dummies*® topics that interest you.

Your feedback helps us determine what books to publish, tells us what coverage to add as we revise our books, and lets us know whether we're meeting your needs as a *...For Dummies* reader. You're our most valuable resource, and what you have to say is important to us!

Not on the Web yet? It's easy to get started with *Dummies 101*®: *The Internet For Windows*® *98* or *The Internet For Dummies*®, 6th Edition, at local retailers everywhere.

Or let us know what you think by sending us a letter at the following address:

...For Dummies Book Registration
Dummies Press
7260 Shadeland Station, Suite 100
Indianapolis, IN 46256-3917
Fax 317-596-5498

™
...FOR
DUMMIES

BESTSELLING BOOK SERIES